CULTURE
AS
HISTORY

CULTURE
AS
HISTORY

THE TRANSFORMATION
OF AMERICAN SOCIETY
IN THE
TWENTIETH CENTURY

WARREN I. SUSMAN

PANTHEON BOOKS NEW YORK

All rights reserved under International and Pan-American Copyright Conventions. Published in the United States by Pantheon Books, a division of Random House, Inc., New York, and simultaneously in Canada by Random House of Canada Limited, Toronto.

Library of Congress Cataloging in Publication Data

Susman, Warren, 1927–
  Culture as history.

  Bibliography: p.
  1. United States—Civilization—20th century.   2. United States—Intellectual life —20th century.   I. Title.
E169.1.S9733   1985   973.9   84-19014
ISBN 0-394-53364-X
ISBN 0-394-72161-6 (pbk.)

Since this page cannot accommodate all the permissions acknowledgments, they appear on the next two pages.

Manufactured in the United States of America

98765

PERMISSIONS
ACKNOWLEDGMENTS

Grateful acknowledgment is made to the following for permission to reprint or adapt from previously published material:

American Quarterly: For "History and the American Intellectual: Uses of a Usable Past," from *American Quarterly,* Vol. XVI (Summer 1964). Copyright © 1964 by the Trustees of the University of Pennsylvania. By permission of *American Quarterly.*

George Braziller, Inc.: For "Culture and Commitment" (originally titled "Introduction"), from *Culture and Commitment, 1929–1945,* ed. Warren Susman. Copyright © 1973 by Warren Susman. By permission of George Braziller, Inc.

Bucknell Review: For "The Frontier Thesis and the American Intellectual" (originally titled "The Useless Past: American Intellectuals and the Frontier Thesis, 1910–1930"), from *Bucknell Review,* Vol. XI (March 1963). By permission of *Bucknell Review.*

Coward-McCann and Martin Secker & Warburg Ltd.: For excerpt from *The Man Without Qualities* by Robert Musil, trans. Eithne Wilkens and Ernst Kaiser. Copyright 1953 by Coward-McCann. By permission of the Putnam Publishing Group and Martin Secker & Warburg Ltd., London.

The Dorsey Press: For "Culture Heroes: Ford, Barton, Ruth," in *Men, Women, and Issues in American History,* ed. A. Quint and M. Cantor, rev. ed., Vol. II. Copyright © 1980 by The Dorsey Press. By permission of The Dorsey Press.

Doubleday & Company, Inc.: For "Socialism and Americanism" (originally titled "Comment 1"), from *Failure of a Dream?,* ed. John H. M. Laslett and Seymour Martin Lipset. Copyright © 1974 by John H. M. Laslett and Seymour Martin Lipset. By permission of Doubleday & Company, Inc.

Houghton Mifflin Company: For excerpt from "America Was Promises," from *New and Collected Poems* by Archibald MacLeish. Copyright © 1976 by Archibald MacLeish. By permission of Houghton Mifflin Company.

The Johns Hopkins University Press: For " 'Personality' and the Making of Twentieth-Century Culture," from *New Trends in Intellectual History*, ed. by John Higham and Paul K. Conklin. Copyright © 1979 by The Johns Hopkins University Press.

Journal of Human Relations: For "The Persistence of Reform" (originally titled "The Persistence of American Reform"), from *Journal of Human Relations*, Vol. XV, no. 3, 1967. Copyright © 1967 by Central State University, Wilberforce, Ohio. By permission of Central State University.

Alfred A. Knopf, Inc.: For excerpt from *The Maltese Falcon* by Dashiell Hammett. Copyright 1929, 1930 by Alfred A. Knopf, Inc. By permission of Alfred A. Knopf, Inc.

Macmillan Publishing Company and New York City Mission Society: For excerpt from *The People Are the City* by Kenneth D. Miller and Ethel P. Miller. Copyright © 1962 by New York City Mission Society. By permission of Macmillan Publishing Company and New York Mission Society.

The Queens Museum: For "World's Fairs: The People's Fair" (originally titled "The People's Fair: Cultural Contradictions of a Consumer Society"), from *Dawn of a New Day*, ed. Helen Harrison. Copyright © 1980 by The Queens Museum. By permission of The Queens Museum.

St. Martin's Press, Inc.: For "The Culture of the Thirties" (originally titled "The Thirties"), from *The Development of an American Culture*, ed. Stanley Coben and Lorman Ratner, 2nd ed. Copyright © 1983 by St. Martin's Press, Inc. By permission of the publisher.

"Culture and Communication" originally appeared as "Communication and Culture" in *Mass Media Between the Wars: Perceptions of Cultural Tension, 1918–1941*, ed. Catherine L. Covert and John D. Stevens (Syracuse, N.Y.: Syracuse University Press, 1984).

"I have always depended on the kindness of strangers." That simple exit line Tennessee Williams provides for Blanche Dubois always rings with a special tragic resonance for American audiences. Yet a literal reading outside the special context of the experience in the play provokes serious question. Why does the line (possibly an early attack on the "Therapeutic Society") so move us? Is it the dependency, the strangers, or the special combination that strikes at some basic cultural attitudes? In my own case it is difficult to assume the tragic pose. I admit readily to the dependency. But I have always depended and have been able to depend on the kindness of special friends. It is to some of those sustaining friends that this volume is dedicated. Some, officially, have been my teachers; some, officially, have been my students; all have taught me. At critical moments they have sustained me. Always, by the force of their example—scholarly, intellectual, personal—they have enriched my life and my work.

Merle Curti
Paul W. Gates
Alan Trachtenberg
William Taylor
Neil Harris
Marvin Levich
Donald Meyer

Traian Stoianovich
Rudolph Bell
Lloyd Gardner
Donald Weinstein
Henry D. Shapiro
Michael Lesy
André Schiffrin

Claire Sprague
William Leach
Mary O. Furner
Michael J. Lacey
Lewis Bateman
Arthur Wang
Sacvan Bercovitch

CONTENTS

PREFACE

In the beginning there are the words, all kinds of words from all kinds of places: words from philosophical treatises and tombstones, from government documents and fairy tales, from scientific papers, advertisements, dictionaries, and collections of jokes. There are, of course, other sources of information: images, sounds, objects of use and of enjoyment, ledgers of debits and of credits, gathered statistics—countless cultural artifacts, each of enormous value but analyzable only when translated into words. Thus the historian's world is always a world of words; they become his primary data; from them he fashions facts. He then can go on to create other words, propositions about the world that follow from his study of those data.

This creation of fact is never an easy task. The historian must discover the precise nature of the human experience the words attempt to describe, the particular attitudes toward that experience they define. Thomas Hobbes warned us centuries ago that "words are wise men's counters, they do but reckon with them, but they are the money of fools." The historian must learn to tell the wise man from the fool—and then learn from both of them. He must learn how people do in fact "reckon" with words.

But the good historian is not done when he has presented the facts. He must be able always to take words seriously but not always literally. He must pay special attention not only to what writers

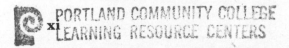

"*parade* but what they *betray*": the unstated assumptions that make the stated words intelligible. The historian searches not only for truth but for meaning. In that process the very words the historian uses become symbols themselves. Each age has its special words, its own vocabulary, its own set of meanings, its particular symbolic order. This is true of the world *about* which the historian writes; it is equally true of the world *in* which he writes. Turning facts into interpreted symbols, the final stage of the historian's craft, becomes the most difficult and the most intellectually dangerous.

The essays in this book are literally about words, often the ones that Raymond Williams has labeled "key words" of our time, crucial to social discourse—*history, ideology, culture,* and *civilization.* We may use them commonly now, but that does not make them any more clear or less controversial. To complicate matters even more, the essays are in turn part of an ongoing dialogue between the historical meaning and usage (in the past) and the historian's meaning and usage (in the present). The historian's reconstruction and analysis of the past represent a necessary, continuous interaction of past and present, for in the end the historian composes a set of words that are to be words of his time.

The work here spans some twenty years, and appears precisely as it appeared originally in various publications or as it was given as papers or addresses in various public forums. My repeated concern with certain major themes may seem obsessive: the revolutions in communication and organization, the significant role of a new middle class, the battle between the party of culture and that of civilization. Traditional historical narrative does not lend itself to the expression of the logic of culture, and the writing of cultural history has always meant a search for a new form, a new language, a new perspective: theme and variation, a fugue-like principle of over-all organization, perhaps repeating but also discovering new notes to describe and probe. I see also how the individual essays reflect some of the intellectual and political debates of the time in which they were written. I should be unhappy if this were *not* the case, but unhappier still if they seemed only period pieces.

I flinch slightly at the rhetorical quality of some of my prose, but I have let it stand, remembering that each and every piece was not only an act of scholarship but also one of persuasion. In each piece you may hear me debating—with my material, with myself, with my colleagues, and especially with my students. In a sense, all historical writing attempts to persuade and all historians are teachers. I have always sought the kind of scholarly work that could initially be addressed to the needs and interests of my students. They have shared their understanding of America with me and have influenced my own understanding; I have deliberately tried to influence theirs as well.

The writing of history is as personal an act as the writing of fiction. As the historian attempts to understand the past, he is at the same time, knowingly or not, seeking to understand his own cultural situation and himself. When I began my own studies of the 1930s, a most distinguished historian in the field of cultural history praised me for my willingness to undertake such a serious intellectual struggle with my father and therefore my immediate past. I was stunned by the suggestion. I had supposed my undertaking an act of disinterested scholarship. But if works of history can often be read as autobiographical, this does not mean that that is all they are. All historians select the problems they will examine and the questions they will ask. Clearly their interests and experiences will help in making those decisions, but each must finally be judged by how much he does in fact enable us to understand the world he is analyzing. This is the world I felt I needed to know. I hope that need provides others something they need to know as well.

ACKNOWLEDG-
MENTS

This book exists because André Schiffrin insisted. He is thus totally responsible for it. Jim Peck and Wendy Wolf held my hand all through the process of making the book; a still-nervous author perhaps appreciates that even more than the significant editorial contributions both made. An old friend, Lewis Bateman, graciously and meticulously read the proofs and offered important suggestions. Owen D. Jones provided important help in compiling the illustrations. But most of all there was, as always, Beatrice. All of the things that can be said about the important contributions of a scholar's wife have long ago been said. But my wife deserves not only all those praises but more, the ones that somehow cannot even be put into words.

AMERICAN HIEROGLYPHICS
A NOTE ON THE ILLUSTRATIONS

Early in the twentieth century, Vachel Lindsay argued that America was becoming a world of visual images, of signs and symbols—in short, a "hieroglyphic civilization." This transformation probably actually began closer to the 1850s, when Americans found themselves able to purchase as well as view an increasing number of inexpensive prints offered by companies like Currier and Ives and the very special new images of life provided by the new profession of photography. These images—prints and photographs—were among the first "mass-produced" objects of an emerging consumer society in the 1850s. They were also to be a major source for a whole series of special *American* hieroglyphics.

Since the consumption of images is basic to an understanding of the culture, I have selected a series of important but often separate, even contrasting, images centered around several critical themes: "Our Father" (George Washington); "Our Skyscraper"; "Our Daily Bread"; "Our Flag"; "Our Town"; and "Our Church." In this world of images-turned-icons we can often literally see the fundamental tensions that help define the very nature of the "hieroglyphic civilization" itself.

Library of Congress

Portland Art Museum

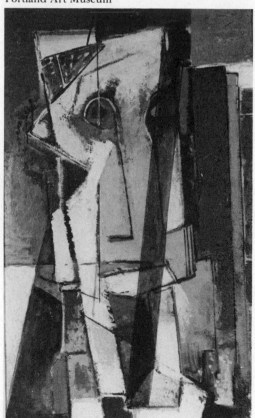

Our Father

In 1932, joint exhibits celebrated the centennial of the birth of the famous Currier and Ives artist Louis Maurer and the bicentennial of the birth of the Father of Our Country, a favorite Currier and Ives subject and one of their perennial best-sellers. Alfred Maurer, Louis's son, was a leading modernist painter, but in 1932 he was uncelebrated, out of money, and cut off emotionally and aesthetically from his father. As if in response to the double celebration of Washington and his own commercially successful father, Alfred offered his own portrait of the Founding Father.

INTRODUCTION
TOWARD A HISTORY
OF THE CULTURE
OF ABUNDANCE:
SOME HYPOTHESES

E*veryday life, a compound of
significance united in this concept, responds
and corresponds to modernity, a compound of
signs by which our society expresses and
justifies itself and which forms part of its
ideology. . . . This study of everyday life
affords a meeting place for specialized
sciences and more besides; it exposes the
possibilities of conflict between the rational
and the irrational in our society and our time,
thus permitting the formulation of concrete
problems of production (in its widest sense):
how the social existence of human beings is
produced, its transition from want to
affluence and from appreciation to
depreciation.*

Henri Lefebvre

When I began to organize a collection of my pieces for this book, I
discovered a deeper sense of order, progression, and even purpose
in their chronological sequence over the past quarter century than
I had suspected. (That sequence, with a few notable exceptions, is
repeated in the essays that follow.) Over the years, while struggling

to articulate for myself and my students some definition of what our culture is like and how it got this way, I find that I was developing almost unconsciously a way of understanding American culture: I was coming to see America through the notion of the "culture of abundance."

Simply put, one of the fundamental conflicts of twentieth-century America is between two cultures—an older culture, often loosely labeled Puritan-republican, producer-capitalist culture, and a newly emerging culture of abundance. If twentieth-century American politics rarely carries the burden of ideological conflict, there was nonetheless a significant and profound clash between different moral orders. The battle was between rival perceptions of the world, different visions of life. It was cultural and social, never merely or even centrally political.

My work on the 1930s led me increasingly to probe the question of a world somehow suspended between two quite distinguishable systems and ways of life. The crucial and perhaps climactic stage of that battle, these essays suggest, was fought in the 1920s and 1930s. Historians, to be sure, have readily seen and studied other basic cultural conflicts in American history: between classes, between regions and sections, between urban and rural worlds, between native and immigrant populations, between races and ethnic groups, and more recently between genders considered as cultural groups. These essays propose another kind of cultural conflict that offers additional perspective on such work, and that, I believe, can help explain much of the dynamic conflict over values in our century.

Perhaps what I mean by the "culture of abundance" best emerges against the background of a summary of what a range of historians have revealed in their study of social change in American life from the nineteenth to the twentieth centuries.* Any examination of the technological order immediately comes face to face with a series of exceptional inventions that, coupled with new sources of energy, made possible the amazingly rapid movement of people, goods, services, and ideas. Historians have rightly called this the "Communications Revolution." Any study of the culture of abundance begins with the obvious cultural consequences of the new communications. It is not simply that these inventions made abundance available to many and made possible increasingly effective distribution. Consciousness itself was altered; the very perception of time and space was radically changed.

---

* Several essays in this volume contribute directly to this outline.

INTRODUCTION

Perhaps no previous culture was as significantly shaped by the available communications technology. New cultural forms previously unknown developed; those that continued were reshaped repeatedly. At the same time, no other culture expended so much of its energy and resources discussing and analyzing communication and its problems. That became a characteristic of the culture itself. Some observers began to wonder whether anyone could really communicate at all. ("What we have here is a problem of communications.")

Perhaps the most important result of the Communications Revolution was its role in creating a new social order. Some historians and social scientists have spoken of an "Organizational Revolution," and there is an excellent and vast literature on the American tendency to organize and its effects in the late nineteenth and early twentieth centuries. Social scientists have analyzed effectively the bureaucratization so characteristic of the period. Yet such organization (especially over national and even international areas and markets) could never have been possible without transformations in communications. In large measure, the office and the office building are products of the new communications; they are unthinkable without the telegraph and telephone, the typewriter and business machine, the elevator, and the railroad.

Yet the Organizational Revolution had its most important consequence in the establishment of a new social class. Historians are of course always inventing new middle classes, but this one is of special significance because the culture of abundance was originally the culture of this new class. Defined in the simplest way, it is a class of bureaucrats: managers, professionals, white-collar workers, technicians, mechanics, salespeople, clerks, engineers (Veblen's favorites)—generally people on salary rather than wages. Again, there is a considerable literature (and even more debate) about this class, its nature and its social and political function. Here is a class undreamed of in our philosophy: Locke imagined a world increasingly populated by freeholders and American liberals, and Lockeans supposed for a long time that more and more people would share in owning property.

Karl Marx as well as other radicals saw more and more property in fewer and fewer hands. They often did not see the possibility of the emergence of a class that would attempt to hold power without holding property. Indeed, not all members of this new class agreed politically; nor did the ideology they shared necessarily reflect a solid front on issues of power and its uses. Yet there was a common ideology: their position in the social order affected their perceptions, their consciousness, and the way they performed in their everyday life.

Furthermore, this middle class provided the source and the inspiration for the new modal psychological type that was to become the ideal for the new culture. Every social order creates such an ideal. Of course, not every one can attain this ideal, but cultures provide means (education of various sorts) to help all move toward the ideal. The older culture—Puritan-republican, producer-capitalist—demanded something it called "character," which stressed moral qualities, whereas the newer culture insisted on "personality," which emphasized being liked and admired (Chapter 14). These terms are simple ones, although there is more than enough evidence of the persistent shift from one to the other to suggest a deeper social and cultural transformation. This shift raises important questions of social roles (questions raised seriously for the first time in social science literature as well as in more popular literature at the turn of the century) in ways that challenge all previously accepted social relationships.

The new middle class also helped articulate a new ideology. Often, before an ideology can be fully stated, another one must be attacked and, if possible, destroyed. This helps explain the wholesale assault on American Puritanism in this period. (See the chapters in Part I.) It helps account as well for the unusual number of revisionist studies of the Founding Fathers and the Constitution in the initial decades of the twentieth century. Further, the search for a positive ideology often led thinkers in the Progressive movement to turn away from Jeffersonian Republicanism and seek a political version more material, more influenced by expertise, more "scientific."

If we begin to look away from the traditional version of politics sanctioned by the older culture (with its insistence on party realignment as its major dynamic and hence its assumption that fundamental structures should remain in place), we can begin to pay attention to some unusual developments. For example, many Progressives demonstrated a particular interest in the arts. Jane Addams was not unique; in the story of her life at Hull House she concluded with a discussion of the role of arts and crafts, a characteristic aesthetic movement of the period. Progressive philosopher John Dewey devoted as much attention to aesthetic issues as he did to political ones, and his masterpiece, *Art as Experience* (written in the 1930s), sums up much of his social thought as well. In a sense, Progressivism was also an aesthetic movement: it proposed as a social *and* political end the opportunity for each man and woman to know some experience that was creative and satisfying, an aesthetic experience that was the

INTRODUCTION

consequence of communal and political life. This kind of vision is strikingly new as a political goal in America.

Perhaps it is even a mistake to talk about the Republic in any traditional sense after 1900. Sometime during or after the Civil War the Republic died and began to live more in rhetoric than in reality. Certainly, voter participation declined dramatically and has continued to do so. So, too, did the idea of the Republic decline as it had been defined in terms of total communal participation. The Founding Fathers had not wanted to create a State in the European sense. In fact, they had done everything possible to avoid creating one. The central government they established was unable to touch the individual citizen in any crucial regard: the definition of citizenship, the question of individual taxation, the issue of possible military service. The Civil War and the postwar years were to change all of that: the burgeoning of an enormous public bureaucracy with vast numbers of bureaucrats and experts making increasingly crucial decisions led to the emergence by the turn of the century of a State equal in kind to any in Europe. Americans might pretend the Republic still existed when civil servants and experts made more of the fundamental decisions affecting peoples' lives and fewer and fewer citizens exercised their right to vote, but it was clear that even though older forms remained a new polity was emerging as part of a new kind of culture. "Leadership" became one of the key words at the end of the century. Schools began to offer courses in it, and Presidents of the United States indulged in learned lectures about it.

Social training for leadership was but one side of the newly minted coin. The new polity dwelt increasingly and lovingly on "public opinion" sought new ways to exploit it without traditional resort to elections alone. Students of politics and public relations contributed to a new interest in, and an understanding of, how to influence mass belief and behavior. In a new world of personality and public relations (to say nothing of the new communications), the older republican vision seemed very distant.

It is in the context of this rapidly changing world that the culture of abundance can be understood. My contention emerged from a series of questions that arose when the usual clichés about urbanization and industrialization failed to explain satisfactorily the developments I was finding in the world of everyday life. Was not a new cultural order based, for example, on new and different assumptions—social, political, psychological, ideological—developing out of the very belly of nineteenth-century American society? Did not this newer order propose itself as an alternative to the existing order, providing a challenge resulting in a dialectical relationship between the two? Had not the doubling of per capita income in the United States between 1850 and 1860 important cultural consequences? And what of the huge surpluses of the late nineteenth century that raised serious contemporary questions about overproduction and underconsumption? Did not the study of everyday life suggest that even during the depression that ended in the 1890s many people began to dream of the possibility of a new world based on fabulous plenty and newfound affluence?

It is not a question of whether such abundance was a real possibility. The significant issue is the belief that it was. Franklin Roosevelt's speeches during the worst Depression times argued for a world of abundance; only some technical difficulties with distribution somehow kept the American people from their rightful share in that abundance. I submit that a whole culture was built on this vision.

Initial investigations to answer such questions yielded suggestions of significant transformation. Key words began to show themselves: *plenty, play, leisure, recreation, self-fulfillment, dreams, pleasure, immediate gratification, personality, public relations, publicity, celebrity.* Everywhere there was a new emphasis on buying, spending, and consuming. Advertising became not only a new economic force essential in the regulation of prices but also a vision of the way the culture worked: the products of the culture became advertisements of the culture itself.

All this seemed to stand in opposition to those words and ideas associated with the more traditional Puritan-republican, producer-capitalist culture that envisioned a world of scarcity (or at least one of significant limits), hard work, self-denial (William Graham Sumner translated these last two terms as labor and capital), sacrifice, and character.

As early as 1852 the distinguished New York minister and social activist Henry W. Bellows defined the New York Crystal Palace exhibition (in a sermon on the Crystal Palace) as a "popular advertisement." Even more notably, he defined advertisement as

a plan for letting the people know what is to be had, and who has it—a scheme for creating wants by exhibiting ingenious means of supplying them, and thus developing new forms of labor and new markets for them.

"Creating wants" suggests something new and important. Long ago, Vico told us that not only did each new age have its own problems and its own ways to solve them, but it also had its own needs, capabilities, and ways of seeing the world. Certainly, our literature has not been without enormous interest in needs and

INTRODUCTION

desires, yet is there something new and important about both the nature of the needs and desires in our age of abundance and our discussion of the problems created by them?

Perhaps the word "comfort" can supply an appropriate symbolic instance of such changes. Originally, it meant "to sustain, to encourage, to give relief," as a verb. "Comfort," as a noun, was precisely that which was given. Only in its listing of a sixth meaning introduced in the nineteenth century does *The Oxford English Dictionary* offer us the more common contemporary usage: "the state of physical and material well-being with freedom from pain and trouble, and the satisfaction of bodily needs; the condition of being comfortable." (One of the O.E.D. citations is from Lord Macaulay, surely one of the enthusiastic supporters of the new middle-class world order.) Earlier sources of comfort included religion and whiskey. J. F. Cooper tells us that frontiersmen called whiskey "Western comfort." And there are few objects as touching as the bags children and women made for Civil War soldiers. They contained buttons, needles, thread, a cake of soap, and above all a little tract or a Testament, as Mitford M. Matthews reports in his *Dictionary of Americanisms*. The soldiers universally called them "comfort-bags."

Of course, Americans still get comfort from whiskey and the Bible; it is still appropriate to comfort the poor, the sick, and those who have lost a friend or relative. The older culture remains. Meanwhile, however, a newer, more joyous vision of comfort emerged. In 1847, the "comforter" was patented, a thing of warmth and lightness, providing "relief" from the cold and a positive state of well-being and satisfaction. By the turn of the century necessities could be turned into something slightly more than utilitarian or relief-giving: the "comfort station" was born.

All of this is meant to be broadly suggestive of the kinds of transformations that are examined in these essays. The environment in which people lived and worked was altered. I do not mean merely the factory and the city street, significant as they surely were. The electric light could actually change the nature of night and one's sense of time. Chemically produced colors made possible a world of color never seen before. Photography and new methods of printing flooded the world with images, the effects of which we are barely beginning to understand. A series of inventions created an exceptional world of sound: a culture transported through the telephone, phonograph, radio, and talking pictures. Historians are well aware of the consequences of moving from a world of oral forms of communication to a new literate world of print. But what are the consequences of a new world of oral communications developing within a literate culture increasingly dependent on print? What is the result of all the visual images bombarding the eye (that "hiero-glyphic civilization" Vachel Lindsay called America) and of the new means of producing and transmitting sounds to the ear?

In that environment, there was a new interest in the body itself: physical culture, health, diet, food and its preparation, "eating out," nutrition and vitamins, obesity. How the body looked and how it felt took on new importance. Significant alteration occurred in how people lived (what they ate, the changing American diet) and how they died (different major causes of death), to say nothing about how and when they dined and how they were buried. The body had to be dressed and beautified in a world of fashion and cosmetics.

This culture had its own institutions that were to play special roles: department stores ("palaces of plenty"), restaurants, hotels— all specified a new way of life. But there were as well bathing beaches, swimming pools, and amusement parks, planned suburbs and the new profession of interior decorating. In fact, there was a new definition of "home." There were new entertainments and new ways of using older ones. There were new roles for women in the theater, for example, that had previously been virtually denied to them. There were new kinds of music, new rhythms, new dances, new musical institutions, and newer visions of the cultural role of music.

Indeed, a multitude of cultural forms native to this period developed: the comics, the poster, the photograph, the phono-graph, the telephone, the radio, moving pictures, advertising, pulp magazines and with them certain genres of fiction and nonfiction stories, and, perhaps most centrally, the automobile. We have, of course, had many studies of these phenomena but seldom in terms of their consequences for a definition of a culture and its ideology.

Among some of the special interests many of these forms reveal, the investigator finds a new and important interest in fairies and fairy tales, a new kind of fantasy, a fascination with magic, an interest in dreams and dreaming. Freud's great work appeared in 1900, but there was a huge popular literature before and after that appears to have owed nothing to him. Furthermore, there was a radically reoriented literature for children, a wide-scale interest in what might be called anthropology (popular as well as scholarly), an enormous outpouring of utopian vision, and not simply those found in the commonly discussed utopian novels of the period.

Thus in a world of tough rationalization and bureaucratiza-tion, science and magic seemed for a moment to come together in strange combination. Sir James George Frazer in his study of some of man's basic myths offered the hope that "the dreams of magic may one day be the waking reality of science," while some of America's most distinguished practical scientists—Edison and Burbank are examples—were presented to the enthusiastic and interested American public as "wizards" rather than scientists. Wizards abounded on the stage and in popular fiction for children. *The Wizard of Oz* and its overwhelming popularity might well prove a key to our understanding of the whole culture transformation.

"Transformation," as I suggest in Part IV, becomes a key word in this period. Taking on meaning in the new worlds of physics and modern biology, it was also used in connection with a fairy world where rocks changed to gold and frogs became princes. It could, and often did, suggest a world of ambiguous sex roles where girls might easily "be" boys and even boys might "be" girls. Transformations seemed to be what the new culture was all about.

All this suggests several lines of inquiry only barely hinted at in the current literature. For example, how much of what was happening in the new popular arts had a surreal quality? Certainly, this was true of many of the comics, many of the early films, popular music in its transformation from the sentimental ballad, advertising (especially the posters), and popular fiction. The strong emergence of the dream theme is only one indication. Serious American painting might indeed have become more "realistic" (though I am not sure that this is the case) with the emergence of the Ash Can School in the first decade of the twentieth century, but who would ever call Windsor McKay's Nemo a "realistic" portrayal of an American boy or see his nightly trips to Dreamland as part of any realist tradition? Yet the full import of the surreal tendency in the popular arts has never been assessed.

The new arts, moreover, are also in large part related to the creation of new associations of people in the society. Celebrities soon had their fans, beginning, I believe, in the world of sports and spreading to the matinee girls, who created matinee idols, and finally in around 1910 to the most fanatic of them all, the movie fans, following the creation of the star system.

The very world of consumer goods and advertising immediately created their organized opposition, however, in various consumer groups and movements as well as in a constant stream of satire, parody, indignant sermonizing. New dialectical forces began to shape new cultural tensions in important cultural dialogue. Those for and against lined up in new associational forms. Virtually every popular cultural form inspired instantly an opposition that urged its banning or at least its censorship. The movies were only the most sensational example. The organized hostility to the motion picture was as significant a phenomenon in our cultural history as was the temperance crusade, although a very different kind of struggle with different results.

The existence of the two cultures creates special problems for the investigator. To anyone committed to the values of the original tradition, and therefore to hard work, self-denial, and even sacrifice for the cause, the ideals of the new culture with its emphasis on pleasure and self-fulfillment and play might well seem offensively frivolous and anarchical. We do have a vast literature of social criticism directed against "consumer culture" and the "therapeutic society." Surely both of these categories are part of any defined culture of abundance. Yet the very terms used deliberately limit the dimensions of that culture in ways designed to denigrate and criticize it. Virtually every critic of consumer or therapeutic society brings with him or her an ideological position and values representative of the older order. Whether Marxist radical or middle-class liberal, the critic of the culture of abundance brings to bear the Weberian vision of material possessions as an "iron cage," a contempt for mass culture and its products; a dread of the "technological and bureaucratic organization of life"; a conviction that modern communications manipulates and distorts; a sense that the culture has brought with it a marked decrease in human freedom.

Our foremost historians of utopian thought, Frank and Fritzie Manuel, depict an important crisis in the early nineteenth century (as the social thinkers of that era saw it): "a crisis in man's capacity to find satisfaction in his work and emotional relationships." At least three great visions propelled some of the leading socialists of the period. Saint-Simon and his followers advocated a world socially engineered for the collective good, a society organized upon principles of science to create a world that fitted the needs of men and women as they really were. Fourier called for an environment in which all could fulfill their desires to the fullest, a world without repression, one that maximized libidinal gratification. And Marx, also concerned about human needs, sought a world in which it was possible to wrest a realm of freedom from a realm of necessity.

Such ideals—if not the general and more specific proposals—of these great socialists were in some fundamental sense shared by the culture of abundance. At least some of the ends proposed were approached and achieved in that culture. If new problems arose, if the results did not produce a utopia, if a great many things went wrong, if we now question whether there were not serious dangers implicit in some of the efforts to achieve this vision of freedom, and if in the end there are new kinds of determinisms, new necessities that frustrate any definition of true freedom, none of that negates the historical significance of the attempt. Even Marx and Engels

INTRODUCTION

could praise the achievements of the bourgeois overthrowers of the feudal order, which, however, did not make them enthusiastic supporters of continued bourgeois domination.

Many who attack the modern world are clearly unhappy living in this century. They have little sympathy for anything that is for the masses, seeing always some sort of fascism or Stalinism around the corner. Not all of these accounts are simply polemical; often they are based on scholarship of high quality. For example, none of us who work in this field can fail to respect what the Frankfurt School accomplished and therefore enabled us to do. But often the works of scholars in this tradition, concerned and worried about hegemony in the contemporary late (we hope) capitalist order, speak from a position of the Left but end up extolling the values and institutions of the older capitalist order of the nineteenth century (see Chapter 5).

Let me make my own position clear. The original enthusiastic support for the culture of abundance was often utopian. Many saw in the promise of the new culture a solution to fundamental human and social problems, a new world of fulfillment and even liberation. Many intellectuals (Simon Patten is an outstanding case) welcomed in the new world of abundance the emergence of a new man and a new society. Quite possibly, the culture of abundance and its believed promises help explain better than any other factor why Marxian socialism did not take deep root in the United States. Many who might have chosen the socialist way went instead with the hope of a culture of abundance.

Buying things (consumption) and getting professional help (therapy) do not, I think, represent things that are intrinsically wrong. Nor does entertainment enjoyed by huge numbers of people (mass culture). The culture of abundance was not largely the result of evil machinations to control and distort human life (I retain an initial sympathy for some of its values and dreams), and it would be a serious methodological error not to attempt first to understand the culture on its own terms.

Further, critics often make another serious methodological error. They assume that the world today (whatever its nature and however correct their critical evaluation) is simply the direct and only consequence that could follow from the world developing at the turn of the century. Therefore, they conclude, it must have been all bad from the start. No other view is possible if we look at where we are today. But this is simply bad history. If the culture of abundance has become manipulative, coercive, vulgar, and intolerable in all the ways these critics would have it, why did this happen? Did it have to follow? Were there alternatives? Only a historical view—a vision of that culture as it developed and changed over time and in interaction with the traditional culture itself—can provide hope of getting at these crucial issues. Perhaps there is still hope for a radical rebuilding of the world on the ideological vision of a culture of abundance. Perhaps this is a proper "socialist" view. Only a careful study of history can provide us with the necessary knowledge and the special insights to see whether this is possible.

To see the utopian possibilities in the culture of abundance and to insist on a dialogical or dialectical reading of both its repressive and its liberating possibilities is not to commit oneself to the culture itself, to accept all that it proposes, or even to agree that its end can be achieved only within this particular economic and social structure. Such a reading does not eschew critical evaluation: it insists on making distinctions, on understanding first and criticizing from some stated position afterward.

This is the new world and the new culture that my studies in history (consciousness), ideology (perception), and culture (forms of order) have helped me to propose. This is the order of things that my studies of transition and transformation have suggested. This is the outline of the undeveloped dialectic that might make American culture more open to analysis and understanding.

I | HISTORY AS MYTH AND IDEOLOGY

Our Skyscraper

No structure seems more typical of both modern America and the triumphant technology so admired by Americans than the skyscraper. No skyscraper was so symbolically significant as the Empire State Building. Designed and begun in what appeared to be the era of capitalism's greatest achievement, it was finished in the midst of one of capitalism's greatest crises. For photographer Lewis Hine, the building of the structure offered an opportunity to present the dramatic saga of men at work in "The Sky Boy," an almost romantic merging of man and technology. Only a few years later in 1933, the same building appears as a central icon in the movie *King Kong,* but takes on a darker, more ambiguous significance.

International Museum of Photography at
George Eastman House

Movie Star News

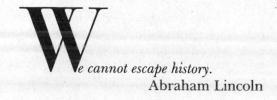

e cannot escape history.
Abraham Lincoln

Great political leaders are usually masters of the great rhetorical flourish. Memorable and frequently useful, such statements are brilliantly ambiguous: as false as they are true, as banal as they are profound, as meaningless as they are full of meaning. One thinks immediately of Franklin Roosevelt's "The only thing we have to fear is fear itself." Really? In 1933? Such statements cannot stand too close scrutiny.

Yet Mr. Lincoln's warning represents a characteristic American attitude. Not only do Americans believe they cannot escape history; few seem to want to. From the founding of the colonies, Americans have sought—almost as a kind of secular conversion—justification and sanctification from history. William Bradford began writing his great history of Plymouth Plantation, perhaps our first great book, our *Iliad* or *Odyssey*, within a decade of the establishment of the colony itself. The Founding Fathers thought of history as the "lamp of experience," the source of significant moral and political lessons. By the nineteenth century, Americans could find in history a way to become immortal: being part of history meant being part of eternity. History was and persisted in being a way to position oneself and one's group and community in the world, now and forever.

Long before history became a profession and historians became fixtures in colleges and universities, Americans read history with enthusiasm and had realized almost unconsciously the lesson George Orwell felt he had to teach in *1984*: he who controls the past controls the future. Nothing else explains the almost constant demand for a "new" history to replace the current and "officially" sanctified version of the past. The established view supports an order to things of which we disapprove; if we want a new order of affairs, we must rewrite our history to justify it. Thus history was from the start a crucial aspect of the culture. Not satisfied merely with destroying the older vision, such thinkers felt the need to provide a substitute vision.

There was the case of Edward Bellamy, that exceptional late-nineteenth-century socialist. For much of his writing career he engaged in a rare struggle against the menace of memory. Bellamy would have his fellows forget the past and dwell only in the present and the future. The destruction of memory was an essential part of his social philosophy because he was convinced that, socially and personally, memory was repressive: it prolonged a sense of guilt and sin. But even while he engaged in his crusade, Bellamy undertook the research for and the writing of one of the most memorable American historical novels; he felt, somehow, that he must put right the official, but quite erroneous, version of Shays' Rebellion. Thus even the enemy of memory yielded to the act of providing a more usable past.

The essays in this section attempt to explore the problem of history and culture. The first and most theoretical piece was an almost inevitable consequence of a lifelong fascination with the problem as I first came across it as a high-school student. I had acquired a copy of Charles and Mary Beard's *The Rise of American Civilization,* and I carried this fat volume with me everywhere, obviously to impress my fellows and to intimidate my teachers. But I read and reread it whatever my evil motives, and I fell in love not only with the sweep of that narrative but also with the basic questions it asked about history as it happened and about history as it was written. The two questions proceeded hand in hand, as I saw them. The Beards remain for me the starting point. Their work was as all great historical work should be: dialectical. Of course, I have long since come to wonder whether in fact they picked the right dialectical opponents, but the general method has stood the test of time as has their insistence that somehow the two questions of history as experience and history as record must be related and be considered together. This is what I have tried to do.

The Frontier Thesis essay was intended as homage to my best undergraduate teachers of history at Cornell. I had come to Cornell full of Beard and Parrington. There Curtis P. Nettels and Paul W. Gates introduced me to, saturated me in, the writings of Frederick Jackson Turner and his critics. Nettels had written a brilliant piece on Turner and the New Deal; he was a colonial historian, of course, but he taught me that great historians are people of rare and shimmering imaginations. And Paul Gates made me always face up to the material base of things, the reality in which all ideas and ideals of vague young would-be intellectuals must be grounded. My materialism came from Paul Gates, not from Thomas Hobbes and Karl Marx (although I suspect they helped), and so this essay was for them.

The essay on the Puritans was strictly for myself. I had been fascinated by why so many people had fought for so long over what the Puritans were really like, and knew there must be more to it than a simply historiographic battle. I had some ideas then; I am even surer now that I am on to the answer. And it is not unrelated to that persistent probing of recent years about group and gender identity that seeks an effective past and continues the basic cultural tradition I have tried to define and study.

History, I am convinced, is not just something to be left to the historians. In fact, in recent years the interest in history has grown while professional historians have felt increasingly left out. Some understanding of the role of history in American culture would help them to understand why. Not any kind of historical reconstruction will do. The age—like all previous ages—demands history as the myth or ideology it needs.

1 HISTORY AND THE AMERICAN INTELLECTUAL: THE USES OF A USABLE PAST

Writing during what must now appear to many as halycon days of faith in the possibilities of social studies, Charles and Mary Beard could declare: "The history of a civilization, if intelligently conceived, may be an instrument of civilization."[1] Buried within what was clearly for the Beards a significant normative proposition—the call for a special kind of history—there rests a fundamental truth even more important for the student of a civilization. The idea of history itself, special kinds of historical studies, and various attitudes toward history always play —whether intelligently conceived or not—a major role within a culture. That strange collection of assumptions, attitudes, and ideas we have come to call a "world view" always contains a more or less specific view of the nature of history. Attitudes toward the past frequently become facts of profound consequence for the culture itself. Many students of historiography, of course, have expended much worthwhile energy in attempting to unearth the cultural causes of various approaches to the study of the past. This paper, however, suggests, with a series of broad hypotheses, the possibilities involved in a full-scale examination of the cultural consequences of special attitudes toward the past and the uses of history within a culture. In order to do so, I first would like to suggest in the most general sense how two kinds of treatments of the past, designated "mythic" and "historical" for purposes of the discussion, are related

to each other and to culture. The rest of the essay proposes a basic
outline of the history of some of these key relationships throughout
American history.[2]

The idea of "history" itself belongs to a special kind of social and
cultural organization. In status or community societies there is no
written "history," although there may be epics or chronicles.[3] Myth
predominates in the prevailing world view: a special class—most
generally a priesthood—exists in whose hands the monopoly of the
interpretation of the myths of the society resides. Few question the
nature or kind of social order. The institutional and normative pattern remains relatively static. The myths are sufficient to unify the
whole, to answer the largely emotional needs of the members of the
community, and to provide, when necessary, the collective dreams
of the society about the past, the present, and the future in the same
instant. The myths "explain" all. The function of myth is largely
utopian: it provides a vision of the future without providing in and
of itself any essential dynamic element that might produce the
means for bringing about any changes in the present order of
things. Ritual is generally enough to assure the fulfillment of the
promise of the myth.

History, however, comes into existence in contract or associational societies. Here, the social order is changing in ways that contrast dramatically with the more static nature of a status society.
New institutions and values arise; associations become increasingly
defended not because they exist but because they fulfill a function
that can be more clearly seen and understood. The social order itself
must be rationalized; reasoned explanations are called for. It is
history that can more reasonably explain the origin, the nature, and
the function of various institutions and their interaction. Further,
history seems able to point the direction in which a dynamic society
is moving. It brings order out of the disordered array that is the
consequence of change itself. As a result, history is often used as the
basis for a political philosophy that while explaining the past offers
also a way to change the future. History thus operates ideologically.
But by the nature of its enterprise and the kind of society that calls
it into existence, historical interpretation cannot be effectively mo-
nopolized for long by any special class or group.[4] Its study is open
to all who can reason and to all who participate in the various contractual or associational aspects of the society.

Obviously what I have presented in excessively brief form is a
contrast of two models of social organization and one significant
element in the world view an investigator might be expected to
discover in each. In status societies the prevailing attitude toward

the past is mythic and its function utopian; in a contract society the past is viewed historically with consequent ideological uses. Probably no such ideal types ever existed. Certainly, for example, a contract society does not surrender its mythic elements; the psychological and social need for myth seems to persist in the most dynamic and rationalized social organizations. For it is the realm of myth, in my usage, to provide much of the vision, the hopes, and the dreams of any group. Myth, therefore, continues as what I call the utopian element in any world view, although I would like to suggest that in a complex contract society the number and kinds of myths are multiplied and frequently conflict more dramatically than they would in an ideal status society.[5]

What is significant, then, about a historical approach to the past in the newer social order is not that it replaces a mythic approach or even that history sometimes finds itself in conflict with myth. I am not proposing only a battle between mythos and logos (although surely this too does exist) but a special interaction between myth and history, utopianism and ideology, that has significant cultural consequences for any society. History is frequently called upon to play a new role in relationship to the older, mythic views. Perhaps a metaphor will explain what I have in mind. Myth traditionally provides the central drama of any social order—witness the sacred drama of the Christian myth. But history offers something vastly different in its ideal form. Since it is concerned with change, movement, the ongoing course of action and ideas, since it is more clearly related to the dynamic aspects of social life, it provides what I have called an ideology as distinguished from a utopian vision. But the two frequently work hand in hand: myth provides the drama and history puts the show on the road. Myths often propose fundamental goals; history often defines and illuminates basic processes involved in achieving goals.

Philosophies of history—attitudes toward history as process—frequently influence the *kind* of action (or retreat to inaction) men adopt as a result of belief in a fundamental myth. If one needed further proof about this important relationship between myth and history, a brief examination of millennialist interpretations of history would prove most illuminating. All Christians believe in the central myth (and therefore promise) of their faith; but this belief clearly has different consequences culturally when coupled with different theories of history. Millennialism, as a special theory of history, is itself of crucial cultural importance. But those who hold a premillennialist view are going to act far differently in the world from those who hold a postmillennialist position, as any student of eighteenth- or nineteenth-century American intellectual and social history can attest, in spite of their fundamentally shared view of the truth of the Christian myth.[6]

In the complex relationship between myth and history within a culture it is clear that there are conditions that frequently lead to the attempt to use each cultural force—myth and history—in ways that emulate the natural function of the other. We are perhaps most clearly aware of the consequences that result from an attempt to make history into myth (or at least make history *perform* mythically). W. Lloyd Warner's extended discussion of the particular uses of American history in his latest Yankee City volume provides a most graphic instance. Here history has in fact become myth, complete with ritual, pageant, and even a kind of priesthood. A relatively complex contract society is unified, the existing social order justified, basic values reinforced, and community goals sanctified—all by resort to major incidents in Yankee City's history treated in mythic ways in which all citizens of the town are invited or perhaps socially compelled to share. In the process, however, something significantly different is made from history—and even the history of Yankee City and the U.S.A.—from what we usually think of it.[7]

But there is also a drive to make the myth something historically real; that is, to turn the utopian promise into a specific kind of ideology. The nineteenth century began its detailed search for a historical Christ, for example, undoubtedly to provide a rational basis for a belief in the Christian myth. But that very process of putting Christ *in* history has enormous cultural consequences for society and for the nature of Christianity itself. For once the chief mythic character of the Christian religion, the man-god who died and was reborn, became a figure within the limits of rational historical inquiry, he became subject to special interpretations and uses. Jesus became a great "representative man"—an idea that in its very nature was a threat to the mysteries of the Christian myth—who was a great moral teacher and prophet. By the end of the century, the American people could be told that if they would truly walk "in His steps" they ought to become Christian socialists. They were presented with a set of immediate social consequences if He came to Chicago. Within a few decades, He would become Comrade Christ, the social revolutionary.[8] Ideological consequences of a striking kind result from the effort to make a mythic vision of the past function as history. But, if only to emphasize the problem, that very act of making history out of myth, the act of treating Jesus as a historical figure shaped by historical conditions and circumstances and shaping in turn his society and world, as any great man might, opens the way to a variety of ideological uses, not just one. History is seldom the monopoly of the few, as the interpretation of the mystery of myth may indeed be in some cultures. And as a result, it is this same historical Christ who could become in 1925 the subject of a book entitled *The Man Nobody Knows,* by the eminently successful salesman-businessman Bruce Barton.

I have selected two extreme examples of history becoming myth and myth becoming history to establish my basic hypothesis. Yet somewhere in between there is a special meeting ground between history and myth that frequently provides a key to the central tensions within a culture. It is in this area of the tensions between established myths and developing ideologies, between the efforts of converting history to mythic ends and of using history in its more traditionally ideological way, where much of the story will have to be told. This conflict is often quite clearly recognized by many intellectuals within the culture. Artists, especially, are able to see and use this important intellectual and cultural fact. Two novels will perhaps indicate the existence of this awareness. In Melville's *Billy Budd* many commentators have seen the significant use of both the myth of Christ and the myth of Adam. But too few have seen that these mythic representations are put into a very special and carefully defined historical context. For Melville goes to great lengths to set his scene within history—precisely and in some detail, with dates, events, and all the trappings of historical reality. We see the mythic enactments against the backdrop of meticulously established historical detail, a particular time and place, a particular series of historically true events. It is the tension between the historical demands (ideology) and the mythic ones (utopia) that gives the novel its tragic pertinence. Sixty years later, William Faulkner was to use the same kind of central tension in *A Fable.* The enactment of the Christ myth is again presented against a most specific and realistic historical background. Not only does Faulkner place his tale during the First World War as Melville did his during the aftermath of the French Revolution, but he also uses an amazing number of details that come from the actual history of that war. Thus it is this very tension between the mythic beliefs of a people—their visions, their hopes, their dreams—and the ongoing, dynamic demands of their social life recorded by the students of the real past and the actual present (with perhaps an often implied future) that provides many artists with their theme, a theme reflecting a basic conflict within the culture itself. This is in fact one of the basic tensions that help define the nature and kind of culture that exists.

American civilization begins with a unique set of cultural circumstances. On the shores of New England, a group of able intellectuals —some ministers, others reflecting their important university train-

ing—established a kind of social order that was clearly, by definition, a contract society. It was organized on the theoretical base
composed of a series of major compacts; it was prepared to carry
out an ongoing mission within history, the task no less than the
reformation of the whole world. It was also, however, a social order
committed with grave earnestness to a belief in the Christian myth.
But intellectually, for its particular kind of organization to survive
and its mission to be fulfilled, the myth alone, no matter how interpreted, would not suffice. It is always important to remember that
this was a society dominated largely by those we would today call
intellectuals. The nineteenth-century image of the alienated intellectual would surely seem strange to these Puritans, even to the
Hutchinsons and Williamses and Taylors who were driven from the
colony or forced to keep their private thoughts very private indeed.
And these intellectuals who functioned as leaders from the very
beginnings of the enterprise carried with them a special view of
history; they made the study of history and its interpretation a vital
part of the cultural development of the colony. The view of history
that the settlers and those who followed brought was one that clearly
explained, defined, and justified the specific kind of contractual
society they proposed to establish and develop. The writing of history, the keeping of journals, at least in part for historical purposes,
the discussions of history in various sermons and addresses make
clear the central role—second only, I would argue, to the expound-
ing of the Christian myth itself and its meanings—of historical inquiry to the colonizing efforts. For it is history that provides the
ideology, the dynamic view that makes possible the onward movement of the society to its historically appointed task. The tension
between the promise of the Christian myth and its obligations upon
man and the promise of their special view of history and its demands forms a central theme in any analysis of the culture they
built.

By the end of the seventeenth century, that brilliant series of
covenants and compromises, that essential tension between myth
and ideology directed by America's first intellectual elite, had broken down forever. In an almost final gesture, Cotton Mather characteristically resorted again to history in an effort to restore the old
order socially and intellectually. But the age was over, the tensions
too great; nothing—not even Mather's monumental and most significant history—could save it. Two important groups, both denied
an effective place within the old order, were now ready to face each
other in a major struggle reflecting again a basic tension in the
eighteenth century. Each had its own view of the nature of the
process of history, derived in some measure from the original Pu-

ritan synthesis but each stressing its special aspects as ideology for its own kind and class.

The revivalists of the Great Awakening took the millennialist and providential elements of the old synthesis as their own. In their frankly supernatural view of history they saw in the revival movement itself the hope of the coming millennium. In their enthusiastic and optimistic view they were committed, then, to a theory of history that might provide an effective threat to the social order and stability in the name of the currently disinherited. On the other hand, the new leaders of the American social order, who had taken over after the older Puritan leadership had faltered, found it necessary to fight back with a philosophy of history and a view of American development that could be used to defend the newly-arrived-at contractual order in which they were now the elite, intellectually and socially. Stow Persons has shown with acute awareness how these men developed a cyclical theory of history without significant reference to the Christian myth and yet without attempting to deny this mythic vision directly. Rather, they stressed the law and order that ruled the universe in terms of clearly discernible moral qualities, qualities reflected most effectively in the accumulation of property and position, in the special moral character exemplified by their own group in society. Thus their theory of history justified the new social order and their place in it and sought to counter the "dangerous" theories of the enthusiasts and millennialists of the revival movement.[9]

The intellectual tensions of the century—and in some sense the real social tensions as well—were reflected in a basic conflict of historical theories, one in which the Christian myth was about to be actualized in time and thus posed a radical threat to the stability of the social order, and the other in which the Christian myth itself had become some sort of regularized goal at the end of history, a goal that might be best achieved through the orderly and moral progress of men under the leadership of those of good character and sound social position. The conservative philosophy of history of the Enlightenment in America largely dominated public policy, and the newer intellectuals who espoused it continued to maintain effective control in society as had an earlier elite in Puritan New England.

By the second and third decades of the nineteenth century several important new factors could be witnessed on the American cultural scene. First, the intellectuals in the society could no longer easily assume that through the professions of the ministry or the law social power would be assured to them within the American community. The problem of vocation for the intellectual in America became for the first time a serious issue: for this reason Emerson's soul-searching struggle to find a proper vocation becomes a key symbolic instance for the student of the role of the intellectual in America. Secondly, the emergence of the idea of progress in its variant forms provided an easy view of the nature of history for every man and an all too easy rationalism that engulfed all before it. So much had history taken hold in American society that the very mystical and intuitive nature of fundamental myths seemed to lose place and meaning for many. So easily did the notion of progress adapt all events past and present to its use that the whole social order became too readily (for some) justified—any change, any development, any direction.

For those who felt these dislocations there were several courses open. They might reject history in its currently accepted sense and seek beyond it or apart from it some sense of the importance and meaning of life. This, of course, was the path of Emerson and Thoreau, who refused to allow rational historical analysis to take away from them the transcendental vision of the basic myths they still wished to and needed to believe in. If history did have a value, it was not the history as ongoing process but rather the study of what might be abstracted from the past as a standard in the present —exactly those transcendent virtues and ideas that were unaffected by the relativities of the historical process itself.

This particular use of the past was, of course, not new nor was it uniquely the property of Emerson and his followers. The eighteenth-century elite had drawn on its studies of the classical world for models of behavior and conduct; the nineteenth century frequently found ideal patterns for society and morals (as well as art and architecture) in a special and static vision of the Middle Ages, Gothic, and Romanesque; the later nineteenth century and early twentieth century looked especially to the glories of the Renaissance for standards of taste, virtue, and judgment; and in the early twentieth century the American humanists (following what they believed to be the lead of the Renaissance humanists) again proposed a vision of the classical world as ideal. But such a use of history—abstract, outside of time and circumstances, detached from the whole process of development—was largely a device to overcome, to halt, to stem the tide of the ongoing process itself. It was almost always the tool of a small elite and its effect was seldom widely felt. It was, in my terms, essentially an antihistorical use of history. Its function was mythic in purpose, but it failed too often to elicit a proper mythic response from the mass of society—no matter how monumental and overpowering its architectural representations all over the American landscape.

Perhaps more effective but still limited in appeal was the resort to myths of a purer kind in which more of the community might easily share. R. W. B. Lewis has sketched for us the story of *The American Adam,* which deals with a major aspect of that effort. And if Emerson and the transcendentalists generally failed to reaffirm the vital mystery of their particular vision of the Godhead to large numbers of Americans, the continuing revivalist tradition did keep alive a more readily emotional and social response to the Christian myth, although in this case once again usually related to a millennialist historical view, whose considerable consequence I have previously suggested. The transcendentalist and revivalist attempts to reassert the value and function of myth in American society are, after all, parts of a single process and in some very real sense transcendentalism can well be considered a kind of revivalism among the intellectuals.

But there were intellectuals in this period who did not turn away from the study of history itself. One of the most significant aspects of the intellectual history of the mid-nineteenth century is the effort made by American intellectuals to recapture control over the study of history itself as a vehicle of intellectual and social influence and power. Most of these intellectuals had been trained, initially, for either the law or the ministry, the previous career patterns available to those intellectuals who sought power in American society.[10] These intellectuals trained themselves in the best of the methods provided by the newer "scientific" historical scholarship then thriving in Germany. They were, moreover, much admired and much read by a goodly segment of the American community. In an age when a special kind of historical imagination flourished, these intellectuals discovered that through the writing of history itself they might achieve some of the ends their more ahistorical fellows were unable to achieve.

But in capturing, in some meaningful sense at least, part of the intellectual leadership through their study of history, what ends were the Bancrofts and the Sparkses, the Prescotts and the Parkmans actually seeking? David Levin has ably shown how they conceived of history as a "romantic art" and how clearly they used the major devices of that art in their works of scholarship.[11] They wrote colorful narrative history; they made characters and events come alive. But such history—and it is again being called for in our own age—with all its serious and studied scholarship yields itself to fulfilling the very kind of mythic function (albeit much more popularly received) in a way that the more self-conscious nonhistorical mythic efforts of the period seemingly failed to do. Almost always narrative history attempts a mythic function, and the more carefully analytical history (most characteristic in the monographs and studies in the period from 1890 to 1940) lends itself to ideological uses. In the unstable world of the nineteenth century, filled with change, teeming with developments bent on upsetting the fundamental nature of the social order itself—developments that were to include a civil war—these great historians of the middle of the century produced American epics. They provided, perhaps, a way of understanding what was happening through an almost mystical notion of the divine law of progress, as in the case of Bancroft. Here is history offering hope without program, faith without a searching investigation of basic issues and problems. In the words of R. W. B. Lewis, Bancroft's kind of history was a demonstration "in historical terms of the validity of the hopeful legend, the legend of the second chance." [12] In the case of Parkman, on the other hand, history became a kind of tragedy, the unfulfilled promise of both savagery and civilization. But whether optimistic or pessimistic, the histories of the period provided certain fundamental values, a certain commitment to moral law, certain reinforcement through examples of exemplary social and political behavior. In spite of all their scholarship and science, then, these epic accounts are mythic in consequence of maintaining older social arrangements and values, utopian in essence and objective. These historians try to speak out as high priests in charge of interpreting a newer and more scientifically composed mythology. It is perhaps not surprising that a scholar like R. W. B. Lewis should discover mythic elements in their work similar to that in the work of some of those who rejected traditional historical analysis.

Mid-nineteenth-century American intellectuals adopted an approach to the study of the past that led to a fundamentally utopian outlook; the method of analysis was primarily mythic—no matter what the more formal trappings. This attitude toward history and toward the world reached a most dramatic climax in the 1880s—the decade in which more Americans sought to outline in print their utopian visions than perhaps any other decade in our history.[13] Significantly, however, most of these attempts to devise a utopia were presented without any ideological basis that might indicate how the existing social order could propel itself toward the achievement of such a new and ideal ordering of society.

The intellectual historian fond of dramatic contrasts might delight in comparing the essential utopian outlook of much thought of the 1880s with the fundamental return to the historical vision of the 1890s. Such a contrast might easily, it is true, be overdrawn. But nevertheless, here, amidst a series of basic problems too harsh to be overlooked, too earnest and demanding of immediate attention to be judged on the basis of a mythic view of some distant future, history again emerged as a vehicle for the intellectual with a new and special set of functions significantly in line with the ideological usefulness of certain attitudes toward history.

Many defenders of Frederick Jackson Turner and many critics have tried to sum up his greatness. Many have pointed to a considerable group of forerunners or precursors who held views similar to his. But the genius of Turner was essentially a simple and yet vital one culturally. He took a major American myth and made from it effective history. He took a utopian set of attitudes and beliefs and made them ideologically effective for his own times. First, he compiled no great narrative, used almost none of the current literary conventions. His was an effort in analysis. His starting point was not some vague feeling of instability but a set of specific problems in the American scene that were of moment in his own era—labor unrest, the farmers' revolt, the consequences of a vast new immigration, the rise of urban problems, a worldwide depression in the face of a worldwide transportation and communications revolution. He wanted to account for these problems; he wanted to suggest why they had not arisen previously in our history. He made, therefore, the Frontier Thesis, a long-established myth as many authorities agree, a major tool for social analysis. What is more, since he could reveal *why* America had developed the way it had, since he knew the key ingredient in producing the kind and quality of social institutions and character types that made America unique, his analysis might more easily provide some clues about what must be done to preserve that order. Thus his analysis might make it possible for one to act—not resign oneself to the myth of a second chance with some inevitable progress under God's benign direction, nor surrender to the essential tragedy of the human condition, nor carry on precisely as one had in the past under the leadership of one's betters.[14]

I hope this analysis will not be taken as approval of the kind of approach Turner and his followers undertook, or the kind of ideology that emerged in part because of that approach. Rather, I am suggesting that what followed from this kind of history was precisely that: an ideology, and moreover one that was in striking ways to become in part the official American ideology since at least 1893. If from 1893 to 1963 Americans find themselves committed to a search for new frontiers to replace the one Turner announced was no more, they do so in large part because the study of history pointed the way ideologically. It is precisely because this did become a major ideological force, adapted to many ends in the America of the twentieth century, that there has been such a wide-scale public debate on the validity of the so-called Turner thesis and that important groups of American intellectuals found it necessary to discuss the values that followed from a frontier America, values that some were trying to preserve in our century while others equally vigorously were trying to disavow them.[15]

Out of the historical awareness that dawned in the 1890s in America came still another example of the importance of history as ideology. This involves another pattern of historical inquiry. If Turner turned a myth into history, others in the period, again for ideological purposes, attempted to take the mythic out of what had previously passed for history. All through the nineteenth century there had been a rumbling of dissatisfaction with the inheritance from seventeenth-century Puritan theology and social organization and values. One can point to many landmarks along the way that reveal the challenge to the Puritan tradition which had become so important a part of official American mythology. But the real explosion occurred in the 1890s—an explosion that was to continue to reverberate throughout American intellectual life until the 1940s.

For any student of culture, one question must seem apparent at the outset. Why should anyone bother to attack the life and ideas of men long dead or of a social order no longer in existence? Why, after all, in any culture should anyone, save perhaps those professionally involved with the study of the past, care about what the seventeenth century was *really* like? Yet in that great era of historical awareness beginning roughly in the 1890s, American intellectuals *did* care. They cared because they realized the vital ideological importance in a society like ours of history and the "proper" attitudes toward it. They cared because they realized that views held about the past generally had consequences for the present. It was not simply that the past "determined" the present in some rather simple casual order of things, but that the way one viewed the past had significant consequences for the way one acted in the present. It was precisely because in our kind of social order history becomes a key to ideology, a key to the world view that shapes programs and actions in the present and future. At least this was a fundamental view of the majority of American intellectuals in the period between 1890 and 1940. Since current ideology is based on a particular view of the nature of the past, since present problems are frequently solved by reference to the way past experience dealt with similar problems, the control over the interpretation of the nature of the past becomes a burning cultural issue. This is, in effect, the driving force behind the movement James Harvey Robinson called the "New History" in 1913; it colors the achievements of other professional historians like Charles Beard and Carl Becker.[16] And it is not beside the point that these historians, like Turner, played significant roles in the general culture of their era that went far beyond their purely professional responsibilities These attitides in fact came generally to be held by a generation or more of intellectuals who were in no sense profes sional historians.

There is, of course, still a further assumption behind this historic struggle within history itself. Not only is it important that we have the "right" view of the past, the proper attitudes toward history, if we are to operate effectively in the world today and tomorrow, but also the right view, the proper attitudes *can* help us to solve our problems and change the course of the stream of history itself. This is why Van Wyck Brooks' call in 1918 for a "usable past" made sense to American intellectuals all through the period under discussion, no matter how they might agree or disagree about which view of the past was most especially useful. There was a basic agreement that an intelligent reading of the past might make possible man's intelligent direction over the future course of history.

The preoccupation of the brothers Adams with special phases of the American past is well known by students of our civilization. Further, there has been extensive discussion of these remarkable men against the background of the very special problems they faced as intellectuals in a society in which they seemed to have, in the current social order of their day, little place or function. They fit rather easily into the image of the alienated intellectual, that image which began to emerge significantly on the American scene in the nineteenth century. But the special relationship between this seeming lack of function and their interest in the study of the past has not been sufficiently explored. For as "aliens" seeking positions of intellectual authority and power, they did not follow the path of the transcendentalists in turning against the past or the tradition of the historians of the earlier days of the century who would become high priests for society by turning history into a special mythic form, an epic art. Rather, they turned to the study of the past in an effort to find a new ideological position that they could offer in refutation of accepted contemporary ideologies, ideologies justified by a view of the past currently in vogue and for them significantly untrue and dangerous.

If they told the story of the antinomian controversy, for example, they did so not simply to set the record straight. (How few historians, professional or otherwise, really seem interested in the pastness of the past!) They did so because they believed that the defense of Puritan America, which had become part of the official creed, perpetuated values and social attitudes intolerable to them, impossible for the America they would see develop. If Brooks

Adams, more forcefully than any figure before him and in advance of the more sophisticated analysis of the same relation made slightly later by Max Weber, undertook to relate the development of modern capitalism and the Reformation, he did so because he found Puritan values reinforcing capitalist values and the resultant social and economic organization destructive of the kind of culture he wished to see flourish in America. If as a result of the new economic man who emerged as a major social type from the fusion of capitalism and Protestantism it was, as he believed, impossible to have a decent art, architecture, and literature, and it was unlikely that an effective civilization could endure in the United States, obviously something must be done to modify if not overthrow the ruling ideology that perpetuated this social type. *The Law of Civilization and Decay* was in effect a kind of "New History." The philosophies of history advanced by Brooks and Henry Adams were not simply statements of pessimistic surrender to the world as it was, but a new reading of how the world got that way: an effective, critical beginning of a search for a new ideology that might produce a culture more agreeable. It would not be easy to achieve this reorganization, but the place to begin was clearly with a reexamination of the past and the effort to discover from such study the possible new laws that might provide a new dynamic approach to the world's problems. At the same time, of course, it might provide a new role for the intellectual as agent of discovery, critic of the old history, the old social order, and the old ideology and liaison to the new men of power bringing them a new history, a new ideology, new insights for the development of programs of action. If the older view of the Puritan past sanctified the purging of individualist dissent or the more vicious values and consequences of capitalism, it must give way to a new view, a true view of what the Puritans *really* were.

This form of intellectual activity became common in the period after 1890. The whole of American history and its official version came under the scrutiny of American intellectuals in a way unique in our development. The frontier past and its consequences for culture, the Puritan tradition and its results were but two areas of growing concern on the part of those who sought from a newer version of the American past some new orientation for American civilization itself.[17] It became especially the function of the intellectual to find a useful past, a version of American history and of the nature of history itself that would propel America onto the road to a desirable culture or at least provide the critical tools with which to overthrow the official view—the view Van Wyck Brooks suggested put a "Talmudic seal" on institutions, values, and policies repellent to these intellectuals. Brooks and Lewis Mumford, for example, felt they must rewrite our literary history, if only to provide some new basis for literature in their own time and some worthwhile relationship between the artist, the intellectual, and his society. Other intellectuals joined suit; their useful pasts frequently differed and they quarreled about this among themselves. Southern agrarians, for whom the nature of the Southern past became a matter of vital concern, an obsession that led literary men to write history and biography, found their view of the past directly challenged, for example, by the views of a growing number of Marxist intellectuals. Some were concerned only with "debunking" the past—a new and rather common pastime, introducing a new word into the language itself; others developed more profound philosophies of history. But the fundamental point remains: during this era in our intellectual development attitudes toward history played a key role in many debates, and all seemed to agree that some special view of the past was necessary, some view of history that challenged the assumed truths about the past and the ideological positions based on such "truths."

The extraordinary importance placed on the control of the past was reflected in all fields of activity. The Social Gospel movement depended upon its special version of history and its special view of Christ's mission in history. Certain factions of the so-called Progressive movement made the New History a key ally. It is ironic to think that a book as dry, painfully detailed, and scholarly as Beard's *An Economic Interpretation of the Constitution* could become a work of political significance— but it did for some Progressives. The New Criticism in literature (and the new literature itself), while frequently believed to be antagonistic to historical study, was in fact simply antagonistic to special versions of history. Many literary figures found themselves, in their battles with the entrenched literary standards of the day, forced to rewrite the whole of literary history to support their own critical and creative activities. T. S. Eliot is but one outstanding example of a New Critic who gave us, in rough outlines at least, a brand-new version of European literary history. The most advanced movements in the arts frequently were based in large part on a profound restudy of the past, be it in painting, in architecture, or in music, in an effort to support the newer visions.

It is striking to examine from this perspective some of the major literary figures and their most important works. Here again the artist believed that somehow it was his special function (a function that would afford him special status, a way out of alienation) to make history his own, to offer in his art a vision of that history that would be more meaningful for culture. Ezra Pound became deeply involved in the study of America's past—as well as the past of Europe and China. The *Cantos* represent a major effort to come to grips with historical materials and to use them in a special mythic way. To many students of our civilization it must seem strange indeed to discover in the body of this complex and difficult work not simply allusions to John Adams and Martin Van Buren (two of Pound's special American heroes, whom he believes American official history has ignored) but also long passages from the writings of these men and other historical figures. For Pound was trying to "make it new" in this as in other areas, to provide for his audience some newer insight into what he believed was the true nature of the American tradition and therefore the special promise of American life. Hart Crane's *The Bridge* likewise insists on a special historical vision. And the career of William Carlos Williams can be assessed in terms of a persistent effort—from his earliest work to the end of his brilliant career—to make meaningful his nation's history in a special mythopoetic way. Williams is especially clear about his objective: he wished to make the past alive and important in the present. Official, or "scientific," history was for Williams a lie. It was the kind of history that "portrays us in generic patterns, like effigies or the carving on sarcophagi, which say nothing save, of such and such a man, that he is dead." It is the pastness of the past that is dangerous for a culture. We need history, for when we regret the past, not realizing that "what we are has its origins in what *the nation* in the past has been," we lose immeasurably because of our ignorance. The past, as brought to new and meaningful light by the artist's imagination, which makes it present to us all, is "our greatest well of inspiration, our greatest hope of freedom (since the future is totally blank, if not black)."[18]

Thus the culture of America in the period between 1890 and 1940 was based in large measure on a view of the importance of history in solving human problems on every level and on a firm commitment to the special role that the intellectual might develop for himself in a world in which he felt alien as critic of the official ideology and champion of the truer meanings of the nation. Toward the end of this period, it is clear, what Richard Chase has called "the Quest for Myth" again became a major occupational and imaginative concern for many artists and intellectuals. The need for myth began to reassert itself—be it the Christian myth or any number of mythic visions out of history. As depression and world war engulfed the world, the stabilizing and utopian function of myth again seemed important. But throughout the major portion of the period, leading figures dealt directly with the tensions created between history as myth and history as ideology in a brilliant effort to make a new civilization and to make it move in directions established by a newer historical view. It is this fact which gives special tone to the period and can in part be held responsible for the very special kind of cultural consequences that developed.[19]

The last two decades in America have been marked by a singularly antihistorical spirit among the leading figures of our intellectual life. This trend, of course, had existed as a sharp undercurrent during the previous era as part of the everpresent tension between myth and ideology. I have already indicated the beginnings of what were to be a ground swell of interest in and search for (even conscious creation of, if that is possible) myth. T. S. Eliot's career can be seen, from one perspective, as a continual lyric battle raging within the poet himself between the mythic and the ideological, between the utopian vision and the historical. The "cunning passages, contrived corridors" of history that Eliot speaks of always presented for him dangerous traps from which man finally must escape. In *Four Quartets* it becomes clear to the poet that "right action is freedom from past and future also," a vision of man in relation to history that stands in effective contrast to the views of his contemporary, William Carlos Williams, cited previously.

In the realm of religion the historically oriented Social Gospel no longer commands the allegiance of the major Protestant intellectual leaders. The existential eye sees no historic Christ and no Christian mission that can be accomplished within time. The ideology of the Social Gospel depended upon a specific role of Christ in history and a view of the nature of history that made possible the achievement within history of a Christian society. The existential temper sees in the mythic Christ a "concrete absolute" that provided the model for those who would have the "Courage to Be" but who realize that within the relativities of history it is not really possible for man to solve any important problem facing him.

Many of our newer literary vogues—some of them brilliantly evocative of major moral dilemmas of our time to be sure—are deliberately wedded to the present moment alone. For the Beat Generation, the past—and even the future—is an enemy, threatening man with a vicious traditionalism (sometimes called conformity) or a series of problems to which there is no solution except individual action. They return to an almost Thoreau-like ritual burning of the past, preferring the immediate sensation, the experience of the moment, or the escape into timelessness offered by some oriental philosophies (or their versions of them) that are strictly ahistorical. Our leading movements in painting, especially Abstract Expressionism and Pop art, offer the most immediate kind of experience, more clearly divorced from any sense of history than any other movement in painting since the Renaissance.

The study of history as a discipline has again become major literature, frequently superbly written and compiled, but often based on an underlying assumption clearly taken from American existential theology and stated most effectively by one of our leading intellectuals who is himself the writer of much admired history:

History is not a redeemer, promising to solve all human problems in time; nor is man capable of transcending the limitation of his being. Man generally is entangled in insoluble problems; history is a constant tragedy in which we are all involved, whose keynote is anxiety and frustration, not progress and fulfillment.[20]

It is a history, then, that escapes from ideology (in my sense) by returning to the mythic and dramatic. It specifically attacks the ideologies and the theories of history from which they came in the previous era. In its hostility to a Beard or a Turner it offers no new system of analysis, no new theory of the operation of the historical process. Rather, it disapproves of such theories and such ideologies. Once again, as in the middle of the nineteenth century, we return characteristically to the multivolume narrative historical work. In Arthur Schlesinger, Jr., we discover our new Bancroft, ironically a pessimistic Bancroft. In Allan Nevins we find our own Parkman, albeit a surprisingly optimistic Parkman. And in Admiral Samuel Eliot Morison's brilliant and many-volumed history of the Navy during the Second World War we have perhaps the greatest literary achievement by any historian in our century. But in these works we look in vain for a vision of the past that will enable us to remake the present and the future. Here ideology is specifically rejected. Here we find a history that offers a reinforcement of current moral values and no effective challenge to the decision makers within the social order who *do* most frequently operate in terms of some view of history, some ideology. It is characteristic, in fact, of many American intellectuals these days to talk about how Americans have traditionally solved the problems that faced them—when they were in fact able to solve them at all—pragmatically and without reference to ideology. But the fact remains that there are many ways to solve a given problem, and the choice of specific solution is frequently determined by a set of attitudes toward history that may be unarticulated but are within the consciousness. And if this paper has any validity at all, it should be clear that a retreat from ideology to the mythic use of the past has its special cultural consequences as well. Thus our own age retreats from history or derives intense excitement from what is often called "history" in its most brilliant mythic or theological forms—witness the enthusiastic response to the works of Toynbee and Niebuhr. The escape from history leads us to the world of myth. And yet, surprisingly, in terms of my definition of myth, the new mythic vision seems almost anything but utopian, seems to offer no happy goals for man or culture. We are left with a mythic past, an anxious present, and an anti-utopian, Orwellian future.

What I have briefly attempted to sketch in roughest and most general terms were five major periods reflecting the relationships between history and myth as they were developed by American intellectuals responding to the circumstances of their own eras. In the first social order, intellectuals led the way in attempting to stabilize the tension between myth and history in order to protect the very special contract society they had organized and to enable it to fulfill its mission within history. In the eighteenth century, in the wake of the failure of the first position, the newer intellectual and social elite continued to dominate with its own special conservative philosophy of history, highly rationalized and secularized, removed from the power of the Christian myth. This myth, however, supported by a millennialist philosophy of history, continued to galvanize the sons of the Great Awakening, who found themselves in intellectual and social battle with the sons of the Enlightenment. With the special conditions and problems of the early nineteenth century came an entirely new approach to the problem, and American intellectuals became, through the use of history but with the repudiation of its rational powers, essentially the mythologists of America, the creators and revitalizers of a series of major myths that dominated the culture and determined its significantly utopian intellectual quality. In the last decade of the century, a new intellectual order was born on the heels of a new social order created in part by the communications revolution, an order in which a special kind of historical awareness contributed a dynamic element and where once again the intellectuals, removed from seats of social or political power but frequently anxious to achieve such power or contribute to its effective use, brought to life for their own present a special new tension between the mythic and the historic, stressing the ideological significance of their work. Finally, in our own day history has become once again the enemy, useful only if it points up the mythic tragedy of our inability to solve our problems in any meaningful sense.

Of course there are still those conscious of history, although ironically it would seem that, these days, to have some view of the past that has clear-cut ideological consequences for the present and future is generally thought of as a special function of what is left of

HISTORY AS MYTH AND IDEOLOGY

a radical tradition. But it is not unfair to see in the major intellectual trends of the years since World War II a fundamentally antihistorical view of the world. It is in fact a view that has been praised as marking the end of innocence or the end of ideology. But the cultural consequences of this triumph, so-called, over ideology, so-called, have yet to be assessed. In a world where leading intellectuals become committed to a view that human problems cannot really be solved, where the public ideology therefore too often goes unchallenged in our incredibly bipartisan age, where history flourishes most brilliantly in epic or mythic or theological forms, and yet where enormous problems do continue to confront us, there are grave dangers to the culture itself. But the fundamental tensions between the mythic and the ideological still remain, even though the balance may be tipped more to one side at the moment. Perhaps we are simply reenacting the plot of our story as it was played out in the middle decades of the nineteenth century, where once again great and frightening changes seemed too often more than man could handle. Perhaps there will yet be a reawakening, as there was in the 1890s, to the other real need and function of history in our kind of society. Perhaps there will even be another kind of social order.

2 THE FRONTIER THESIS AND THE AMERICAN INTELLECTUAL

When Van Wyck Brooks issued his call for the creation of a "usable past" in 1918, he was making explicit a kind of activity that intellectuals have almost always accepted as a part of their function,[1] For when Carl Becker insisted that Everyman is his own historian he was suggesting that every man creates for himself a past he finds useful in the pursuit of his life and mission. The particular problem of what constitutes such a "useful" past, of course, presents a series of difficult decisions, especially for the intellectual, who is more self-conscious and more analytical than Mr. Becker's Everyman. No matter what the difficulties, however, every intellectual finds himself committed to at least some philosophy of history—some notion of the operation of history as process—and generally also to some particular analysis of the past of his own nation or the world that he frequently makes the basis of the analysis he develops of the current situation in which he finds himself. Such useful pasts are the commonplaces of intellectual history and part of the *Weltanschauung* of intellectuals that the intellectual historian must examine.

But what is frequently overlooked in analyses of "usable pasts" is that they almost always assume, also, the rejection of some part of the past or some view of past history as "useless." Before any useful view of the past can be erected, the current and useless view must be put down. One of the most striking facts about the period under

HISTORY AS MYTH AND IDEOLOGY

discussion is the enormous interest in the study of American history shown by intellectuals who are not themselves professional historians or even professors. Brooks himself, Waldo Frank, Lewis Mumford, John Gould Fletcher are only a few of the intellectuals of the period who reveal this fascination with the American past. Certainly a generation of intellectuals spent—as Waldo Frank suggested in his discussion of several Midwestern authors of the period—considerable "vehemence in attack upon the Past from which they should be free. They are not free. They attack the Past because the Past is still so emotionally real; because it holds them back from full bestowal upon the Present. . . . We attack only what hinders and holds. . . . The protest against American ghosts shows how fearfully America is still haunted by them. . . . The Past is still with us in this land. At best, the Present is a feeble growth."[2] Thus the call for the creation of a "usable past" was in effect a call to exorcise a past that had proven "useless."

These intellectuals were committed to at least one of the several propositions advanced by what James Harvey Robinson christened the "New History," another characteristic intellectual trend of the period. For John Gould Fletcher, the Arkansas Imagist poet educated at Harvard, the study of the past was worthwhile only "if we are able to use historical criteria, the values of the past, as a means of not only judging but also directing the latent powers of the present and the future."[3] But the problem as Brooks and others saw it was not so much that the American past was without "elements that might contribute to some common understanding in the present, as that interpreters of that past experience have put a gloss upon it which renders it sterile for the living mind. . . . Instead of reflecting the creative impulses in American history, it reaffirms the values established by the commercial tradition; it crowns everything that has passed the censorship of the commercial and moralistic mind. . . . The past which survives in the common mind of the present is a past without living value."[4] The debate about the nature of history was therefore a debate about the nature of values seemingly sanctioned by history or those who wrote and used history, values that were indeed of consequence for the present and the future.

For these intellectuals coming to maturity in the period between 1910 and 1930 there was at least one such view of the past that many in the East found especially sterile—a view of the past that was used to reaffirm values these intellectuals themselves wished to repudiate. Historians, committed to the nineteenth-century search for origins, have told us much about the intellectual and historical setting out of which the Turner thesis emerged, but they have spent perhaps too little of their attention on the consequences of Turnerism after 1893.[5] Frederick Jackson Turner himself and his doctrine have a special place in the period discussed in this paper. It was in 1910 that Turner moved from his post at the University of Wisconsin to a leading position in the East at Harvard University. It was in 1910 he received the national recognition of his fellow historians by election to the presidency of their professional association. His famous essay on the significance of the frontier, along with other seminal studies, received publication in volume form only in 1920. The awarding of the Pulitzer Prize in 1925 for history to Frederick L. Paxson, a Turner disciple, for his history of the American frontier, marked another stage in the wide-scale acceptance of the frontier thesis. Turner was awarded his only Pulitzer Prize for his collection of articles on sectionalism the year after his death in 1932.

The popularization of Turnerism had many consequences for the intellectual life of the period.[6] But at least one of the major themes of the era centered around the revolt *against* the frontier, an attempt to renounce the American pioneering experience. The history of the American frontier, a history becoming more thoroughly and popularly studied in this period, was a useless past that must first be attacked if any usable past could be created. It was a history that clearly failed to provide the kinds of values necessary (to some intellectuals) for the modern era.

This is not to suggest that the enterprise was an entirely new one. The influence of the frontier on American life had been under severe attack before. Indeed, almost from the beginnings of the American experiment there were those who bewailed the effects of pioneering on American institutions and character. Perry Miller tells us of a preacher before the General Court of Massachusetts in 1705 who held that many worldly evils came from those men outside the confines of "orderly society" on the frontier.[7] Henry Adams could report, in his study of the Americans of 1800, that foreign travelers and "the educated, well-to-do Americans of the sea coast" could "seldom see anything to admire in the ignorance and brutality of the frontiersman" and therefore feared for the Republic itself.[8] Turner himself cites the initial antagonism of Timothy Dwight to the contribution of the frontier experience to American life.[9] But the fact remains that by the time Turner codified into historic law his thesis about the significance of the frontier in American development it had become part of the American mythos to attribute almost all that was desirable in American life and character to the effects of the pioneering experience.

That was precisely the difficulty: from an analysis of the role of the frontier in American history, various ideological consequences, various values announced as essential to preserving the nation, were deduced. It was this attempt to sanctify particular ideological positions and values by an appeal to history against which these intellectuals were revolting. Instead of questioning the procedure itself—for there remains a serious question about the relationship of ideology to history—the intellectuals of the period frequently sought to counterattack by redefining the consequences of the historical experience itself as well as the particular values that might be derived from it. Accepting as legitimate the enterprise that attempts to use the past as a basis for an ideology in the present, these young men simply insisted that others had failed to learn the proper lessons from the past they had examined. What rendered the frontier past useless was the uses to which that past had been put in the present, generally by individuals and groups regarded by the intellectuals as nonintellectual or even anti-intellectual. In the name of the life of the mind, they fought the "popular" images of the frontier past that were used for purposes they opposed. To understand the position of the intellectuals discussed in this paper, one must see their particular strictures against this specific backdrop. For while they did not always make this clear, they were in fact participating in a debate—a debate about the past that was indeed a debate about the present.

The most characteristic use of the frontier in this period was the largely sentimental effort to retain what was considered to be the picturesque glamour and glory of the Old West. The announced disappearance of the frontier seemed to create an ever-growing market for articles and stories of the American West and of frontier adventure. Even a cursory examination of the number of titles of such pieces listed year after year in the *Readers' Guide* indicates the enormous growth of this literature. The frontier had been, in Percy Boynton's word, "rediscovered." [10] Some bemoaned the disappearance of the Old West and urged a search for new myths to replace it. [11] Others condemned the "taming" of the West and sought the preservation of some of its characteristics. [12] Here Americans sought a native epic, an epic that extolled the virtues of extreme individualism, courage, recklessness, aloofness from social ties and obligations. In this "aristocratic West" some hoped to find qualities and traits of character that might continue to withstand the onrush of standardization and conformity. [13] While the preservation of individuality and the survival of personality were vital issues to the intellectuals of the period, they regretted the particularly romantic, dangerous excesses of this sentimental search for an epic West. They knew the need for stability and order, and such frontier traits were not to be desired in the new era. [14]

It became commonplace, for example, in this period to assign any lawlessness in American life to the consequences of the frontier experience. Serious scholars here provided the lead. Zechariah Chafee, writing in that brilliant critical symposium *Civilization in the United States,* which in effect excoriated American civilization, laid American hostility to law to the frontier:

Habitual obedience to law was a spirit which could not develop in men who were largely squatters, and who, from the outset of our national history, disregarded the Congressional statutes which required that public lands must be surveyed before they were settled. Sometimes, as in this instance, the settlers' resistance to law was successful. More often they were overpowered by the strength of civilization and submitted to the law sullen and unconvinced.[15]

Following this line, James Truslow Adams could find—as did in part the famous Wickersham Commission Report—that American lawlessness so characteristic of the 1920s in some areas, the failure of Americans to obey the Prohibition amendment, stemmed directly from the lawless traits that pioneering experience had developed and extolled.[16] If frontier individualism meant lack of law, the younger intellectuals knew that their kind of individualism could be developed only within a society of law.

Frequently, however, serious use was made of a far different, in fact contradictory set of personal characteristics derived also from the frontier experience. It was this very ambiguity—eccentric individualism and cooperative conformity—that Turner himself failed to resolve in his own picture of the American character. And looking more particularly to the Midwestern frontier (Turner's own frontier) rather than to the Far West, many Americans found that frontier traits were essentially those that made for effective social conformity. The Western type developed by the pioneering adventure was one that had learned the lesson of necessary subservience to general social standards established by the conditions of the frontier life itself. To those conservatives who heaped praise on *The Valley of Democracy* and *The Westerner*—like Meredith Nicholson and William Cook, for example—the frontier had created the perfect small-town bourgeoisie: stable, reliable (i.e., Republican), uninfluenced by immigrant blocs and foreign radical ideas, the safeguard of the Republic.[17] This product of the West posed even a greater problem for the intellectuals of the period, who found the villager and the farmer most opposed to the high culture and social reform they most desired. The frontier thesis in effect had made the contemporary Middle West "the apotheosis of American civilization," and that was exactly the problem for the Eastern intellectuals, who could insist with Randolph Bourne that that area had failed to create "very vigorous and diverse spiritual types." [18]

American business enterprise had also appropriated the frontier past for itself and insisted that the pioneer spirit was being carried forward by modern industrialism, an image that Turner himself had suggested. As early as 1906, Albert Shaw, in an address to the students of Trinity College, had used the legacy of the pioneer to defend the status quo:

All the conditions of American pioneering were such as to create a wonderful spirit of individuality, independence, and self-direction in the average man. Never in the world has there been anything to equal this development of personality, and the capacity for private and individual initiative.

Even though America has now entered a new stage "of buoyant, progressive maturity," however, Americans cannot disregard frontier virtues that were still necessary because the problem remained one of creating new wealth. However, he cautioned, these same virtues should of course keep individuals from concerning themselves about problems relating to the distribution of wealth. [19] The business literature of the 1920s constantly suggested that American industrialism was simply a continuation of the frontier process. "A frontier still confronts us, and only in the frontier spirit can we meet it," Guy Emerson maintained in a volume he dedicated to his fellow bankers, "true pioneers on the new frontier." [20] Still another defender of the businessman in America, Archer Hulbert, identified business efficiency as a new frontier. [21] The use of the frontier past and its extension into the present and future mark a central cluster of images applied in defense of the processes of American enterprise in the twentieth century. [22] It is no wonder, then, that many of the intellectuals of the period accepted the same basic set of images, although for purposes of attack rather than defense. Matthew Josephson, vigorous opponent of the values of a business civilization and of what he believed to be frontier traits and values, saw industrialism as "the final drama of the frontier" and of a culture based upon principles of preemption. [23] For Van Wyck Brooks the culture of industrialism was the culture of an age of pioneering with all the evils that adhered to such an age and such a culture. [24] Harold Stearns found that the entrepreneur was simply an individual carrying on the American pioneering tradition—and did not like him any better than he did the original pioneer. [25]

If the businessman and his apologists of the period discovered in the frontier experience a particularly useful past, the leaders of American government and politics were not blind to the ideological possibilities of such a history in defense of their special theories of government and society. Theodore Roosevelt, himself a historian of frontier America, had early in the century discussed "The Pioneer Spirit and American Problems."[26] Calvin Coolidge could assert with as much feeling as he could ever muster, "This is still a new and young country. The frontier still lingers. The hardy pioneer still defends the outworks of civilization."[27] Herbert Hoover's defense of "American individualism" is clearly rooted in the lessons he would have us derive from a study of frontier history. Again and again, Mr. Hoover makes clear that whatever greatness the nation has achieved it owes to those values that were promoted "by ceaseless contest with the wilderness in an ever extending frontier."[28] But unlike Mr. Turner, Mr. Hoover refused ever to believe that the age of pioneering was at an end. Even in the dark days of the Depression, Hoover never suggested that Americans surrender their "frontier traits." Rather, he informed them that they had not reached the last frontiers—that science, industry, invention, human inspiration would always provide new frontiers, which themselves could only be conquered if older frontier ideals and ways were retained.[29] It was for this very reason that *The New Republic* saw fit to urge editorially that frontier morality ought to cease to be operative in the United States; such morality would simply perpetuate the view of governmental theory and practice identifiable with the policies of Herbert Hoover, policies the magazine found intolerable.[30]

Views of history frequently entail views of human nature, and the discussion of the consequences of the frontier experience provides no exception. Throughout the analyses of this past, the "pioneer type" has been made the equivalent of the American type.[31] This "type" was almost always described as a personality with little time for reflective thought, an anti-intellectual individual committed to material things, an exaggerated extrovert. All of this had, of course, been suggested previously. The significant point here is that the kind of character produced by the pioneering experience was no longer valued in any way by an important body of American intellectuals. For all of them—and their language is significantly similar in most accounts—the experience meant for Americans "a sacrifice of some part of their own personality."[32] This sacrifice meant as a consequence a warped man in a warped culture.

In an era when Freudian analysis dominated much of the thinking of American intellectuals, it is not surprising to find the resultant character of Americans depicted in what can only be described as the jargon of the new psychology. But what is surprising is to discover that frequently Freudian consequences are assigned as products of what might be called Turnerian causes.[33] For it is the

frontier process that produced in the American character particular
psychic maladjustments. To any student of either Turner or Freud,
such a linking of the two analyses must appear very strange, but the
fact is that the marriage of these two great Romantic world views of
the nineteenth century is one of the most interesting intellectual
developments of twentieth-century America.[34]

Waldo Frank was one of the earliest leaders in the movement.
For Frank, in his effort to analyze the particular qualities of America
and American character, the backwoodsman was in large part responsible for the traits he could discover in the American of 1919.
His brief examination of our frontier past revealed how this particular type came about. "The backwoodsman needed a rationale for
pressing on: he needed to make the bitter sacrifice of self, the sacrifice of culture, in order to carry through the job in his Age—the
unfolding of the American empire. *His* progress was best served by
the suppression of Desire."[35] What resulted was neither a superb
individual—self-reliant, Emersonian, or Whitmanesque—nor a decent culture. That which had been considered for generations the
natural, the supremely natural, life of man on the American continent—the conquest of the wilderness, the establishment of a community—was now labeled "unnatural." John Crowe Ransom and
Lewis Mumford both insisted upon this point. Ransom maintained
that "the pioneering life is not the normal life, whatever some
Americans might suppose."[36] When Lewis Mumford came to write
his important study of American cultural history—his own attempt
to find a useful past and to dislodge from prominence a useless past
—he summed up the attitude of a whole generation of intellectuals
on this point. "The truth is that the life of the pioneer was bare and
insufficient: he did not really face Nature, he merely avoided society. . . . [Man] can reside for long in the wilderness only by losing
some of the essential qualities of the cultivated human species."[37]
Meanwhile, the newer biographies of the period reinforced this
view, with Van Wyck Brooks' study of Mark Twain perhaps the
classic account of the cultural and intellectual deficiencies that can
result, in part, from the frontier experience.[38]

One of the most thoroughgoing analyses of the consequences
of the pioneering past made during the period was John Gould
Fletcher's intriguing attempt to compare the effects of the two frontier experiences, that of the Americans and that of the Russians. It
was Fletcher's Turnerian contentions that "the whole course of
American history may be summed up as the history of the spread
of the pioneer and his type of mind into every department of
human effort."[39] The other intellectuals who joined in this view
pointed to specific areas of American life in which the vicious con-

sequences of this experience showed themselves. In spite of the frequently made contention that this experience produced a demo cratic spirit, these intellectuals discovered that the frontier had in fact produced no adequate social philosophy, but simply anarchic individualism. Since all agreed that the process itself left little time for reflective thought, many blamed all the political deficiencies of the nation on that experience. The pioneer was innocent and naive about matters of politics and morality. He saw all problems as simple. He was reinforced in all prejudices and intolerances.[40] Thus, for example, the development of an adequate foreign policy was impossible in a land where unsophisticated pioneer traits and values dominated.[41] There could be no decent community life—simply lawlessness or intolerable social conformity—*The New Republic* warned, if frontier morality were allowed to continue.[42]

As early as 1912 one of the founders of that magazine insisted that it was the frontier experience that made impossible the kind of democratic state he desired. In *The New Democracy*, Walter Weyl argued:

The conquest of the wide-stretching continent lying to the west of the Appalachians gave to American development a tendency adverse from the evolution of a socialized democracy. It made America atomic. It led automatically to a loose political coherence and to a structureless economic system. The trust, the hundred-millionaire, and the slum were latent in the lands which the American people in their first century of freedom were to subjugate . . . [This conquest] entrained a series of developments which still vitally affect every American life. Today we cannot tear down a slum, regulate a corporation, or establish a national educational system, we cannot attack either industrial oligarchy or political corruption, without coming into contact with the economic, political, and psychological after effects of the conquest. . . . The western march of the pioneer gave to Americans a psychological twist which was to hinder the development of a socialized democracy.[43]

Others on *The New Republic* staff ten and twenty years after Weyl had written his indictment of this useless past were to continue to iterate the same themes and the same general complaints.[44]

If the frontier experience seemed to make impossible decent social and political arrangements in America, it also made impossible anything resembling high culture. Matthew Josephson found the whole history of the frontier inimical to artistic production and further insisted that even the possibilities of that history as a source of materials from which an American epic or a literature of value might be produced did not exist. The only way in which the West might serve for literature and the arts was by way of repudiation of the whole experience itself.[45] This was a direct challenge to those who looked to the West for a mythology and the basis of a unique American literature. John Dewey went even further; he attributed the fear of science—as seen in Bryan's campaign against the teaching of evolution—to the same old set of frontier conditions. For while Dewey agreed that the frontier may have produced a sense of philanthropy and political progressivism (a fact denied by other intellectuals of the period), it was responsible for the development of an area that never "had any interest in ideas as ideas, nor in art and science for what they may do in liberating and elevating the human spirit." The frontier was—and persisted in being—a "limit beyond which it was dangerous and unrespectable for thought to travel."[46]

Dewey's analysis indicated another fact of much importance for the intellectual life of the period. This was an era in which the menace to a healthy cultural life was frequently designated as "Puritanism."[47] But Dewey insisted that what most intellectuals were really attacking was largely the kind of religion associated with frontier revivalism. He saw in Bryan a typical frontier revivalist. Brooks, too, realized that what he called Puritanism was in fact the perfect philosophy for an age of pioneering.[48] Dewey's discussion of "The American Intellectual Frontier" suggested that "we are not Puritans in our intellectual heritage, but we are evangelical because of our fears of ourselves and of our latent frontier disorderliness. . . . This is the illiberalism which is deeply rooted in our liberalism."[49] Those cultural villains of the era—the Puritan, the Philistine, and the Pioneer—were the product of the same historical experience.[50]

The frontier became the scapegoat for all that was wrong with contemporary America. It had created a dangerously incomplete psychological type that reigned as national character; it was responsible for American lawlessness and for political corruption; it strengthened the hold of social conformity on American communities; it was basic to the establishment of conditions in America that made it impossible to generate intelligent political, social, or economic arrangements nationally or in the international arena; it made the achievement of a high culture, of outstanding work in art, science, or ideas, difficult if not impossible; it created an environment that was simply hostile to the life of the mind.

The revolt against this particular "useless past" was part of a larger revolt against what was considered to be the Midwestern domination of American life and values. It was made by intellectuals who were born or educated in the East, the urban United States.[51] But, significantly, it accepted in general outline the same essential thesis about the nature of American history that had been advanced in most striking mythic form by Frederick Jackson Turner at the turn of the century: It admitted that American development had been the creation of the frontier process. Yet it insisted that the consequences of that process had been detrimental to the creation of a valuable political and cultural life. The debate, therefore, between the western Turnerians and the eastern Turnerians (if they may be so categorized) was largely a debate over values—not an unusual or surprising turn of affairs in the annals of historiography. But by accepting the Turnerian analysis—no matter what value judgments they assigned—these Eastern intellectuals played into the hands of those they most consistently attacked. By granting the initial premises of the opposition view, they seemed in one important sense to join the professors Van Wyck Brooks had attacked for putting "a sort of Talmudic seal on the American tradition."[52]

Yet the assault on the useless past and the stress on the problem of values and ideologies related to the study of the past itself may not have been without important consequences. It is more than possible that this very effort may have been in part responsible for a search among professional students of history to discover for themselves a more usable past, a new way of viewing the history of America that might enable Americans to develop values and programs of action calculated to reestablish the "creative impulse" Brooks talks about in his essay. These vigorous exposures of what these intellectuals conceived to be the consequences of the pioneering process may have led others to a reexamination of the value of the Turnerian analysis itself. For only in the late 1920s did any systematic critique appear that questioned the truth and the efficacy of the Turner thesis itself.[53] The beginnings of the serious anti-Turnerian tendency in professional historical circles can be traced to the last years of the Twenties and the early years of the Thirties. No doubt in part the Great Depression of 1929 stimulated thinking anew of the problems of our history as the depression of the 1890s perhaps stimulated Turner's original effort. But it is not unlikely that the two-decade bombardment of the frontier process as useless past by American intellectuals provided the necessary intellectual background, in part, for the movement that led some to repudiate Turner's explanation of American development as sufficient.

Historians turned to new methods of analysis, to new explanations of American developments. From these visions of the American past the intellectuals might better find their more usable past, a past from which the present might develop new values and ideologies that would be of greater significance in creating the kind of future for which the intellectuals of the earlier period had been striving. By 1927 two major syntheses embodying the newer vision were ready for presentation to the American people. Both had been in preparation for many years and had been preceded by more specialized studies that suggested a new line of investigation and interpretation. Both were hailed by many of these same Eastern intellectuals with great enthusiasm.[54] Ironically enough, both were the creations of Midwestern Americans brought up in large part in that very environment that was under such heavy attack in the East. Charles and Mary Beard's *The Rise of American Civilization* and Vernon L. Parrington's *Main Currents in American Thought* rapidly became for many a new official history. These works were to be the basis of what many felt truthfully could be called a usable past in the decades that followed. But the irony of usable pasts was to overtake both works. Just as the Turnerian past became useless to the intellectuals of the period 1910 to 1930, so too were the works of Beard and Parrington under serious attack by the late 1940s and the early 1950s. This new "usable past" had become for many simply a new "useless past."

3 USES OF THE PURITAN PAST

During the last two decades, the teaching of history has become much more sophisticated. Not only do we introduce even our beginning students to some of the source materials from which the historian develops his own studies, but also we have begun—a movement perhaps heralded on a major scale by the now-famous Amherst Series begun in the late 1940s—to reveal to these students one of our deepest and darkest professional secrets: historians often disagree (and violently) over the interpretation of historical fact, event, and development. Today, even high-school students know about the great disorder within the house of the historian. The clash of historical opinion and the diversity of approaches have become so central that students often can detail the historiography of particular issues far better than they are able to present their own understanding of such issues!

To be sure, such new techniques have given a new liveliness to the study of our discipline. They have raised important questions about the historian's procedures, helped develop significant analytical and critical tools, and made students even more aware of the complexity of the problem of truth and use of evidence. Perhaps these new efforts have been the real and lasting contribution of the long, three-decade debate over "historical relativism" that preceded the Second World War.

There is, however, one area of significance overlooked consis-

tently by most historians—and especially those who teach history—
that ought to be more earnestly pursued. Historians, these days well
attuned to the discovery of the cultural implications of developments in science and technology and the teachings of a variety of
other disciplines, have simply failed as a body to concern themselves
with the cultural implications of the study of the past itself. What
historians will not devote considerable discussion to the cultural
consequences of the theories of a Newton or a Darwin, an Adam
Smith or a Herbert Spencer? But how many of these same historians
bother to consider the general intellectual impact of the theories of
a Turner or a Beard? The question of the cultural consequences of
attitudes toward the past is a vast and important area. Our general
world view and therefore the way we behave in the present is determined perhaps more than we are aware by our views of the past
and our theories about developments out of the past.

We care about the past and how it ought to be viewed because
it appears to make a significant difference to us, not simply because
(as professionals) some of us seek the truth. Frequently, we care
because we believe that the past and its peculiar problems impinge
on us in a special way: we share the same problems or are still trying
to solve similar ones. We feel that we are somehow what the past
has made us. We seek models of behavior, and for many of us—
rightly or wrongly—the past offers such examples. We seek a new
future and think we can attain it only if we can throw off what the
past has bequeathed to us. These attitudes are not common to all
men and all cultures, but they are strikingly characteristic of the
cultures roughly grouped under the rubric of Western Civilization.

We call constantly on the past. In the simplest form of this
tendency, American revolutionaries and some of their French coun-
terparts dreamed of a return to the image of a society of virtue and
order embodied in the Roman Republic. Jacksonians called for a
return to the golden age of Jefferson, and New Dealers gloried in
recalling the marvelous age of Jackson. Republicans in the 1950s
urged one another to "get right with Lincoln." Out of the study of
the past could come a tradition that could sustain us; out of the
study of the past could come a vision of the future that could move
us to revolutionary change.

Some view of the past or some theory of how that past happened is significant to us in our daily life. Debates over the nature
of the past are not merely textbook exercises for our students, demonstrating the difficult task of obtaining the truth. They are (consciously or not) public debates over values and developments that
count in culture. It makes a difference *how* you view the past; unless
this is understood, simple exercises concerning who is *right* in a

particular conflict of historical interpretations cannot be seen in its fullest light. For history is not the monopoly of the historian. The key debates go on—often without any notion of what is happening in libraries and classrooms—in a more public forum with consequences for public policy, as well as other aspects of the culture.

The debate over the image of the Puritan makes this theme clearer and reveals something of the cultural dimension involved in using the past. My purpose is not to discuss what the New England Puritan was really like, nor to analyze the historiography of Puritanism in America. I wish rather to demonstrate the general kind of cultural debate that in using the image of the Puritan and his past illuminates the larger context of the uses of history.

Perhaps no other historical image, except that of the frontier, has been so crucial during the development of our culture. Almost unchallenged has been the contention that Puritanism and the Puritan past somehow determined much that has become characteristic of the nation: the sense of the burden or the glory of this particular past has been present in almost every decade.

Puritanism, for the purposes of the general historical debate, centered around four issues, sometimes discussed individually, sometimes examined as a complex of related ideas. Each issue was capable of two interpretations, each of which assumed (without much concern for scholarly accuracy) to represent what did in fact exist in seventeenth-century New England. Therefore, when something or someone was labeled "Puritan," the image called into focus was supposedly a historical one, a "real" one.

(1) Puritanism has been hailed as the creed that highlighted self-restraint and control over appetites and emotions. It was the expression of dedication to a higher ideal than self, of God-centered men awaiting direct confrontation with the Almighty. However, inherent even in original Puritan theory as practiced in the New World was another doctrine that almost seemed the reverse side of the same coin. New England Puritan theology promised the hope of individual conversion and fulfillment in God, and at least one strain of Puritanism interpreted this as promising self-expression and individual liberation from man-made law in the name of newly found conscience.

(2) Puritanism has meant community, a strong sense of earthly order and law, cooperation in establishing a social system, subordinating individual will to social welfare, the planting of a city on the hill that might become somehow the City of God itself. For others, however, this sense of community meant little more than intolerance, persecution, and frustration of individual liberty and freedom

of self-expression—a theocracy, a despotism ruled by an elite, a vicious totalitarian state.

(3) Puritanism has meant morality, a stern and demanding code of ethics, that bent men not merely to the law of the state but to the higher, ideal, and just law of God. For others, Puritan morality meant nothing but a sterile moralism, codes of conduct imposed from above without personal meaning or social purpose. They were simply a device to maintain order and control by a few who regarded themselves as morally superior.

(4) Puritanism has become identified with a particular set of attitudes toward success in a material sense, a sign of salvation (the Protestant ethic) stressing industry, thrift, achievement of wealth. Such an ethic, creating a vibrant modern capitalism, was the true safeguard of the whole economic and social order. On the other hand, such an ethic could be damned as religious sanction for crass materialism and a vicious, morally unworthy economic and social system, strangling truer values and more worthwhile cultural enterprises—the arts and sciences.

During the nineteenth-century, the Puritan generally enjoyed a good press. Throughout most of the century (see chapter 1), the function of history was largely mythic. That is, the past was called upon to furnish the present—a period of intense social, economic, and political change—with a set of values, standards of personal and institutional behavior designed to maintain what could be maintained of the status quo. The Puritans were, after all, our Founding Fathers. They represent the origins of our liberties; their institutions are the basis of our democracy. Their conduct showed us the proper standards of personal and social behavior, the proper moral code in an era when morality itself and the basic institutions of the social order (especially the family) seemed threatened with destruction. The Protestant ethic continued to rally Americans to a belief in the growing capitalist order, seemingly explaining satisfactorily economic and social distinctions in the world, the existence of poverty for some and great wealth for others. Indeed, the moral code of the Puritan seemed to support the moral reform movements of the day, especially those such as the temperance movement that were concerned with personal conduct.

By the 1890s the leaders of the American intellectual community seemed to have put a seal of approval on almost every aspect of Puritanism. Resisting the pressures that threatened a breakdown of the social and political order, most Americans in positions of intellectual and public authority persisted in offering the Puritan past as an ideal for their more uncertain present. David Starr Jordan hailed

John Brown as the last of the Puritans, indicating his praise and admiration for those who could put individual conscience and higher law over mere civil law. This potentially radical doctrine (a strange notion of true Puritanism for some modern scholars), however, became somehow tame in his hands. It was long ago, the battle had been won. The distinguished Franklin H. Giddings, longing to preserve the genuine sense of community in America that he saw fast disappearing in a world of impersonal industrialism and urbanization, argued that the Puritan experience and its ideals provided the main source for the model of community in America. Puritans, after all, had insisted that the community itself should regulate personal conduct in the interest of the whole social body; they placed ideals over material ends and persisted in treating every man as his brother's keeper. For Giddings, therefore, Puritanism provided the essential "ethical like-mindedness" for meaningful community to survive. In a series of lectures before the Brooklyn Ethical Association in 1893, one of the speakers praised the Puritan spirit as the origin of all worthwhile American political institutions and quoted with approval John Fiske's glowing tribute to the lofty ideals of the Puritans, which, if carried out, would indeed build the City of God on American soil. And the influential William Graham Sumner could pay his special homage to the teachings of his ministerial ancestors in Puritan New England by adopting the language of the Protestant ethic when he called the more modern economic terms "labor" and "capital" "hard work." and "self denial" and praised the savings bank depositor as the hero of civilization.

Thus by the end of the century almost every aspect of what was taken to be historic Puritanism was called upon as part of the bulwark of the prevailing order. But what is most distinctive about these statements of the 1880s and 1890s is that they actually represent a defense against a new attack then beginning to be mounted against Puritanism. To be effective, this attack had to return to history itself and destroy the favorable image of the Puritan past generally held throughout the century. It is not difficult to understand why the Puritan past should have been glorified in the particular ways it was in the nineteenth century. But why the vigor and the violence of this assault on Puritanism (and those long-gone seventeenth-century figures) that was an intellectual hallmark of the period between 1886 and 1940? Why should anyone really care what the Puritan world was really like? Why should history—any part of the past—become a villain? What harm could the past do in the present? It is precisely because the past *had* been used to support aspects of the present, because the Puritan past *had* been developed into a bulwark, a mythical defense of the status quo, that those who wished to see a new and different America felt they must begin by the destruction of this image of the past.

Two conditions help explain the nature of the debate in the years after 1886. First, there was the problem of alienation, personal and social. The vision of the intellectual as alien that nineteenth-century intellectuals saw when they looked into their mirrors became a cliché during the twentieth century. This plight is hinted at, and even strangely defined, in many of the major figures of our mid-nineteenth-century intellectual life: Hawthorne, Emerson, Melville—the list could be extended almost at will. Not surprisingly, many of these striking personalities, feeling themselves out of tune with their society, nature, the universe, and even God, doubted much of their inheritance. While many American intellectuals rejoiced in the Puritan past, many of these doubters, often beginning with deep concern over problems of personal salvation and individual relationship to the natural and social order of things, turned to that Puritan past with a more quizical, if not hostile, attitude. Hawthorne's deep interest in the Puritan past was no mere antiquarian concern. His romances and tales turned on historical situations, frequently centering on problems that haunted many of the original Puritans. He sought a key to unlock his own and society's nineteenth-century problems in probing the Puritan past.

One of our most popular novelists, Harriet Beecher Stowe, came back time again to historical novels or stories that tried to recreate New England life of the previous century in all its detail, indicating in striking and clear fashion the deep personal and social consequences of Puritan doctrine and social organization. Moreover, in at least two important novels, *The Minister's Wooing* (1859) and *Oldtown Folks* (1869), she devoted separate and significant chapters to a discussion of Puritan ideas, theological, political, and social. Like Hawthorne, Stowe undertook a searching interpretation of Puritanism and its consequences. Both authors found issues that continued to have meaning in an era far removed from that past. Neither simply wrote "historical novels"; instead, their works are historical interpretations meant to bear on the present (personally for the artists and socially for their society), and with the four aspects of the Puritan theme detailed above. They are more than an artist's device; they are the substance of the writers' concern.

Perry Miller has brilliantly sketched out the possible linkage between two seemingly unlike thinkers as Edwards and Emerson by insisting on the continuity of their personal, cultural, and intellectual problems. Emerson belongs with those intellectuals haunted by a Puritan past who began the modern search for meaningful readjustment and fuller expression of self. Ironically, John Jay Chapman, in his brilliant essay on Emerson (1896), blames Puritanism both for stifling him and for contributing to his greatest strengths. Chapman's Puritanism exalted conscience and moral law; the result was a kind of social and political conservatism. The harsh creed preached a distrust of human feelings, passion, and love, leaving Emerson but half a man. Emerson himself might well have made the same charges against the doctrines that dominated New England generations before him.

Chapman's support for a breakthrough against the forces that stifled emotion and limited free and meaningful self-expression (thus destroying both men and art) became one of the dominant ideas in American letters after 1890. Van Wyck Brooks proclaimed this for the younger generation in *The Wine of the Puritans* (1908) and repeated it in volume after volume. For Brooks, Puritanism as idealism was valuable. But the fact that "theocracy is the all-influential fact in the history of the American mind" made our history "intolerable." Brooks therefore had to destroy this history and find a more usable past. His general attitude and approach can be found over and over in such critics of the period as Waldo Frank and Lewis Mumford. With the introduction of Freudian thought (misunderstood and misinterpreted as it surely was) into American intellectual life, the theme emerged of liberation, self-expression, the need for art and beauty, and the denunciation of Puritanism as repressive and hostile to expression, beauty, and even to nature itself.

From here, it was an easy step to yet another assertion: Puritanism was, in fact, simply moralism—a phony morality without meaningful social purpose, a brake on worthwhile human instincts and desires that offered no effective system of morals that an intelligent man could accept. Santayana, in 1911, found Puritanism necessary and even effective as a doctrine for a particular time and special set of circumstances. But its continued hold in a new America made for a pale and ineffectual "genteel tradition." H. L. Mencken's analysis of "Puritanism as a Literary Force" (1917) attacked a creed and a culture that incapacitated men for looking at the world as it really was and refused to allow men, through institutions such as censorship, to express themselves. Randolph Bourne's deep concern over "The Puritan's Will to Power" (1917) expressed fear of a moral elite incapable of understanding true leadership and human nature. In effect, the new image of Puritanism became a weapon against developments that many once had hailed as reform and that earlier nineteenth-century radicals had argued for in the name of virtuous Puritan ideals: temperance, censorship—a whole range of so-called reformist ideas. The new Puritan history became an ideological weapon against such "moral" actions of men and governments previously defended as a culmination of the Puritan tradition and dream for America. By 1927, with Parrington's devastating and popular attack on Puritanism as essentially foreign (an English import), as well as elitist and antidemocratic, the new Puritan historical image had been fully forged and become fully effective ideologically.

One other significant development in the late nineteenth century helps explain the newer trends. Between 1870 and 1910, a new middle class was in the process of creation in the United States, and for this class and its champions an entirely new ideology appeared necessary. For this new middle class was not a class of property holders; yet in no sense were its members proletarians. They were managers, engineers, professional bureaucrats, and technicians of all kinds. The key to the new world they sought to create was order, but a rationalized order that was not based simply on property-holding in the tradition of John Locke or Adam Smith. Such an order would not fulfill the prophecies of Karl Marx. Rather, the future belonged to the managers and the engineers, to the scientists, the men of reason and efficiency, an order where profits were not as significant as the corporate good, but where the corporate good must itself be determined not by outmoded religious ideals or ineffectual moral leadership but by the actual, scientifically determined nature of man's abilities and needs. For these men, Puritan moralism and the Puritan social and political order so long admired became the enemy, enshrining an improper kind of moral elite and improper values for the new rationalized order. The Puritan ethic epitomized all that was wrong.

As early as 1886, Brooks Adams began his search for historical laws, admiring from the start the possibilities of the new sciences and the possibilities of a new scientific order. His starting point, *The Emancipation of New England,* was a full-scale attack on the old Puritan world. In Puritan New England, Adams found absence both of liberty and of intelligent social order. The theocracy fostered neither personal liberty (his defense of the antinomians) nor the good society. In his famous volume of the 1890s, *The Law of Civilization and Decay,* Adams went beyond this analysis to a study of the Reformation in England and there discovered the origin of a blight that threatens civilization itself: the Protestant ethic (defined as the basis of modern capitalism at least a decade before Max Weber's work on the subject). For in a world where Economic Man dominates, there can be no truly good society, no arts worthy of the name, no culture.

Nor was Adams' account—perhaps the most complex, difficult, and philosophical—singular. John Dewey advanced a parallel position. In 1913 in *A Preface to Politics,* Walter Lippman assured his readers that reform could not work as it was attempted by Puritan New England: by abolishing "with a law or an axe the desires of men." In a provocative chapter on "Drift," in *Drift and Mastery* (1914), Lippmann specifically attacked the kinds of history men make for themselves, the false utopias to which they long to return, be it the Romantic's longing for the state of nature or the Puritan's dreams of religious revolt. For Lippman, the Protestant revolt led to disorders of enormous consequence. History therefore became for Lippman an enemy (at least in the ways it currently was being used) every bit as much as it was for Brooks and the others. Such enemies must be first destroyed if a good society can be built, a society based on a scientific analysis (with the aid of Freud) of the true nature of man and his needs, something obviously lacking from any examination of the Puritan moral code or of reformers in the Puritan tradition. Reinhold Niebuhr and others took up the challenge of R. H. Tawney's *Religion and the Rise of Capitalism* (1925) in an effort to undermine the more pernicious features of the capitalist order that seemed so clearly underpinned by Puritan social values. During the 1920s, the anti-Puritan movement reached its height. It is little wonder that John Maynard Keynes could find that "puritanism . . . neglected the arts of production as well as those of enjoyment" and could label William Graham Sumner's hero, the savings bank depositor, a newfound enemy!

The Puritan past in the literature from 1890 to 1940 is perhaps too well known. But it was, clearly, a major concern touching on all four aspects of the Puritan issue. As early as 1906, William Vaughan Moody's heroine in *The Great Divide* is haunted by the portraits of her Puritan ancestors that hang on her cabin wall. The inability to lead the good life, to escape from her repression, is specifically traced to a Puritan past. The free and liberated West triumphs over a Puritan past; the Puritan ethic generally fails in the face of Western freedom. Nor can one forget the many historically based plays of Eugene O'Neill, written during the 1920s, with their brooding Puritan menace, personal and social. The explicit attacks of Theodore Dreiser and Sherwood Anderson, of e. e. cummings and T. S. Eliot in their New England poems, and of Edward Arlington Robinson's "New England" (1925) all repeat similar themes. William Carlos Williams' imaginative attempt to create his own usable past —especially the brilliant *In the American Grain* of 1925—deals with the historical question. Somehow, many of the major artists of America in the period have felt, like Glenway Wescott's Alwyn in *The Grandmothers* (1927), that they must come to grips with the American past and that a knowledge of it must include some real

understanding of the Puritan experience so crucial to the making
of contemporary America.

Not all American intellectuals rejected the Puritan past. There
was a debate, although the defenders of Puritanism were far out-
numbered. The Humanists, for example, insisted that Puritanism
still revealed what self-restraint might achieve. In 1923, Stuart Sherman, in one of the most balanced accounts, insisted that much of
validity in the Puritan tradition remained, for the Puritan experience was valuable in terms of its moral achievements and its
strengthening of individual will. By 1936, Gilbert Seldes, who had
been hot in pursuit of Puritan vices during the 1920s, could issue a
countercharge against American critics in his *Mainland*. He defended Puritanism in its own setting, rebutting the critics by arguing
that it was in fact the breakdown of Puritanism that was the most
conspicuous moral event of the nineteenth century. All through the
1920s and 1930s, indeed up to his last statements, William Allen
White, a reformer of the older tradition not so taken with theories
of social engineering and new middle-class management, could
argue that the basic social and moral values of the true Puritan were
the only basis for liberty and justice, that the Protestant ethic was
still viable, that reform in any meaningful sense could come only
out of a noble Puritan tradition, kept alive primarily in the American West.

In the period since the Second World War, the scales have
tipped in the Puritan's favor. Not only has scholarship risen to the
defense of those long dead, but also the general tone of the cultural
debate has indicated a more favorable reaction. In the wake of that
great war and the firm establishment of the new technological, administrative state system in America (so desired by many of the
reformers associated with the new middle class at the turn of the
century), there have come new doubts about the corporate order
and its social and personal achievements. In an age in which relativ-
isms of all kinds are under attack, Ralph Barton Perry's wartime
Puritan "moral athlete" looks impressive. Appeals to higher law and
moral absolutes are strikingly in favor once again. The various attacks on the affluent society seems to sound a return to some "Puritan" values long denied as worthwhile. The Puritan model of a
community once again looks attractive in our era of the "Gemeinschaft grouse." And in a recent polemic directed against the cultural
consequences of a new ethic that arose to replace the old Protestant
ethic, Richard LaPiere explicitly states that the decline of that old
ethic and the rise of excesses under the new Freudian ethic are
causes of real concern.

In this age of A-bombs and existentialism, the Puritan-agonized conscience (long an object of derision) once again makes sense. A whole series of American poets—John Crowe Ransom, Richard Wilbur, Robert Lowell, Wallace Stevens, John Berryman, to name but a few—have reexamined the Puritan and his private experience and found sympathetic understanding, even something of profound value for an understanding of our own experience today. In the late 1930s, Katherine Anne Porter had already begun her study of Cotton Mather, a remarkable undertaking by a Texas author delving deeply into Puritan history. John Cheever's fiction frequently underscores what American life and community lost when the Puritan disappeared—a far cry from the cruder satire of J. P. Marquand, who took New England for his province in the 1930s and 1940s. And the fascination with the actual personal and social experience of the Puritans in Arthur Miller's *The Crucible* (1953) makes that play anything but a simple attack on Puritanism and witch hunting, then or now.

Clearly, the cultural debate continues, and it continues in spite of what professional historians may write or say. For the vision of the past and its interpretation do not belong to the historian alone, nor are they simple issues for classroom discussion. It makes little difference if we tell ourselves that our vision is simply a rationale for what we want in the present or the future. The point is that in Western society history is culturally important. It will continue to be used, mythically or ideologically, whether we like it or not. Man will insist on a historical view and he will use it, come what may, to help him determine his present and his future. What the role of the professional historian ought to be in all of this is too big a question for this occasion. But it is important that we know that what is said about the past *is* important, *is* culturally significant. Too easily intimidated by what appears to us to be the significance of science in our cultural life (and worried because scientists themselves fail to realize this fact), we historians have often forgotten that what we deal with is of enormous cultural consequence, too.

II IDEOLOGY AS CULTURE

OURS...to fight for

FREEDOM FROM WANT

Library of Congress

Our Daily Bread

Norman Rockwell's effort to translate the abstract language of Franklin Roosevelt's Four Freedoms into significant iconographic form became itself a part of the fundamental mythic structure of "Americanism." Issued by the U.S. government, these posters outsold all previous posters produced in the United States. The ideal they represented —one that many Americans clearly wanted to embrace as their own—contrasted markedly with the reality of daily experience, which gave rise to a very different but equally powerful iconography, glimpsed here at the drugstore lunch counter.

Thereweremarxistswhode-nounced it as "false consciousness" imposed in ways that led people to operate against their own best interests. Neo-Conservative and Liberal social critics of the 1950s and 1960s hailed its disappearance in a world where increasing scientific and technological understanding would give us the good society now that *it* no longer influenced political judgment. That "it," of course, was ideology, a word and concept introduced into European and American discussion at the end of the eighteenth century and a source of angry debate about its nature and role ever since.

It is not perversity that leads me to argue that ideology is one of culture's fundamental gifts to its participants. Louis Althusser has rightly called it "the very 'lived experience' of human existence." Erik Erikson has defined the ideological as "a universal psychological need for a system of ideas that provides a convincing world image." So important is our way of perceiving the world in giving us an identity and anchoring us to our social substance that we surrender it with great hesitancy, often refusing to accept the reality of our experience if it interferes with our preconceptions. The learned and scientifically astute Thomas Jefferson could not, near the end of his life, accept the possibility that fossil remains indicated that some forms of life had simply died out. Believing in a fixed, finished, finally formed universe where no existing forms could disappear and no new forms could somehow appear now, he could not bring himself to accept such a threat not simply to his view of nature, but to his view of politics and society as well. Ideologies become systems that account for everything. Shatter one assumption and it is difficult to keep any of the rest.

Yet ideologies do give way; the confrontation with experience does force old assumptions (often in time) to yield to new ones. Class experience, historical developments, and social and economic differences often produce conflicting or contradictory ideological positions within a culture that tries to find ways of mediating these conflicts. The American colonies were founded at a unique moment in world history. Three revolutionary developments preceded their founding:

the Protestant Reformation, the commercial revolution and the beginnings of capitalism, and the rise of the modern state system. Each of these great movements had ideological consequences or made ideological demands.

In 1678, for example, John Bunyan published what was to be one of the most popular of all English books. *The Pilgrim's Progress* was allegorical in form and spiritual in purpose. Its interest was in tracing Christian's progress "From This World to That Which Is to Come," as the rest of the title tells us. It is a Puritan tale based on the Puritan perception of life and death. In 1719, Daniel Defoe published a far different kind of adventure story. *Robinson Crusoe* was no allegory but an almost journalistically observed account in realistic detail. And while Bunyan presented his readers with the journey of a man toward sainthood, Crusoe's life manifested the development of a shrewd, ingenious, enterprising new man of the bourgeois world. There are important ideological differences, no matter how much this account of the two books may exaggerate them. Yet they were books that coexisted; both were widely read and played a major role in Anglo-American culture. Such ideological tension is an important part of any cultural analysis.

At the same time, there is often an effort to exaggerate the differences between ideological approaches that actually share some significant common elements. Cultural analysis requires an appreciation of both tensions and convergences. The very idea of culture presupposes some common ground. These are the problems addressed in the pieces that follow. Acknowledgment again must be made here to Charles and Mary Beard. The last volume of their great *The Rise of American Civilization* is called *The American Spirit*. It is a work not well known even among professionals and not much admired by those who know it. Yet I find it masterful in its development of the concept that the Idea of Civilization became the focus of an American world view, an American ideology. My own attempt to define American conservatism starts from their analysis, although it soon goes in other directions. That paper, never before published, was originally prepared for and given at the first Socialist Scholars' Conference at Columbia University in 1965. This was a special moment in the intellectual history of the Left in America, a point when American left intellectuals and scholars were trying more urgently than for many years to define their role and function. My paper was memorable, to me, for two reasons: my colleagues, who claimed some interest in what I had to say, were upset because I had no seemingly orthodox Marxist position *and* because I quoted with apparent approval reactionary poets and intellectuals. Our audience contained many Old Left activists who were frankly appalled by the refusal to come up with specific political proposals to fight rising fascism in the United States. I will always recall the angry woman who grabbed the audience microphone at the end of the session. "If this is the way socialist scholars behave, long live the peasants and the workers!" I had somehow become, in spite of myself, an enemy of the people.

In the early 1970s, John M. Laslett and S. M. Lipset organized an interesting project; several sympathetic scholars were asked to participate in a joint stocktaking about the fate of socialism in America. Some of us were asked specifically to comment on previous writers who had addressed the problem of socialism in America. I was asked to respond to a piece by Leon Samson. I reprint my analysis exactly as it appeared in *Failure of a Dream?* although I am now convinced that I failed to realize sufficiently the exceptional development in Marxist and left scholarship taking place during the 1960s and the 1970s—the parade of intelligent and thoughtful journals from every part of the country, the heights of scholarly excellence achieved in American history by a figure like Eugene D. Genovese, the initial successes for several years of the Socialist Scholars Conferences. Yet the fact remains that out of all that came no new ideological position, and the strictures as well as the hopes expressed in my article are even more to the point today. If Americanism wouldn't do, simple-minded anti-Americanism or antimodernism won't do either.

Reform is one of those wonderful words in America that are generally greeted with enthusiasm by all. Americans seem to love reformers, even when they appear to mock them. I am less convinced that the position is a meaningful one. Once again, my heroes appear to be those on the Right like John Adams and Orestes Brownson who at least were willing to face the problem of society and reform squarely and realistically. This article also stresses something that is now obvious after several generations of fine scholarship: no analysis of American culture makes any sense if it fails to realize that this was from the start and largely remains a Protestant nation in which the role of religious ideology in the shaping of other ideological positions is key.

4 THE NATURE OF AMERICAN CONSERVATISM

In 1882, when admittedly the world was less complex and therefore easier to comprehend, England's most profound students of matters social and political offered extraordinary insight into the problem of conservatism. Their mouthpiece, Private Willis, was on his own testimony "an intellectual chap," and the brilliant reflection he was able to provide came, naturally, while he was "exercising of his brains" during an evening's sentry duty:

> I often think it's comical
> Fal, lal, la!
> Fal, lal, la!
> How Nature always does contrive
> Fal, lal, la, la
> That ev'ry boy and ev'ry gal
> That's born into the world alive
> Is either a little Liberal or else a little Conservative
> Fal, lal, la! Fal, lal, la!
> Is either a little Liberal or else a little Conservative!
> Fal, lal, la!

Now, it is no wonder that Gilbert and Sullivan's *Iolanthe* is undoubtedly the definitive analysis of conservatism—and indeed perhaps of the intellectual—that the nineteenth century could produce. For at that time and in that country, the words "liberal" and "conservative" had precise and original meanings, clear in reference to a specific historical social structure and political and economic organization. But those of us who must discuss "conservatism" today are rather faced with a series of what those equally eminent logicians (before Russell and Whitehead) would surely call most ingenious paradoxes.

In 1953, Daniel Boorstin's *The Genius of American Politics* is hailed by *Fortune* as definitive evidence that the American tradition in reality follows in the wake of the great Edmund Burke; in 1955, Louis Hartz assures us that the particular American dilemma is the consequence of our having *no* conservative tradition whatsoever but only an unchallenged "liberal" one. And if that weren't sufficiently confusing, Gunnar Myrdal's earlier massive inquiry into what he insists is *An American Dilemma* results in the profound and even brilliant observation that "America is . . . conservative. . . . But the principles conserved are liberal, and some, indeed, are radical." Self-styled conservatives unfortunately haven't helped. Stuart Sherman insists that tradition plays a vital, if not the most vital, role in American life, but that in America tradition includes the tradition of revolt, the tradition of change. Historians speak easily of the American Revolution as a conservative movement. And in what must be the final irony in our intellectual history, one of the key themes of the last two decades has been the self-conscious search for an American conservative tradition, a search that not only has brought to the center of the public arena some of the strangest characters yet, but also has found professed liberals helping with the search, urging the writing of "conservative" history, arguing with one another about who *really* belongs in our conservative tradition! What a marvelous opera Gilbert and Sullivan might have written about all of this, especially when in a final aria or grand finale America's greatest conservative seems to be a British politician who is for some reason ranked as a great political theorist, Edmund Burke.

Yet in some sense the subject is better fit for tragedy than comedy. Having quite deliberately used three of the favorite and fashionable words of those who seek an American conservatism— paradox, irony, and tragedy—it is time to explain more precisely why this state of affairs in some sense requires their use.

First, this strange quest for an American conservatism, so bewildering to elegant foreign commentators like Bernard Crick, is final evidence of the failure and collapse of the buoyant liberal faith, the optimistic, expansive, and expansionist vision that has been called the American Dream, which shaped so much of our thought and action. On the defensive at least since the crisis of the 1890s, traditional American liberalism did make historically great contributions to the theory and practice of equality and liberty, no matter its great weaknesses. We traditionalist historians must therefore be saddened. But, more significantly, the sense of failure and frustration that begets a search for conservatism produces fear, repression, and the inability to respond reasonably to the problems and challenges of our own era.

Having suggested one tragic aspect of the search for conservatism since 1945, let me point to at least one element of irony as well. Much of what most frequently is designated as characteristic of conservative attitudes already dominates in America and is central to the current Cultural Establishment. One need look no further than the intellectuals who twenty years ago were regarded (at least by themselves) as radicals or than the so-called leftist magazines such as *Partisan Review, Commentary,* and *Dissent.* What are the overriding issues, and how are they approached? The most attention is paid to the notion of the "mass society" and its cultural and psychological consequences. The attack on "mass society" is of course not new, but it does seem strange to find so many liberals or even radicals seriously worried about excessive equalitarianism and its effects on culture—a worry that finds its parallel in earlier thinkers such as Ortega, Marcel, Jaspers, Eliot, all conservatives by almost any definition. And those who quoted (or misquoted) Marx in the 1930s now without fail quote Tocqueville.

Further, the fear of the debasement of cultural values in a mass society or in popular culture spawns a self-conscious elitism among the academic and periodical guardians of cultural values; they propose themselves as arbiters, the last hope for continued "excellence." On occasion, such critics reveal a remarkable change of emphasis in their careers. Witness Dwight Macdonald: as late as 1957 he could publish his *Memoirs of a Revolutionist,* which he subtitled "Essays in Political Criticism." The bulk of these essays were from his remarkable journal *Politics* (1944–1949), certainly one of the most provocative leftist magazines in our recent past. As he moved from Marxism to other political positions—strange and wonderful on occasion—he always saw himself as a radical and distinguished himself from liberals and progressives. His autobiographical essay in the volume, which he calls "Politics Past," is in many ways extraordinarily suggestive. By 1946, he insisted that a radical was aware of the dual nature of man, evil as well as good; was skeptical about the ability of science to explain things; was aware of the tragic element in man's fate in *any* society; always stressed the

individual conscience rather than any collective. Clearly, some of
these contentions are remarkably similar to many that self-confessed
conservatives normally reserve for themselves. But in 1946 Macdonald still insisted that the radical had no interest in history, no concern with what *is* happening, only a concern with what he wants to
happen. If these values distinguish the radical from the conservative, his final emphasis on morality, the *ought* rather than the *is*,
again suggests what conservatives frequently insist is their own view.
But this transition gives way to what seems a transformation: in
1962 he published another collection of essays. The subtitle of
Against the American Grain makes clear the nature of the change, for
these are essays on the effects of mass culture: no words devoted to
the political order, no insistence on the label "radical." And in a
striking passage, Macdonald refers to the academics who compile
"Great Books of the Western World," who remake the King James
version of the Bible, who debase thought and language by compiling
a new edition of the unabridged dictionary, who by their very
profession ought to defend rather than undermine our "cultural
traditions."

If they lack respect for tradition that remote ages instinctively felt, they also
lack that historical sense that was introduced in the Renaissance, that feeling
for the special quality of each moment of historical time which, from Vico
to Spengler, has enabled us to appreciate the past on its own terms. Here
we have, as in the Stalin period in Russia, a simple obliteration of what has
gone before. . . . The trouble is not only that the predecessors had something to teach us but also that a people which loses contact with its past
becomes culturally psychotic.

Mass society, cultural values, debasement of popular culture,
the need for a cultural elite—are these the new radical concerns?
And what of those two other ideas, in article after article, book after
book—alienation and community? Indeed, they are mutual terms:
the "communal roots of the old nourishing Gemeinschaft have been
torn up by the soulless, impersonal, mechanized society." Such concerns and discussions, no matter how important, how truly vital, are
no monopoly of a radical or liberal tradition. They belong at least
equally (if not primarily) to traditional definitions of conservatism:
the organic society, the need for order, for roots, for place.

Against such conservative themes is set the preoccupation with
"place" in society by those intellectuals who do not regard themselves as conservatives. For discussion of the role of status, "status
anxiety," "status politics," or "status revolutions" seems to over-
whelm all other explanations of historical and current developments. While it is true, I believe, that few of these writers would

THE NATURE OF AMERICAN CONSERVATISM

echo Russell Kirk's preference for a return from an era of contract society to some form of status society, their implication is that we in fact *have* a status society and that the solution of "status anxiety" would solve all our basic problems. Yet here reemerges the conservative theme of Gemeinschaft, the romantic vision of a folk society as against a technological order. The same theme is also an old *non-*conservative lament, and perhaps its most significant and popular development came in the 1930s in Stuart Chase's important and influential book on Mexico where the findings of Robert Redfield in a Mexican village were contrasted favorably with the discoveries the Lynds made at about the same time in an American city.

The issue of order and social organization that might most dramatically link current dominant intellectuals with what has traditionally been called conservatism is the search for an American aristocracy. Thus the Kennedys and their friends served the American cultural establishment very well. (Imagine: Robert Frost at the Inaugural and Pablo Casals playing at the White House! America might be saved after all!) America's First Family was indeed a First Family. Here was frank enthusiasm for this kind and quality of aristocracy, with its "democratic" character, its development through the genius of American social mobility in but a few generations, its genuine social, cultural, and intellectual leadership. Here, in short, was a spectrum of attitudes about the need for leadership of a special kind. Historians enthusiastically discovered that Theodore Roosevelt had made it respectable for "gentlemen" to interest themselves in political affairs. And if the notion of an aristocracy, hereditary or not, is crucial to traditional conservatism, once again contemporary intellectuals provided what might be regarded as a living, ready-made conservative movement for the seekers after an American aristocracy.

The significance of this concern for status and for aristocracy is even more remarkably revealed in the attack on populist democracy. I am referring not only to the attack on Populism with a capital P, but also to the concept of democracy founded in popular will, majority rule, and mass participation. Richard Hofstadter, more moderately than some, states the issue clearly: democratic institutions and equalitarian sentiments *cause* anti-intellectualism in America. As a result, American intellectuals find themselves in a difficult position: they try, as Hofstadter wrote in *Anti-Intellectualism in American Life,* to be "good believing citizens of a democratic society and at the same time to resist the vulgarization of culture which that society *constantly* produces" (italics mine).

Intellectuals seem to have found a special function as missionaries preaching culture against growing anarchy. I pick these words

IDEOLOGY AS CULTURE

carefully, for one striking aspect of recent cultural development is
the self-conscious adoption by a group of cultural critics of the role
of a modern Matthew Arnold, with Lionel Trilling and Richard
Hofstadter perhaps heading the list. Reading Hofstadter's analysis
of anti-intellectualism constantly provides a striking recall of the
phrases, attitudes, and interests of Arnold in his various lectures:
the attack on debased Protestantism (evangelicalism); the enthusiasm for gentlemen and scholars in public office; a deep concern for
standards and values in education; and the fear of the dangers of
equalitarianism—all without the surrender of some general commitment to "democracy." And Trilling has been, in addition to a
major cultural critic in the tradition of Arnold, a leading interpreter
of Arnold for our time.

This important group of cultural critics generally speak for a
segment of a middle class whose liberal political attitudes have been,
as one writer has suggested, "disillusioned by current reality." They
are in some sense more sophisticated than Arnold because they can
draw on an acquaintance with Marx, a deep interest in Freud, and
an understanding of sociology (especially through the work of
Mannheim). Yet while they provide a basic criticism of contemporary culture, while they play the role of Arnold in America, their
own vision is strictly limited by their desire to maintain *one* way of
life, to cultivate *one* kind of sensibility. Not only does this limit their
ability to analyze American culture as a whole (as it limited Arnold
in his analysis of his culture), but their stress on the survival and
continuity of *a* way of life, *a* sensibility, also seems to mark them as
conservatives—although, ironically, conservatives (self-styled) see
them as radicals!

The triumph of Neo-Orthodoxy and the towering stature of
Niebuhr and Tillich in contemporary intellectual life also reveal a
potential source of conservatism—with the deep concern for sin,
the nature of evil, the tragedy of human life and the assault on the
optimism and rationalism of the Enlightenment. Both are monumental figures; both have made good use of their study of major
currents in recent intellectual history, including the work of Marx
and Freud. Both have suggested important relationships between
religious ideas and values and the political and cultural order. Their
relevance, culturally, was in their rejection of "liberal" America and
its relativism, its optimism, its dream, its mission, its materialism.
And yet, in spite of what might seem to be values their work could
easily share with that of some conservatives, especially those who
insist with Viereck that conservatism is after all nothing but the
secularization of the idea of original sin, few who seek a conservative
tradition find Neo-Orthodoxy as relevant as they find, for example,

the Neo-Thomism that still flourishes in some departments at the University of Chicago.

And, finally, more than one critic has pointed to the fact that scholars today, in social science, in history, and in philosophy, have surrendered an interest in theory, in system, in what is often called rationalism, and have retreated to gross empiricism. Philosophers surrender metaphysical interests as meaningless and concentrate on the uses of language; sociologists gather vast bodies of data and eschew massive theoretical analysis; historians supposedly reject philosophies of history and theories of interpretation and settle instead for the presentation of fact; psychology pays major attention to behavior, to clinical studies; economics concentrates on measurement and mathematical computations. This is the age of the computer, the end of "philosophizing." If this is the case, aren't we once again fulfilling the necessary conditions for conservativism, which traditionally has called for the limitation of man's system-building based on assumptions of the power of reason, and restricting ourselves rather to an empirical investigation, limited though it must necessarily be, of the way the real world is and how it does in fact operate?

These are but a few suggestions about the present state of culture in America that reveal the irony of the current search for the conservative tradition. For in terms of many of the traditional definitions of the nature of any conservatism, many trends in our intellectual life today might very well qualify as basic to conservatism.

There are, to be blunt, certain key notions that are generally associated with conservatism. But when they appear in modern culture, they are not, by the majority of thinking Americans anyway, regarded as "conservative." Rather, in some strange, almost perverse, sense they seem to reflect a redefined liberalism or even radicalism!

Let me introduce my discussion of paradox by presenting two concrete cases. Frank Tannenbaum argued that no matter how the trade-union movement conceives of itself, as conservative, radical, or revolutionary, it is actually revolutionary. The very existence of the union, the cooperation of its members, the small changes it manages to make in the structure of wages, hours, and working conditions constitute a revolution. Clustering people around their work and substituting cooperation for individual competition ends the atomization of society and the isolation of workers from their fellows. But, he assures us, the consequence of the revolution are conservative. It restores order, harmony, balance, community; it eliminates strife and creates peace; it minimizes dissent and unrest.

Thus it embodies the highest principles of Western Civilization by giving men *both* freedom and security. It develops the whole man and the whole society organically—the desired ends of such great thinkers as Shaftesbury, Dickens, Coleridge, Carlyle, Ruskin, and Kingsley.

Arnold Paul, in his discussion of conservatism and the law during the crisis of the 1890s, provides us with another example. Here the problems of the years after 1886 seemed to threaten the existence of the nature of the constituted social order. The fear grew of anarchy, revolution, and socialist takeover. The defense of property rights had always been basic to the American structure of constitutional government, although the role of the rule of law and of the courts placed strict limitations on the power of both property rights and the powers of government. However, when faced with such a crisis, certain conservative lawyers persuaded even the most traditionalistic practitioners of the need to heighten the power of law and order, especially the role of the courts. What happened, in effect, was a revolution carried out by conservatives in order to defend the social order from assault. As Paul writes in *Conservative Crisis and the Rule of Law:*

The resultant constitutional and legal revolution was, from the conservative point of view, indeed creative, in its way as significant for the laissez-faire conservatism of the 1890s as the constitutionalism of 1787 for the conservatism of that era. Due process, once primarily procedural, was now solidly substantive as well; the police power, once freely malleable as an adjuster of social imbalance, was now encased by freedom of contract; the ancient process of equity, once applicable only to named individuals and as a safeguard for physical property, was now an instrument of public policy applicable to "all persons whomsoever." . . . Traditional legal conservatism, forced to choose between *traditionalism* and *conservatism*—ironic choice— had chosen the latter. The conservative attachment to the ordered society, demanding as it seemed the firmest judicial interposition in the protection of property from social upheaval, had outranked in value the more formalistic virtues of legal tradition.

The result, Paul believes, was the unintentional sweep of laissez-faire philosophy as *the* tradition of the courts; but it was a tradition newly born and without plan.

These examples are offered not to establish that conservatives *actually* can do revolutionary things or that revolutionary movements frequently have conservative consequences. Rather, I want to stress that there may not be a necessary or logical connection between intent and consequence. Such a perspective allows us to reach a fuller understanding of *American* conservatism as a consequence of *American* experience. For there is indeed an American conservative tradition, and whatever its intent there are reasons for those who possess a radical vision to value it. It is, for example, perfectly obvious that the fundamental motive behind American conservatism is the defense of property rights. Private property—no matter what the particular working definition of the nature of capitalism at the moment—is basic, though what is of value in the conservative tradition does not *depend* on that fundamental assumption. The aspect of conservatism that is of importance today emerges only when seen against the liberal-radical tradition of individual fulfillment, individual conscience, salvation of personality and the self from the forces that seem a threat.

Werner Stark, in *America: Ideal and Reality*, offers a convenient starting point. Stark indicates through a systematic study of several key European social philosophers that, at the start of American national existence late in the eighteenth century, considerable enthusiasm was aroused among the optimists—and even among those who had doubts that the beautiful dream could long survive. To them, America represented the bourgeois ideal come to life: at last a society that would enable men to conform to nature, in which all institutions would develop and all habits would be established within the true patterns of God's benevolent laws of nature. By conforming to nature, men would be finally truly free. Here would be a society organized on a simple, semirural basis, an ordered and yet free community of truly independent members, without rich or poor, masters or slaves, a commonwealth of artisans and peasants—equals among equals—a perfect harmony of all, with peace and freedom, the absence of class and distinction. Natural laws of distribution, moral and intellectual development, pleasure rather than pain, and one's possessions neither enormous nor numerous—such was the dream. Equality *and* liberty, order *and* freedom. As late as 1788, Jacques-Pierre Brissot could write:

I transport myself sometimes in imagination to the succeeding century. I see the whole extent of the continent, from Canada to Quito, covered with cultivated fields, little villages, and country houses. (America will never have enormous cities like London and Paris which would absorb the means of industry and vitiate morals. Hence it will result, that property will be more equally divided, population greater, manners less corrupted and industry and happiness more universal.) I see Happiness and Industry, smiling side by side, Beauty adorning the daughter of Nature, Liberty and Morals rendering almost useless the coercion of Government and Laws, and gentle Tolerance taking the place of the ferocious Inquisition. I see Mexicans,

Peruvians, men of the United States, Frenchmen, and Canadians, embracing each other, cursing tyrants, and blessing the reign of Liberty which leads to Universal Harmony.

How soon Brissot's exceptional vision of the future of America gave way to harsher realities. As Stark makes clear, the notion of private property and the developments that created the industrial revolution doomed the bourgeois ideal.

Thus the new nation begins with a dream of paradise, a dream shared by European intellectuals as well as by Americans. But the dream quickly confronts capitalist reality. For the bourgeois ideal, I believe, was doomed from the start once certain fundamental assumptions were adopted. No eighteenth-century radical, not even Paine, ever advocated, for example, the elimination of private property in America. The equalitarian state found itself almost immediately a rapidly developing class state. The ideal of what the United States *might* be after the Revolution did not die. Yet significant adjustment had to be made to the newer realities of the capitalist class state that was obviously emerging. One year before Brissot's extraordinary vision, John Adams had published his great *A Defense of the Constitutions of Government of the United States of America*. In it, Adams described and justified the new system designed to provide within the framework of growing inequality some equilibrium of class forces, some mechanism to maintain order, social peace, and material advancement. The genius of Adams rests on many things; no doubt it would be easy to relate him to the Puritan heritage and to the Arminianism designed by those in new positions of social, economic, and therefore (in the eighteenth century) political power and responsibility and emphasizing the significance of community, the importance of social organization, and the moral traditions of Puritanism rather than the pietistic elements. No doubt his philosophical studies and his efforts in political theory were justifications of his class and its right, even its responsibility, to rule. What is more significant here, however, is that American conservatism at this juncture meant a positive response to the *reality* of American conditions.

Adams and other great American conservatives were interested first and foremost in what Charles Beard has called "the American Spirit"—the world view subsumed under the new Idea of Civilization. (Such categories can be too-sharp or too-arbitrary shorthand, but I hope to provide at least *some* conceptual basis that may lead to a fuller understanding of the value of conservatism in the American experience and the weakness of radicalism or liberalism.) The Idea of Civilization involves, primarily, a deep and abiding concern for the structure and organization of life and society. It assumes from the start that institutional patterns are crucial, that they are made by men to solve the problems that the real world presents in terms of existing social and economic conditions. It speaks in terms of social order that, while it may rhetorically make reference to Laws of Nature, never believes for a minute that man can or should be allowed to live in Nature. Rather, it assumes, happily or not, that man must live in society, that any other possibility is denied him, and that society therefore must be organized, must provide for a maximization of order, peace, harmony, and stability so that it will be possible to provide the conditions for progress. It assumes the fundamental importance of morality, although it does not necessarily insist on religious sanction or authority if it can indeed discover other possible sanctions or authority (the police power of the state, the mechanisms of education). It is committed, in the American experience, to "democracy" or "republicanism," although its definition of these terms may rest on ideas of limited suffrage. It values the study of history, *not* tradition, not the prescription of the past (I can think of no American who has argued this view), but of history as human experience from which lessons could be drawn. Undoubtedly, Fisher Ames is remembered as the most hidebound of conservatives, and yet his description of the making of the Constitution is most remarkable:

The body of the Federalists were always and yet are essentially democratic in their political notions . . . willing to hazard the experiment of an . . . almost unqualified proportion of democracy. . . . The Federal Constitution was as good, or very nearly as good, as our country could bear . . . Our materials for government were all democratic; and whatever the hazard of their combination may be, our Solons and Lycurguses in the convention had no alternative, nothing to consider, but how to combine them. . . . We should have succeeded worse if we had trusted our metaphysics more. Experience must be our physician, though his medicines may kill.

Of course, the best should rule. Would anyone argue against that proposition? However, the best did not mean, even for Adams, a hereditary aristocray but a natural one, no matter how difficult it might be to determine such leadership or how difficult institutionally it might be to arrange. Above all, in accepting the necessary obligations of Civilization, in rejecting the possibility of a return to Nature in any meaningful form in encouraging the importance of inventing institutions and of the necessity of adapting institutions to changing circumstances (*all* things must and would change), conservatives saw their task as the minimization of pain and the creation of the least possible hurt and of the least *possible* limitation on individual development. The acceptance of the idea of limitations and the sacrifice of some individual possibilities for the progress of the whole was inherent from the start, in the Arminian branch of the Puritan tradition as well as in the eighteenth-century development as a full-scale American conservatism. That there could be no civilization without private property went untested and is the one significant area of intellectual weakness I see from the start. They were committed to capitalism but certainly not to any specific form of capitalism. Upon reading Adam Smith, Rufus King, for example, found himself puzzled. He wrote: "If his [Smith's] theory is just, our plans are all wrong."

Nor did conservatism mean, in America, any particular form of institutional order. In his able recent study, David Fischer writes of what he calls (more irony!) *The Revolution of American Conservatism,* in which he shows how the younger, yet very conservative, Federalists broke with the old ways and adopted the techniques, the rhetoric, and even some of the more advanced "democratic" ideas of the Jeffersonians without changing their aims or surrendering their desire for power. Even old Fisher Ames could write to John Rutledge in a most modern manner: "We must court popular favor. We must study popular opinion and accommodate measure to what it is."

In our greatest conservatives, the Idea of Civilization implies a wholeness of view and a moral concern. Taking the social order as central necessarily makes conservatives moralists; it is hard to think of major ethical theories that derive from the American Left. Frequently, the decisions conservatives make in order to "save" civilization are painful ones: Orestes Brownson suffered a long, personal search for the proper instrumentalities and in the end realized the painfulness of what he had to surrender to maintain civilization. George Fitzhugh, too, as Charles and Mary Beard quoted him in *The American Spirit,* saw his problem as painful:

The last battle of civilization is the severest; the last problem the knottiest to solve. Out of all the multitudinous ingredients and influences of the past; out of the conquest of nature, and the victory of freedom; out of the blending and intermixture of all previous forms of policy and modifications of humanity, has arisen a complex order of society, of which the disorders and anomalies are as complex as its own structure. We are now summoned to the combat, not with material difficulties, not yet with oppressors nor with priests, but with an imperfect and diseased condition of that social world of which we form a part; with pains and evils appalling in their magnitude, baffling in their subtlety, perplexing in their complication, and demanding far more clear insight and unerring judgment, than even the purity of purpose, or commanding energy of will. This conflict may be said to date from the French Revolution; and it has been increasing in intensity ever since, till it has reached to a vividness and solemnity of interest, which surpasses and overshadows the attractions of all other topics.

The Idea of Civilization is basic, then, and it assumes the need for some sort of material and moral progress for the whole. It assumes the need to respond to real problems of the real world and not to metaphysical speculations, and it knows the real world through a careful study of society and history. No wonder that the first to adopt the new science of sociology in America were the conservative defenders of antebellum Southern society. No such comprehensive effort to deal with the nature of the social structure in all its aspects existed in the North at the same time.

Thus the Idea of Civilization, conceived and based on historical and social analysis, led to the development of a self-conscious, often articulate, ideology. For in ideology there was a way to view the social order and its problems as a whole and to plan for the solution of those problems. The consequences are clear: such total ideological frameworks have given the conservatives untold advantages in our history. Mark Hanna and Herbert Hoover, for example, were hardly great political theorists; yet they were committed ideologists, and their commitment enabled them to view the world with special shrewdness, to see major problems and challenges, and to plan responses and organize for the future in order to insure a continuation of Civilization as they viewed it. No liberal or radical group in American history could ever have created as successful and important a body as Hanna's National Civic Federation.

All of this implies a basic criticism of the liberal-radical tradition in America. From the days of the antinomian controversy to the present, this tradition has been largely one of dissent. It was from the start concerned not with Civilization, but with self, with the promise of fulfillment of the potentials of the self. In the nineteenth century, it sought not the progress of civilization, but Nature. It wished to return to the conditions whereby the bourgeois ideal might somehow be fulfilled. Even Thorstein Veblen found "savagery" more appealing than civilization, and if he welcomed the machine and its discipline, it was largely because he hoped that somehow the machine would destroy all institutions and man would somehow be transported back to his own nature, his basic instincts. Objecting to civilization as mere materialism in the hands of selfish men uninterested in individual development, the liberal-radical tradition often sought "reform" that was sometimes even institutional, but only of *some* institutions. For it sought to return to a previous social order (for example, the need to return to the old family

IDEOLOGY AS CULTURE

structure, disrupted by industrialism, runs like a thread through several of the reform movements of the nineteenth century). It often envisioned a social ideal based on communities that were no more or that were not undergoing great technological change. Yet significantly, it rarely attacked the basic principle of the Idea of Civilization, and the role of private property. It might try communal ownership on a small scale for a few as a "patent-office model," but it rarely accepted the challenge of a full-scale attack on the fundamental structure of society. In *Uncle Tom's Cabin,* Mrs. Stowe provides, at the core of her book, one of the most devastating critiques of American capitalism in nineteenth-century literature. Nevertheless, her attack amounts to little because she has no full ideological vision. In the end, she presents us instead with our first existentialist hero, our Uncle Tom, who finds liberty in Christ and death. Religion and saving grace are more important than economic or social adjustments. It is the strangest case for abolition on record that I know of.

To put this in another way, the liberal-radical critique centered not on the Idea of Civilization, but on another great nineteenth-century idea: Culture. Interested in the maximization of individual pleasure and the achievement of individual grace and fulfillment, the tradition emphasized conscience and man in nature ("real" man, "basic" man) and feared social involvement. Above all, it was singularly uninterested in history. (Thoreau's *Walden,* for example, is a ritual burning of the past.) As late as 1911, James Harvey Robinson bemoaned the conservatives' monopoly on the use of history and, try as he might, he was unable to persuade radicals of the value of history for their cause. Until the twentieth century, the study of history was a function of the conservative elements in our social order and provided a basis for ideology. In my terminology, the liberal-radical tradition relied instead on myth. It cut itself off from possible uses of history and thereby from the chance to build an ideology. The men and women of this tradition were interested in Culture—not in the organization of life but in the conditions of life, the quality of life, the elimination of pain and evil. These are admirable goals. But goals are not enough, nor is piecemeal reform or analysis. Emerson sounds the keynote in his famous address "The American Scholar" in 1837. We have become cowed, trustless, blinded by custom and habit. He insists he has nonetheless hope, hope provided by his doctrine that Man is One.

I believe man has been wronged; he has wronged himself. He has almost lost the light that can lead him back to his prerogatives. Men are become of no account. Men in history, men in the world of to-day, are bugs, are spawn, and are called "the mass" and "the herd." Men, such as they are, very naturally seek money or power; and power because it is as good as money —the "spoils," so called, "of office." And why not? for they aspire to the highest, and this in their sleep-walking they dream is highest. Wake them up and they shall quit the false good and leap to the true, and leave governments to clerks and desks. This revolution is to be wrought by the gradual domestication of the idea of Culture. The main enterprise of the world for splendor, for extent, is the upbuilding of a man.

In the Idea of Culture, the liberal-radical tradition offered important criticism of the ongoing society: the failure to uplift man. But in its appeal to Nature and its assumption that somehow Civilization and Culture were not significantly related (a position that showed up in interesting ways in some early professional sociology and anthropology in the late nineteenth and early twentieth century and, to some students, seemed a characteristically American social-science confusion), the liberal-radical tradition failed to develop a substantive ideology that would work effectively to replace the older order. True, the social sciences of the late nineteenth and early twentieth century showed in some sense a new turn of affairs. Yet William Graham Sumner's *Folkways* seemed more daring and damaging to the defense of the then-vision of Civilization than the work of others. In part, the new social sciences began to surrender the demand of a return to Nature—although they frequently did demand a return to Community, to the conditions of rural America, they often did suggest an overwhelming nostalgia.

The twentieth century was to find a substitute for Nature in art. It is striking how many American liberal reformers saw in art and in the aesthetic experience the end of man and the basis of his spiritual fulfillment. Recall how fundamental this notion was to John Dewey. Although often thought of as singularly committed to science as the key to democracy and community, Dewey insisted time and again on the ultimate value of shared aesthetic experience. One of his mentors, Charles Peirce, argued that the proper pursuit of science—for its own sake, without interest in practical application —is in the end a glorious aesthetic experience, a spiritual experience. This notion is similar to Veblen's strange belief in "idle curiosity" and its function. Simon Patten also saw the goal of the community, its fullest climax, its greatest maximization of pleasure, as a kind of aesthetic experience, and he makes clear the high value he places on "climax" over "product," on the individual experience of joy over material achievement. Similarly, Frederick C. Howe keenly concluded that Lincoln Steffens was not really a reformer but an artist, and Jane Addams devoted considerable space in her memoir of Hull House to the importance of the arts and aesthetic experience.

In some sense, the entire tradition of which I write is one that seeks for individual men individual *experience*, spiritual fulfillment, gratification. This experience may be religious; it may be through communion with nature; it may be in art—but such is the aim.

There is of course a further problem with those who maintain the Idea of Culture. Certainly, it offers a significant critical stance, a series of major objections to the existing order—or it *may* do so. But after all, transcendentalism demands no particular political or social view: generally, English advocates of the same set of ideas are thought of as conservatives (witness Coleridge). Further, the Idea of Culture, as our intellectual history shows, often declines into a Genteel Tradition—for Santayana's tradition of that name is clearly the tired extension of the vigorous movement of previous years. James Russell Lowell, for example, shared clearly the basic transcendentalist dream, yet by his late years the revolt against tradition had itself become traditional; the Emerson he describes in *My Study Windows* (or even the one John Jay Chapman depicts) is a very different sort of American Puritan than we see in the context of his own time. Lowell, of course, found in Thoreau nothing worth keeping alive: the ashes of a Puritan passion that burned out quickly; a selfish man, a morally empty man, a man with a morbid desire to escape to nature. (Lowell also preferred art to nature as an experience for man, and in the days from Lowell to Babbitt experience became confined to books, libraries, and galleries.) Slowly, the Genteel Tradition added what the transcendental revolt lacked: an appeal to the past, but a past that provided comfort and substance, the warmth of the study rather than an ideology for the active life. By Lowell's final days, democracy, he said, "properly understood, is a great conservative force" and America is a "democracy with conservative instincts."

I do not mean to suggest that the Idea of Civilization, which defines for me the nature of American conservativism, is without its failings. It may stumble most seriously because it had assumed and maintains an active, ongoing role in the world of affairs. Also, ideologies lose their meanings; they fail to adjust to new realities; they force the real world into patterns that provide for dangerous misunderstandings. And since conservativism in the sense I have used the term is the product of fear, the product of the dangerous changes necessitated by the recognition of the failure of one ideal and its replacement by a newer reality, that very fear, while at moments socially desirable and admirable when contrasted with a wilder optimism that perceives no problem, can be a blinding factor.

This brings me back to the present. For there is no effective conservativism, in my sense, operating in America today. Those who seek it, or say they seek it, are already too blinded by fears that have a real basis but demand a greater intellectual capacity than they make to see the whole of our contemporary reality. The changes in the world have come too fast and too dramatically, and yet after its vigorous launching in the 1930s into its new orbit and in its new form, the Idea of Culture fails as well, in spite of its discovery of existentialism and of Neo-Orthodoxy, its recovery of Dostoyevsky, its fond affection for Herman Melville and Henry James (whose fundamental understanding *is* of the nature of civilization and the intricate moral problems it creates). So a Niebuhr is a pillar of the establishment, politically as well as intellectually, with a position that originally was a clear affront to that order. No wonder the worried seekers after a new conservativism cannot buy the current crew of cultural critics. They are trapped with an Idea of Civilization that no longer represents the current reality.

And yet both traditions at least in their history—have value for those who seek to create a new radicalism today. Brooks Adams is important not because he was critical of his society but because he offered a view of Civilization. What we learn from the conservatives is primarily the value of ideology, an Idea of Civilization based on a meticulous analysis of the nature of the total reality of our world as best we are able to discover it, no matter what our dreams, our illusions, and our desires. Those who warn us away from ideology, rather than from *some* ideologies, give us no hope of confronting the world meaningfully. On the other hand, we owe our champions of the Idea of Culture great homage as well, for their efforts to seek for individual men not merely liberty and equality but also a set of worthwhile human experiences. I do not know where the balance will be struck between the search for pleasure and the avoidance of pain. I am impressed with Herbert Marcuse's *Eros and Civilization* and sense that somehow in the dilemmas with which Freud presented us in *Civilization and Its Discontents* there may be the answer to the problem of maintaining both Civilization and Culture. This is, after all, the basic problem with which Freud (both a great conservative and a great radical) was working at the end of his life. Meanwhile, we must tackle the problem head on, unafraid to move beyond our empirical data, unafraid to learn from those with whom we disagree. Our greatest conservatives have much we can profit by.

"Here error is all in the not done / All in the diffidence that faltered," wrote Ezra Pound. There are, indeed, occasions when a poet whose commitment to repulsive doctrine can tell us more about the human conditions than one whose vision of the future is closer to our own but insists on informing us tritely and perhaps even meaninglessly "First Bread, then Morality." We must demand a more complete vision than that.

5 SOCIALISM AND AMERICANISM

The problem of revolutionary politics might well be illuminated by a brief reference to the injunction repeatedly put upon the solid middle-class Puritans who came to American shores in the seventeenth century, not merely to found their own "City on a Hill" but to undertake the even more breathtaking task of reforming the Reformation itself—and thus the whole world. They must remain, they were constantly reminded, *in* the world but they must never become *of* the world. The enormous difficulty in obeying that injunction informs the whole history of the Puritan experience. It is also, in effect, the same challenge that faces any group determined to alter radically the world in which it finds itself, the very world in which the group must continue to live while laboring to transform it.

Those who wish to see a socialist America might well learn from the history of those who strove to create a Christian America. As H. Richard Niebuhr brilliantly demonstrated in *Christ and Culture*, Christianity could and has served as a compelling counterculture, providing an often devastating judgment against the ongoing patterns of a culture. But at the same time conversion to the Christian creed might very well serve a far different function of mitigating feelings of oppression and even thus becoming an ideology sustaining the very culture to which it originally offered critical opposition. Thus in 1921, Frank Tannenbaum (a socialist attracted both to the IWW and to John Dewey, to whom he dedicated his book) warned in *The Labor Movement* against political movements, suggesting that they functioned much like "a Billy Sunday meeting . . . dime novels, drink, baseball scores, moving pictures" as rationales or "a means of emotional dissipation in things."

The Socialist Party differs from other political organizations in that it concerns itself consciously about those things that *seem* to be most vital to the worker's life and labor. By its agitation it helps to crystallize discontent, gives it meaning and sets for it a definite goal. It must, however, be noted that the Socialist Party concerns itself *about* those problems *rather than with them.* It tends to postpone immediate activity by centering interest in things outside the sphere of daily contact and function in which the worker operates, and *thus in a measurable degree unconsciously participates in the work performed by all other agencies that go to distract the worker's attention from his immediate problems.*[1]

Tannenbaum saw the revolutionary transformation as coming primarily as an inevitable end of the process of unionization; yet in his work he realized that the labor movement itself could and would have "conservative consequences," stabilizing and ordering the social system, eliminating friction and discord and creating harmony and true community. And as early as the turn of the century the leaders of American industry realized, in the formation of the National Civic Federation, the desirable role organized labor might play in rationalizing the new industrial order. By 1948, when C. Wright Mills published his *The New Men of Power,* few Americans on the Left retained any illusions about the significant role organized labor had in fact played in sustaining the existing American system.

The problem of how to function *in* the world and yet not become *of* that world is thus the crucial question of strategy and tactics; that problem has been immeasurably complicated by a set of special conditions in the American experience. There was from the outset the problem of the relationship of theory to that experience itself. Both American and European socialists have repeatedly raised the question of American uniqueness, the "special" nature of American history and development.[2] Some have seen the problem in terms of the relationship (or the failure to establish such a relationship) between a theoretical or ideological viewpoint and some form of political action. Others have insisted that the key question rested in the definition of the potential "mass base" of any such movement, some praising ventures (like the almost legendary IWW) dedicated to and centering around those "marginal" to the ongoing system: unskilled and unorganized labor, immigrants, blacks, women; others calling for a movement that could draw the widest possible support, including the resources of the intellectuals, the established trade unions, sympathetic members of the middle class. And while political activity of some sort has been central to many who sought a socialist America, some would insist the initial struggle must take place in the community, within local institutions, while others believed an attempt at national power was paramount. Others, in effect, renounced all political activity and proposed in its place activity in the cultural area, often in a vision of a special kind of literary or cultural radicalism.

But in almost all of these cases there was the persistent and very special question: how does or can socialism relate to the specifically American experience? And often the question was put even more crudely: was socialism a "foreign" ideology or was it actually a "native" movement that belonged within the American Way? One of the many paradoxes of American history is how a nation of immigrants could be at the same time a nation that could so often be roused to fear and even hysteria over ideas, movements, and people labeled "foreign," or how often other ideas, movements, and people could be defended and even enthusiastically supported if they could be thought of as "native"—or accepted if they could be proven to have been effectively "Americanized."

It is vital to the history of socialism in America to realize that the very years that witnessed the growth of considerable interest in and support for socialist ideas and the Socialist Party itself were the years that saw as well the development of "Americanism" as an ideology, especially the first few decades of the twentieth century. Certainly by the 1920s, as Elwin H. Powell contends, the whole new order created in the United States under the reign of Progressivism and tightened by the experience of the war itself "was 'sacralized' or sanctified by the mystique of Americanism, which replaced the older Protestant ethic as an ideological foundation of corporate capitalism."[3] And it is further true that the experience of the Depression and still another world war extended the sway and power of the vision of an American way of life.[4]

Even the most superficial reading of history suggests there was a greater appeal in a socialism under the leadership of a man like Eugene V. Debs, for example, who for all of his references to Marx and class struggle gave the appearance of "native" American radicalism in his person, rhetoric, and even conduct than in the growing power of foreign-language federations on the Left of the American socialist movement or in the IWW, with its methods ("anarchism," "violence," uncharacteristic unionism) and membership (with its appeal to "bums" and marginal men). Historians, too, have argued that the growing power of foreign-language federations and the

IDEOLOGY AS CULTURE

emergence of the new Communist Party in the 1920s tended to reflect European events, especially the experience of the Russian Revolution and its consequences. In his superb essay on "The Collapse of Socialism," Christopher Lasch sums up the characteristics of American radicalism from the 1920s until the present: "sectarianism, marginality, and alienation from American life."[5]

Precisely. In this great century of "Americanism," socialists worried the problem of their "alienation from American life," but they made every effort (consciously or unconsciously) to overcome that sense. "Perhaps the most important symptom of the progress of Socialism in America," wrote Upton Sinclair jubilantly in 1911, "is the flood of Socialist books which are pouring from the presses nowadays, books written by native-born Americans and dealing with American questions from American points of view."[6] The literary radicals of the period who also felt themselves aliens regarded themselves most often as socialists while they eschewed any political path to the revolution they sought. Rather, with one of their leaders, Van Wyck Brooks, they struggled to create an American cultural renaissance. One of their most important magazines, *Seven Arts,* stated in its opening editorial: "It is our faith and the faith of many, that we are living in the first days of a renascent period, a time which means for America the coming of that national self-consciousness which is the beginning of greatness." And even those who sought in part to make their revolution in terms of a life-style that would challenge the American middle class with departures in dress, in experimentation in a wide variety of life experiences, new attitudes toward sex and traditional institutions and values (culminating perhaps in the Greenwich Village "Bohemian") often chose as a model or culture hero a figure like Jack London or John Reed or the tramp, vagabond, social outcast. As James B. Gilbert shrewdly observes, "A characteristic American social type was now depicted as a social revolutionary, but he could now be seen as the creator of a new sort of culture contained in songbooks and IWW newspapers and as a prophet in his own life, a man on the fringe of society, yet capable of seeing clearly to its center." Yet it is significant that such a figure has American roots in Walt Whitman, in Mark Twain's Huck Finn, in a long American tradition that was in fact slowly being pieced together and brought to stand in the service of a counterculture dedicated to overturn (as George Santayana observed) the sterile Genteel Tradition that no longer stood for life and experience in America but only in support of the established order. Thus socialists adopted a wide range of techniques, but they did so in reference to putting themselves in some kind of proper relationship with the Americanism of the era.

It is clearly possible to propose that the socialism of the era—in whatever form—had an impact on American developments. Indeed, the newly defined Americanism of the period was increasingly broad in its definition to encompass many things Americans might once have rejected as "socialistic." The new liberal social thinkers in their revolt against formalism had also been in revolt against the more ruthless forms of individualism that had generated the robber barons and the chaos in corporate capitalism that made for inefficiency. The whole Progressive effort to rationalize the new industrial order had led as well to a renewal or continuation of the search for community, a search as old at least as John Winthrop's famous "Model of Christian Charity" written aboard the *Arbella* in 1630. The trend toward "socializing the services and goods of the community and placing them at the disposal of the individual" was an outstanding characteristic of the American Way by the 1920s, as Frank Tannenbaum wrote in *The Labor Movement*, published in 1921:

We have socialized things as water, public highways, education, lighted streets, bridges, medical service for the sick through public hospitals, dental services for children in public schools, parks, museums, books through libraries, and information services of various kinds. . . . To this must be added sickness insurance, unemployment insurance, care for the old through old age pensions and for the young through maternity pensions, factory and mine inspections, and legal enforcement of protection against dangerous machinery.[7]

To this list Tannenbaum might well have added the income tax among other transformations of governmental roles previously held to be socialistic attacks on private property and even the gradual but grudging respect to the workers' rights to organizing and bargaining collectively. It might very well be in fact that all of these "socialized things" were part of an effort to rationalize the industrial order; it might very well be that they were designed primarily to aid the middle class and the organized and that millions of Americans did not benefit significantly or directly from them. But the fact remains that such transformations could lead a Buffalo newspaper to declare editorially in 1917: "We are all more or less socialists nowadays. Some of us call our socialism by the name State Regulation or Municipal Ownership or Organized Benevolence. But it is socialism pure and simple as distinguished from the individualism of Herbert Spencer."[8]

Even that radical new life-style that presented such a deliberate affront to middle-class Americans, and especially to those mid-

IDEOLOGY AS CULTURE

dle-class values so long associated with the Puritan work-save ethic, proved in the end supportive of the new Americanism (although it clearly did as well play a role in significantly altering American life and manners and morals generally). As Malcolm Cowley has shown, the very things valued by the new ethic of Greenwich Village provided a necessary new ethic of *consumption*, encouraging people to spend and buy, changing the nature of American habits, and helping to create the consumer aspect of Americanism so necessary if the new industrial system was to survive. Cultural radicalism could be accepted (in part at least); Americanism could encompass this variant of socialism.[9]

On the Fourth of July, 1935, *The Daily Worker* announced in a bold headline: TOWARD A SOVIET AMERICA. The goal was by no means new; the means appeared to be. No longer would a major thrust in American socialism be "alienated" from the American world (as it appeared to many to be in the 1920s). On page 2 the reader of the *Worker* would find, side by side, pictures of the two great revolutionaries, Lenin and George Washington. A reprint of the Declaration of Independence completed the obvious message. American socialism had joined Americanism with a vengeance. Communism became twentieth-century Americanism. "We," Earl Browder would say of his comrades, "are the only true Americans." No matter what the formal policy considerations—and of course the idea of the Popular Front was by no means singular nor an American development conditioned by unique American circumstances—it was but another step in the whole history of the special relationship between Americanism and socialism, an almost predictable part of the shift and countershift that mark the whole history of the interplay between socialism and the American experience in our century. Leon Samson has argued that Americans, unconscious socialists all along, had used Americanism as a substitute for conscious socialism. The Popular Front would now try to capture that Americanism as a device for turning Americans into conscious socialists.

This is not the place to assess the consequences of the Popular Front in America. In the 1940s and after, much attention was paid to the supposedly pernicious role the Communists were able to play under the cover of the Front by insinuating themselves into government and a wide variety of American institutions. Too little attention has been paid to the harm done to American socialism itself: out of it came an absurd vision of the American past, a peculiar notion of American society in the present, a ludicrous attitude toward American culture in general. At a most critical juncture in our history American socialists helped us little in understanding ourselves or the world. The effort to partake of Americanism led to gross comedy in which ideas—to say nothing of ideology—took a back seat. A university Communist group could even announce:

Some people have the idea that a YCLer is politically minded, that nothing outside of politics means anything. Gosh no. They have a few simple problems. There is the problem of getting good men on the baseball team this spring, of opposition from ping-pong teams, of dating girls, etc. We go to shows, parties, dances and all that. In short, the YCL and its members are no different from other people except that we believe in dialectical materialism as a solution to all problems.[10]

Irving Howe and Lewis Coser have shown how the Popular Front in fact became a kind of culture. While they may concentrate, perhaps, too much attention on the absurd aspects of that culture (with its social-minded nightclubs, for example), they also brilliantly highlight the contributions it made to the style of mass culture in the United States, a style that they rightly suggest continued long after the Second World War. The Popular Front (like previous socialist confrontations with Americanism) helped shape that Americanism, but few would be willing to suggest that the kind of society and kind of culture that resulted could in any legitimate sense be designated as socialist.

As early as 1936, many Marxist intellectuals had begun to wonder whether indeed Marxism was compatible with the American Tradition, and by 1937 William Phillips and Philip Rahv, editors of the distinguished *Partisan Review*, had concluded that "an essential contradiction existed between Marxism and domestic intellectual traditions that could only be resolved through the 'Europeanization of American Literature.' "[11] (One is immediately reminded of Van Wyck Brooks' early sense of frustration at his inability to find a meaningful basis in the literary life in America for the base of a new socialist culture. For a bibliography in connection with his essay on the subject in Harold Stearns' *Civilization in the United States* (1922), Brooks wrote: "For a sense of everything American literary life is *not,* one might read, for instance, the Letters of Ibsen, Dostoyevsky, Chekhov, Flaubert, Taine, and Leopardi. . . .)"[12] But by 1952— after years of war, hot and cold, and McCarthyism, in a symposium on "Our Country and Our Culture"—many *Partisan Review* authors could again speak of the end of alienation, of the return to America and her traditions, the end of exile and rebellion. Americanism will out.

Yet there is another sense in which Americanism itself must be taken: it stands for industrialism itself. "Industrialism," a group of critics of the entire system, the "Twelve Southerners," argued in 1930,

IDEOLOGY AS CULTURE

is the economic organization of the collective American society. It means the decision of society to invest its economic resources in the applied sciences. . . . The capitalization of the applied sciences has now become extravagant and uncritical; it has enslaved our human energies to a degree now clearly felt to be burdensome. The apologists of industrialism do not like to meet this charge directly; so they often take refuge in saying they are devoted simply to science. They are really devoted to the applied sciences and to practical production. . . . It is an Americanism which looks innocent and disinterested, but really is not either.[13]

Above all, perhaps, as many Europeans already knew in the 1920s, Americanism meant *Fordismus*. Add to our gallery of pictures another pair: it was not at all unusual during the 1920s to find in factories in the U.S.S.R., hanging side by side as portraits of the two men who had "revolutionized" the twentieth century, pictures of Lenin and Henry Ford. Without worrying about ideological consequences or the danger of foreign ideas, the Soviets could admire the genius of Ford and his contribution to the technological developments that transformed the industrial order. American engineers reciprocated: many returning from visits to Soviet factories during the 1920s and 1930s were enthusiastic about Soviet industrialization and industrial organization and progress, again without ideological or political concern but with professional admiration at achievement and production. And in the United States itself Ford's action of January 1, 1914, establishing the five-dollar, eight-hour day for all Ford workers who could pass his Sociological Department's examination "on the clean and wholesome life" (the department also provided services that would enable workers to pass the examination, adjust themselves to proper conditions of home and community living, sound work habits, and the good citizenship required of them), was frequently hailed as a major contribution of a new vision —not merely of man as a producer but man as a member of the American community. Ford himself realized that part of what he was doing created customers for his automobiles, but even here his vision of a car for every man would provide workers a share, not in essential decision-making power in the shop, industry, the community, or the nation, perhaps, but in a kind of fundamental social equality through the ownership and use of energy and mobility resources of a society usually reserved in past orders for the very few. And Tocqueville had said so long ago that Americans preferred equality to liberty anyway. Some writers have gone so far as to insist (not socialist writers, to be sure) that Ford's overall revolution *was* as significant as Lenin's.[14] But whatever one's interpretation of *Fordismus* it was undeniably part of what came to be called Americanism.

And socialism was from the outset significantly related to industrialism. No matter what criticism it might find in the kind of
industrial order that existed under capitalism, it was committed to
that basic order itself. It thefore shared from the start many assumptions and many basic values. If Samson can find in Americanism substitutes for socialist values or socialist concepts turned on
their head, it is possible to see as well in socialism those values and
beliefs associated with industrialism easily acceptable in Americanism: a belief in order, rationality, and science; a respect for production, efficiency, power, discipline, and above all work; the need for
planning, organization, and even bureaucracy and the state (at least
at a certain stage of development); an intense interest in mass culture or the culture of the masses; stress on cooperation, participation, the importance of the well-being of the community; a vision of
Progress, especially under science. Both accepted trade unionism
and both paid special homage to the role of the worker: socialists
argued the worker deserved "full value of his product" and even
Henry Ford spoke of profit sharing (even before profits) in which
workers would receive their "just share." Americanism ordered a
Labor Day while the Popular Front proposed an Americanism Day.
Both claim to seek a stability and order to end insecurity, anomie,
and alienation. Both value the concept of social equality. The list
could be extended with ease: the point is that both are the products
of industrialism.

Thus there *is* a real challenge in the criticism of the Twelve
Southerners quoted previously. These critics called themselves
"Agrarians" and put themselves in opposition to all forms of industrialism. They held that even some critics of the industrial order
find remediation in only more industrialism.

Sometimes they rely on the benevolence of capital, or the militancy of labor,
to bring about a fairer division of the spoils: they are Cooperationists or
Socialists. And sometimes they expect to find super-engineers, in the shape
of Boards of Control, who will adapt production to consumption and regulate prices and guarantee business against fluctuations: they are Sovietists.
With respect to these last it must be insisted that the true Sovietists or
Communists . . . are Industrialists themselves. . . . We therefore look upon
the Communist menace as menace indeed, but not as a Red one; because it
is simply according to the blind drift of our industrial development to
expect in America at last much the same economic system as that imposed
by violence upon Russia in 1917.[15]

I do not accept this analysis, yet I do believe that socialists must
accept the challenge it contains: how much have socialists accepted
of the world in which they find themselves and how much of that

IDEOLOGY AS CULTURE

often uncritical acceptance of Industrialism-Americanism has in fact hampered them from building toward a program with genuine consequences for the quality of human life and fundamental thought about human aspirations?

Socialism has contributed to the American experience in ways that have perhaps broadened the definition of Americanism without significantly altering its fundamental structure or proposing a genuine alternative culture. As it strove to operate in this century in its own strange game with Americanism, it often found itself not only in the world but of it, sometimes dramatically reinforcing the very order it proposed to alter radically. It is true that socialists in America have never been able to sustain a mass movement; but perhaps there is another question of as much significance related to it: why have we produced no Luxemburg, no Gramsci, no Lukács, no Gorz, no Althusser—no theoretical contributions to the great discussion Marx began well over a century ago? why have we produced no school of social analysis equal to the work of the Frankfurt School to help us come to an understanding of the nature of our industrial society? why no school of historical scholars in the tradition of the English *Past and Present* group, for example, to make it possible for us to understand our past and present?

Why have we allowed sentiment and rhetoric to replace the good hard work of analysis and deep thought? Why have we so often found ourselves playing the Americanism game, ending up ironically reinforcing the order we propose to change, contributing more to the "socializing" of things than the socializing of America, supporting too often the liberal American substitute for socialism: the idea of the new middle class of professional as expert, the engineer, planner, designer, social scientist as savior; or the support of movements like trade unionism without seeing it in any large social context? We have contributed to the making of mass culture without developing any position from which to evaluate it. Even our Bohemian Left has often, as we have seen, ended up reinforcing certain values necessary for the system. Have we really been wise in our pursuit of Americanism in an effort to capture it for socialism, or has that very Americanism ended up capturing us because we have not been sufficiently self-aware or self-critical?

Socialists *are* alienated by definition; the end of our alienation we believe will not come through private solutions; it certainly will not come through acceptance of Industrialism-Americanism. We are too often conscious only of our alienation and too little conscious of what that alienation means, too ready to accept for ourselves or our group some more immediate answer to that problem for us with too little attention to what it means in the totality of experience and social relations. Howe and Coser shrewdly point out in a parenthetical remark: "American radicalism has always functioned as a kind of prep school for the leaders of American capitalist society,"[16] Is it not possible to find that place *in* but not *of* the world we have inherited? Must Americanism win?

6 THE PERSISTENCE OF REFORM

The American is most characteristically a reformer and his history a series of reforms. It is possible to spell out in considerable detail the consequences of an almost continual impulse to reform from the days of the first English settlers on this continent who proposed from the start nothing less than the completion of the Reformation itself, nothing less than the reform of a corrupt old Europe and the establishment of the Kingdom of God. The triumph of reform has been for many the special glory of our history, the meaning of Progress: the constant—some would add pragmatic—adjustment and readjustment to change, the peaceful solution of human and social problems, and the advancement toward increasingly enlightened ends. Some historians prefer to see the operation of some metaphoric pendulum with each impulse toward reform followed by an almost Newtonian reaction—albeit never equal in force—or possibly, adopting instead images from quantum theory, waves of reform exhausting themselves but ultimately to be followed by new waves of reform energy. Other historians are impressed with particular periods: from Henry Steele Commager the years between 1830 and 1860 mark The Era of Reform, while Richard Hofstadter finds special reasons for characterizing the period between 1890, and 1940 as The Age of Reform. If this suggests that the years between 1860 and 1890 somehow escape from the reform mania, a brief examination of

86

THE PERSISTENCE OF REFORM

such a work as the monumental *Encyclopedia of Social Reform* published by the Christian Socialist W. D. P. Bliss in the 1890s should dispel such an illusion.

It is difficult to think of a single decade in American history that did not produce its significant reforms or reformers. Many periods thought of as "reactionary" now in the light of new research appear to be far different; they, too, testify to the persistence and extension of reform efforts. The 1920s, among other "progressive things," witnessed an extraordinary growth in the process of the professionalization of reform, with major developments in the field of social work, for example. The very creation of such a profession in effect institutionalized the idea of reform and made it an integral part of "the system." The notion of building reform into the very structure of our culture seems right and proper. Americans know that reform movements occur in other nations and that some reforms have preceded similar achievements in the United States by decades while others have been inspired by the American example. But in the American historical view, European reformers, having had to fight for their lives and reforms, threatened by the overwhelming power of reactionary counterpowers, frequently failed or ultimately gave way to revolutionary change by force and violence. Our historians delight in the "conservative" nature of our own revolution and are ashamed that the Civil War alone mars our record of constant reform achievement. Forms, methods, and techniques may change, but each generation of Americans seems to have had its rendezvous with reform, and it is precisely this constant series of reform achievements that American liberal historians hail as the characteristic feature of our national history.

Such a vision of reform and progress is not false to many of the facts of the historic record. But it does beg a crucial question: *if Americans are reformers brilliantly readjusting their lives and institutions to new needs in terms of changing circumstances, why is it necessary for the process of reform itself to be such a constant fact?* Why can we not solve many of our problems permanently? Why can we not provide a structure that works without the persistence of reformist energy and activity? Why does not the American Way of Life—that concept brilliantly invented in the 1930s—work itself out without the constant need to solve again old problems? Why are we faced with, over and over again, problems with which previous reform generations struggled? Problems of race relations, civil rights, and the existence of poverty, for a few examples, seem to be as persistent in our culture—although the forms may differ—as the idea of reform itself. The very "success" of repeated reform movements somehow ironically indicates as well a basic "failure." If American historical glory resides in its reformist-liberal tradition, why are we somehow repeatedly called to action by age-old problems?

This paper proposes to explore some of the possible reasons for the persistence of the reform phenomenon in American culture. There are many such explanations, of course, already on the books, some of the most persuasive concentrating on the peculiarity of the American social structure in the nineteenth and twentieth centuries, especially the mobility existing within that structure. Other students look to economic variations, cycles of boom-and-bust. Political and institutional arrangements following from the extraordinary environment created by the American Constitution and the increasing democratization of the culture have not been ignored. Even mechanical laws, cycles of reform and reaction occuring automatically every twenty years or so, have been proposed. Intellectual sources, too, have not been overlooked and frequently students have seen the reform impulse from the perspective of the special confluence of Puritan and Enlightenment ideologies, a democratized enlightenment and an evangelized Puritanism. Here I hope rather to examine some of the basic assumptions, the common storehouse of ideas and attitudes generalized from the history of reform experience in America. I shall attempt to define three traditions of reform, bodies of ideas, and experience, of ideologies and social situations that I believe to be basic to our historic development. Possibly an examination of these traditions may add to our understanding of the persistence of reform itself.

MORAL RECTITUDE IN REFORM

Each of these traditions was clearly enough established by the early decades of the nineteenth century. The first represents a striking aspect of Protestantism in America: the moral rehabilitation of the Nation by the exertion of strong moral leadership that would influence individual men to love virtue and shun vice. This moralism insisted on the need to obtain justice in the name of a higher moral law and stressed the need for order and standards of stability in a world of increasing change. It did not threaten the newly emerging social order by a direct assault on its fundamental principles or its basic institutions—and, indeed, in the antislavery movement it might be said to have assisted that new order by its insistence on the removal of an institution no longer compatible with it. Rather, it stressed, initially through the leadership and direction of "the best men," the responsibility of man for his fellow man, the need to be (as Professor Charles Griffin has so effectively shown) one's "brother's keeper."

No longer able to rely upon the power of the church, effectively disestablished by the early decades of the nineteenth century, and initially unable or unwilling in an increasingly mobile society to depend upon the institutions of the state, the moral crusaders generally depended upon two methods of operation. First, there were the voluntary associations, either a variety of missionary groups determined to spread the Gospel and bring men thus to "the way" or societies directed against a whole range of threats to the social order: war, drunkenness, slavery, foreign immigrants—the list is long and impressive, and the leadership of such crusades was equally impressive. Second, the various new revival movements in the mid-nineteenth century, concentrating increasingly in the cities, stressed the effort to Christianize the whole Nation, to bring America in line with God's Plan and Mission for her, God's new moral order.

Frederick C. Howe, in his great personal analysis of the mind and life of a reformer, *The Confessions of a Reformer* (1925), provides this often-quoted and still shrewd insight.

It was with difficulty that realism got lodgment in my mind; early assumptions as to virtue and vice, goodness and evil remained in my mind long after I had tried to discard them. This is, I think, the most characteristic influence of my generation. It explains the nature of our reforms, the regulatory legislation in morals and economics, our belief in men rather than institutions and our messages to other peoples. Missionaries and battleships, anti-saloon leagues and Ku Klux Klans, Wilson and Santo Domingo are all a part of that evangelistic psychology that makes America what she is. . . . [We are dominated by an] evangelical-mindedness that seeks a moralistic explanation of social problems and a religious solution for most of them.[1]

While a moral explanation might provide a way of viewing the world, it did not effectively provide an analysis to the basic system of the society and the economy as it operated. Even in the great days of the Social Gospel movement when men talked of the literal possibility of establishing the Kingdom of God on earth, there was a failure to provide an analysis of the precise nature of the difficulties and therefore failure to make any fundamental thrust against more than discrete symptoms of faults within that system.

It is easy to ridicule this Steward tradition and its moralism. We are assuredly bemused when we read of that famous comment directed at our first President Roosevelt by an associate: "Theodore, if there is one thing more than any other for which I admire you, it is your original discovery of the Ten Commandments." But it was precisely this internalization of such strong moral vision that made it such a force and makes it still a vital factor in reform in our own times as well. No analysis of our history and certainly no discussion of American reform can fail to attend to it carefully and respectfully. It was an effective instrument that over and over recorded successes in a battle to mitigate against the more blatant abuses of a rapidly changing social order and in leading men to demand a satisfactory working of the system.

Yet one is also impressed by the basic conservatism of such reform as well. Many may have disliked the more vicious consequences, for example, of the industrialization of society but few wished to refuse its achievements or deny the basic value of its capitalist assumptions. They wished rather to preserve, in so far as possible, the older values and basic institutions of the past, the older social and moral codes in an effort to blunt the consequences of the more serious dislocations. How strikingly, for example, reform movements for the last century and a half show—especially in their rhetoric—a desire to maintain the older family patterns of an agrarian and preindustrial order. The literature of the temperance and abolition movements are but two illustrations of this from an early period. How consistently, too, we can witness the appeal to the ideal of "community" and the nostalgic desire to retain, as basic, community patterns that also represent the older era of small-town America. Such institutions and the values associated with them are considered designed to function as a stable center of moral and social order.

Only gradually did the moral reformers of the Steward tradition turn from individual exhortation and conversion to the use of instruments of the state for purposes of regulation and enforcement. Little by little they turned in this new direction, and some became prepared to see the possibility of social institutions that might aid man in achieving the moral way. This is especially true, perhaps, after the doctrine of Immanence—that strangely un-Protestant view that God's attributes might be found in the world—grew in importance. Thus from Horace Bushnell's *Christian Nurture* in the 1840s through the Social Gospel movement and beyond, it becomes possible for the moralists to argue the value of nature and of even institutions in the world as helping bring man and the nation to God. Education, even state-directed education, becomes an especially important aspect of the moralist's program for remaking America. But such a positive use of the state and its power was only cautiously and begrudgingly proposed. The moralists wished to create a Christian America according to God's Plan (unfortunately not always clearly seen or understood, not always consistently viewed by all reformers who sought its implementation). But they usually saw the human answer as simple, for were not God's own Commandments simple, and what could be more uncomplicated than Jesus' magnificent Sermon on the Mount? Reformers of this persuasion often dreaded more complex institutional or organization programs. The appeal of a Henry George, for one example, was extraordinary: his language contained the familiar rhetoric of an older order, the rhetoric of John Locke and more especially that of the Bible itself. His solution to social problems required no fundamental change in the nature of the new capitalist order, and yet his Single Tax would enable society to keep the achievements of modern industrial capitalism—Progress—while it restored equality and other social and moral virtues—that is, the end of Poverty—of the older agrarian order. For many, George was a modern translator of the Sermon on the Mount, and for many reformers this was enough. Frederick Howe quotes a telling passage from the reformer Brand Whitlock:

I have gone through every political philosophy. I can see nothing in Socialism. The philosophy of Henry George of a free state in which the resources of the earth will be opened up to use is the only political philosophy that ever commanded my adherence. But the world is not interested in such a simple reform. It wants too much government, too much regulation, too much policing.[a]

THE REFORMERS OF THE EMERGING SYSTEM

Such a view contrasts dramatically with the special vision of the second great reform tradition, also a product of the early nineteenth century. In that era of brilliant and revolutionary breakthroughs in the areas of communications and organization, it was perhaps only logical that a tradition of reform should develop dedicated to the use of new instruments being forged by the newly emerging social order itself, tools already being used with stunning success in business and industry. This was the tradition of the Artisans, of the Technocrats, the believers in the application to society itself of the new devices of organization and communication, the new tools of science and engineering. We see them perhaps foreshadowed early in France, in the men of the École Polytechnique, the followers of Saint-Simon and Comte. In the United States, they developed their position more slowly but by the turn of the century they commanded a considerable following. Edward Bellamy's utopian state of the 1880s is a testament to the magic power of industrial and military organization and to the application of science and technology. Brooks Adams' definition of civilization as centralization, his stress on scientific education, administration, and efficiency, were to become commonplaces. The key words were "power," "efficiency," "science."

Such a view stressed the role of the expert and the manager, of special training and special skills. The Progressive movement was certainly many things; but surely among them was a sense of revolt against politics itself in the interest of a managerial-oriented society, a government of trained and efficient experts who could make the system work to the profit of the whole nation and its citizens, a kind of neomercantilist view of the state and society directed by an elite of experts. Some even urged a new definition of the popular will: a direction of affairs by those who understood psychology and "social science," those who could give the people not what they *believed* they wanted but what they knew, through their training, they *really* wanted (witness Walter Lippmann's special use of Freud and other social thinkers in works like *Public Opinion*).

This tradition of reform sought no wholesale readjustments; it did not, for example, propose any alteration of the system of property holding. Rather, it argued for the logic of the emerging system itself, the clearing away of the obsolete—the older, foolish rugged individualism, the wasteful competition and unscientific use of resources—so that the system might be rationalized and breakdowns and social maladjustments avoided. It called early for civil service, for commissions of experts, for managers in cities and countries; it talked of "social engineering" to achieve the general happiness and well-being of all. These reformers had seen the future and were determined to make it work! They called for the Organizational Society and the Organizational Man to counteract the culture in which they found themselves at the turn of the century; in other words, they called for the very social order and culture now under attack by a current generation of reformers. One of these new reformers, Paul Goodman, in speaking of the "transition from the old tycoon-and-clergyman culture to the new managerial organization" in *Growing Up Absurd,* makes the point this way:

The pragmatism, instrumentalism, and technologism of James, Dewey, and Veblen were leveled against the abuses and ideals of the then dominant class: the Four Hundred and the Robber Barons—academic culture, caste morals and formal religion, unsocial greed. The philosophers were concerned about abundant production, social harmony, practical virtues and more honest perception and feeling, which would presumably pertain to a rising group of technicians, social-scientific administrators, and organized labor. . . . In that early turn of the century, these philosophers failed to predict that precisely with the success of the managers, technicians, and organized labor, the "achieved" values of efficient abundant production, social harmony, and one popular culture would produce even more devastatingly the things they did not want: an abstract and inhuman physical environment, a useless economy, a caste system, a dangerous conformity, a trivial and sensational leisure.[3]

Thus the Technocrat reformers, too, thought they could accept the new order—in this case on its own terms and with its own logic—and yet somehow retain or return to those basic values of an older order: Brooks Adams' admiration for the dedicated man of medieval knighthood; James' effort to retain a meaningful "self" in a deterministic world; Dewey's endless search for "community"; Veblen's desire to see fully expressed basic and primitive "instincts" (most especially his almost mystical "instinct for workmanship"). Yet their very yielding to the essentials of the new order often helped prepare the way for that order and its consequences. No wonder that as early as the 1920s yet other reformers, such as Lewis Mumford, could hurl the charge that the Progressive generation had made a "Pragmatic Acquiescence" to a vicious and unprofitable world order. What was the hope of a new world became the frightening shadow of a *Brave New World* or even a *1984*.

In those glorious days of technocratic promise, Henry Ford would be hailed as a leading Progressive and even considered as a possible Progressive presidential candidate. What he had done so brilliantly in industry might be done on a larger scale more brilliantly for society at large. It is well to remember that Ford had his own school and his Sociological Department—headed by an ex-minister—both institutions dedicated not only to produce men able to adjust to the demands of a new technological order but also to make men morally and socially responsible individuals (as Ford defined "moral"). Thus, the Technocrats and the Stewards were not mutually exclusive groups, and reform traditions could frequently operate effectively together.

PERFECTIONISM IN REFORM

The third tradition, however, frequently complicated the problems facing the other two approaches. It related, initially at least, to the special promise of the Protestant Reformation, the promise, for some at least, of an individual experience of conversion, for salvation or regeneration, the basic "reform," if you like, of the individual. This search for the "perfection" and fulfillment of "self" dominates much of American thought. In a basic sense it is the old antinomian vision and problem. The Perfectionist tradition does not look to institutions to remake man (although once again in an era when the idea of Immanence took new root, some institutions— especially the family and the school as well as the church—assume some new importance). Rather, it seeks God and hopes God will somehow bring about the long-sought-after conversion, the creation of the "new man."

Reform of the world begins with the reform of the individual. The devices ultimately invented in the nineteenth century—the new revivalism of Finney, the "self-culture" of Channing, the "transparent eyeball" of Emerson, the moral, intellectual, and social education of Parker, and the "Christian Nurture" of Bushnell—were only a few forerunners of a whole series of efforts at self-discovery and self-fulfillment believed basic to any meaningful reform of a larger society. William James' pragmatism was, in effect, a defense of the will as a secularized version of the kinds of religious conversion experiences he had studied in his famous book on the subject. Dewey's system of education and Veblen's "discipline of the machine" were in their own way methods of achieving the liberation of the creative individual, a modern, secularized version of the search for regeneration. Sometimes the sought-after experience took an aesthetic form (commonly an analog for the religious experience): Frederick C. Howe realized, for example, that many supposed reformers, like Lincoln Steffens, were artists rather than reformers, seeking in even their accounts of vice and corruption a way of finding for themselves the interesting, the vital, the exciting, and the beautiful. The aesthetic experience plays an essential role in John Dewey's philosophy, as arts and crafts have a special and significant function in Jane Addams' work at Hull House.

In a sense, of course, such Perfectionism, such an essentially antinomian vision, can and has been "radical." But insofar as it relates to general reform in the United States, such radicalism has been limited. Only occasionally did it lead to withdrawal from society for an extended period; rarely did it call for any profound institutional readjustments. Rather, it often ended what should have been a radical critique by making possible the adjustment of the individual to the ongoing society. This is precisely what happened to Dewey's extraordinary discoveries in education and to Freud's even more radical critique of man and civilization in the hands of American Neo-Freudians. The antinomian vision has been part of our tradition—and a major reform tradition—from the earliest days of the seventeenth century. It has asserted the role of the individual and stressed self-development against the social forces that might crush it, sometimes resisting "moral" laws as well as man-made law, minimizing the role of organization and institutions, and realizing and emphasizing that regulations do not in themselves effect reforms.

But the hope for individual regeneration *in* the world was also the belief that such reformations would lead to a fuller, an ultimately social regeneration. In the post-Civil War years, Emerson himself became disillusioned. Where were the new state and the new church that were to emerge from the various efforts at self-discovery? Now all he could hope for was the coming of some special geniuses, some heroes who might lead us to a brighter future—a sad end indeed for the search for "self." But if Emerson grew disillusioned, Americans have not. Once again, as always, the cry goes out that the way to reform is the way of self-discovery. The history of previous efforts—just as the history of previous reforms within the other two traditions detailed above—does not in the least dissuade a younger generation of reformers. For traditions persist; they are an essential part of an American-Protestant culture pattern.

Thus in a profound sense the dilemma of reform in America is analogous to the fundamental paradox of the Protestant Reformation itself: man must be *in* but not *of* the world. American reformers—whatever road to reform they elected—refused to surrender their commitment to the material world as it had developed around them. They wished to maintain the advantages achieved by the changing systems of economic, technological, and social life, while at the same time they hoped to retain the personal, moral, and social values of the world they knew—or thought they knew—from a previous order. They were willing to accept the new world completely, and unwilling to surrender the old world completely. Ironically, such a position left them caught between heaven and hell, *in* the world. Yet in a real sense they did not want to be *of* this world. They wished to accept the world on their own terms. The result was a brilliant series of temporary adjustments that permitted society to continue and frequently to flourish. But time after time their successes led to their own disillusionment. Having achieved, seemingly, their ends, they too often discovered that they had merely helped prepare adjustment to the world, a world they did not in fact desire. So they—or the next generation—had to begin again. But the nature of the culture provided the essential traditions within which they chose to operate, although specific methods might be different.

Generally these reform movements were, as I have suggested, basically conservative. Sometimes, however, the methods adopted were themselves significantly novel and so daring that they might effect changes unanticipated and even unwanted. The Populists, to maintain the yeoman farmer and his private and important place in the American scheme of things, held on to the values of an older era. But they were willing enough to adopt from the new order devices of organization, ownership, and regulation, especially in the areas of banking, communication, and distribution, that could be used effectively to remake much of society in the image of the new emerging social order. The conservative lawyers, at the turn of the century, in an effort to stem possible attacks on the institution of private property, radically extended the nature and function of state police power, power that might in later years be used against the institutions these lawyers sought to defend. Thus the story of reform in America has its dynamics as well as its continuities.

THE PERSISTENT BALANCE IN AMERICAN REFORM

The persistence of reform is made dramatically clear in the *Confessions* of Frederick C. Howe. Howe's amazing self-revelations detail the failure of reform movement after reform movement with which he associated himself, in and out of government, between 1890, and 1920. Yet, he does not surrender hope. In his last chapters, he tries again. New ideas come to him in the disillusion of his wartime experiences (disillusionment of such a serious nature that it is in fact related to a nervous breakdown he suffers). First, he decides he must surrender previous class alliances, and unite himself with the labor movement. Only in labor can he find a group whose self-interest is really in the interest of the whole people. We are almost happy, for his sake, that he did not live to see the very force in which he then put so much faith become in our own time easily adjusted to the current order, and very much a part of the status quo. But again, and most characteristically, Howe has still another hope: a school, a very special kind of intellectual retreat on his own farm:

I would have a herd of my own . . . people who also wanted to escape other herds and be themselves. That was the thing that interested me—finding myself; and I wanted to be surrounded by people who were interested in finding themselves, who wanted to understand life and its meanings.[4]

In the days of the early New Deal, Howe was once again to join "the movement" as an official in the Department of Agriculture; once again he was to become disillusioned. The recurrent pattern is indeed a pattern of our culture.

There were, however, some reformers who did in fact see the failure of American reform efforts as final. Orestes Brownson had been involved in most of the Protestant denominations and their search for individual and social regeneration; he had played a role in many of the major reform efforts of his day. In 1840, in an essay, "The Laboring Classes," he provides a classic critique of such reforms. Insisting that reformers in general answer the urgent needs of their time by concentrating on the regeneration of individual reason or conscience by "priests and pedagogues," he rejected both the ways of religion and of science. Reformers, he found, are "always in league with the people's masters, seeking to reform without disturbing the social arrangements which render reform necessary." (Howe makes the same charge, eighty-five years later, in his *Confessions*.) Brownson's challenge is dramatic and extreme. Even if all men were made Christians, in theory and practice, "the evils of the social state would remain untouched. . . . The only way to get rid of its evils is to change the system, not its managers. . . . You must abolish the system or accept its consequences. No man can serve both God and Mammon."

If this seems like a revolutionary cry, it is well to remember that Brownson's own personal answer was not merely to surrender his Protestantism to accept the hierarchical, authoritarian, traditionalist Catholic faith, but to accept as well the full consequences of the then-current social and economic system, including slavery. In the interest of preserving the social order, he was willing to sacrifice personal and social strivings outside a clearly defined institutional framework. He knew the choice he was making, and he had pointed the way in his 1840 essay.

But most Americans have refused the challenge of Brownson. Even our conservatives have been reformers, wishing not to overthrow the institutional and social order that has emerged under liberalism but rather accepting it, as reformers in America generally have done, while insisting on maintaining certain older values and forms as well. America *is* a nation of reformers. They will not give up the new world, and yet they will not surrender the old either. They still wish to be *in* but not *of* the world. They cling to that difficult paradox of their Protestant heritage defined in American secular terms, and they try over and over again, in the traditional patterns of their culture, to realize what history seems to indicate cannot be.

III | CULTURE AS HISTORY

Our Flag

A nation's flag is always a crucial element in its iconography. During the Second World War, news photographer Joe Rosenthal's on-the-spot record of a key incident in the Pacific became for all Americans a work of lasting symbolic significance, inspiring an actual monument of remembrance. Twenty-five years later, the same flag took on for many a more dubious and even ominous tone in the motorcycle garb worn in **Easy Rider**.

Library of Congress

Movie Star News

In 1940 Caroline Ware edited the collected papers of the annual meeting of the American Historical Association in what should have been a path-breaking volume called *The Cultural Approach to History*. In spite of a rich European tradition of cultural historical writing, American historians had generally avoided such a "cultural approach." Indeed, most American historians, trained in the use of more traditional documents, have been unable to deal with the materials of American culture, especially of recent times, in which new cultural forms tended to dominate. Merle Curti, my own teacher, had pioneered in the use of previously unused cultural artifacts such as dime novels, and his Pulitzer Prize–winning *The Growth of American Thought* was often breathtaking in its variety of sources.

No effective cultural history could be undertaken until historians learned how to deal with the cultural forms characteristic of their times, most especially the popular-cultural forms. The theoretical justification and philosophical rationalization for the use of such materials had, of course, been made by the pioneers in the field, Vico and Herder. But if these giants were known in the United States, they were not known among historians. I was introduced to Vico—an introduction that changed my view of historical studies—not in a course in history but in a course in world literature. And the key translations and scholarship in the case of Vico belong primarily to the post–World War II era.

While the New History movement of the early twentieth century began a systematic assault on the vision of history as past politics that had dominated professional historical scholarship before, it operated first largely in the name of economic and social history, with cultural history often restricted to selected summary chapters. American history textbooks still make their major focus political and increasingly social. Cultural history still finds itself playing a supporting role in occasional chapters.

Only gradually is the effort being made to understand the way people respond in a series of developing cultural forms to the nature of the experience they undertake. The articles in this part, following Vico, stress specifically how people make their own history and examines the popular forms through which that history is expressed. Those who study civilization and its institutions, many of these essays have stressed, represent a conservative vision. The generations of young men who attended American colleges and universities during the nineteenth and early twentieth centuries were all taught their history through the reading of Guizot's great *History of Civilization.* It was the perfect textbook for the training of a liberal elite who would be the statesmen and business leaders of modern American capitalist society. To propose an examination of cultural history is to seek another understanding and to fulfill another mission.

One other disclaimer is required. The essays here represent a tradition in American historical scholarship that demands fuller attention than I can give it in this volume. I have in these pieces resorted to a special and perhaps characteristically American way of seeing the past: as a series of decades that fit neatly into limits imposed by man-made calendars. The Nineties, the Twenties, the Thirties—all of this forces attention on special "events" that are without doubt important but may not be so totally awesome as they might seem in the world of politics, for example. They force an emphasis on discontinuity rather than continuity, on short-range developments rather than longer trends. There appears no room in American scholarship for Fernand Braudel's vision of extended time—there is none in the overwhelming bulk of American scholarship; but is there in any American experience? We hardly ever ask the question. We merrily tick off decades, give them tricky names, and assume that that is what history is all about.

If I have yielded to the convention of decade analysis, I have refused to reduce these decades to clichés that can be explained by prosperity and depression. To attribute unexpected behavior to having too much or to the need to escape from having too little cannot account for the particular *forms* such behavior assumes or analyze such experience in terms that acknowledge the specific nature of the culture itself. Escapism may indeed be an issue, but why and how people choose to escape in the particular ways they do—the choices the culture provides—is a much more important question. I have tried to look beyond what is frequently isolated as high culture, popular culture, and folk culture and to see the tensions and contradictions of a larger cultural whole. These are very initial inquiries that attempt to use a whole range of materials. The secondary literature is usually dreadful in this area because the major historical talent has concentrated on political and, more recently, on economic and social developments. It is ironic that precisely in a world in which cultural forms other than the political play a greater and greater role, and politics itself evidences a considerable decline in shaping the nature of experience, so little attention has been paid to it until recently. When I argue that Mickey Mouse may in fact be more important to an understanding of the 1930s than Franklin Roosevelt, audiences snicker. The shaping of government remains a significant thing, and my respect for the role Mr. Roosevelt played (his cultural role was after all a significant part of that) without limit. But if we want to know how people experienced the world, FDR had his role but so did Mickey Mouse.

7 CULTURE AND CIVILIZATION: THE NINETEEN-TWENTIES

In a prefatory note to a small collection of her essays published in 1936, Willa Cather commented, "The world broke in two in 1922 or thereabouts, and the persons and prejudices recalled in these sketches slide back into yesterday's seven thousand years." Surely, Cather's vision appears excessively melodramatic. And yet it might profit us to attempt some gloss of her bold announcement. Too often historians see the decade all too simply as the consequence of involvement in World War I, or as a time of prosperity or of troubles leading to the Depression—or even as an era between two World Wars. They have been unable to present an overview that satisfactorily relates the period to the overall context of historical development. Too often the decade appears as Ishmael Reed describes it in his recent (1972) brilliant and provocative literary tour de force *Mumbo Jumbo*:

That 1 decade which doesn't seem so much a part of American history as the hidden After-Hours of America struggling to jam. To get through. . . . If the British prose style is Churchillian, America is the tobacco auctioneer, the barker; Runyon, Lardner, W. W., the travelling salesman who can sell the world the Brooklyn Bridge and convince you that tomatoes grow at the South Pole. If in the 1920s the British say "The Sun Never Sets on the British Empire," the American motto is "There's a Sucker Born Every Minute." America is the smart-aleck adolescent who's "been around" and has his own hot rod.

CULTURE AS HISTORY

Historians, of course, have long been aware of the serious tensions that pervade American life in the period. The contradictions in patterns of action, belief, and behavior, in values and ideals, are notable in even the most routine textbook account. They have repeatedly analyzed these and the many significant efforts to deal with them in a number of areas—political, economic, social, aesthetic, philosophical. But if we take Cather's statement seriously, some newer overview of the period may begin to emerge.

Willa Cather's world did not break in two only because of World War I. Indeed, her Pulitzer Prize–winning novel published that year, *One of Ours*, already made clear that much of what she cherished in the world—a rich, agrarian-based family and communal order closely in tune with the natural order—had already been laid waste by the new technological order. Yet she still retained a kind of mystical faith in the survival of the basic values and achievements of civilization in the West. (Sensitive young Americans sufficiently cherished them to be willing to sacrifice their lives for their continuation. Her hero may in fact be the last such hero in major modern American fiction. But after 1922 Cather was no longer so sanguine.)

By 1922 an exceptional and ever-growing number of Americans came to believe in a series of changes in the structure of their world, natural, technological, social, personal, and moral. This awareness was based on the extraordinarily rapid accumulation of both new knowledge and new experiences. At the same time, they found themselves in the process of developing new techniques both for amassing still more knowledge and for achieving even fuller experiences. For the cultural historian, these techniques themselves often were readily transformed into new forms for dealing with the world and its problems in an era that frankly hungered for all kinds of knowledge and yet found itself unable to cope easily with the vast quantities and differing kinds of knowledge with which it was presented. Partly as a result, R. P. Blackmur proposed in his brilliant lectures *Anni Mirabiles, 1920–1925* (significantly subtitled "Reason in the Madness of Letters") that

all our new knowledges—or all the new forms into which our knowledge has segregated and incriminated itself—have come out as techniques for finding troubles in ourselves and in the world. It is almost as if to make trouble had become the creative habit of the general mind.

These conditions, as those living during this period discovered and worried over, did not prevail simply among a very few or simply in one small area of human activity. One of the more striking observed results of the structural changes in the social order was that a larger proportion of it was increasingly engaged in professional seeking to understand it, with a special calling to "know" the world as writers, artists, intellectuals, journalists, scientists, social scientists, philosophers, teachers. Fundamental probing of the "real" world in its various aspects, natural and social, psychological and moral, was not only charted by a brilliant series of artists and writers, but also by equally brilliant (if often startlingly different) achievements in the social sciences, which had come of age as "scientific" disciplines during the period. Meanwhile, scientists and psychologists probed their worlds as well and often provided contradictory ways of seeing as well as different bodies of knowledge.

The growth of such new knowledge appeared to be a cause for great rejoicing; many thought of the New Era as a New Enlightenment. Harold Stearns compared his effort to prepare *Civilization in the United States* (1922) to the work of the eighteenth-century *philosophes*, and Beard, Becker, and even Dewey invoke such comparisons in connection with their own work. Nor was such a sense limited to the United States. The telegram summoning Charles Beard to help in rebuilding Tokyo after the earthquake of 1923 was said to have read, "Bring your knowledge of disaster." In fact, the new world of new knowledge tended rather to heighten the very contradictions the new knowledge itself was often uncovering. Several examples may help make the situation clear.

First, much of the new knowledge was of a quality so highly specialized that it often could not readily be shared. R. P. Blackmur, citing Arnold Toynbee's statement about scientific knowledge, argued that the same proposition was now a fact of increasing concern in poetry and the other arts. If, Blackmur insisted, the reader substituted "poetic" for the word "scientific" in the following passage in Toynbee (written in the 1930s), he would find it equally true for both kinds of knowledge by the 1920s:

Our Western scientific [read "poetic"] knowledge of which we boast, and even our Western technique for turning knowledge to practical account upon which we depend for our wealth and strength is perilously esoteric.

Thus the great fear that runs through much of the writing of the 1920s and 1930s is whether any great industrial and democratic mass society can maintain a significant level of civilization, and whether mass education and mass communication will allow any civilization to survive.

One of the initial answers to that problem in the 1920s was the enormous campaign of "popularization." There were "outlines" of history and science; "stories" of philosophy and mankind. It was a best-selling world of popular psychology. In all (one must remember the Haldeman-Julius "Little Blue Books"), there was a spectacular eruption of highly popular efforts to popularize knowledge. James Steel Smith, one of its leading students, called it "a singular phenomenon." Yet the haunting question of the meaning and usefulness of such knowledge remained. What did that knowledge reveal about man and his world, and what about the techniques by which it sought to make it available and "useful"?

Second, such knowledge often presented contradictions. In 1921, Charlie Chaplin delighted millions of middle-class Americans with his charming and touching film *The Kid*. I do not know whether J. B. Watson ever saw the movie; if he did he might have referred to it as a model of precisely the way *not* to raise a child. For certainly everything that occurs in that happy and warm relationship between the tramp and the orphan is antithetical to the idea of "routine" and "objectivity" recommended by the Behaviorists as a key to the scientific child-rearing they believed so necessary to raising a healthy and independent individual ("Never hug and kiss them, never let them sit on your lap"). The Chaplin way in the film was the way of traditional, common-sense knowledge; the Watson way was the method proposed by newer scientific knowledge. It can, of course, be argued that *neither* way is strictly "knowledge," and yet both visions were strikingly promulgated at roughly the same time to roughly similar audiences.

Americans were made constantly and fully aware that they lived in a new era. Communications was key to this, and no more dramatic instruments of total change had come along than the automobile and the motion picture. Yet almost at the outset of the period architects and their clients chose in extraordinary ways to "house" these revolutionary devices in showrooms that appear contradictory to the revolutionary machines they were to showcase: in the 1920s, we built palaces, not so much for people to live in, but to provide elegant settings for the new machines—witness, for example, Bernard Maybeck's unbelievably age-of-elegance Chrysler showroom in San Francisco and Meyer and Holler's Grauman's Egyptian Theater, which brought Karnak to Los Angeles' Hollywood Boulevard. Like the "popularization" movement or *The Reader's Digest*, which began its career in 1922, these efforts may be examples of ways adopted to provide forms of covering over the break in the world that had come or was coming apart. But we have yet to assess the cultural and psychological costs.

Everyone attempted to face the issues of the new revolution in communications. James Malin, in the very first effort to write a history of the decade, devoted considerable space to its economic and even foreign-policy consequences and a good number of chapters to the way government responded. His analysis, interestingly enough, is perhaps more detailed and better than any overall account we have had since. But here again new knowledge provided no universal meanings, no agreed-upon vision. Our literature frequently played upon the idea that it was ironic and perhaps sad that in a new era of advanced and easy communications men had increasingly little they wanted to, or were able to, communicate with each other. The new and highly creative Chicago School of sociologists made the analysis of communications (with special study of the newspaper) basic to their general social analysis and saw fundamental hope in the newer means of communication for recreating the community. John Dewey, in his *Reconstruction in Philosophy* (1920), could speak of the "mystic force" of communication and the resulting "miracle of the shared life," as a way of overcoming the "hardness and crudeness of contemporary life." Vachel Lindsay spoke of an "American civilization [that] grows more hieroglyphic every day." Others argued that with the coming of standardized and commercialized pictures goes the word and with it the possibility of genuine thought and reflection. The philosopher Paul Arthur Schilpp in 1928 raised serious questions about what it is we really have to communicate: "Stocks and bond quotations, football scores, World Series results, jazz music, and bedtime stories." It hardly seemed worthwhile.

If communications can in effect stand for invention, technology, and the mechanization of the social order, the other great common issue, so contradictorily, was that of community. As Howard W. Odum, the North Carolina sociologist, said during the decade, "Perhaps no greater advance has been made in the after-war period than the increased recognition of the institution of community, whether it be community of organization, of fellowship, of industry, or arts and letters, of learning, of religion, or of citizenship." Such a statement seems out of place to anyone who has read at all in the literature of the period. Even those who valued the order of a social world held only in the memory—Edith Wharton, Willa Cather, Dorothy Canfield Fisher—or those who, like Booth Tarkington, dwelled on the transformation of small-town community in America (only to report its disappearance in the "realistic" world of modern business) tended to regard the idea as something past. From the grotesques of Sherwood Anderson through the satires of Sinclair Lewis, from the weird fantasy worlds of James Branch Cabell to the worlds of Fitzgerald and Hemingway, where the possibility of community did not seem to exist even in the imagination; the novelist and the poet seemed to provide little to support Odum's proposition. And yet, of course, it was a fundamental part of the world and the knowledge of that world, shaped by the social sciences of the period in terms of surveys and studies, anthropological as well as sociological, statistical as well as fieldwork observations. From the Chicago sociologists such as Park and Burgess came discussions of "we-groups" and "we-feelings." There was a fascination with "the gang" and the neighborhood, the lodge and the fraternity. This was the great age of community study. In his brilliant and sadly unknown cultural-historical analysis of America in this period, the distinguished Dutch historian Johan Huizinga comments that "literature in all the great ages of civilization was precisely the perfect expression of the dominant ideals of life." While he suggests that it is probably still present in American literature, too, if you probe deeply enough, the surface shows our literature to have the "character of aversion, protest, and accusation." He says of Cabell, for example, that "aversion to the Western Civilization of his own time" is his major tone. Thus here again we are struck with the contradictory force of two kinds of knowledge, two representations perhaps of a world broken, not quite in two the way Willa Cather sees it, but certainly broken.

For the writer and artist, at least, still another contradiction loomed large. If one wanted to share his knowledge, express his experience, offer his vision, how might he best do it? At least from the time of the Post-Impressionists and the Armory Show in the visual arts and of the Imagists in poetry, the creative worker had (in the words of Marilyn Gaull in her article on "Language and Identity") "become acutely aware of the discrepancy between his environment and the symbols at his disposal for describing it, between his experience and the language available for expressing it." From Ezra Pound's repudiation of Victorian abstractions such as "infinity" and his effort to use the "ideogramic method," with a logic, a syntax, and a grammar not conventional in Western writing, to the Dadaists; from the linguistic experiments of Gertrude Stein to the special prose of Ernest Hemingway's *Farewell to Arms*—"abstract words such as glory, honor, courage or hallow were obscene beside the concrete names of villages, the numbers of roads, the names of rivers, the numbers of regiments and the dates"—there was a growing concern among writers, philosophers, and students of language about the relationship between language and reality. This problem was rapidly becoming a major cultural concern. One cannot help but link the enormous popularity of word games, especially of crossword puzzles in the 1920s, with this increased fascination with the issue, to say little of the growing general interest in the work of Alfred

Korzybski, I. A. Richards, S. I. Hayakawa, Edward Sapir, Stuart Chase, and Thurmond Arnold in the 1930s. The question was not only what could and ought one communicate, but also *how* could one communicate at all?

Thus the new knowledge of the world increasingly included knowledge about the techniques specifically developed to deal with the reality that all seemed so anxious to touch, to understand, to use. Vachel Lindsay's "hieroglyphic civilization" did not seem an impossible dream—or nightmare. After all, there were the cartoons and comics, increasingly visual advertising, and motion pictures. There were also great tabloids, newspapers like *The Daily News* in New York, which began in 1919 to make a heavy investment in photographs (often real, but sometimes artificially concocted), and the playful and sensational use of various kinds and sizes of prints. By the late 1920s, they were essentially designing for well over a million readers a special definition of what was "news." What was clearly involved in the arts and in other aspects of the culture was the emergence of new ways of knowing that stood in sharp contrast with old ways of knowing available in the book and the printed word. It was a significant break for a culture that had taken form under Bible and dictionary.

Finally, the unusual commitment of self-knowledge in the decade, and the resulting flurry of studies in psychology, sociology, history, and anthropology, presented conclusions of enormous importance to the increasingly self-aware American public. At the outset, Americans were becoming more aware of themselves as a public as well as of the problem (as old among intellectuals as the Enlightenment, but newly ordered for a mass audience) of the relationship between public association and social act, between private needs and personal vision. Generally, Americans had grown up to believe in the Protestant work ethic. In the 1870s, William Graham Sumner said that hard work and self-denial equaled capitalism; the savings bank depositor was the true hero of civilization! Now the world really seemed to break in two: the American learned that he was largely to think of himself as a consumer. He was encouraged increasingly (ways were found to help him) not to hoard his savings (a part of the evil of Puritanism) but to spend and spend. He was told he no longer lived in a world of scarcity but in one of abundance, and that he must develop new values in keeping with that new status. Leisure was rapidly becoming almost as important as labor, and he must learn a pleasure ethic, if not to replace, at least to put beside, his work ethic. He often found himself with more leisure, not to speak of the greater educational possibilities (and even more opportunities for education at the adult level).

While millions still labored to produce goods, fewer workers were needed to produce as much, and more and more people found themselves as professionals or in clerical or service trades. More found themselves on salary with all the assurances and possibilities for planning a life that meant.

In the new world of abundance-leisure-consumer-pleasure orientation, more attention could be paid to gratification of personal needs of all kinds; and in fact, as it soon became clear, the new service industry of advertising would make every effort to stimulate those needs and awaken those desires in an effort to use them in creating a market for a whole new set of products. Strict codes of sexual morality would yield to what has been called a Freudian ethic. New assessments of the labor market would make possible facilitation of the birth-control movement, the idea of companionate marriage, and totally new conceptions of child rearing.

The values of home, security, family, and community were constantly pointed to from over the divide, but in this new world the American was urged at the same time to use the new means of communication, especially his automobile, which advertising and the beginnings of a great new road system made unusually attractive. Community and the advantages of joining a host of organizations were somehow considered an admirable way to sustain individualism. It was important to read all the right books, but since he didn't know what they might be, special services were organized for him: a digest so he didn't have to read all the magazines and, in 1926, a Book-of-the-Month Club.

Obviously, the overall social transformation involved had begun long before World War I. But the transformation generally and nontechnically described *did* occur; and it represented a crucial change in the nature of the capitalist order and its culture. There was a striking awareness of the essential conflicts this created for many, reared in the values of the old and now asked to adopt values more clearly in tune with the new. Such adjustments did not come easily. Certainly as far back as Santayana's address on "The Genteel Tradition in American Philosophy" (1911) and the early work of Van Wyck Brooks, particularly *America's Coming of Age* (1915), American critics and writers were deeply aware of the divisions in the American psyche.

There were other signs of the enormous transformation in American life. The leading cause of death, tuberculosis, perhaps more characteristic of a producers' world, yielded to heart attack, often thought to be more characteristic of a business-consumer world. There was a beginning of a fundamental alteration of the national diet, in part because of the discovery of the vitamin. The motion picture developed, especially under Griffith, into the particular kind of middle-class entertainment it was to become. There were many other signs, too. Ford reordered the factory system. But it was not until the 1920s that these and all other *facts* about the transformations were fully developed (nowhere more brilliantly and in keeping with the basic social-science outlook of the period than in *Recent Economic Trends* and *Recent Social Trends*). Furthermore, they became topics of a common body of knowledge and therefore the object of a common source of popular concern in a variety of magazines, newspapers, and popular readings.

We seem a long way from Willa Cather's broken world; yet from a broad variety of perspectives and different definitions there *was* a widely shared view of contradictions in the ongoing order. Some saw them as fundamental. The world had broken; it could not be mended. Others, defining the breach in their own special way, sought through techniques designed to help them understand the world to find a way to bridge the gap.

The final propositions of the argument hinge on the fact that a great many Americans were "aroused by the vision of a civilization in crisis." What followed was, in effect, a most remarkable debate that, no matter what the variation of approach, centered around a key concept: civilization. In 1942 Charles and Mary Beard (themselves participants in the great debate of the 1920s) told us in *The American Spirit* that the word "civilization," as it developed from its origins in the late eighteenth century, was a key to the basic world view of Americans. "At no other time, or certainly never in so brief a period, has so much concern been shown over the nature and future of civilization as in the years that have followed the World War," commented V. F. Calverton and S. D. Schmalhausen, the editors of *Sex and Civilization* (1929). They were correct, both statistically in terms of the number of books and articles specifically containing the word "civilization" in their titles, and, even more so, impressionistically when one reviews the wide variety of work in the period.

In many ways, Calverton and Schmalhausen's introduction is a prototype of many pieces in the period. Initially, the concept of civilization, they inform us, was synonymous with advance and progress; now many people believe that true progress can be achieved only with the destruction of civilization. Of course, the Romantics often have argued that civilized man was in no sense superior to the primitive type. But this was, in reality, they wrote, a revolt against a certain form of civilization in which "aristocratic oppression had reduced society to a state of economic chaos and moral disintegration." Today, because of the enormous changes in the nature of civilization since the Industrial Revolution, the revolt against civilization must be either "a revolt against its entire essence" (as in the case of modern mystics and those who yearn for medieval Catholicism or some Oriental world) or a revolt against "certain manifestations of its controls, which once changed will render it a different entity" (like those who believe that civilization as we conceive of it "has been founded upon institutions that circle about the concept of private property," and who see civilization ceasing and a new culture beginning with the annihilation of that concept).

Calverton and Schmalhausen saw pretense as the key to modern civilization. They sought to apply modern psychology to an understanding of not only the individual personality but its link with society as well. To do this, there must be devised a special *technique,* which in its final form would belong to the domain of a new science. That technique, that new science, would uncover the sources of internal malaise and external maladaptation. It would end the problem of civilization: "Nature and culture . . . destroying one another marvelously. . . . The body and the mind hate one another in queer ways that run the gamut from tenderness to violence. Ambivalence poisons our human nature. We are scientific and superstitious; critical and credulous; conservative and radical; libertarian and autocratic; savage and charitable; intolerant and amiable; educated and shallow; prosperous and empty." The contradictions cause our problems; our techniques (which in effect are our forms of knowledge) cure: civilization creates maladjustments because of contradictions; knowledge and experience yield new techniques that yield solutions that revitalize civilization. The pattern becomes a familiar one.

One of the most popular kinds of anthologies of the period was the collection of original essays attempting an assessment of the status of civilization to date, a sort of balance sheet for the American people. Their titles reveal a special and characteristic rhetoric of the period: *Whither Mankind: A Panorama of Modern Civilization; Toward Civilization; Recent Gains in American Civilization.* In each case, the list of contributors was impressive, the list of fields surveyed extensive. In each case, the essays proposed a kind of popularization of knowledge and achievement in a wide number of areas so as to test how Americans had collectively succeeded or failed. Often, they included pep talks urging on the citizen body and its institutions to still greater "progress." The volumes and their articles had, of course, analogs in hundreds of magazine articles in the period and, finally, in Chicago at the World's Fair of 1933, which dedicated itself to assessing and commemorating "A Century of Progress." These were all efforts sometimes to chasten and always to reassure. There was something jittery, nervous (to use Roderick Nash's characterization of the era's generation), and yet marvelously traditional about this ceaseless need to know where we were at and how to measure how far we had come and to worry about where we were going. Although there was nothing totally new about all of this, there was something special and excessive about it in this period.

So much that was produced during the twenties can be seen and read in terms of a thinking that self-consciously considered itself as part of the issue of civilization and even as a technique or instrument involved somehow in sustaining, modifying, destroying, or creating "civilization." And this view is a possible and meaningful way toward the establishment of an overview of the period. Certainly, the idea was everywhere: during the war Eugene V. Debs had argued that socialism's role was to "civilize civilization"; Fitzgerald could not resist telling us that his first hero, Amory Blaine, was first caught "in his underwear, so to speak," by the "crude, vulgar air of Western civilization," in Minneapolis; Ernest Elmo Calkins wrote of "Business the Civilizer"; Marcus Garvey made a great appeal, even to white Americans, with his idea of the importance of developing a Negro civilization. These are radically different uses of the concept of civilization yet central to a significant body of rhetoric, a crucial group of metaphors around which much of what we associate with the 1920s seem to play.

Perhaps a few brief examples can further illustrate this theme. The first is the most obvious. In 1922, just before a most dramatic farewell to the United States, Harold Stearns published his most famous editorial venture, the cooperative enterprise of those now-famous Thirty Americans, *Civilization in the United States*. It offered itself as a common effort of like-minded men and women to "see the problem of modern American civilization as a whole," in order to provide a "critical examination of our civilization . . . in order to do our share in making a real civilization possible." The unity, the editor proposed, rested on three contentions: (1) in all branches of American life there is a "sharp dichotomy between preaching and practice"; (2) "whatever else American civilization is, it is not Anglo-Saxon," and no headway will be made unless we begin to achieve genuine nationalistic self-consciousness; and (3) social life in America currently is "emotional and aesthetic starvation" and we have "no heritages and traditions to which to cling."

Stearns offered no political or social solution; instead he asked for a change in our hearts. The first step in growing up as a civilization is "self-conscious and deliberate critical examination of ourselves without sentimentality and without fear." The technique was characteristic: more than one commentator had seen this period as part of a new age of criticism where the techniques of examination themselves become the genuinely vital elements, the creative elements. "Critique," R. P. Blackmur tells us in *Anni Mirabiles,* "is the wiggling extreme articulation of vital elements into an order of vision: especially the elements of the new powers and the new troubles." Critique as creation: Blackmur was clearly speaking of criticism in the arts, but the statement could be more widely applied to all fields of knowledge and understanding. The aim of the Stearns volume echoed the issues raised as early as 1915 by Van Wyck Brooks: "To get civilization out of the Yankee stock . . . is the more arduous and the more inspiriting enterprise. Is it possible? Is it in process? The signs are anything but obvious." By 1922, that civilization could be approached only through increased self-consciousness of what our life was like, and this could be achieved only through critique.

It might seem strange to offer as immediate comparison the influential textbook *Introduction to the Science of Sociology* that the famous University of Chicago sociologists Robert Park and Ernest Burgess published in 1921, yet few books have been so important in the field. For our purposes, it provides another insight into the ways knowledge and civilization were related. Significantly, in distinction to many earlier and contemporary works, it insisted on seeing in sociology a science and not a way to do good, a system of inquiry and not a series of solutions to social problems. Technique was uppermost in treatment. "The whole organization of this volume may be taken as an illustration of the method, at once tentative and experimental, for the collection, classification, and interpretation of materials. . . ." It was a manual, in part, stressing observation as well as reading, experience as well as study. Its center was, of course, social groups and institutions, social organization and the processes of social interaction. Its approach shunned any kind of reformism and any announced ideological position. One of the final chapters did deal with the concept of "progress," which was conceived of as the prospect of control through scientific knowledge, including sociology. The book closed with the sentence: "From the point of view of social research the problem of progress is mainly one of getting devices that will measure all the different factors of progress and of estimating the relative value of different factors in the progress of the community." There is no more telling statement. There is here no vision of the end, of what civilization is expected to achieve or of how it is to be judged. But, nevertheless, all through the volume there is the view that man is more likely to achieve what he wants if we somehow build up a sufficient—unspecified—body of useful—undefined—knowledge about society and human nature.

There is a revealing passage in Walter Lippmann's *Public Opinion* (1922) where he discussed the stereotypes represented by such words as "progress" and "perfection." (Here again was the concern for the possible danger as well as value of words and images.) On the basis of their version of progress (fundamentally mechanical invention), Americans created "a civilization which provides them who made it ample satisfaction. . . ." But now, Lippmann argued, there are growing frustrations. Further, the war and the bad peace that followed began to point the way to that split between stereotype and fact leading no longer to useful adjustment but rather to blind spots that threatened the civilization itself and compelled a need to reorder the images in the head to fit the realities in the world. Lippmann's work led him to a special vision of manipulation and advocacy of kinds of social control. The literature of the "new psychology," as Professor James Burnham showed in his thorough analysis ("The New Psychology: From Narcissism to Social Control"), provides a wealth of basic data and analysis for the kind of overview I am trying to develop.

Another major achievement of social science in 1922 was William Fielding Ogburn's *Social Change*. Here, too, the emphasis was on adaptation. Civilization became a series of such adaptations of parts of the culture to other parts. Most particularly, Ogburn stressed the need of adjustment to the often more rapid technological or material changes in the cultural base (the famous theory of "cultural lag") as well as the need for human nature itself to make necessary adaptations to cultural changes. In the very same year another American—this one a Ph.D. from Harvard—also faced the problem of social change. He expressed apprehension that such changes, underway largely as a result of the new mass order, would lead ultimately to the ruin of civilization. Lothrop Stoddard found his answer in yet another science, biology, and he spelled out his argument in *The Revolt Against Civilization: The Menace of the Under Man*. Warning of the dangerous lure of the primitive, demonstrating "the Iron Law of inequality," Stoddard insisted that the only way to assure the protection and advancement of civilization was to bring about control by a neo-aristocracy. This could be accomplished only through the careful practice of eugenics, weeding out the inferior and enlarging the proportion of the fit. It was, after all, simply a matter of biology.

Few works of nonfiction were so important as a part of the history of the 1920s as a major popular interpretation of the whole of human history itself—indeed, the whole of the history of the world even before man. Someday someone will analyze the nature and meaning of the enormous impact of H. G. Wells in his many roles on the culture of English-speaking peoples in the first half of the twentieth century. His *Outline of History* has been one of the most extraordinary "popularizations" of knowledge. It first hit American best-seller lists in 1921 and has remained a steady seller in many editions up to the present. It was exceptional because it refused to see the history of Europe as central and saw it rather in a larger context, of both time and space. It was exceptional because in spite of the disasters it recounted it continued to see the general pattern of history as one of a steady—or at least an ultimate—march of man in terms of progress; it provided a sense of unity and continuity, a steady, continuous path toward some future. It made no claim to original knowledge, but it did claim a significant purpose for the knowledge and the nature of the understanding it provides.

The need for a common knowledge of the general facts of human history throughout the world has become very evident during the tragic happenings of the last few years. . . . There can be no peace now, we realize, but a common peace in all the world; no prosperity but a general prosperity. But *there can be no common peace and prosperity without the common historical ideas. . . . Such are the views that this outline* seeks to realize. It is an attempt to tell how our recent state of affairs, this distressed and multifarious human life about us, arose in the course of vast ages and out of the inanimate clash of matter, and to estimate the quality and amount and range of hopes with which it now faces its destiny.

And yet another best-selling history, the only such work by professional historians ever to make the top ten of the best-seller lists, the Beards' masterpiece of 1927, *The Rise of American Civilization*, not only provided the public with the fullest picture and historical definition of America as a civilization to date, but also insisted in the preface (again recalling the *philosophes*, especially Voltaire) that a history of civilization could become, if properly conceived, an instrument of civilization itself!

Part of this argument rested on the long efforts to reestablish the fundamental efficacy and value or meaning of Western civilization for all Americans in this period. In 1918, for example, John Erskine introduced at Columbia College the first course in the Great Books of the Western World. The following year, the college began its experiment that led to two basic courses in the Introduction to Contemporary Civilization. First was a required freshman course concentrating on the history of Western Civilization from the Middle Ages. A basic second-year course in the humanities—art, literature, music, philosophy—paralleled the work of the first year. These courses became models for the development of programs elsewhere during the 1920s and after. The debate over this move ment belongs not only to the history of education but also to the analysis of the 1920s as a whole and to the theme of this essay. Special value was assigned to the study of its history and its cultural achievement, to the reading of its documents from the past. Certain things were assumed to follow for the present from such study of this particular past.

No doubt *The Education of Henry Adams,* a best seller in 1919, even as it defined the possiblities of a new civilization, continued to make the vision of the European Middle Ages and its civilization fascinating to many readers. And amidst the heroes of the era, there was a very special heroine: Joan of Arc, who finally became St. Joan in 1921. Surely she recalled in a singular way the vision of another era and became an emblem for aspects of Western Civilization many wished to cherish and maintain.

And surely no one has forgotten that 1922 was the year of T. S. Eliot's *The Wasteland.* The poem glories as much in its technique as in its certain awareness of its technique; it shows its tricks, and tricks its reader by showing them. It is the portrait of the world as it is—broken. One thinks of Ezra Pound's "Hugh Selwyn Mauberly" (1920) with its description of civilization: "an old bitch gone in the teeth," a "botched civilization." Men had died, after all "For two gross of broken statues / For a few thousand battered books." Or is it after all a reconstruction of the possiblitities of the creative vision, the individual talent wrestling with the great traditions to put the whole critically back together?

For that is what one might well make out of the work of the American painter Stuart Davis. Starting with *Lucky Strike* (1921), his brilliant abstractions began to create their own language, their own signs and symbols, to both making ironic comment on the nature of "noncivilization" or even anticivilization in America and at the same time by using discarded or chance objects, banal words, parodies of advertising as the key to much of American life. Davis was a serious painter well schooled in the best of the classic techniques of Western Civilization, but he also took seriously the world of popular culture. Jazz thrilled him; he felt the same sense of excitement in seeing a Matisse as he did when he listened to black jazzmen play with their extraordinary precision in a Newark saloon. Does his painting mean that the movement toward Vachel Lindsay's "hieroglyphic civilization" is gathering support?

A full investigation would include some detailed attention to the fascination or temptation of what so many Americans saw as anticivilization: the attraction of cultures and peoples non-Western. This would include the enormous popularity of such nonfiction adventures as Frederick O'Brien's *White Shadows in the South Seas,* the later tales of Richard Halliburton, and Edith M. Hull's *The Sheik* (especially in the film version with Valentino), as well as the considerable attraction of Malinowski's Trobriand Islanders and what appeared to many to be a sexual paradise; and closer to home, it would include the discovery of jazz and the "barbarism" of the "unrepressed" black world.

In his novel *Mumbo Jumbo* Ishmael Reed presents a most impressive reading of the 1920s. In it, the forces of anticivilization plant a disease, Jes Grew, designed to wipe out Western Civilization. (In 1917 Stanton Coit had asked, "Is Civilization a Disease?" and in 1928 Samuel Schmalhausen had said, "Civilization is a study in pathology and perversion.") Jes Grew, using song, dance, rhythm, plus forces designed to remove art from museums and return it to people for use or for destruction, continues a relentless campaign against the forces of civilization. In white America any cause could get help if it "went to the heart of Western Civilization because all agreed on the sacredness of Western Civilization," Ishmael Reed tells us satirically in dealing with elements in Harlem like the NAACP. And that civilization and its history he symbolizes with a building: "Upstairs is a store which deals in religious articles. Above this is a gun store; at the top, an advertising firm which deals in soap accounts."

The 1920s was a period dedicated to knowledge and experience and the effective use of both. It spent considerable time, energy, and talent in trying to mend what had become apparent to many, each often in his own way, as a broken world. It sought to build on knowledge, technique; it sought to find methods and ways of expressing and communicating. (J. H. Denison in his 1928 work *Emotion as the Basis of Civilization* argued that success in civilization *meant* the cultivation of certain key emotions; H. A. Overstreet's *Influencing Human Behavior*, written in 1925, seemed to suggest that civilization meant effectively man having influence over others, and that there was a fundamental responsibility of all to communicate, "to take hold of other men and influence them.") The decade came to an end with two great publishing ventures: the Fourteenth Edition of *The Encyclopaedia Britannica* (1929; James Harvey Robinson in his article on "Civilization" in that work suggested that the encyclopedia was in itself "a description of civilization") and *The Encyclopedia of the Social Sciences* (1933). But no matter how great the achievement in knowledge and in understanding the human condition, in retrospect the decade is still haunted by the telling question T. S. Eliot had asked at its outset, in 1920, in his "Gerontion": "After such knowledge, what forgiveness?"

But all of this was part of what amounted to a major debate in which in one way or another the newer mass society of the 1920s, increasingly self-conscious about itself individually and collectively, faced a time of crisis in its world view. It centered, often consciously, around the concept of civilization, as had the birth of the Republic. Some tried to make a new era of enlightenment, and characteristically following, one might suggest, even historical precedent, some tried to answer with a new Romanticism. The result was an effort to bridge the gap in a world come apart, a social order divided and confused. All bridges, it seemed, were like Thornton Wilder's Bridge of San Luis Rey; they collapsed. Perhaps we, like Wilder, ought to try to find out why. But meanwhile several writers have offered suggestive leads. James Burnham pointed out how those who sought to keep others from destroying the fabric of civilized order devised newer and more effective techniques for the manipulation of men. R. P. Blackmur asked:

Are we not the first age which is self-conscious of its own fictions; and hence the first age of true Pyrrhonism: doubting the value as well as the fact? We believe only in the technique of manipulating and counting. Not in choice, not in imperative, chiefly in opinion. Thus we believe in the analysis of conduct as a meaning of discounting behavior, in the drum-majorette of fourteen as a means of showing sex as a force without having to take account of it. Our age is full of great hymns to the puerile, what in medicine and art are called images of fundamental frustration.

After such knowledge, such techniques, such self-consciousness of self and society, what forgiveness?

8 CULTURE HEROES: FORD, BARTON, RUTH

When Bruce Barton died at the age of 80 in 1967, it seemed almost inevitably and perfectly logical that at least one writer of his obituary should refer to his life story as "legendary in the best Horatio Alger sense." Among the most prominent men of his time, Barton had come out of a small Tennessee town to become one of the most widely read and respected authors of his day. He would serve in the Congress of the United States, run for the Senate, and even be considered as a possible presidential candidate. He was to found one of the most important advertising agencies and to shape the development of the advertising business—so crucial itself in shaping the new mass society of the period—in significant ways. Barton's success in managing his agency can in part be measured by the fact that when he retired in 1961 the company could boast of billings in excess of $230 million. While Barton himself was known to millions of Americans through his writings and public service, his company could, in a special memorandum on the occasion of his death, point to the special meaning of his vast "contacts." "It meant contact with Presidents of the United States, with senators, with cabinet members, with leaders of industry. . . . Bruce could call anyone in the United States and time would be found for him." But perhaps most significant, Barton's life recalls Horatio Alger because, in a sense, he rewrote the American primer on success in a way that most effectively served the middle class of the 1920s. This revision provided a necessary kind of secular religion, a special vision of piety essential to the nation's transformation into a modern industrial mass society. His version of the success story helped ease the transition from an older, more producer-centered system with its traditional value structure to the newer, more consumer-centered system with its changed value structure. Barton's inspirational writings (and in a way this includes his brilliant advertising copy) found a way of bridging the gap between the demands of a Calvinistic producer ethic with its emphasis on hard work, self-denial, savings and the new, increasing demands of a hedonistic consumer ethic: spend, enjoy, use up.

Barton once explained his own success in a tongue-in-cheek article he published in 1919:

We preachers' sons have an unfair advantage over the rest of the world. Out of about 12,000 names in one of the editions of *Who's Who,* more than 1,000 were names of us. In England's *Dictionary of National Biography* we appear 1,270 times, while the sons of lawyers are there only to the number of 510, and the sons of doctors score only 350 times. In fact, we show up so well that any unprejudiced man will agree that all the money given to the church would have been well invested had it done nothing more than enable preachers to raise sons. . . . Not all of us make good, of course. A third of us go to the devil; another third float around in between; but another third rule the world.

A well-known authority on the American idea of success has provided a shrewd generalization: "Whenever Calvinism's stern demands bit deep, as in Woodrow Wilson, Henry Luce, Norman Thomas, Robert Hutchins, Adolf A. Berle, Jr., DeWitt Wallace, or John Foster Dulles [all sons of preachers], there was a moral earnestness, a mission—and often a destiny." William Eleazar Barton instilled this evangelical sense and moral purpose in his son. Bruce Barton, in his writings as in his life, provided convincing evidence of his deep dedication to and the profound influence of his Congregational minister-father.

William Barton, a descendant of a soldier in the American Revolution, was at the time of his son's birth in 1886 a circuit rider working out of a small church in Robbins, Tennessee. Bruce Barton was the eldest of five children. His father's missionary zeal led him to seek further education even after he had started his family. Moving on to Oberlin Theological Seminary, William Barton graduated at the top of his class when he was almost 30 years old. That same zeal plus a special flair for writing and preaching enabled him to move from one important church to another. At the same time, he lectured at seminaries, edited a magazine, wrote a series of books (significant among them were detailed and scholarly studies of Abraham Lincoln and a biography of Clara Barton, no relative, the founder of the Red Cross). Eventually, he became a famous preacher and at one time was Moderator of the National Council of Congregational Churches. In speaking of his childhood, it pleased Bruce Barton to insist: "We were not poor; we just didn't have any money." The family's wealth included a library, with books coming before cakes in this intensely intellectual household. His mother, who was a schoolteacher, helped establish such priorities. Barton delighted in the memories of that environment of books, simple living, and countryside trips with the father he worshipped and whom he held onto as they both rode on the back of the family's white mare. Meanwhile, he was also being prepared for a more sophisticated life in commerce and journalism.

In the hallowed Alger tradition, Bruce Barton had a paper route by the time he was nine. The family eventually settled in a fairly comfortable middle-class professional life with a ministry in the Chicago suburb of Oak Park, Illinois. He went to high school there, and received his initiation into the business world. Arranging with an Ohio uncle to sell maple syrup tapped from trees on his uncle's farm, young Barton netted some $600 a year. Simultaneously, he was also developing his skills as a journalist, serving as writer, editor, proofreader, and copy-runner on the high-school newspaper. Barton also found work as a part-time reporter (at three dollars a week) on a community newspaper. His intellectual interests did not slacken; and as graduation approached, he determined to go to Amherst College.

Although William Barton had no objections, he induced his son to spend at least one year at Berea College in Kentucky, where all students worked part-time to pay for tuition. Bruce Barton's own accounts make clear that his father's desire was not prompted by financial necessities or by loyalty to Berea, which had been his own alma mater. Reverend Barton's object was simple: to guarantee that his son remain sympathetic toward those who must work for what they want. At Berea, Barton chose the printing office, where he learned to set type, read proof, and handle a press—for eight cents an hour.

After his freshman year, Bruce Barton did transfer to Amherst. There he was elected to Phi Beta Kappa, headed the Student Council, served on the debating team in outstanding fashion, and even managed to play some football as a substitute lineman. Predictably, he worked his way through college (by selling pots and pans) and was elected the member of his class "most likely to succeed"—the whole pattern of his biography demands such things.

Bruce Barton's postgraduation plans, however, were not consonant with this formula for worldly success. He had decided that being a professor of history would be a sufficient goal and was delighted at the prospect of a fellowship from the exciting department at the University of Wisconsin. But 1907 was a depression year, and Bruce Barton felt the need to work. After weeks of job hunting in Chicago, one of his father's parishioners found a position for him—as time-keeper in a western Montana construction camp. Working ten hours a day, he earned $65 a month; he valued the experience because it taught him to get along with tough men in a tough job.

Bruce Barton returned to Chicago at the age of 21 to sell advertising space for three magazines. He was soon working as a public relations counselor and as editor of a small religious paper. His paper was nearing bankruptcy, but the crisis, Barton's biographers love to recall, did not lead to personal failure; rather it served to heighten his "enterprising spirit." It also gave him his first opportunity to write an advertisement. He asked for, and received, permission to take back salary in advertising space and made arrangements with a friend who operated a travel agency. He would drum up customers for a Bavarian tour, this being the year of the Oberammergau Passion Play, and would receive a fee for every customer he secured. "Just a few dollars will take you to Europe to see the Passion Play" was typical ad copy, as salesmanship and religion united. The result: enough money to take Barton to New York City, where he settled in at the YMCA, first to work at *Vogue* magazine and then as managing editor of another religious weekly that soon folded. P. J. Collier and Son soon hired him as assistant sales manager. His flair for promotion and sales led to increased self-confidence and a firm belief in the value of salesmanship. His copy for Collier's Five-Foot Shelf of Harvard Classics (sometimes known as Dr. Eliot's Five-Foot Shelf of Books) helped lift that work to fame and played a significant role in the popularization of knowledge and culture so characteristic of this age. It was Bruce Barton who successfully urged countless readers to "let Dr. Eliot of Harvard give you the essentials of a liberal education in only 15 minutes a day."

From 1914 to 1918, Barton served with the Collier company as editor of *Every Week*, a Sunday supplement with a format that presaged the modern picture magazine. His editorials and articles brought him a flourishing literary career, and one article in particular, about Billy Sunday, the evangelist, attracted the attention of an editor of the *American Magazine*. Invited to contribute to this journal, his articles, especially his interviews with famous people, stressed the inspirational and uplifting aspects of life and long remained popular. Indeed, these articles were so admired that they were reproduced in a series of volumes during the 1920s; their titles suggest the over-all theme: *More Power to You, It's a Good Old World, Better Days, On the Up and Up.*

During World War I, the federal government asked Barton to coordinate fund drives of the YWCA and YMCA, Knights of Columbus, Salvation Army, and Jewish Welfare Board. Out of this experience two significant developments emerged. First, Barton's effort to help publicize the Salvation Army inspired one of his most famous slogans—indeed one of the most famous in an era of sloganeering—"A man may be down but he is never out." Second, the fund-raising campaign itself led him to enlist the aid of two advertising men, Alex Osborn of Buffalo and Roy Durstine of New York. That this campaign did not begin until Armistice Day failed to discourage the trio, since the funds were still needed. Their determination was justified: They topped their goal of $150,000,000 by some $50,000,000 more. Out of their successful team effort came the creation of a new advertising agency, Barton, Durstine, and Osborn, in January 1919. In 1928, the company merged with another agency, the George Batten Company, to become the highly publicized BBD&O. Its fame was hardly limited to professional advertising men. The agency was well known to the general public and was very much the product of a transformed America, of a new era of the consumer-oriented mass society. Jokes, cartoons, and other popular references to its kind of activities made the agency's name a commonplace. By the time of Barton's retirement, it was the nation's fourth largest advertising firm. Its clients included many of the industrial giants—General Electric, General Motors, United States Steel. Founded on a $10,000 loan, the company had become a multimillion-dollar enterprise. Barton, who never seemed to seek money, attracted it with extraordinary ease. At the beginning, legend has it, he took a salary of only $5,000 a year from the agency, claiming that it was all anybody needed. He and his family obviously lived well (although never extravagantly) in later years, but it is probably true, as Barton delightedly used to insist, that "it would be a scandal if people knew how little I make as chairman of BBD&O. I think it's almost a disgrace for a man to die rich." He was always equally generous with his contributions to charity and with the time he devoted to public service work.

Barton's original fame rested on his prolific and unsubtle contributions to inspirational literature. Some found his work sentimental, even cloying, but there seemed to be a ceaseless public demand for it. Many of these qualities appeared in his most famous advertising copy. What Bruce Barton possessed was an insight into human nature, especially into the character of the American middle class in a period of transformation. He had a special sensitivity to its fears and hopes, yearnings and ideals. Richard M. Huber rightly finds him a man "with a knack for retailing simple homilies"—very much like the poet Edgar Guest. It seemed both easy and natural when "this leading retailer of values poured most of his energies into retailing products." But perhaps Alistair Cooke was most perceptive of all in seeing the meaning of Barton's career in advertising. Writing in his column for *The Manchester Guardian* on the occasion of Barton's death, Cooke stated: "He came as close as any one will to achieving a philosophy of advertising, because he saw the whole of human history as an exercise in persuasion."

Bruce Barton understood the power of communication in an era when new techniques of communications were remaking the social order. In a memorable piece immediately after World War I, "They Shall Beat Their Swords into Electrotypes," he pleaded for a new effort in the cause of international understanding. Each nation, he said, should pledge itself to spend at least one percent of its war costs in international advertising, "explaining to the rest of the world its own achievements and ideals; and seeking to eradicate from the character of its own people those characteristics which are a source of irritation to their neighbors." In the same article, he urged the international exchange of newspapermen, clergymen, professors—of every group that had "in its power the shaping of public opinion." And he continued, "In all these ways—plus the regular use of the printed word and motion picture—I would make the people of the world to know each other, knowing that ultimately they would come to like each other." These are ideas very much in harmony with so-called advanced thinking in an era fascinated by the power of new agencies of communication and mass culture. In the early 1930s, Barton's article "Let's Advertise This Hell" proposed an entirely new series of ads that would be offered to any publication that could be persuaded to print them as a way of keeping the United States out of another war. Late in 1923, he was busy proposing to Calvin Coolidge's political advisors a publicity campaign for the President's 1924 bid.

Barton's famous "Creed of an Advertising Man," first delivered as an address in 1927, is even more characteristic of his thinking and greatly contributed to an understanding of his 1920s vision of the importance of advertising in the social order. He writes:

I am in advertising because I believe in business and advertising is the voice of business. I recognize the waste and inefficiencies of business. I recognize the cruelties of competition, and the dishonesty that still stains too many business operations. Yet I believe that in the larger development of business and the gradual evolution of its ideals lies the best hope of the world.

I am in advertising because advertising is the power which keeps business out in the open, which compels it to set up for itself public ideals of quality and service and to measure up to those ideals. Advertising is a creative force that has generated jobs, new ideas, has expanded our economy and has helped give us the highest standard of living in the world. Advertising is the spark plug on the cylinder of mass production, and essential to the continuance of the democratic process. Advertising sustains a system that has made us leaders of the free world: The American Way of Life.

If advertising sometimes encourages men and women to live beyond their means, so sometimes does matrimony. If advertising is too often tedious, garrulous and redundant, so is the U.S. Senate.

Advertising, then, was persuasion and persuasion could and would change the world; but advertising at the moment was doing its greatest and most necessary service in its special relationship to business—by publicizing products and urging consumers to buy them. (His method of dealing with Communism, stated later in life, is characteristic: "Give every Russian a copy of the latest Sears-Roebuck Catalogue and the address of the nearest Sears-Roebuck outlet.") The genius of Barton's own advertising copy was based on the assumption that the use of products advertised effectively contributed to growth and progress, sometimes of the nation but more often of the individual himself. The most successful ads would seek to employ the products of a business in the service of the sanctity or betterment of human life. Witness, for instance, one General Electric ad: "Any woman who is doing any household task that a little electric motor can do is working for three cents an hour. Human life is too precious to be sold at the price of three cents an hour." Or that ad for the Alexander Hamilton Institute (a two-year correspondence course): "A wonderful two years' trip at full pay. But only men with imagination can take it. Only one man in ten has imagination, and imagination rules the world." Or that for General Foods: the creation of Betty Crocker as "the kitchen familiar of every lonely American housewife." The ad shaped for each situation sought to provide everyone with a simple way to understand a rapidly standardizing and mechanizing way of life. In a world of increased complexities, mass technology, and fearful changes, such advertisements offered a chance to retain human dignity as well as individual meaning and development. Bruce Barton, the great master of the uplift essay, without doubt had put uplift at the service of American business enterprise; without doubt he did so largely because of that learning he had received as a young boy at his father's table.

Bruce Barton, it is clear, had been fascinated by ideas about salesmanship and religion many years before writing his 1925 best seller *The Man Nobody Knows*. He had often commented, in writing and conversation, what a great textbook the Bible could be for an advertising man. Barton's writings delighted in Biblical-like parables and even his advertising copy had a Biblical quality to its prose. But it was only in 1925, the year of the Scopes Trial and William Jennings Bryan's fundamentalist interpretation of the Old Testament, that the Republican business-oriented Barton finally provided his important and widely read interpretation of the New Testament, which especially emphasized the life of Jesus.

Ever since the nineteenth century had sought and found a historical Christ, it had become increasingly popular to see him in ways that suited the historical needs of a given moment. Jesus had been recreated as a fairly respectable Christian socialist or a not-so-respectable proletarian revolutionary. Now, in the 1920s, Barton claimed him for yet another historical role. He set out specifically, we might argue today, to give Christ a new image. In the process he provided a new vision of Christianity. Such a vision was consistent both with the tough demands of a more difficult and rigorously ordered mass society and with a new religious glow destined, not as a simple justification of capitalism and the virtues necessary to sustain it, but as a means of sanctifying the new order of modern business—one organized through the instrumentality of salesmanship to serve the newly emerging consumer-based mass society. In a society where the older ideal of the stewardship of wealth could no longer serve, a new idea evolved: business—all business—as service to others and something fundamental to the development of self. Barton, Richard Huber observed, "soaked the idea of success in the sanctity of the New Testament." He moved American Puritanism, in a profound sense, from a more traditional dependence on the God of the Old Testament to a greater reliance on a carefully reexamined and reconstructed vision of the New Testament.

The initial task at hand was to develop a necessary new view of the personality of Jesus and the basic values that went with it. Barton took particular aim at the Sunday School image of Jesus: a weakling, a killjoy, a failure, a sissy, meek and full of grief. In its place there was a new Jesus: the physically strong carpenter, a healthy and vigorous outdoors man, a sociable companion, a strong and effective leader. "A killjoy! He was the most popular dinner guest in Jerusalem! . . . A failure! He picked up twelve men from the bottom ranks of business and forged them into an organization that conquered the world." Barton insisted on Jesus' masculinity, suggesting his attractiveness to women, stressing his role as a father figure, even emphasizing the role of Jesus' own "historical" father, Joseph. Jesus emerges, as it were, a consumer himself, enjoying life and parties, turning water into wine. His methods are those of advertising; he is the founder of "modern business" and modern entrepreneurial tactics. Barton's understanding of what Jesus meant by his "Father's business" is the key to his own analysis. God seeks, Barton tells us,

to develop perfect human beings, superior to circumstance, victorious over Fate. No single kind of human talent or effort can be spared if the experiment is to succeed. The race must be fed and clothed and housed and transported, as well as preached to, and taught and healed. Thus *all* business is his Father's business. All work is worship; all useful service prayer. And whoever works wholeheartedly at any worthy calling is a co-worker with the Almighty in the great enterprise which He has initiated but which he can never finish without the help of men.

The Man Nobody Knows first appeared in serial form in the *Woman's Home Companion* and then for several years in the late 1920s continued to ride high on the best-seller lists. Barton followed it in 1927 with *The Book Nobody Knows,* a study of the Bible. These works have never been without an audience since they were first published, but they remain peculiarly documents of the 1920s and in a sense the high points of Barton's career.

Barton, of course, continued with his agency and his writing. He was elected to Congress from Manhattan's East Side Silk Stocking District in 1937 and easily reelected in 1938. Earning a considerable reputation, among reporters at least, for his ability and service in the House, he was a vigorous opponent of Franklin Roosevelt's New Deal. He lost a bid for the Senate in 1940 and retired from politics—only after the President borrowed something from Barton's book with a little sloganeering of his own. His jocular condemnation of three outstanding GOP House critics with the repeated phrase "Martin, Barton, and Fish" delighted his audience and gave Bruce Barton still another claim to national fame.

But it is fair to say that the major impact of Barton's life and ideas rests in the 1920s. Somehow his special vision of the world served these pre-Depression years in a special way. Barton's optimism, his defense of business, and especially his often profound sense of the importance of communications, of techniques of persuasion, of the significant role played by salesmanship and advertising in the new order of things served this period most particularly. Of no less service to the 1920s was his basic and old-fashioned evangelism, which he carried with him from the nineteenth century and which was transformed in a way that coincided with the needs of millions of middle-class Americans living in a time of clashing values and sharp institutional change. Much of Barton, of course, today seems camp, unsophisticated, self-serving, unreal. We know that most of his ardent beliefs were being attacked or mocked even during the period in which he wrote. Yet Barton tried to accept the new order as well as redefine older values without abandoning what he deemed best in the latter—ideals of self-development and individual human dignity in an era of mass technology, mass organization, mass society. He tried to redefine Christianity and made it again a potent moral force.

Barton's salesman as hero replaced William Graham Sumner's savings bank depositor as hero for the conservative sons of American Puritan ministers—much as though one age of social order were in effect replacing another. At a time in which the values of a producer society dominated, Sumner, the Yale sociologist, could claim that the man who saved his money and practiced self-denial was the hero of civilization; in an age of increasing consumer orientation stressing sales and spending and joy rather than self-denial, Barton, the advertising man, glorified the salesman-businessman. The type, of course, was subject to Sinclair Lewis' bitter satire at almost the instant Barton was creating him. Later, by 1935, novelist Thorton Wilder would present his extraordinary study of both modern salesmanship and modern Protestantism in *Heaven's My Destination*. And during the 1940s and 1950s, the images of the salesman that emerged from works like Eugene O'Neill's *The Iceman Cometh* and Arthur Miller's *Death of a Salesman* have the appearance of tragedy and perhaps even symbolize the whole tragedy of American life. Only in the mid-1960s, with the Maysles brothers' documentary film *Salesman,* does the salesman image evoke neither heroism nor tragedy; rather pathos and perhaps a touch of comedy. But these are other times.

To return to the 1920s, however, it is apparent that we will not understand this decade until we understand Bruce Barton's life and contribution to it—or better yet, why so many Americans responded to Barton's message in quite the way they did. A successful salesman best served the world, Barton firmly believed, and in the 1920s he was perhaps the best salesman of all. A secular piety and a new priesthood. Preachers' sons might indeed rule the world.

By the time of Henry Ford's death in 1947, at least one of the crucial ideas in Bruce Barton's life and work—the proposition that business was service—was firmly fixed in American thought. Notwithstanding depression and World War, the idea of business success had also become sharply identified with the business of being American. Maybe Calvin Coolidge had said it crudely in the 1920s, but the overwhelming majority of the public opinion makers in 1947 seemed to agree: the business of America *was* business. This identification was so complete that Ford himself as well as his achievements seemed to be, as *The New York Times* declared, the very "embodiment of America in an era of industrial revolution." Yet Ford's career had been made possible *because* of the American system itself; he was the product of our "free enterprise" way while also serving as the living symbol of its achievement and success.

This account of the relationship between Ford and America produced a series of complex intellectual problems. First, the portrait of Ford was that of a simple man who sought neither a vast fortune nor luxuries, whose constant concern was for "the great multitude," for the "common man." Second, his great accomplishments, possible "only in America," were ultimately based on a "single-minded devotion to fundamentals as he saw them: hard work, the simple virtues, self-reliance, the good earth. He profited by providing what was new, but he also treasured that which was bygone." None of this enables us to come to grips with the essentially radical, if not revolutionary, consequences of Ford's achievement. Nor do we necessarily understand why, even outside America and indeed in the very heart of socialist Europe, Ford and his system—*Fordismus,* the Europeans often called it—was hailed in the 1920s as a major contribution to the twentieth-century revolution by Marxists as imposing as Vladimir Lenin. Indeed, it was not at all unusual to find Ford's portrait hanging alongside that of Lenin in Soviet factories. (Nor was Ford himself unappreciative of the achievement of Soviet engineers and factories.) Ford's favorite authors may have been Horatio Alger and Ralph Waldo Emerson; he may have repeatedly quoted homilies from the McGuffey *Readers,* which appear to be his only source of formal education, but he was nonetheless considered a major architect of the new social order that came into being during the first two decades of the twentieth century and must be understood if we are to grasp the nature of the 1920s.

Biography, then, includes both the subject's achievements and the way these provide for continuity and/or change in society. It also tells us, by the use some elements in society make of a man's life, something about that society as well. The Ford as Horatio Alger hero—simple mechanic to industrial giant; the Ford as living evidence of the success and meaning of the American way; the Ford as villainous autocrat, brutally exemplifying the worst features of class warfare; the Ford as genius whose wisdom gives him the right if not the responsibility to speak with authority on all human and social problems; the Ford as revolutionary who remade the modern world in his own vision—the "legends" of Henry Ford are in many ways as significant to an understanding of history as is any study of the "true" achievements of a life's work, properly assessed.

Ford was 57 years old in 1920 (Bruce Barton was 34, and Babe Ruth 25). The decade saw the culmination of his major work and witnessed even the beginning of the decline of the system he had dreamed and schemed to create. Like Barton, he was a man with a mission and the story of that mission and what happened to it in the 1920s dominates this discussion. Roger Burlingame has insisted, "It is hard to deny that Henry Ford was ridden by two obsessions: mechanical perfection and the 'common man.' " Those obsessions, the way they often conflicted and the attempts to achieve some kind of effective balance between them, are important here. They are explored not only because such an approach helps us to understand more fully the life of Ford himself but because in a profound sense their story is the central theme of our century, a theme that reached a peak of sorts in the 1920s.

Henry Ford did not worship his father. William Ford was a prosperous farmer of pioneer Scots-Irish stock, well established on a largely self-sufficient and profitable farm near Dearborn, Michigan, when Henry was born in July 1863. The farm had its own sawmill and gristmill and machinery for making homespun of wool that was sheared from William Ford's own sheep. There were, of course, many chores for a farm boy, but Henry from earliest childhood seemed to loathe such work. From the outset, however, he seemed attracted to and useful in dealing with the machinery on the place. By all local accounts, he had a special mechanical aptitude and a kind of intuitive mechanical logic. At an early age, for instance, he developed a passion for timepieces and spent considerable time fixing things; that is, "tinkering"—a fine old Yankee tradition. Mechanization even in the years of Henry's boyhood, had become important to Midwest farm life, especially in more prosperous regions. Significant, too, was the increasing industrialization occurring around the Ford farm in Wayne County. But the boy's fascination with the machine and with mechanics did not please his father, who not only disliked the new industrial and urbanized world growing up around him but also had other needs for the boy's labor. When the boy was sixteen the arguments between the two proved too much: Ford's dislike of farming, his disagreements with his father, and the attraction of work in a machine shop led him to Detroit. It was around this time, Ford himself tells us, that his dream of making something in quantity without reduction in quality began to take hold of his imagination.

Evidence indicates not only little formal education in Henry Ford's life, but also almost no use at all for books; further, there seems to be no sense of any religious training or commitment. Even before Ford left home for the first time in 1879, and though he was unaware of it, George Selden had already applied for his celebrated patent for a gasoline-motored car. (It would later play a significant role in the development of Ford's company.) Clearly, then, people —both in the United States and abroad—were responding to the possibilities inherent in new sources of energy. Ford himself experimented with steam engines before he began to study the internal-combustion engine. But from a very early age his commitment was to engines and to production in quantity, not to the manufacture of luxury items for the few.

Ford did return to the farm for a period. His father, hoping to give him a worthwhile occupation that would provide independence and a livelihood, bequeathed forty acres of timberland to Henry. Ford used the opportunity to get married, to build himself a house as well as a machine shop—and to avoid any farming whatsoever! By 1891 he had left the rural homestead for good for a position as an engineer with the Edison Illuminating Company. He advanced rapidly and became chief engineer. In his spare time, he worked at home on a small motor-driven vehicle of his own design. By 1893 the Duryea brothers successfully had demonstrated the first American gasoline automobile. Two years later, a meeting with Thomas A. Edison, perhaps Ford's only hero, encouraged him to continue work on his engine. By 1896 he had demonstrated his own first car; by 1899 the company asked him to choose between his hobby and his job. Ford made his decision: a full dedication of his future to the automobile.

Detroit was taking young Ford seriously as a builder of automobiles, and the nation as a whole was increasingly fascinated by the possibilities of the "horseless carriage." Yet Ford's first corporate venture, the Detroit Automobile Company, was short-lived; within a year a new firm had been formed, the Henry Ford Automobile Company. But it, too, did not survive. Such detail is significant only because it documents Ford's intense difficulties in working under conditions in which he lacked complete control, and he vowed never again to be in a position where others could give him orders. Meanwhile, between 1899 and 1902, Ford had used his time well. He was becoming famous. He knew that one of the central propositions of the new age was self-advertisement and publicity, and that car speed was the way to it in the automobile business. Ford himself did not believe that high speed added to a car's value, but he was aware that breaking speed records made one a celebrity in the social world at large. Furthermore, such records cornered the attention of the rich and, notwithstanding his growing dream, they alone could afford this new toy—expensive as such handmade objects inevitably had to be. And when Ford began to win races at fashionable tracks such as that at Grosse Pointe, Michigan—at one event he reached the speed of 70 miles an hour—international publicity came to him. Finally, the famous driver Barney Oldfield broke all records at the Grosse Point course in the "999," a car Ford had built.

By 1903 the Ford Motor Company was a reality. Incorporated with basic capital investment of only $28,000 provided by a Detroit coal dealer (most of that in the form of shop, machinery, patents, contracts), the company managed to assemble an extraordinary group of businessmen, engineers, etc. Within five years it had become one of the leading automobile manufacturers. There was little to distinguish the company's product. Ransome E. Olds had already pioneered in producing inexpensive cars. "Mass production" meth ods were available to all manufacturers. But, as Roger Burlingame tells us, the automobile of 1903 was still in an early experimental stage:

No detail of engine or transmission was settled, no design of any part frozen; there was no standardization of tools or processes, and it was not until four years later that true interchangeability of parts even among supposedly identical cars made in a single factory was demonstrated. . . . In 1903 there were more than 25 American manufacturers of passenger cars and, with the exception of Olds, no manufacturer sold more than a few hundred cars each year. The automobile, therefore, was for the most part a strictly handmade article.

Meanwhile, the famous public fancy was increasingly captured by the possibilities of the automobile. There was clearly a rising demand although obviously most cars remained too expensive for the wide and hungering middle-class market. Woodrow Wilson actually feared the motorcar mania because, he suggested in 1906, the automobile might very well bring socialism to America by inciting the poor to envy the rich!

In 1907, against "sound" advice, Ford announced his mission and his dream:

CULTURE AS HISTORY

I will build a motor car for the great multitude. It will be large enough for the family but small enough for the individual to run and care for. It will be constructed of the best materials, by the best men to be hired, after the simplest designs that modern engineering can devise. But it will be so low in price that no man making a good salary will be unable to own one—and enjoy with his family the blessing of hours of pleasure in God's great open spaces.

From the vantage point of the time it was issued, this extraordinarily simple statement is breathtaking in its implications. It is, in fact, a prediction of a new social order, an introduction to the world that was to be in the 1920s. It had enormous significance for the individual, the family, the mass society—and perhaps even in a sense proposed a serious redefinition of each. It hinted at a new definition of work and of production. It projected the likelihood of a new lifestyle. It implied a new kind of possible egalitarianism unheard of in the world's history—and it did all of this not in the name of needs, basic requirements of life, but in terms of possible pleasure: here, indeed, was a consumer vision of the world.

The creation of the Model T—the Tin Lizzie, or the flivver, as "she" was also called—is the climax of the story, the final convergence of Ford and history. It called for a series of key decisions, each Ford's fundamental responsibility no matter where the original idea came from. First, there was the matter of the huge new plant covering over 65 acres at Highland Park and the start of a major effort to cut back on dividends to stockholders, to plow some of the profits into new production. Second, there was the decision to make one car and only one car: "The way to make automobiles is to make one automobile like another automobile, to make them all alike, to make them come from the factory just alike—just like one pin is like another pin when it comes from the pin factory." In this decision, of course, Ford simply followed the well-established tradition of mass production as developed in the United States but never applied to the automobile industry. It meant the search for a car design suitable for mass use rather than one simply for cheap manufacture. Third, there was the need for low-cost production techniques. It resulted in the introduction of the famous moving assembly line, which involved an enormous financial commitment in terms of tools. The idea of continuous movement seemed simple enough, and it rested on two seemingly simple principles: (1) the work must be brought to the worker and not the worker to the work, and (2) the work must be brought waist high so no worker would have to stoop. Taking almost seven years to perfect, the system at Highland Park was an established fact by 1914, and the production revolution had been wrought. Men and machine, through the central conveyor belt, had been in effect merged into one gigantic machine. It made possible a dramatic reduction in the time required to produce a car. By 1920 one completed Model T rolled off the line every minute; by 1925 one every ten seconds. Production rose from 39,640 in 1911 to 740,770 in 1917. In 1920, every other car in the world was a Model T Ford.

By the early 1920s, Ford commanded over 60 percent of the American output. Never before had such a complex mechanical process been devised or such production been possible. The achievement required a spectacular degree of synchronization, precision, and specialization. Yet this in itself created newer problems that led to still further revolutionary consequences. For instance, such mechanization meant that little real skill was required by any particular worker. Only the top engineers and designers had to know anything about the total process. It suggested the possibility of an easily obtainable work force, but it had inherent drawbacks—in the form of the sheer monotony of the work, which led to an alarming turnover in the labor force.

With production methods already radically altered by 1914, Ford announced yet another daring step. He proposed a new wage scheme, a kind of profit sharing (in advance of actual profits) in which the minimum for any class of work would be (under certain conditions) five dollars a day. At the same time, he reduced the working day from nine to eight hours. The key fact here was that in *no* sense was pay tied into productivity. There were conditions attached to the minimum pay stipulation: certain minimum standards of conduct and behavior as outlined by the company; that is, standards by which the company judged men to be "good workers." Ford, in effect, doubled the wages of those "who could pass his sociology examination on the clean and wholesome life," stated John R. Commons, who reported on the operation of Ford's plan with considerable enthusiasm. Not only did the resultant stable work force please Ford, but he was able to show an increase in profits as well. And, as he was well aware, he had also made every workman a potential customer.

There was still one more remaining piece in the mosaic of a new order of work and life, production and consumption. Ford established a "Sociological Department" (later called the "Education Department"), initially under the direction of an Episcopal minister. Its aim was paternalistic: to teach Ford's workers how to live the exemplary life, how to budget their newfound high wages, to encourage them to refrain from liquor or tobacco, to provide elemental lessons in hygiene and home management, to suggest steps helpful in the "Americanization" of the huge numbers of foreign-born in the company's work force. Under pressure from those who opposed such paternalism and charged Ford with spying or a special kind of tyranny, the scheme was eventually given up. But it was in effect replaced by the company's extraordinary trade school, with perhaps more lasting effects. Nonetheless, it is important to see the social aspects of Ford's thinking about his world and to see how the whole dream finally produced a totally new order, the object of Ford's mission and dream, whether or not he fully realized it.

By the 1920s, then, Ford and his new system were being widely hailed as the American System. The miracles he had wrought in production and consumption made his name synonymous with American success. A national figure, his advice sought on all kinds of issues, Ford began to yield to pressures to go beyond the world of automobile manufacture. With war raging in Europe, he sailed off in 1915 on his famous and much maligned "peace ship," a venture in personal diplomacy by which he hoped to dramatize the crusade for peace. In 1918, at the urging of Woodrow Wilson, he ran for the Senate from Michigan and lost in a close contest in which voter fraud was later established. Ford's writings grew more voluminous on many subjects; he owned his own newspaper, *The Dearborn Independent,* in which he conducted "his own" column (it was obvious that he increasingly relied on ghostwriters for much of his published work, although this dependence, of course, did not relieve him of responsibility for what was said in his name). The blatantly anti-Semitic material published in the paper, for example, was one of the worst mistakes of his career. It cost him countless followers and threatened him with court action as well.

Ford's national dreams in the 1920s led him to propose the development of Muscle Shoals (site of the later TVA) under his own auspices. It was a grand scheme to bring industry to the countryside and to decentralize industrial concentration while offering the advantages of industrial life to isolated rural areas. George Norris and others in the Senate blocked this private takeover. Ford continued to remain a much-sought-after man politically. There was even talk of his running for the Presidency in 1924, but he finally decided against encouraging such a move.

Meanwhile, in Ford's immediate world, potential disaster turned almost literally to gold. He had lost a stockholders' suit to compel the payment of special dividends. Company stockholders were more and more frightened by his apparent lack of interest in profits; the "socialism" of his Five-Dollar-a-Day wage scheme and the Sociological Department; the idea of profit-sharing; and the projected society of the common man. Ford was now determined to obtain complete control to carry out his plans. Taking a daring chance, he bought out all the stockholders. But he hated banks and bankers, and refused to borrow from them to achieve his goal of complete family ownership (something unique for an industrial corporation of that size and wealth). To obtain increased operating capital, he put a squeeze play on Ford dealerships. He pushed through a production speed-up, forced cars on unwilling dealers, threatened franchise losses if they didn't pay for cars, ordered or not, and forced them to go to *their* banks, leaving Ford free and clear and, finally in the 1920s, his own master.

The 1920s initially seemed to bring increased growth. Ford's organization weathered the 1921 depression better than any other company in the industry. Meanwhile, he continued his struggle for full integration in production. He sought to make his enterprise completely self-sufficient, acquiring raw materials and methods of transportation to achieve an even flow of raw materials into the process of production and then an even flow of finished goods coming off the production line—a kind of universal and unceasing procession of the universal car, the Model T.

Ford was unable to create the final realization of his vision on either the technological side (with the system of complete integration) or the social or human side (with the reshaping of human lives by means of the Sociological Department) any more than he had been able to transcend Highland Park and later River Rouge. The wider regional or national dreams remained unfulfilled. But the impact of Ford's revolutionary mission continued to unfold in the United States and through the rest of the world. *Fordismus* had created a 1920s different from what the decade would have been without it. Nevertheless, other forces had begun to threaten the basic assumptions on which Ford's radical revision of things had been partly based.

In 1927, the Ford Motor Company made its crucial decision to end production of the great Tin Lizzie, the Model T, and to begin work on the replacement Model A. Ford had perhaps belatedly learned a fundamental fact about the new and affluent mass society he had done so much to shape, if not to create: price and efficiency alone would not dictate consumer choice. Many of his competitors already knew as much. This new world of mass consumption was also a new world of mass communications in which national advertising and newer forms of national media (radio, film, the new journalism) helped play upon human needs and desires, hopes and fears. Ford was not familiar with the world of Bruce Barton; he did not sense the need for individual and even private fulfillment; he had not perceived that the common man did not want to *feel* common; mechanical perfection, although often desirable, was not enough.

Ironically, of course, it was profits (or lack of them) that forced Ford's move. He himself was clearly uninterested in simply making money for its own sake; his whole career is a testament to that observation; his own simple and sometimes even austere way of life are sufficient evidence. But the company did exist as part of a capitalist order and survival meant coming to grips with competition— no matter how much Ford might wish to rely on internal strengths and isolate himself from external dangers, and no matter how "false" for him were the values that led to the rejection of the cheap, ugly, durable, efficient, simple, and black Model T. Having in a sense created the 1920s, he failed to see what else had also been created.

The retreat of 1927—with the decision to end the Model T— was a fateful one. Except for some of the production miracles he contributed to during World War II, Ford's life was increasingly given over to a bitter series of struggles—within management and with labor, the latter often being bloody affairs. To 1927, the seemingly progressive Henry Ford of 1907 seemed unable even to understand the world of the 1930s. The Ford of the Five-Dollar-a-Day and the Sociological Department could not believe that workers really wanted unions and that strikes could ever achieve a real purpose.

Even in terms of the day-to-day operation of the business, Ford could admit in 1933 that the new plant at River Rouge "is so big that it isn't any fun any more." Increasingly (again, ironically for the man who "made" the twentieth century), he continued to turn to the past: new interest in rediscovered folk dancing; republication of McGuffey's *Readers;* historical collecting for his special museum or for Greenfield Village, which was a kind of sentimental reconstruction of his own past, that past that he had run away from so many years ago. We face a strange portrait: the man who invented the future now carefully rediscovering the past.

Was there an answer to the fundamental problem his life so startlingly posed? Could the ideals projected by the phrases "mechanical perfection" and "common man" ever really be reconciled? Would even a totalitarian regime be able to achieve the perfect reconciliation? Ford tried and we have seen the outcome in the America of the 1920s. Yet the question continues to haunt us— partly because of how far Ford went, because we are still feeling the consequences of that accomplishment, because we still respond to the experiences of the 1920s with a continued sense of hope and fear.

When George Herman Ruth, Jr., died in 1947, *The New York Times* devoted more than two of its large eight-column pages to him. While each column clearly supplemented the other, they were vastly different in tone and method of presentation. The headline on the first read:

Ruth, Baseball's Great Star and Idol of Children, Had a Career Both Dramatic and Bizarre/World-Wide Fame Won on Diamond/Even in Lands Where Game is Unknown, Baseball's Star Player Was Admired

There followed a traditional and detailed obituary, rich in sentiment of recalled moments of sorrow and joy as well as prosaic biographical fact, with strenuous effort to recount both significant achievements and recapture an extraordinary personality. The second headline presented something else:

Ruth Set Fifty-four Major League Records and Ten Additional Marks in American Circuit/Slugger Starred in 10 World Series/Ruth Set Major League Homer Mark on Total of 714—Hit Over 40 Eleven Seasons/Had Most Walks in 1923/All-Time Batting Great also Struck Out Most Times in Career Lasting 22 Years

The page itself had no prose story. It was simply a serial listing of all kinds of records, a careful selection of complete box scores of games important in Ruth's career, a carefully outlined and specially headed box that listed his yearly salary from the first days in Baltimore ($600) in 1914 to the final year in Brooklyn ($15,000), for a lifetime total of $925,900.

In these two descriptions of the career of one of the great sports heroes of the 1920s (so often called "The Golden Age of American Sports"), it is perhaps possible to see two aspects of the enormous appeal spectator sports held for this decade. The mechanization of life generally, when combined with the mounting effort to rationalize all aspects of man's activities, produced a particular middle-class delight in what could be measured and counted. (How fitting, then, were statistics on the "home run," with both numbers hit and distances traveled by the ball.) Americans could delight in the data that Ruth and other players provided. Athletic records provided a means of measuring achievement—success—in sports as such statistics did in other aspects of the mechanized and rationalized life. Most especially, salary figures also assisted in judging success.

But no matter how fascinated a society may be with this mechanized aspect of the life that its athletes lead (which naturally transfers to the games people play or watch), it apparently was not enough. "Star," "Idol," "Dramatic," "Bizarre" were words featured in Ruth's official obituary, suggesting that the public demands something more. Perhaps in an increasingly mechanized world more was called for. Grantland Rice, the sports writer, once wrote this about the great sports figures like Ruth:

They had something more than mere skill or competitive ability. They also had in record quality and quantity that indescribable asset known as color, personality, crowd appeal, or whatever you may care to call it.

And if our sports mirror other aspects of our lives in a significant way, it might not be inappropriate to propose that what Rice suggests about sports figures was the lesson Ford had bitterly learned by 1927 when he discovered that his "common man" was no longer willing to settle for record-book cheapness, mechanical efficiency, and the like. People, he discovered, also wanted "style" (a favorite subject of Henry's son Edsel, with whom old Henry constantly fought) in their cars; that is, "color, personality, crowd appeal."

Also in 1927, another major American corporation was enjoying huge success. Colonel Jacob Ruppert's New York Yankees was the best baseball team in the world; there are those that claim it was the greatest baseball team of all time. Ruth hit 60 home runs that season, Lou Gehrig drove in 175 runs, the Yankees won the pennant by 19 games and swept the World Series against the Pittsburgh Pirates in four straight games. Babe Ruth earned $70,000 in 1927 for simply playing under contract with the Colonel. And Ruth was worth every penny to Ruppert's corporation, which owned a gigantic stadium (often known as "The House that Ruth Built") with 70,000 seats to fill. This was big business for the Colonel and the Yankee organization—and seeing the Babe perform and produce was something big and special for the fans. It was more than a question of team loyalties, more than winning or losing the game. The *New York Times* account of one 1927 World Series game perhaps captures a little of this sentiment:

His majesty the Babe had sent 64,000 folks in a paroxysm of glee by clubbing a screaming liner into the right field bleachers. . . . The big time came in the seventh. The Yanks had the game safely stowed away and the sus pense was over . . . but the fans still stood up and demanded that Mr. Ruth get busy and do something for home and country. . . . "A homer, Babe! Give us a homer!" ran the burden of the plea, and the big fellow pulled his cap on tighter, took a reef in his belt, dug spikes into the ground and grimly faced [the pitcher]. . . . Upward and onward, gaining speed and height with every foot, the little white ball winged with terrific speed until it dashed itself against the seat of the right-field bleachers, more than a quarter of the way up the peopled slope. And now the populace had its homer and it stood up and gave the glad joyous howl that must have rang out in the Roman arena of old. . . .

This description is revealing evidence of another pertinent aspect of the world of George Herman Ruth, Jr., perhaps an aspect helping to "make" him into the heroic Babe he would become. The new mechanized era of mass society was one of mass communications as well, and the media demanded suitable material for copy. A new group of reporters and writers—Ring Lardner, Grantland Rice, Heywood Broun, John Kiernan among them—were ready exploiters of achievement and personalities, anxious to expand the traditional meaning of "news" for a whole series of publications, radio broadcasts, sometimes even films, that constantly demanded copy to feed a growing number of hungry consumers of this kind of news. They invented along the way an often brilliantly different and always special kind of rhetoric and style. Their unique prose delighted readers, sold more copies, appealed to more advertising agencies with products to sell—which was done through buying space in publications or time on the radio. "The Ruth is mighty and shall prevail," Haywood Broun wrote in 1923. It is still quoted by enthusiasts of the special sportswriting prose of this golden age of sports and of sports promotion.

The "mighty Ruth" of 1923 was born among the most lowly in a poor, third-floor apartment over a saloon in the waterfront section of Baltimore, Maryland, in 1895. His parents, both children of immigrants, constantly struggled with poverty in a home described as an "angry, violent, desperately poor place, tense with all the frustrations of extreme poverty and shabbiness." Ruth confessed that he hardly knew them, and the major recollections of his father seem to be those of repeated and brutal beatings. "I was a bad kid," Ruth tells us in his autobiography. Unable to take care of their 7-year-old son and describing him as "incorrigible," his parents put Ruth in St. Mary's Industrial School in Baltimore. He would remain there— with occasional returns to the parental home—until he was 19.

The story of Ruth's upbringing reads like a stereotype of Victorian childhood among the lowliest urban poor, a kind of Dickensian horror tale without any cheerful relief, without any sentimental moments of escape from nightmare. The school stressed order and discipline; it tried to educate but clearly did little in the case of Ruth: he could barely read and write. There was no privacy. And there were few if any friends for Ruth, who was the object of unkind verbal abuse because of his size and shape. After leaving school, he continued to have—and to retain almost until the end of his life—the most primitive of personal habits and the crudest of manners. There is little evidence that the strict Catholicism administered at St. Mary's had any significant effect on him. Ruth's excessive and obsessive interest in gambling, sex, and drinking appear to be schoolboy products he carried throughout his life. When at home, he lived near the harsh waterfront, mixing with rough sailors and bums. In effect he was an abandoned child. "I had a rotten start," he tells us, "and it took me a long time to get my bearings." St. Mary's appears to have been of little help in getting those "bearings," and Ruth's life story leads one to wonder whether he ever really got them. Perhaps this upbringing accounts for what appears to be his genuine fondness for the countless number of children who idolized him during his great career and for his willingness to visit children in hospitals and homes throughout these later years.

St. Mary's did try to give Ruth a vocation. He was assigned to the shirt factory to learn the tailor's trade, and the assignment indicates that the brothers noted no special potential or skills during his many years with them. But two positive things did emerge from his life at St. Mary's. First, he appeared to learn (as Ken Sobol, his ablest biographer tells us) that his "personal crudities" became "uproarious crowd-pleasers" in the presence of an audience. This was certainly important preparation for the "colorful" personality and always willing performer Ruth was to become. He would be eager to provide "good copy" and to delight fans off the field as well as on. (The shy, educated, craftsmanlike Lou Gehrig, for example, never learned to be a showman and never earned the kind of vast following or the money that Ruth did.) Yet St. Mary's most important gift was not any special training but a special opportunity. Baseball was about the only recreational outlet given to the boys at St. Mary's. So it was here that Ruth learned to play the game and to develop the enormous native skills, the coordination and power, that would make him the most spectacular ballplayer of his time.

Baseball had been a successful professional activity since the 1870s, and by 1903 it had become sufficiently developed and well organized to create the beginnings of a mass audience and the source of significant careers for many young men. For Ruth—a man without learning, traditional skills, or alternate route—it offered a miraculous escape from the treadmill of poverty. Baseball could provide him with effective social mobility. Ruth was certainly neither the first nor the last of the children of fairly recent immigration and urban poverty to find their way to national status and success. Yet in many ways his career was among the most spectacular. One of St. Mary's brothers recommended Ruth to the owner of the Baltimore club, and he signed his first professional contract in 1914. That same year, his contract was sold for $2,900 to the Boston Red Sox, and with that organization he soon matured into a pitcher of rare ability.

While at Boston, Ruth also began to show remarkable prowess as a hitter. Baseball fans started to talk of his home runs, and by 1919 he was more often in the outfield than on the pitching mound. The following year was a turning point in both Ruth's career and in the game itself. The Yankees purchased his contract for $100,000 and also guaranteed the $350,000 mortgage on the financially shaky Red Sox stadium. It was a record sum—but the Babe delivered with a record number of home runs and enthusiastic fan response. The winter of 1920–1921, however, produced a scandal that rocked the entire structure of professional baseball. Gamblers had managed to buy the services of several members of the Chicago White Sox (subsequently labeled "Black Sox") to "throw" the 1919 World Series. The owners then reorganized baseball's business structure and appointed a stern federal judge, James Kenesaw Mountain Landis, as new high commissioner with unlimited power to assure the sanctity of the sport, though they still worried whether this reform would be enough, whether the fans would return. Many historians of the game attribute Ruth's brilliant performance during the following season as the most important factor in reviving spectator enthusiasm. Nine to ten million fans annually paid to see major league baseball in the 1920s.

By the end of the 1921 season (again to quote Sobol), more words were written about Ruth "than had ever been devoted to any other athlete in any single year. More people had watched him play than any other player. And more citizens of America, young and old, knew his name and could even recognize his homely round face than ever heard of Ty Cobb or John J. McGraw." Sportswriters vied with one another to provide him with appropriate nicknames ("Sultan of Swat"), but somehow he always remained "Babe" or "Bambino" (a change from "Nigger-lips," which he was often called at St. Mary's). He was the nation's great boy child, and Americans loved their big boy who often did so many childish things.

Whatever his achievements on the field, his growing contributions to the record books, the Babe also delighted millions of his countrymen by the sheer bigness of his affable personality and even by his awesome inability to curb his overwhelming appetites. Most Americans seemed to tolerate at least some of the indulgences of their big boy. No Ford or Barton, Ruth enjoyed spending money as well as earning it. An incorrigible gambler, and for large sums, he never seemed concerned about winning or losing. He loved expensive and fancy clothes. His interest in sex seemed limitless, and he frequented the better brothels even while in training or on tour with the ball club. His gluttony became equally legendary; he often overate and overdrank to the point of actual severe physical illness. Like so many celebrities in our modern mechanized age, Ruth's frequent illness, physical collapse, even hospitalization became almost routine. The Babe's most publicized collapse and hospitalization occurred during spring training in 1925, and the public apparently accepted the official explanation that his illness was the result of influenza and indigestion; the real cause, it appears, was a serious case of syphilis. A much concerned public watched intensely for reports of Ruth's condition. One well-known sportswriter called it "the stomach ache heard round the world."

Ruth was a heroic producer in the mechanized world of play. He was also an ideal hero for the world of consumption. Americans enjoyed the Babe's excess; they took comfort in the life of apparently enormous pleasures that Ruth enjoyed. Seldom if ever (even in this age of the rising popularity of Freudian thought) did they seem aware of what might exist behind this pattern of excess and illness. "Babe Ruth," Bill McGeehan said in 1925, "is our national exaggeration. . . . He has lightened the cares of the world and kept us from becoming overserious by his sheer exuberance."

Ruth found a way of making all of this pay; he made himself into a marketable product. In 1921 he hired an agent—or perhaps Christy Walsh snared Ruth. Walsh saw the vast possibilities in this extraordinary era of communications. He originally developed a ghostwriting syndicate especially in the sports field: writers who would sell articles and books under the name of a contracted sports figure. Increasingly the ghostwriter was becoming important in the public relations field. More and more distinguished Americans who wished to be heard or read (for example, Henry Ford), or from whom the public would like to hear (for example, Babe Ruth) contracted with professional writers to do the job. Soon there was no field without such literary talent, and the number and range of such ventures increased markedly in the 1920s. Walsh provided Ruth with a great deal more than ghostwriting: as agent he worked out product endorsements for advertising; he solicited special assignments in movies (Ruth made a few but was never very successful in this field); he arranged and booked barnstorming tours during the off-season or even tours on the vaudeville circuits. In 1926, for example, Ruth played 12 weeks in vaudeville—in effect, just appearing on stage so that fans in dozens of small towns could see their hero close up—for over $8,000 a week. This sum was considerably more than many notable show business people with special talents for entertaining were earning. Barnstorming around the country in 1927 and playing with hastily arranged teams of local citizens, Ruth added over $30,000 to his already sizable income. Press agent activity was hardly new; neither was Walsh's. He served as a kind of business manager, arranging investments, bank accounts, and the like in an effort to keep Ruth from squandering all his money. But what he did for Ruth added in a special 1920s way to the ballyhoo that promoted a professional athlete into a celebrity of ever-exaggerated proportions.

The year 1925 marked a low point in Babe Ruth's career and few believed he could recover. His "stomach ache heard round the world" was followed later the same season by failures to maintain training and to perform effectively. Manager Miller Huggins, in exasperation, fined him $5,000 for "misconduct off the ball field," and his decision was upheld by Colonel Jacob Ruppert, the Yankee owner. Ruth, with his own special arrogance, had originally taken the whole thing as a joke but now began to pay greater attention to his work, the management of his affairs, and possibly even to his image. His exceptional comeback in the 1926 season became, according to Sobol, a "symbol of continuity." Ruth was 30 and no longer a boy; he had suffered a kind of depression, and the fact that he could recover gave the whole country a sense of hope. Increasingly, the writers waxed sentimental over him and his generosity to the kids. (Ruth himself may have begun to believe the new image the writers had projected of him; he even began to color his days at St. Mary's in terms of kindnesses done him by some of the brothers.) Increasingly, the press transformed him into an older, less boyish "idol of the American boy." They began to forget the excesses and the crudities. His relationship with Mrs. Claire Hodgson may have also contributed to the change in his life. He married her in 1929 after the death of his estranged first wife. He paid greater attention to training, developing a shrewder interest in investments. The new Mrs. Ruth provided structure and order in his life: a tighter rein and necessary stability. It is difficult to avoid speculating on whether she was not providing as well the kind of love that Ruth never received from his mother so long ago in Baltimore.

But the Bambino of the 1930s and 1940s—the sentimentalized and reformed "idol" of American youth—is not the hero of the 1920s. Historian William E. Leuchtenberg may be somewhat unkind in describing Ruth in 1934 as "a pathetic figure, tightly corseted, a cruel lampoon of his former greatness" when he took off his Yankee uniform for the last time. For Ruth by now was out of place and out of time. He might be transformed into a sentimental figure by sentimental writers. Perhaps the times called for that kind of hero. But for the 1920s he was the perfect creation for an increasingly mechanized world that still hungered for the extraordinary personality, that tired of the Model T automobiles and yet was also appreciative of their virtues—wanting only something more, something bigger than life.

What kind of personality did Ruth bring to the era he so aptly characterized? And what was the price to himself and to the kind of society that enjoyed and admired "our national exaggeration?" What does it say about our values and his values, about the tragic set of conditions and circumstances that may lurk beneath the surface of his life and as well as of the life of his nation in the 1920s?

One series of probing questions, at least, is suggested in a passage from the work of a great Dutch historian who made a significant effort to come to an understanding of American history and especially the current American culture during the First World War. He is writing, in effect, about the onset of the 1920s and is considering what will follow. I do not know whether or not he saw Ruth during his own visit to this country during the Babe's comeback year (1926), but he most certainly must have heard about him. It would be interesting to listen to him discuss this view with special reference to Ruth's career. Perhaps we can do it for him:

One of the preeminent elements of modern civilization is sport, in which intellectual and physical culture meet. In it too mechanization seems to attain the opposite of its purposes. Gregarious modern man tries to save his individualism, as it were, in sport. But sport is not just the strictly physical development of skills and strength; it is also the giving of form, the stylizing of the very feeling of youth, strength, and life, a spiritual value of enormous weight. Play is culture. Play can pass over into art and rite, as in the dance and in sacred stage presentations. Play is rhythm and struggle, The competitive ideal itself is a cultural value of high importance. Play also means organization. But now, as a result of the modern capacity for very far-reaching organization and the possibilities created by modern transportation, an element of mechanization enters sport. In the immense sport organizations like those of football and baseball, we see free youthful forces and courage reduced to normality and uniformity in the service of the machinery of rules of play and the competitive system. If we compare the tense athlete in his competitive harness with the pioneer hunter and the Indian fighter, then the loss of true personality is obvious.

Johan Huizinga
America

9 THE CULTURE OF THE THIRTIES

So far as I am concerned, what had been the twenties ended that night. We would try to penetrate the fogs to come, to listen to the buoys, to read the charts. It would be three years before we took down a volume of Kunstgeschichte *from our shelves to be replaced by a thin narrow book in red entitled* What Is to Be Done?, *by V. I. Lenin. Then in a few years it would be taken down to be replaced by another. And so on.*[1]

The time was August 23, 1927; Sacco and Vanzetti had been executed. But for Josephine Herbst this political event, significant as it was, did not in itself mark the end of an era. For it was also on that day that she and John Herrmann were forced to abandon their 23-foot ketch after a difficult passage through a thick fog.[2] In her brilliant memoir of the year 1927, "A Year of Disgrace," Herbst demonstrates the extraordinary complexity that results from the mixture of private misfortune and public joys, public disasters and private triumphs, personal seekings and social developments. In April, for example, there were: the discovery of John Herrmann's illness and the happy preparations for the boating venture in Maine; the scandal and excitement of Antheil's *Ballet-Mécanique* at

Carnegie Hall and Herbst's unfulfilled longing to be moved by the
music as her friends had been; and the death sentence irrevocably
passed on Sacco and Vanzetti, crushing to those who had come to
believe so fervently in their innocence.

This very mixture of events of different kinds and qualities
provides a lesson. The past is not preserved for the historian as his
private domain. Myth, memory, history—these are three alternative
ways to capture and account for an allusive past, each with its own
persuasive claim. The very complexities of the record raise questions about the task of reconstruction in any form. Herbst, for example, is wise enough to ask:

But is there such a thing as the twenties? The decade simply falls apart
upon examination into crumbs and pieces which completely contradict each
other in their essences. The twenties were not at all the museum piece it has
since become where our literary curators have posed on elevated pedestals
a few busts of the eminent. Even individual characters cannot be studied in
a state of static immobility. It was all flux and change with artistic movements evolving into political crises, and where ideas of social service, justice,
and religious reaction had their special spokesman.[3]

So complex, so varied are events and motives that Erich Auerbach
shrewdly suggests, "To write history is so difficult that most historians are forced to make concessions to the technique of the legend."[4]
For no matter how great the difficulties, each of us—in his private
capacity or as propagandist or as historian—demands some order,
some form, from the past. (In spite of her own questions about the
nature of the 1920s, Herbst's personal reconstruction dates the
"end" of the period with precision.) Yet for the maker of myths,
the propagandist for a cause, the memoirist, and the historian, there
are frequently different, compelling psychological and social needs
dictating different forms and different ways of reconstruction.

Memory is often the historian's most potent ally. But hovering
as it does in that strange psychological zone between nostalgia and
regret it can often strike out on its own, producing not so much the
ordered vision of the past the historian aims to develop as a picture
of The Past (even a lurid Past) in the Victorian sense. What had
seemed so right at the moment it happened becomes in retrospect
not only wrong but criminal.[5] The personal needs of the present
demand of the memoir writer a strangely skewed version of what
happened.[6] In the time of Hiss trial and McCarthy accusations, the
1930s appeared to be a period dominated by ideological commitment to Stalinism. Even for those who opposed witch hunting, there
was a lesson to be learned from the "tragic innocence" of the 1930s;
avoid any ideology at all cost.[7] Yet sober historical evaluation, con-

firming the fact of an obvious movement toward the political Left by many American intellectuals, raises serious questions about how deep and how significantly "ideological" such political interest was.[8] An examination of the literature of the period reveals an enormous number of tracts, and polemics, political, social, and economic analyses; yet when one looks for major contributions to the literature of ideology—if such a phrase can be used—the only work that seems to stand out as read by "everyone" and regarded as a "powerful instrument" is *The Coming Struggle for Power* by England's John Strachey.[9] Today it is hard to regard that work as a serious ideological contribution, and the historian must be a little puzzled that a period regarded as so heavily ideological failed to produce a Lenin or a Gramsci, or indeed even a moderately significant contribution to the literature of ideology. Ideology may indeed have been important in the Thirties, but many of the most brilliant and long-lasting contributions to political analysis written in the period were distinctly anti-ideological.[10]

Certainly there was a movement toward the Left; certainly there was a change in the intellectual and literary climate. As George Orwell put it when discussing the English-speaking literary community:

Suddenly we got out of the twilight of the gods into a sort of Boy Scout atmosphere of bare knees and community singing. The typical literary man ceases to be a cultured expatriate with a leaning towards the Church, and becomes an eager-minded schoolboy with a leaning towards communism. If the keynote of the writers of the 'twenties is "tragic sense of life," the keynote of the new writers is "serious purpose."[11]

But it is all too easy to see a political Thirties contrasting dramatically with an apolitical Twenties. And while memory seems to demand of the figures of the 1930s a *mea culpa* for having joined the Communist Party or having been a "fellow traveler" (as that period itself demanded of the writers of the 1920s a *mea culpa* for having been duped into expatriation or into some "art-for-art's-sake" movement), history demands an examination of the deeper issues that underlay such cries of regret.

The 1960s forced memory to look again at the 1930s and this time with considerable nostalgia. Fashions in clothes and furniture return to the decade for inspiration.[12] Some of what Susan Sontag has characterized under the rubric of "camp" represents an effort to recapture the mood of the Thirties, its films, its radio programs, its heroes. The literary marketplace suddenly rediscovers novels virtually unread and critically ignored in the period and now hailed

as significant: Nelson Algren's *Somebody in Boots,* the works of Na-
thanael West, Daniel Fuchs' trilogy, Henry Roth's novel of immigrant life, and even Horace McCoy's "existentialist" treatment of
the dance marathon craze, *They Shoot Horses, Don't They?*[13] Several
anthologies of the writings of the period have appeared, each discovering a verve and importance in the literary output of the period
previously denied or overlooked.[14] And some of the collected memories of the period reinforce significant new scholarship that reveals
not only a fascination with the "proletariat" and a literature and
reportage concerned with industrial workers, strikes, and coming
revolution, but also a widespread agrarian utopianism, in the North
as well as in the South, a deep interest in communitarian ventures
that smacks more of the America of Brook Farm than of the
U.S.S.R. of Five-Year Plans.[15]

The past summoned up before us by the forces of memory is
important; it is part of the record that cannot be ignored. But because it serves the special functions that memory demands, because
it is often colored by nostalgia or regret, the historian must be on
his guard. He is obligated to seek some more solid foundation that
will hold in spite of the psychological and social demands of the
moment. In building this vision of the Thirties, the historian does
not seek to debunk what the memoir writers recall or what has been
written previously about the period, but rather to understand it all
in a way that helps, at least, account for the complexities and contradictions, the confusions of flux and change.

In sketching this structure, no fact is more significant than the
general and even popular "discovery" of the concept of culture.
Obviously, the idea of culture was anything but new in the 1930s,
but there is a special sense in which the idea became widespread in
the period.[16] What had been discovered was "the inescapable inter-
relatedness of . . . things" so that culture could no longer be considered what Matthew Arnold and the intellectuals of previous
generations had often meant—the knowledge of the highest
achievements of men of intellect and art through history—but
rather reference to "all the things that a group of people inhabiting
a common geographical area do, the ways they do things and the
ways they think and feel about things, their material tools and their
values and symbols."[17] The remarkable popularity of Ruth Bene-
dict's *Patterns of Culture* (1934)—surely one of the most widely read
works of professional anthropology ever published in the United
States—provides us with a symbolic landmark. Its impact was significant; but more important, her analysis of the possibility of different
cultural patterns and the way such patterns shape and account for
individual behavior was part of a more general discovery of the idea

itself, the sense of awareness of what it means to *be* a culture, or the search to *become* a kind of culture. "The quest for culture," one student of the problem suggests, "is the search for meaning and value." [18] It is not too extreme to propose that it was during the Thirties that the idea of culture was domesticated, with important consequences. Americans then began thinking in terms of patterns of behavior and belief, values and life-styles, symbols and meanings. It was during this period that we find, for the first time, frequent reference to an "American Way of Life." The phrase "The American Dream" came into common use; it meant something shared collectively by all Americans; yet something different than the vision of an American Mission, the function of the organized nation itself. [19] It is not surprising that H. L. Mencken believed (erroneously, it appears) that the expression "grass roots" was coined in the 1930s, for during the decade it became a characteristic phrase. [20] The "promises" that Archibald MacLeish insisted were America contrast dramatically in image, rhetoric, and kind with those in *The Promise of American Life* that Herbert Croly discussed in the Progressive era. For Croly that promise depended on a definition of democracy and the creation of new institutional patterns divorced from history; it involved political, social, and economic readjustments. But for MacLeish the promises could be best found within history, a special kind of folk history:

> Jefferson knew:
> Declared it before God and before history:
> Declares it still in the remembering tomb.
> The promises were Man's; the land was his—
> Man endowed by his Creator:
> Earnest in love; perfectible by reason:
> Just and perceiving justice: his natural nature
> Clear and sweet at the source as springs in trees are.
>
> It was Man who had been promised: who should have.
> Man was to ride from the Tidewater: over the Gap:
> West and South with the water: taking the book with him:
> Taking the wheat seed: corn seed: pip of apple:
> Building liberty a farmyard wide:
> Breeding for useful labor: for good looks:
> For husbandry: humanity: for pride—
> Practicing self-respect and common decency. [21]

Clearly the two works differ in form and purpose. Further, it is obvious that we can discover common values and beliefs in the writings of the Progressive and the poet. But it is still proper to suggest that in the work of the Thirties MacLeish actually proposes a redefinition of the promise of American life, placing great emphasis on what we might call the cultural visions, questions of life-style, patterns of belief and conduct, special values and attitudes that constitute the characteristics of a special people.

It is said all too often that certain extremely popular works of fiction obtained their popular hold because they provided a means of escape from contemporary problems. It is not possible to deny this. Yet from the point of view of an increased interest in a particular life-style, in patterns of belief and their consequences, as well as in the consequences of the destruction of such cultures, it becomes possible to read in a different light the enthusiastic reception given to Oliver LaFarge's *Laughing Boy* (1929), with its touching, even sentimental plea for cultural pluralism (only one of many works in the period recalling a rich American tradition of works dating back at least to Cooper in which the Indian's admired "culture" is threatened by the white man's "civilization"), or to Margaret Mitchell's *Gone with the Wind* (1936), with its historical reconstruction of the destruction of a way of life (again, only one of many historical romances in the 1930s recounting in extraordinary detail life-styles and values different from those of the 1930s).[22]

In 1931 Stuart Chase produced a best seller, *Mexico: A Study of Two Americas*. The book was to play an important role in the whole discussion of the nature of culture, especially "popular culture."[23] But even more important, it made explicit for a large audience the kind of distinction that became increasingly characteristic of the period. Drawing specifically not only on his own experiences but also on the works of American social scientists (the Lynds' study of *Middletown* and Robert Redfield's analysis of a Mexican community), Chase sharply contrasted the urban-industrial culture of the United States and the folk culture of a more primitivist and traditional Mexico. While the United States might well have the advantages that come with "civilization," the author of *Mexico* clearly found special benefits in the simple folkways of Tepoztlán. It was a community free of the business cycle and mechanical civilization, an "organic, breathing entity." Although it had no machines, it was "impossible for Mexicans to produce the humblest thing without form and design." Time was measured by sun and climate, not by clocks. The clock was "perhaps the most tyrannical engine ever invented. To live beyond its lash is an experience in liberty which comes to few citizens of the machine age." The villages are self-sustaining. The men want neither money nor the things money can buy. And perhaps most important, Chase frequently sees in Tepoztlán echoes of what American life itself once was before machine-age Middletown developed "a culture which has found neither dignity nor unity." "While each family harvests its own fields, community spirit is strong—as in old New England barn raisings. For machineless men generally, it is both necessity and pleasure to assist, and be assisted by, one's neighbor" or "When all is said and done [the government, a kind of village communism] is 'a form of play.' Thus the working of the sublime principles of Jeffersonian democracy in Tepoztlán."[24]

As early as 1922, William Fielding Ogburn had defined the concept of "cultural lag."[25] But again, it was in the 1930s that the phrase and its implications became part of common discourse. "The depression has made us acutely aware of the fact that our brilliant technological skills are shackled to the shambling gait of an institutional Caliban," one of our most brilliant and widely read sociologists declared; his was an urgent appeal for a social science devoted to the study of the whole culture in the endeavor to develop the consequences of such knowledge for man.[26] And the distinguished historian Carl Becker mournfully announced:

Mankind has entered a new phase of human progress—a time in which the acquisition of new implements of power too swiftly outruns the necessary adjustment of habits and ideas to novel conditions created by their use.[27]

This is a far cry from the glorious hopes of a Progressive era when "progress," "power," and indeed "efficiency" or "organization" were magic words; when it was felt that the application of the very techniques of the communications revolution might create a more desirable community and society.

It is in fact possible to define as a key structural element in a historical reconstruction of the 1930s the effort to find, characterize, and adapt to an American Way of Life as distinguished from the material achievements (and the failures) of an American industrial civilization. Civilization meant technology, scientific achievement, institutions and organizations, power, and material (financial) success. The battle between "culture" and "civilization," between the quality of living and the material, organized advancement of life, was anything but new as an intellectual issue.[28] But the theme becomes central in the 1930s, and even those older followers of the Progressive tradition who valued the march of civilization and progress sought to emulate Thorstein Veblen and make from an industrial civilization a meaningful culture or way of life.[29]

However, civilization itself—in its urban-industrial form— seemed increasingly the enemy. It stood for the electricity that was used to destroy Sacco and Vanzetti; [30] or, as the hero of Algren's novel muses, " 'Civilization' must mean a thing much like that mob that had threatened his father." [31] Writers as different in other ways as Reinhold Niebuhr and Lewis Mumford wondered whether the civilization that had triumphed was worthy of the highest aspirations of man. The increased interest in the social sciences in the period and the tendency to point to the failure of the natural sciences to solve man's problems are additional evidence for a new-found cultural awareness; we may add the growth of serious study of popular culture, of cultures other than our own, or the remains of folk or other subcultures within our own. [32]

Again, the effort to define precisely the nature of American culture—as it has been historically and as it was now—characteristic of so much of the writing of the 1930s is no new effort, but it appears more widespread and central than in any previous time. (This effort is also distinctly different from that which seeks to show the development of the achievements of civilization in the United States.) Constance Rourke's *American Humor,* significantly subtitled *A Study in National Character* (1931), and her essay on "The Roots of American Culture" provide special landmarks. Rourke did not devote herself to an analysis of the great contributors to Culture; she sought rather to find the significant cultural patterns to which she might relate such figures and from which they could and must draw their material. And when Van Wyck Brooks emerged from long silence in 1936 with *The Flowering of New England* to begin his monumental multivolume cultural history, he had not so much changed his way of thinking—he still sought a usable past, some meeting ground between highbrow and lowbrow—as his method of analysis. Following in some sense the lead of Constance Rourke, he attempted in his own way to discover the basic patterns of culture, basic values and attitudes, using minor and forgotten figures as well as the major writers to show the underlying structure of the culture from which they came. [33]

The issue, then, is not that the 1930s simply produced a new era of nationalism. [34] Certainly few, if any, decades in our history could claim the production of such a vast literature—to say nothing of a vast body of films, recordings, and paintings—that described and defined every aspect of American life. It was not, then, simply that many writers and artists and critics began to sing glowingly of American life and its past. It was rather the more complex effort to seek and to define America as a culture and to create the patterns of a way of life worth understanding. The movement had begun in the 1920s; by the 1930s it was a crusade. *America in Search of Culture* William Aylott Orton had called his not always friendly analysis of this phenomenon in 1933. The search was to continue throughout the decade in the most overwhelming effort ever attempted to document in art, reportage, social science, and history the life and values of the American people.[35]

If there was an increased awareness of the concept of culture and its implications as well as a growing self-consciousness of an American Way or a native culture of value, there were also forces operating to shape that culture into a heightened sensitivity of itself as a culture. The development of systematic and supposedly scientific methods of measuring the way "the people" thought and believed is certainly one important example. The idea of public opinion was an old one (it can be traced back at least to Tocqueville) and the political, social, and even economic consequences of such opinion had been studied by a number of serious students: Lowell, Lippmann, and Bernays, to point to the most obvious examples. The Creel Committee of World War I days had already paid careful attention to the advantages and special techniques of manipulating such opinion. But it was not until 1935, when George Gallup established the American Institute of Public Opinion, that "polling" became commonplace in American life. Now Americans had "empirical" evidence of how they felt and thought regarding the major issues of the day and generally shared attitudes and beliefs. It was easier now to find the core of values and opinions that united Americans, the symbols that tied them together, that helped define the American Way. It was not just the discovery of techniques that might be manipulated by experts to produce desired results, although this was a part of what happened; the polls themselves became a force, an instrument of significance, not only for the discovery and molding of dominant cultural patterns, but also for their reinforcement.[36]

Other technological developments played an even more vital role. The decade of the Thirties was a most dramatic era of sound and sight. It is impossible to recall the period without recourse to special sounds: the "talkies," the machine-gun precision of the dancing feet in Busby Berkeley's musical extravaganzas, the "Big Bands," the voices of Amos and Andy, to say nothing of the magic of Franklin Roosevelt's Fireside Addresses. For our immediate purposes, examples of the consequences of a new age of sound can best be found by looking briefly at some of the effects of national radio networks. Through their radio sets a unique view of the world and a way of interpreting it came to the American people. Nothing more dramatically illustrates the power of this newfound sound medium than the response of the Orson Welles Mercury Theater dramatization of H. G. Wells' story of a supposed Martian invasion. Using the recently developed news broadcasting techniques expertly, Welles' company made thousands accept (as they were used to accepting) the rhetoric of a radio show as a description of reality, the resulting panic is famous.[37] Sound helped mold uniform national responses; it helped create or reinforce uniform national values and beliefs in a way that no previous medium had ever before been able to do. Roosevelt was able to create a new kind of Presidency and a new kind of political and social power partly through his brilliant use of the medium.

The photograph and the film, too, changed the nature of cultural communication in America. Unlike the printed word in newspapers and books, the photograph affected even those who could not or would not read. The Thirties brought home the impact of the image created by the photograph in a more universal way. *Life,* founded in 1936, can perhaps be credited with the invention of the "picture essay"; however, it is but one example of the novel way Americans could experience the world. Luce's extraordinary empire also produced "The March of Time," the most brilliant of the newly developed newsreels that provided a fresh way of understanding events. The whole idea of the documentary—not with words alone but with sight and sound—makes it possible to see, know, and feel the details of life, its styles in different places, to feel oneself part of some other's experience.[38]

We are not yet in a position to evaluate the full consequence of these events. But certainly it is possible to suggest that the newly developed media and their special kinds of appeal helped reinforce a social order rapidly disintegrating under economic and social pressures that were too great to endure, and helped create an environment in which the sharing of common experience, be they of hunger, dustbowls, or war, made the uniform demand for action and reform more striking and urgent. The unity provided deserves some special role in the story of the 1930s. Whatever else might be said about the New Deal, its successes and its failures, it is obviously true that it was a sociological and psychological triumph. From the very outset of his presidential campaign in 1932, Franklin Roosevelt showed himself fully aware of the importance of symbols. "Let it be symbolic," he told the Convention that had nominated him, in his acceptance speech made after an unprecedented flight to Chicago to receive personally the leadership bestowed upon him, "that I broke the tradition. Let it be from now on the task of our Party to break foolish traditions."[39] The history of the ill-fated NRA offers a series of examples of a brilliant sense for the symbolic in the administration itself: the Blue Eagle, the display of flags, the parades. Roosevelt on radio was to reach out to each American in his living room and make him feel that the Administration was thinking specifically of him, that he had a place in society. The film and the picture essay brought the figures of power, in every aspect of their activity, personal as well as public, into the immediate experience of most Americans.

Even the lowly soap opera, the most frequently mocked of radio's innovations, played a role in reinforcing fundamental values and in providing the intimate experience of other people's lives so that millions of housewives knew they were neither alone nor unique in their problems. Timeless and consistent in portraying patterns of crisis and recovery, they provided a sense of continuity, assuring the triumph of generally shared values and beliefs, no matter what "reality" in the form of social and economic conditions might suggest.[40]

It is possible to see in the notorious "soaps" the operation of what might be called the force and power of myth. In his famous American Writers' Congress address in 1935, Kenneth Burke analyzed the function of myth in society. He argued that a myth was "the social tool for welding a sense of interrelationship by which the carpenter and the mechanic, though differently occupied, can work together for a common social end."[41] He was concerned, it is true, in this paper with the role of revolutionary myths and symbols, but an analysis of the 1930s reveals how significant a role the new media played in providing a huge public with a body of symbols and myths. In this sense, it might not be unfair to consider the extraordinary mythic role the absurd soap opera played. The form may appear ridiculous to some today, but then so do many myths once socially operative that are nonetheless later discarded.

The photograph, the radio, the moving picture—these were not new, but the sophisticated uses to which they were put created a special community of all Americans (possibly an international community) unthinkable previously. The shift to a culture of sight and sound was of profound importance; it increased our self-awareness as a culture; it helped create a unity of response and action not previously possible; it made us more susceptible than ever to those who would mold culture and thought. In this connection, it is possible to see how these developments also heightened a growing interest among social and political thinkers in the role of symbol, myth, and rhetoric. Kenneth Burke's study of the significance of Hitler's rhetoric and of the importance of the careful development of revolutionary symbolism in the United States showed how important such factors were in shaping cultures, the vast power (and therefore dangers) involved in language and symbol.[42] The major works of Thurmond Arnold, one of the more original thinkers of the period, deal with political life, not in terms of ideology or the rational implementation of philosophies, but in terms of the role of "folklore" and symbols.[43] And perhaps the leading academic student of political life, Harold Lasswell, developed a whole school of political analysis dealing with psychological and sociological factors barely touched on in previous periods.[44] While a Progressive generation was much interested in problems of communications and even made small but significant use of the photograph, the painting, the cartoon, it is not possible to compare this with the developments in the 1930s, when an unusual sense of sight and sound, a peculiar interest in symbol, myth, and language, created a novel kind of community, breaking down barriers, creating often new common experiences for millions. For no matter how great their interest in communication, how deep their concern for the social role of the arts, the Progressives relied primarily and most profoundly on the written word, the rational argument on the printed page. They were a generation of writers who produced an enormous political literature; but they did not and could not make their appeal to the ear and eye, with a sense of symbol and rhetoric that compared to the stunning techniques and effects developed during the 1930s. One significant difference between the two eras is this: the Progressives were people of the book; the children of the 1930s were people of the picture and the radio.

In a stimulating essay on "The New Deal as a Cultural Phenomenon," T. V. Smith suggests that "sportsmanship is the key to contemporary American life." Speaking of the American way of life itself, Smith argues:

The *game* is a fitting symbol. Long before baseball came to furnish the chief metaphor of American life there was (and there remains) another game— a game of cards: "poker" it is called—in which "to deal" was but to initiate a cooperative activity that could be its own exciting reward, even to those who "lost their shirts" in its honor. Politics is in common American parlance a game, and in expert parlance it is "the great American game." Moreover, the symbolism carried over into business: a deal is a trade, any transaction for gain from which both sides are presumed to profit. Thus the very name of the Rooseveltian movement in question raises connotative echoes in the culture organic to America, in its full multi-dimensionality.[45]

In this passage Smith has done more than to suggest additional evidence about the cultural responsiveness of the New Deal in its selection of symbols. For culture is reflected in and shaped by its games, something analysts writing in the 1930s themselves understood.[46] Most social historians take great pains to point out the significant increase in popular participation in sports, the development of new games and fads, the enormous increase in various forms of gambling in the period.[47] Too often, once again, these facts are explained as the search for escape—a truism to be sure—when they demand more fundamental analysis in terms of the *kind* of escape they propose. The dramatic increase is in special types of gaming, games of competition and chance, games frequently involving co-operation and carefully arranged regulations and limits. The "de-mocratization" of golf and tennis in the 1930s provides a special outlet for the competitive spirit the traditional values of the culture demands and which cannot easily be satisfied in the "real" world of economic and social life. The Parker Brothers' fantastically success-ful board game "Monopoly" enables would-be entrepreneurs to "make a killing" of the kind the economic conditions of the times all but prohibited. Dance marathons, roller derbies, six-day bicycle races, flagpole-sitting contests, goldfish-swallowing competitions—these are not just foolish ways out of the rat race, but rather alter-native (if socially marginal) patterns duplicating in structure what institutionalized society demanded and normally assumed it could provide. Thus the bank-nights and the Bingo games, the extraor-dinary interest in the Irish Sweepstakes, the whole range of patterns of "luck" and "success" offered on the fringes of social respectability but certainly within the range of social acceptance—these provided a way to maintain and reinforce essential values, to keep alive a sense of hope. Roger Caillois, in his brilliant book *Man, Play and Games*, suggests that there are "corruptions" of games as well as cultural forms found at the margins of the social order: resort to violence, superstition, alienation, and even mental illness, alcohol-ism, and the taking of drugs.[48] Certainly, there is evidence that among some elements in the population such corruptions could be found in the 1930s. Yet the striking fact remains that the increase in the particular kind of games that did dominate that aspect of life in the 1930s tended to provide significant social reinforcement. Even the dances of the period marked a return to an almost folk-style pattern of large-scale participation and close cooperation. The holding of block parties that took place even in slum areas of large cities indicates special qualities of life in the 1930s, a fact not over-looked by those whose memory of the period is colored by nostalgia. As Caillois tells us:

Any corruption of the principle of play means the abandonment of those precarious and doubtful conventions that it is always permissible, if not profitable, to deny, but arduous adoption of which is a milestone in the development of civilization. If principles of play in effect correspond to power instincts . . . , it is readily understood that they can be positively and creatively gratified under ideal and circumscribed conditions, which in every case prevail in the rules of play. Left to themselves, destructive and frantic as are all instincts, these basic impulses can hardly lead to any but disastrous consequences. Games discipline instincts and institutionalize them. For the time that they afford formal and limited satisfaction, they educate, enrich, and immunize the mind against their virulence. At the same time, they are made fit to contribute usefully to the enrichment and the establishment of various patterns of culture.[49]

Commentators are right, then, to indicate the importance of the kinds of games played in the 1930s.

There is also the widespread and continuous use of the game metaphor—not only in the business and politics of the period— useful to writers in indicating the meaning or the meaninglessness of life. When Robert Sherwood sought an appropriate image for the fatuous and yet vicious forces of nationalism and international business, he too selected a game of cards. In his pacifist assault on those forces, insensitive to the human condition and hell-bent on destruction, he allows his heroine to speak of God:

Yes . . . We don't do half enough justice to Him. Poor, lonely old soul. Sitting up there in heaven, with nothing to do, but play solitaire. Poor, dear God. Playing Idiot's Delight. The game that never means anything, and never ends.[50]

And from another perspective entirely, William Saroyan built his sentimental tribute to the gentle, innocent, and good American people out of a whole series of games and toys. Most memorable, perhaps, is the pinball machine that the bartender assures Willie he cannot beat. Willie undertakes to try; he

stands straight and pious before the contest. Himself vs. the machine. Willie vs. Destiny. His skill and daring vs. the cunning and trickery of the novelty industry of America, and the whole challenging world. He is the last of the American pioneers, with nothing more to fight but the machine, with no other reward than lights going on and off, and six nickels for one. Before him is the last champion, the machine. He is the last challenger. . . .

In the last act of *The Time of Your Life*, Willie finally beats the machine. Saroyan tells us "the machine groans." And then

the machine begins to make a special kind of noise. Lights go on and off. Some red, some green. A bell rings loudly six times. . . . An American flag jumps up. Willie comes to attention. Salutes. "Oh boy (he says) what a beautiful country." A loud music-box version of the song "America." (Everyone in the barroom rises, singing). "My country, 'tis of thee, sweet land of liberty, of thee I sing." Everything quiets down. . . . Willie is thrilled, amazed, delighted. Everybody has watched the performance of the defeated machine. . . .[51]

The analysis of the structure that underlies an historical picture of the 1930s suggests some tentative conclusions at this point. First, there was in the discovery of the idea of culture and its wide-scale application a critical tool that could shape a critical ideal, especially as it was directed repeatedly against the failures and meaninglessness of an urban-industrial civilization. Yet often it was developed in such ways as to provide significant devices for conserving much of the existing structure. A search for the "real" America could become a new kind of nationalism; the idea of an American Way could reinforce conformity. The reliance on basic culture patterns, stressed by further development of public opinion, studies of myth, symbol, folklore, the new techniques of the mass media, even the games of the period could and did have results far more conservative than radical, no matter what the intentions of those who originally championed some of the ideas and efforts.

Other studies bear out this conservative trend—no matter what memory may tell us about disorganization and a Red menace. The Lynds' return to Middletown in the 1930s led to the discovery that the schools of that community, for example, had had their heyday of freedom in education in the 1920s; by 1935 "the culture was tightening its grip on the schools to insure that 'only the right things' were being taught."[52] And perhaps the most significant experiment in higher education in the decade under Robert M. Hutchins at the University of Chicago can be considered an effort to reassert traditional values and standards in a retreat from the educational philosophy of the supposed followers of John Dewey. An important study of white acceptance of jazz documents the fact that when such music left the confines of the smaller black subculture and achieved wide-scale circulation and popularity in the larger national community through radio, records, and the Big Bands of the period, the lyrics of older jazz and blues as well as new works created tended to lack the bite and social criticism found in the jazz of the 1920s and earlier. In fact, lyrics tended to be bland, mouthing even more forcefully the commonplace and accepted values and beliefs, personal and social.[53]

In no field, however, was the consequence of the new approach stressing the role of existing patterns of culture to be as significant and striking as in the realm of popular psychology, or in that strange combination of religion and psychology that frequently ruled in the 1930s as a substitute for liberal Protestantism, as Donald

Meyer has brilliantly shown.[54] Any student of the 1930s cannot but be impressed with the enormous body of literature designed to instruct and inform on ways to succeed.[55] It was the great age of the how-to-do-it book. But what is most unusual about all such literature, in view of the enormous critical assault on capitalism and even the widely held assumption among many, right, left, and center, that capitalism was doomed, is its initial principle: failure is personal, not social, and success can be achieved by some adjustment, not in the social order but in the individual personality. Dale Carnegie's *How to Win Friends and Influence People* was the best seller of the period, and its publication in 1936 is a landmark for the study of American popular culture. In simplest terms, Carnegie called for adjustment to the existing order. Everyone wanted to feel important; the way to get ahead was to *make* other people feel important. Smile! In the same year Henry C. Link published his best-selling *The Return to Religion*. In it religion joined hands with psychology "to promote not ego strength but surrender." Urging people to "behave themselves" rather than to "know themselves," Link emphasized the importance of work and of just keeping busy (even by dancing, playing cards, or joining clubs). Most important of all was the development of personality. Link's work in psychological testing led him to invent a method of "testing" personality, a way of measuring "Personality Quotient." PQ was clearly more important than IQ. Make people like you; fit in; develop habits and skills that "interest and serve other people." Here again the radio soap operas played their reinforcement role. They repeated the line of Carnegie and Link: Just Plain Bill kept smiling and Ma Perkins kept busy. Everyone tried to fit in and be well liked. The wisdom of the sages of the soaps—and few were without their wise man or woman— follows closely the patterns of advice suggested by the Carnegies and the Links and the Norman Vincent Peales who offered similar proposals during the decade. The stress on personal reasons for success and failure is also typical. New business ventures, relying heavily on the new methods of advertising, made possible by the new media, proposed a host of products to help individuals guard against failure and perhaps even achieve success. New "diseases" could be countered with new remedies: bad breath, body odor, stained teeth, dishpan hands. Advertising also assured us that a host of new mail-order courses might help us achieve success by home study; all we needed to do was improve our spelling or our vocabulary, learn how to develop our personalities, develop our talent for drawing or writing.[56]

All this stress on conforming to what was demanded by society around us, all this emphasis on "fitting in," had its more sophisticated counterpart in the newly emerging field of human relations management. In his important work in the 1930s, Elton Mayo urged adjustment to the patterns of industrial organization from the perspective not of the worker, aiming to "get ahead," but from that of the manager, anxious to provide an effective and happy work force.[57] Mayo speaking from a post at Harvard Business School is certainly a more learned and sophisticated student of human affairs than Dale Carnegie or Henry C. Link, and yet his work strangely seems of a piece with theirs insofar as it seeks adjustment to the existing and ongoing patterns of cultural development. Other intellectuals not influenced by development in popular culture might find, interestingly enough, something at least analogous happening in other areas of professional psychology in the period. For the intellectual community the emergence of what has been called American Neo-Freudianism is undoubtedly the most important development. It may well be that in the Thirties no representative work of the group was more widely read and influential than Karen Horney's *The Neurotic Personality of Our Time* (1937). Her analysis of the problem of anxiety argues that it is the contradictions within the culture that bring about specific neurotic patterns in individuals. The attitudes that prevail within the culture to which we relate provide us with the basic conflicts that create our neuroses, and our culture itself is patterned by the very nature of our anxieties, providing institutionalized paths of attempted escape from anxiety. The neurotic personality reflects the conflicts within the culture; the culture provides the mechanisms to escape from anxieties. It is not without reason that the Neo-Freudian position has often been accused of advocating an adjustment to the patterns of culture as a way of curing more serious problems of anxiety, and it is not completely unfair to read Neo-Freudianism in this aspect as a high-brow translation of what we have already suggested marked the mainstream of popular psychology in the 1930s.[58]

If the idea of culture and the self-awareness of cultural involvement play crucial roles in a structuring of the history of the 1930s, another idea—not unrelated as we shall see—also cannot be overlooked: the idea of commitment. A commonplace of contemporary language, the idea and its current forms came to significant fruition in the 1930s.[59] Hemingway's heroes of the 1920s had a sense of obedience to a code, to be sure, but perhaps nowhere in our fiction is the basic idea brought so much to the center of consciousness as in the mystery writing of the 1930s. This genre was extraordinarily important in the period; more significant (in quality and in number of volumes published) detective fiction was produced in the decade than in any previous period.[60] Unfortunately, too few historians have followed up Professor William Aydelotte's superbly suggestive article, "The Detective Story as a Historical Source."[61] Here we cannot detail all the consequences of the popularity of the form in the 1930s. But we can look at an early and archetypical detective hero of the period and see the form the idea of commitment begins to take. Sam Spade first appears in Dashiell Hammett's masterpiece of 1930, *The Maltese Falcon,* and was immortalized in Humphrey Bogart's portrayal in John Huston's film version of the novel. Few who have read the book or seen the film can forget Sam's last great speech to Brigid O'Shaughnessy, the woman he loves, the woman who offers him love and money (both of which the culture values highly). Yet Brigid is a murderess and Sam vows to surrender her to the police. His argument forms a whole new cultural stance for several generations:

Listen. This isn't a damned bit of good. You'll never understand me, but I'll try once more. . . . When a man's partner is killed he's supposed to do something about it. It doesn't make any difference what you thought of him. He was your partner and you're supposed to do something about it. Then it happens we were in the detective business. Well, when one of your organization gets killed it's bad for business to let the killer get away with it. . . . Third, I'm a detective and expecting me to run criminals down and let them go free is like asking a dog to catch a rabbit and let it go. It can be done, all right, and sometimes it is done, but it's not the natural thing. . . . Fourth, no matter what I wanted to do now it would be absolutely impossible for me to let you go without having myself dragged to the gallows with the others. Next, I've no reason in God's world to think I can trust you and if I did this and got away with it you'd have something on me that you could use whenever you happened to want to. . . . Sixth, . . . since I've got something on you, I couldn't be sure you wouldn't decide to shoot a hole in *me* some day. . . . It's easy to be nuts about you. . . . But I don't know what that amounts to. Does anybody ever? But suppose I do? What of it? Maybe next month I won't. . . . Well, if I send you over I'll be sorry as hell—I'll have some rotten nights—but that'll pass. . . . If that doesn't mean anything to you forget it and we'll make it this: I won't because all of me wants to—wants to say to hell with the consequences and do it—and because—God damn you—you've counted on that with me the same as you counted on that with the others. . . . I won't play the sap for you.[62]

This is a remarkable passage, and it is in its way especially a passage that could have come only out of the 1930s: hard, yet romantic (Spade will wait for Brigid until she is released from prison); pragmatic, yet with rigid adherence to a special code of belief and values; commonplace, yet strangely elevated in mood. Most remarkable of all, Sam expects Brigid to understand and accept, and Hammett expects his audience to understand and accept. It represents a remarkable effacement of the desires of the ego and yet its adherence to a particular scheme of values (meaning at the same time the rejection of still other things of value) allows for survival itself.

The very nature of the period and of the new dominant approach in the idea of culture created special problems for the individual. To be sure, the problems suggested by "individualism" as early as the 1830s, when Tocqueville coined the expression, was whether or not the individual could survive in an age of mass civilization and industrialization. But the effort could be made nonetheless: witness the frequently wild antinomian spirit that infected so many of the young intellectuals of the 1920s with their hopes of asserting the supremacy and persistence of their unique personalities and the survival of their own egos. But the "cultural" approach of the 1930s seemed (even as it resisted the claims of "civilization") to pose still further problems rather than easy solutions. As John Dewey explained:

The function of culture in determining what elements of human nature are dominant and their pattern or arrangement in connection with one another goes beyond any special point to which attention is called. It affects the very idea of individuality. The idea that human nature is inherently and exclusively individual is itself a product of a cultural individualistic movement. The idea that the mind and consciousness are intrinsically individual did not even occur to any one for much the greater part of human history.[63]

Thus individualism can exist only if the culture permits it, that is, if it can have a necessary function within the structure of culture itself.

There was a deep current of pessimism in the Thirties about the possible survival of individualism. In 1935, Robert Sherwood gave Broadway audiences *The Petrified Forest,* a play in which the rootless, wandering poet-intellectual and the fiercely independent gangster both represent types doomed to extinction by society, types as dead as the trees of the Petrified Forest itself. The drive for unity and conformity (ideals often reinforced by the concept of culture itself) that appears such a striking fact in the history of the period —no matter how noble and desirable the end—threatens the survival of individualism. Karen Horney's discussion of solutions to the problem of anxiety nowhere suggests a rebuilding of the ego so it can stand alone.[64] Yet the hunger for such survival of "I" remains; the search for immortality persists as an acute source of anxiety.

Observe Edward G. Robinson's memorable characterization of the title role in *Little Caesar,* a film of 1931. In an early scene, he explains to his friend why he must have a major career in crime. He is not fighting back against social injustices done him; he is not trying to escape from the ghetto and the slum. The women and the money fail to attract him, and he expresses no interest in the excitement of a contest between law and outlaw. He is Rico, he announces proudly, and "I want to *be* someone." In the film's final scene, lying shot and dying under a billboard, he exclaims almost without belief, "Mother of Mercy, is this the end of Rico?"

Thus, too, the "movements" and "ideologies" of a period—and certainly of the 1930s—helped people to "be" somebody. Malcolm Cowley comments on the advantages Communist Party membership afforded:

There was an enormous prestige at that time for people who belonged to the party. They were listened to as if they had received advice straight from God; as if they weren't quite inspired prophets, but had been at meetings where the word was passed down from Mount Sinai. . . . So they had a sort of mana that surrounded them. . . .[65]

One of the first novels written in the period that could be called political, Tess Slesinger's *The Unpossessed* (1934) treats with considerable satiric effect the social and psychological uses to which middle-class intellectuals and writers put their involvement in the political Left.

Yet status and prestige represent only one part of the story of the survival of the ego. The period was one in which social anxieties heightened personal anxieties. Cowley, commenting on the large number of breakdowns among intellectuals, expressed his own belief that Party membership provided a way of helping "these people with psychological problems [who] were looking for some cure outside themselves."[66] Certainly the method could easily fit into one or more of the "dodges" Karen Horney tells us we build into our culture in our effort to escape our anxieties. Katherine Anne Porter, writing in 1939, saw the political tendency since 1930 as

to the last degree a confused, struggling, drowning-man-and-straw sort of thing, stampede of panicked crowd, each man trying to save himself—one at a time trying to work out his horrible confusions. . . . I suffer from it, and I try to work my way out to some firm ground of personal belief, as others do. I have times of terror and doubt and indecision, I am confused in all the uproar of shouting maddened voices. . . . I should like to save myself, but I have no assurance that I can. . . .[67]

"I suspect that it was the question of my own fate that took me to Spain as much as it was any actual convulsion going on in that country," Josephine Herbst shrewdly comments.[68]

There is, of course, a significant difference between becoming a gangster and joining the battle against fascism, no matter what a crusader against the Red Decade might think. But the act of commitment itself had a psychological and sociological significance often unrelated to the specific nature of the profession or movement. For some the act itself could be defined in ways that made it sufficient in itself. For Ernest Hemingway, the Spanish War presented an easy and positive answer for the individual (Herbst tells us that Hemingway was "at home" in Spain and that she was not). For him the war offered

a part in something which you could believe in wholly and completely and in which you felt an absolute brotherhood with others who were engaged in it. . . . Your own death seemed of complete unimportance; only a thing to be avoided because it would interfere with the performance of your duty. But the best thing was that here was something you could do about this feeling and this necessity too, you could fight.[69]

The simplicity of such an act of commitment almost overwhelms, especially in Hemingway's rhetorical flight. This act Hemingway describes is simple, clear, direct; it is obvious and essential.

Yet not everyone could find such immediate satisfaction in his act of commitment. The act might be necessary, but there still remained in fact new dilemmas developed as a consequence of the act itself. Compare Herbst's response with Hemingway's:

I was probably trying to find some answers to the confusions in my own mind. The thirties had come in like a hurricane. An entire young generation had been swept up in a violent protest against the realities of events. But the answers were numbing. The slogans were pieces of twine throttling something that was struggling. Phrases like "the toiling masses" did not answer terrible questions. There were always people, real people, each was an individual spirit with its own peculiar past. The Spanish War was doubtless the last war in which individuals were to enter fully with their individual might. But what a welter of conflicting views this implies! The soldier is not only fighting *against* an enemy but also *for* something beyond.[70]

The special dilemma for the intellectual that this passage reveals is central to any serious study of the 1930s, but Hemingway's contemporary response was perhaps more characteristic of writers of the times.

How important was the ability to make some commitment, to associate with some idea of culture, may best be seen if we look briefly at those who lacked it. Frederick J. Hoffman tells us:

The age of the Great Depression . . . was of course the time of the marginal man *malgre lui*. Time and again, he moves by necessity from place to place, vainly seeking employment, dreadfully aware of his lack of status, his emotional reaction varying from extreme despair to extreme anger.[71]

The 1930s had its forced wanderers, its vagabonds, its tramps. Indeed, such "marginal men" became the subjects of a literature that has emerged as a special legacy from the period. Such marginality is not desired or accepted voluntarily; life on the road is not romanticized, nor is it a source of any genuine pleasure or special wisdom. It is not a journey that ends in discovery or explanation. There is little to suggest the appeal of any particular ideology (even anarchism, so popular in the literature of marginal men in previous periods, is almost strikingly absent). Seldom can the wanderer find alleviation of distress and anxiety by adherence to a group or a community of any lasting kind. Marginal men do not participate in any culture, real or imagined. They do not listen to the radio, go to the movies, or read *Life* magazine. They do not participate in sports or play traditional games. Here, rather, among the marginal men we find those corruptions of games of which Caillois speaks; here is the violence (sometimes personal, sometimes social, but generally in the end without meaning), the alienation, the drunkenness, the unacceptable and antisocial forms of "play." Even the strike takes on this aspect; it seems almost a perversion of sport without purpose or meaning, since it is generally lost or blunted. It can provide, for the moment, common purpose and brotherhood, the suggested beginnings of a pattern of belief or a way of life—as other events or acts also can do on occasion—but such common action is too easily dissolved, and the individual marginal man is on the road again, the road to nowhere. He has no commitments and no culture (in the sense that these words are used here). The phenomenon produced a strong body of literature: Edward Dahlberg's *Bottom Dogs* (1930), Jack Conroy's *The Disinherited* (1933), and Nelson Algren's *Somebody in Boots* (1935) are among the very best. These works, however, have become more admired and treated with fuller critical seriousness in our time than they were in the Thirties.

Only one novel that might be said to be of the same genre was greeted with considerable enthusiasm when it appeared, John Steinbeck's *The Grapes of Wrath* (1939). Yet it is a novel of the enforced wanderings of marginal men with a difference, in fact with several crucial differences. Marginal man here was not alone; the strength and power of the family as a unit went with him. Frequently, he shared with other travelers a strong sense of common purpose and destiny, even the incipient form of a culture. There was an end in view: sometimes a romantic agrarian utopia, sometimes at least a sense of revolutionary enthusiasm and optimism. And the Joad family most especially, therefore, had what can be defined as a sense of commitment.

Thus it was characteristic in the 1930s for the idea of commitment to merge with some idea of culture and to produce, at least for a time, participation in some group, community, or movement. The 1930s was *the* decade of participation and belonging. This is obvious on almost every level of cultural development. The 1920s saw a growth of spectator sports; the 1930s mark a new era in sports participation. The 1920s found the intellectuals in revolt *against* the village; the 1930s witnessed the intellectuals in flight *to* the village. Such generalizations are obviously extreme, yet they do suggest a basic truth about the decade: the need to feel one's self a part of some larger body, some larger sense of purpose. Harold Clurman's excellent memoir of the Group Theater and the Thirties, *The Fervent Years* (1945), makes clear that it was not only the excitement of new plays and new theatrical ideas, or even a new sense of social purpose, that made the venture memorable. It was the sense of working together, sharing ideas and beliefs, the sense of being a "group."

It is not possible to come away from wide reading in the literature of the period without some sense of the excitement—even the enthusiasm and optimism—shared by many. They *were* "fervent years." A participant in the intellectual life of the decade comments that there was an "almost universal liveliness that countervailed universal suffering."[72] The historian must wonder whether the "facts" warranted such enthusiasm. Depression problems were not solved during the period, although they were considerably alleviated. Yet even while political events at home suggested some grounds for hope (although surely no grounds to anticipate any "revolutionary" triumph of the workers), abroad the international order was rapidly collapsing and the menace of fascism constantly growing. One explanation for this mood may very well be found in the additional "fact" of increased participation: in groups, in movements, in what appeared to be the major action of the time.

Political "participation" has most consistently attracted the attention of scholars and citizens who revisit the 1930s. The growth of the Communist Party and its position as a rallying point, at least for a time, of considerable numbers of outstanding American intellectual and artistic figures helped create the image of the decade as heavily political. Such political participation has received excellent scholarly treatment recently; we are now able to understand such activity more fully than ever before. Yet the historian analyzing the culture of the Thirties must attempt to appraise this activity in terms of the total record. There were political tracts; there were petitions and manifestoes. The Communist Party did receive considerable political support, especially in 1932, from leading intellectuals. But somehow there also seems to have been a paucity of political ideas and, more significantly, an inability to maintain effective political stances except on negative issues: against Franco, against the menace of fascism, against the dehumanization of Depression America. When it came to vital issues of political involvement as distinct from commitment to ideas and often vaguer ideals, that is, issues of power, strategy, and organization, which are the lifeblood of actual political movements, the Party soon found itself divided; each issue of genuine political importance brought not only division into factions but actual withdrawal of increasing numbers of intellectuals from the Party itself.[73] It was easy, as Herbst suggested, to be against; it was harder by far to look beyond for something.

The genius of the Communist movement of the 1930s was its ability to use the obvious social and psychological needs of the period. It recruited effectively individuals who had no other place to go and who sought to belong and to do, those who had a commitment to ideals shared by those in the Party if not complete knowledge or understanding of its ideology. There were sentiments and values that united members; there was in those remarkably confused and complicated times little political knowledge and intelligence among intellectuals, whose training and preparation usually left them ill-suited to face the political realities of a collapsing capitalist order. And the Party offered more than political participation: there were its camps, its discussion groups, its magazines, even its dances and social affairs, its lecturers, its writers' congresses. For the first time in the twentieth century, the Party had attempted to organize writers and intellectuals, and to bring them together to exchange views, political and aesthetic, to feel themselves an important part of the American scene. This was an important development—and a major contribution of the Party—for writers who had grown up in the 1920s with the view that America offered no place for the artist and the intellectual. (The New Deal, of course, in this area offered considerable competition, with its own projects in the arts, in the theater, and in the Federal Writers' Project.) There was, furthermore, great satisfaction for many in

the idea of uniting themselves with the mass or the group, and being not leader, but just one in the ranks of the great army that was marching toward a new dawn. If they could forget themselves, they could solve their psychological problems. So there was a great deal of almost religious feeling going on at the same time among people you would never suspect of having it, and who tried to hide their religious feeling in talk of Marxian dialectic. . . . The feeling was there.[74]

It is all too facile to describe the commitment to the Left as a religious surrogate, and yet it is a fact of some importance that American Protestantism was suffering in the 1930s. Liberal Protestantism had tended to disintegrate into a strange breed of mind-cure and positive thinking; the Social Gospel found itself usurped by the political magic and action of the New Deal; and the mighty search for "political realism" among intellectual leaders of Protestantism was just itself in process.[75] The rise of Neo-Thomism at the University of Chicago and the efforts of the Southern Agrarians in the period offer additional evidence of an effort to make religion and religious values relevant to society. It is therefore not far-fetched to see for some in the movement to the political Left quasi-religious motives.

In a sense, Granville Hicks came to Communism through youth groups of the Universalist Church, theological school, and the teaching of Bible at Smith College. But there was perhaps something even more important, as a reviewer of his memoir of the period has observed:

His native feeling for the decentralized, for the communion of the small group, for collective action coming from individuals drawn together for a common purpose, acting out their parts of a common aim, is thoroughly consistent with his life pattern as it is revealed to us in *Part of the Truth*.[76]

Thus Hicks' participation in the Communist movement of the 1930s seems somehow related to his later enthusiastic efforts to make the small town an operative factor in American culture.[77]

Mary McCarthy selected a most apt image when she called her novel about the 1930s *The Group*. In addition to the Communist Party, the various groups within it, and the leagues of authors, there were the Southern Agrarians, who in 1930 issued a group manifesto, *I'll Take My Stand,* and joined in yet another, *Who Owns America?* in 1936. Allen Tate indicated his desire to participate in more genuine and meaningful group life than offered by industrial capitalism: a producers' capitalism, the peasant community, the religious community, or a sense of regional community.[78] Ralph Borsodi was not only a widely read critic of modern urban living who wrote a *Flight from the City* (1933), but he also organized Homestead Units, one of many communitarian ventures in the period. Arthur Morgan, of Antioch College and the TVA, founded in 1939 an organization designed "to promote the interests of the community as a basic social institution and concerned with the economic, recreational, educational, cultural, and spiritual development of its members."[79]

In part this was a continuation of a tradition well established during the Progressive era, and perhaps traceable to the mid-nineteenth-century movements, but there is little question that the 1930s saw a general revival of communitarian concern. Stuart Chase's description of the Mexican village has already been cited. Lewis Mumford looked forward to the creation of a new, human city while he looked back with considerable enthusiasm to the achievements of the medieval city.[80] Black Mountain College, which opened in September of 1934, advanced a special communitarian ideal of college living. There was an unusual equality between students and faculty; they built the institution together, literally sharing even tasks of physical construction. The students developed a strong tradition of native arts and craft work as a part of their college experience.

Thornton Wilder's sentimental hit of 1938, *Our Town*, provided a far different picture of village life than, for example, Sherwood Anderson's *Winesburg, Ohio*, his "book of grotesques" published in 1919. Clifford Odets treated the idea of the strike almost as ritual: *Waiting for Lefty* (1935), his vision of labor solidarity and common action, also created a sense of audience participation in a special community with the workers in the play. The unions were or tried to be more than economic institutions: union membership meant group consciousness, and the union supplied important social functions, sometimes even cultural ones; for example, *Pins and Needles* (1937), the International Ladies' Garment Workers' marvelous theatrical review, which delighted audiences of the 1930s and once again audiences in the 1960s. The MacDowell Colony, a center affording artists the opportunity to work and live away from the demands of jobs and other kinds of social pressures, seemed to some almost a communitarian dream come true in this period. And Mary McCarthy was to satirize in *The Oasis* (1949) the kind of communitarian venture attempted by some intellectuals in the 1930s. There was a new interest in "the folk society" that led to a reappreciation of Indian life, especially pre-Columbian Indian life, despoiled by the coming of European civilization.[81]

Individual acts of commitment led to particular visions of culture, often through participation in specific groups or movements or hoped-for participation in ideal ones. This search often involved a new emphasis on tradition. Mention has already been made of the search for an American tradition. But the movement went beyond this. Robert Penn Warren has said, "The past is always a rebuke to the present,"[82] and the 1930s indeed demonstrated this special use of history, so different from the uses to which history had been put in the Progressive period or in the debunking 1920s. Not only did the Agrarians attempt to create a picture of the pre–Civil War

South as an aid to the development of their twentieth-century Agrarian stand; even those of left-wing persuasion found much in the past—miniature class wars, slave revolts, revolutionary heroes —as V. F. Calverton shows in his *The Awakening of America* (1939). Gilbert Seldes' *Mainland* (1936) found much to praise in our past; as a work it stands in sharp contrast to his depressing and negative report on Depression America, *The Year of the Locust* (1932). The professional historians' more favorable assessment of previously despised Puritanism led to a reassessment of our entire intellectual past. And the work of Mumford, once again, sees much in early history destroyed by the coming of modern technology and urban civilization.

The idea of tradition itself—and most especially the supposed tradition of civilization in the West before the Industrial and the French Revolutions—becomes increasingly important in the period. Not only was there an appeal to the Southern Agrarian tradition and various versions of an American tradition; the Humanists, Irving Babbitt and Paul Elmer More, also offered a lively source of debate in the early 1930s and were widely read in intellectual circles.[83] T. S. Eliot, long interested in "The Tradition and the Individual Talent," placed considerably more of his attention on the tradition in the Thirties, especially in *After Strange Gods* (1934) and *The Idea of a Christian Society* (1939). At the University of Chicago, Robert M. Hutchins not only organized the institution but also produced a significant defense of his version of university education in *The Higher Learning in America* (1936). His work was a direct confrontation to the previous work of Thorstein Veblen and a specific challenge to the pragmatists. He would use the tradition to help shape and reinforce the culture:

In general education we are interested in drawing out elements of our common human nature; we are interested in the attributes of the race, not the accidents of individuals. . . . We propose permanent studies because these studies . . . connect man with man, because they connect us with the best that man has thought, because they are basic to any further study and to any understanding of the world. . . . Real unity can be achieved only by a hierarchy of truths which show us which are fundamental and which subsidiary, which significant and which not.[84]

The pragmatists, already under attack in the 1920s, found themselves fighting for their intellectual lives under the heavy assault of the traditionalists and the antinaturalists.[85]

Even the writing of the period, diverse and different as it was in form and content, shared a common commitment, no matter what the individual participation, in various movements. The Marxist critics may have tried to mold a special kind of proletarian writing but they did not succeed, even among Party members; the movement was surprisingly brief in spite of all the attention paid to it. However, Joseph Freeman's interesting introduction to the anthology *Proletarian Literature in the United States* (1935) is worth examination:

Art, then, is not the same as action; it is not identical with science; it is distinct from party program. It has its own special function, the grasp and transmission of experience. The catch lies in the word "experience."[86]

That is indeed where the catch did lie. Even John Dewey had defined art as experience and the word "experience" had been a crucial one for the Progressive generation. Freeman himself argued for the virtues of the avant-garde in America from the poetic renaissance of 1912 to the economic crisis of 1929. In this period, American writers had repudiated "eternal values" of traditional writers and had emphasized immediate American experience.

The movement has its prophet in Walt Whitman, who broke with the "eternal values" of feudal literature and proclaimed the here and now. Poetry abandoned the pose of moving freely in space and time; it now focused its attention on New York, Chicago, San Francisco, Iowa, Alabama in the twentieth century.[87]

The next stage was to be a rendering of the experience of the class struggle itself as it emerged to consciousness with the depression of 1929, and finally there would come, it was hoped, a literature of The Party.

But literature in general—no matter what the political allegiance of individual writers might be—did not generally respond to the demands of political leadership. There was a new sense of a widening range of experience dramatically brought home because of the events of the era and their widespread transmission by the media. Jack Conroy was associated with Party activities, but *The Disinherited* is not an ideological novel. As Conroy himself remarked, "I, for one, considered myself a witness to the times rather than a novelist. Mine was an effort to obey Whitman's injunction to 'vivify the contemporary fact.' "[88] Allen Tate was a Southern Agrarian, but as he has suggested, "The success or failure of a political idea is none of my business; my business is to render in words the experience of people, whatever movement of ideas they may be caught up in."[89] And Alfred Kazin, recalling his own *Starting Out in the Thirties*, declared:

What young writers of the Thirties wanted was to prove the literary value of our experience, to recognize the possibilities of art in our own lives, to feel we had moved the streets, the stockyards, the hiring halls into literature —to show our radical strength could carry on the experimental impulse of modern literature.[90]

But in many cases this aim, this search for experience and ways to record it (some interesting new forms were produced, especially the "documentary" techniques characteristic of the period, not only in Dos Passos' *U.S.A.*, but in various Federal Theater productions and works like Agee and Walker Evans' *Let Us Now Praise Famous Men*) was related to the discovery of significant myths, symbols, and images from the culture itself that might also serve as a basis of reinforcement or indeed the re-creation or remaking of culture itself. William Faulkner in his novels of the South and Hart Crane in *The Bridge* (1930) self-consciously strove to use our history, and even our technology, mythically and symbolically. The most persistent symbol to emerge from the bulk of the literature of the period, however, was "the people." It was the theme of Burke's lecture on "Revolutionary Symbolism in America." In 1936 Carl Sandburg insisted, at extraordinary length and with much sentimentalism: *The People, Yes*. Others pointed to the "workers" (Burke's preference for "people" rather than "workers" created something of a literary battle at the First American Writers' Congress),[91] to brotherhood, or even to Man (always capitalized).

This self-conscious interest in myth, symbol, and image (to become in succeeding decades a special branch of criticism and philosophy, if not a cult among writers and scholars) was in the 1930s a way in which literature could once again relate experience to culture, not necessarily to political action. Herbert Agar, in his introduction to *Who Owns America?* (1936), declared that the social and economic system in America was on the rocks. There was a need to "build a better world" and to provide some picture "in human terms" of what this would be like. Reformation was necessary, and social and economic theories were not enough: "if a reformation is even to begin, it must be based on an ideal that can stir the human heart."[92]

In an age demanding an image—or a myth or symbol—did the social and political movements provide one effective enough? Josephine Herbst has asked whether a phrase like "toiling masses" is enough, and in 1941 Edward Dahlberg, a former "proletarian novelist" at one time associated with left-wing politics, was to write, devastatingly, of the failure of the Left to provide meaningful symbols and myths. The mystery of the Mythic Strike, for example, was not enough: "The strike fails as tragic purification, as psychic ablution; the strike is barter, a pragmatic expedient, not a way of seeing." Thus he demanded of ideology more than it can provide, indicating in his extraordinary rhetoric a dissatisfaction with communism and fascism that may have led others out of the kinds of political involvement they sought earlier in the 1930s. "The drama of Bread can never be a substitute for the Wine and the Wafer, because man must not only have his loaf of bread, but he must also have an image to eat. Communism and fascism fail as awe and wonder. They are weak as image-making sources."[93] Dahlberg demands what others in this decade so interested in myth, symbol, and image tried to find in a variety of ways. Perhaps in the long run, too, the New Deal succeeded even in its limited way because it, rather than the artist or the intellectual, the Communist Party or other political and social movements such as Technocracy, commanded the set of images, symbols, and myths with most meaning for the bulk of the American people.

At least two recent critics of the 1930s have argued that one of the great failures of the period on the Left was the effort of the Left to associate itself with the "folk" rather than the "intellectual" tradition in America, that is, with "mass culture."[94]

The most important effect of the intellectual life of the 30's and the culture that grew out of it has been to distort and eventually to destroy the emotional and moral content of experience, putting in its place a system of conventionalized "responses." In fact, the chief function of mass culture is to relieve one of the necessity of experiencing one's life directly.[95]

William Phillips has suggested that the writers of the Concord School mark the first appearance of an American intelligentsia. In their revolt against commercialism and the Puritan heritage, he suggests, "they set out consciously to form, as Emerson put it, 'a learned class,' and to assimilate the culture of Europe into a native tradition."[96] In the 1930s, it might be argued, the self-conscious American intelligentsia set out to become 'an unlearned class,' to assimilate the culture of the "people" into the inherited European tradition, perhaps especially those ideas and forms brought back from long stays abroad in the 1920s.

Whether or not the criticisms voiced above constitute a valid perspective on the period, the fact remains that there is in much of the literature and thought of the period a kind of sentimentalism, a quality of intellectual softness all too often apparent: Saroyan's "gentle people,"; the extraordinary messages of hope with which Odets so frequently ended his plays, and for which the content of the plays provided no warrant; Carl Sandburg's positive nod to "the people,"; MacLeish's hymn to Man. The idea of commitment frequently led, when combined with the idea of culture, not to revolution but to acquiescence.

Significantly, there emerged in the decade of the Thirties two other voices from two other rooms, but they achieved full cultural voice and power primarily in the post-Depression period. One may be called the commitment to irresponsibility as a cultural stance; extreme antinomianism, glorying in the experiences of the self and saying to hell with everything else. At first in a kind of underground of the literary world, Henry Miller emerged in 1934 with *Tropic of Cancer*. George Orwell, home from the Spanish War, was to hail Miller in 1940 as "the only imaginative prose writer of the slightest value who has appeared among the English-speaking races for some years past." [97] Miller was neither a defeatist nor a yea-sayer. "Where Miller's work is symptomatically important," Orwell explains,

is in its avoidance of any of these attitudes. He is neither pushing the world-process forward nor trying to drag it back, but on the other hand he is by no means ignoring it. I should say he believes in the impending ruin of Western Civilization much more firmly than the majority of "revolutionary" writers; only he does not feel called upon to do anything about it. He is fiddling while Rome is burning, and, unlike most of the people who do this, fiddling with his face toward the flames. . . . he feels no impulse to alter or control the process that he is undergoing. He has performed the essential Jonah act of allowing himself to be swallowed, remaining passive, *accepting*. [98]

Miller's is an act of commitment in which the act itself is the most important thing. There is no need for "participation," no sense of "belonging" as part of a group or a culture, real or imagined. If he is part of a tradition, it is personal tradition picked up among fragments left behind in history. In Miller there is little sense of history; there is a religious sense, but again antinomian and highly personal. His work attempts a direct expression of his own experience, unstructured by philosophy, ideology, society, by traditional myths or symbols. There is no glorying in the "folk" or special interest in the culture of the "people." American history means no more to him than European, and the America that interests him is only the America of his own experience. Miller's stance belongs to the cultural history of the Thirties: it represents an important modification of the idea of commitment, and one that was to become increasingly important in later decades. For Orwell, Miller's writing is symptomatic: "it is a demonstration of the *impossibility* of any major literature until the world has shaken itself into its new shape." [99]

The other room might be called "Kierkegaardian" in its décor (and it is important to note that this Danish philosopher was translated for the first time into English in the 1930s, although it is not proper to say that the movement under discussion depended upon his thinking). In 1932 Reinhold Niebuhr "loosed his bombshell on individualistic and utopian social thinking, *Moral Man and Immoral Society*." [100] From this time on Niebuhr and other like-minded theologians (generally called Neo-Orthodox) developed a position that was eventually to rule advanced Protestant thinking and ultimately to supply many intellectuals in America with an important world view.

Any generalized picture of the basic structure of the Neo-Orthodox position necessarily risks becoming a parody. But it is fair to suggest that it demanded of man a most difficult commitment. He must live in the world but not be of the world; man is both creature and creator; he is involved in history and yet transcends it. Restoring the doctrine of original sin to a central position, Niebuhr asked man to continue to participate in the job of political reform knowing full well that his limitations would make it impossible for him to succeed fully. He dramatized the distinction and the tension that must exist between the Biblical view of history and the "modern" or "progressive" view. Life was a paradox that must be taken with due seriousness. Sydney Ahlstrom offers this summary of the major features of the movement that emerged as the Protestant Neo-Orthodoxy sought some alternative to the types of cultural surrender implicit in both liberal Protestantism and Social Gospel Protestantism:

Its critique of group, class and personal complacency; its demand for personal appropriation of Christian truth; its insistence that man's moral obligation under the Gospel cannot be stated in terms of legalistic precepts; its warning against the dangers of rationalizing the great Biblical paradoxes; its emphasis upon a radically personalistic understanding of the self, and of God; above all, the reality, the objectivity, and the sovereignty of God and His judgments. [101]

The fundamental role of Christ was, in effect, to stand in opposition to culture. Man was somehow caught in between. Christ was to offer a constant criticism of life in the world, of culture; yet man must continue to operate within the culture with a more realistic sense of the situation. There was no essential morality in any group, party, or class. Ultimately, man was alone in his struggle within culture and had to rely on his commitment, his belief in Christ, to sustain him.

Thus by the end of the decade two new general positions emerged from the confusions of the period and from the idea of culture and the idea of commitment itself, two positions implying significant criticism of the other views of culture and commitment that had characterized the period. With the growing acceptance of these positions by American intellectuals during the Second World War and after, the Thirties came to an end.

Yet, in our effort to achieve an honest understanding of what the decade did achieve, a postscript is called for. In 1941 James Agee and Walker Evans finally published their extraordinary book (begun in 1936) *Let Us Now Praise Famous Men*. It may be the decade's great classic, for the book represents much of what was characteristic of the Thirties' finest contributions. It is, of course, a "documentary"; it deals in intimate detail, not with "the people," but with specific members of three families of sharecroppers in the American South. Brilliantly combining photographs and texts, it responds especially to the demands of an era of sight and sound. Significantly, Agee tells us the text was written "with reading aloud in mind . . . it is suggested that the reader attend with his ear to what he takes off the page: for variations of tone, pace, shape, and dynamics are here particularly unavailable to the eye alone, and with their loss, a good deal of meaning escapes."[102] The text was intended to be read continuously "as music is listened to or a film watched." He wishes he did not have to use words at all, but could put together pieces of cloth, lumps of earth, bits of wood and iron, phials of odors, plates of food and of excrement.

"Above all else; in God's name don't think of it as Art." For Agee struggles to achieve a direct confrontation, by his audience, with the experience of these people themselves, their style of life, their very being. The true meaning, he argues, of a character in his work is that he *exists* "as you do and as I do and as no character of the imagination can possibly exist. His great weight, mystery, and dignity are in this fact."[103] Thus the concentration on the direct experience and the recreation of the total cultural environment in rich detail marks the work. It is a work of passion, a work that involves a fundamental act of commitment by its authors, a belief in the meaningfulness of the lives of such people, a belief in human dignity. There is a moral intensity, albeit without a particular "social" or "political" lesson to teach or doctrine to preach. There may be, as Lionel Trilling suggests, a refusal to see any evil in the universe and thus a moral flaw in the work, but the passion and the innocence are also ways of seeing, perhaps characteristic ways of seeing in the best of the work of the 1930s, ways of seeing that we may forget are part of a genuine and valuable legacy of the decade.[104] Later critics were to hail the end of innocence—that lack of a sense of personalism, the sentimentalism, the failure to see complexity and inherent evil in the world, the optimistic faith in simple solutions to all human problems. These same critics greeted a newer "realism" with considerable enthusiasm. The innocence of the period can be documented; that it was all weakness, perhaps not so easily. The decade was also to be criticized for its commitment to "ideologies," but alas we cannot comment on this charge because there is so little evidence that such a commitment existed. Rather, what appears to have been the stunning weakness of the decade was that innocence *replaced* all ideological sense, when *both* may in fact be essential.

The Thirties this essay has attempted to portray and understand may not correspond to the decade as it exists in myth and memory. It had more than its share of grave weaknesses. But the fact remains that the era made a significant contribution to our development in the acculturation of the idea of culture and of the idea of commitment. Later decades would determine whether better use could be made of these discoveries.

10 CULTURE AND COMMITMENT

I

An eminent British historian had a most effective rhetorical device for shaming his audience into easy acceptance of propositions some might otherwise have found original or even dubious. He would preface such statements with the phrase "every schoolboy knows" and those, often long out of school, who read him would blush and acquiesce, no matter what the initial ignorance or doubt. This is not the case here, for every schoolboy *does* know that in the period between the crash of the stock market and the surrender that marked the end of the Second World War the American people suffered two extraordinary experiences: a prolonged and deep economic depression and the burdens of involvement in a protracted global war. He is also aware, albeit often more vaguely, that these experiences had a profound and often shattering impact on the lives of millions of Americans, with significant consequences for our history.

Yet in spite of what every schoolboy knows, there is little interest here in those experiences. And since they are so central to most accounts of the period under study, some explanation is in order for what I do not do as well as for what it proposes. The current trends have tended to emphasize and perhaps overemphasize the art of historical reconstruction to enable us to reexperience the experience of the past: what was it like, how did it feel? In its most popular forms, such history becomes a kind of nostalgia; objects from the past allow us to relive our youth, or allow those who did not live it then to experience it now.

The cultural historian does not seek to know past experience, that is, to reexperience it in any sense. Rather he seeks to discover the *forms* in which people have experienced the world—the patterns of life, the symbols by which they cope with the world. For no individual comes to an experience like some kind of Lockean tabula rasa; he comes conditioned to receive experience in certain ways, using certain patterns of response, certain established forms. Frequently in the course of such confrontation with experience, new forms are created or older patterns altered. The cultural historian keeps his eye on the changing shapes of these forms; he does not plunge into the experience itself bringing with him only his own culture, his own patterns, symbols, forms.

But the problem is a complicated one for the historian, for in order to do his job he must, as a matter of fact, also create forms so that he can best understand the forms that make up the culture he is studying. "Every work of history," the great cultural historian Johan Huizinga tells us, "constructs contexts and designs forms in which past reality can be comprehended. History creates comprehensibility primarily by arranging facts meaningfully and only in a very limited sense by establishing strict causal connections." Two interesting ideas follow. First, the historian deals with the culture he is studying very much like the culture itself deals with the experience with which it is confronted; in the effort to cope and make meaningful, people create culture, a set of forms, patterns, symbols with which to deal with experience. So, too, does the historian deal with his "experience," the culture under analysis. And second, the historian's contexts and forms are of course summoned out of his ongoing culture and his history is therefore part of that culture—part of its context and forms.

My focus here is on the forms, patterns, and symbols that a largely middle-class America used to deal with the experiences of depression and war, and not on these experiences themselves. But just as I as historian find myself trying to make this cultural history "comprehensible" by designing forms and constructing contexts, so too I discover that in this period the people under study are trying to make their own world comprehensible by their self-conscious awareness of the importance of the idea of culture and the idea of commitment, their self-conscious search for a culture that will enable them to deal with the world of experience, and a commitment to forms, patterns, symbols that will make their life meaningful.

In 1926 the great historian of the classic world M. I. Rostov-tzeff asked a series of haunting questions at the end of his most extraordinary work:

But the ultimate problem remains like a ghost, ever present and unlaid: Is it possible to extend a higher civilization to the lower classes without debasing its standard and diluting its quality to the vanishing point? Is not every civilization bound to decay as soon as it begins to penetrate the masses?

And while these characteristic questions of the late 1920s and 1930s remain in mind, there are others raised that specifically haunt my work. What happens to a culture that suddenly discovers it is a culture? What are the consequences for culture of a self-conscious awareness not only of culture but of the *idea* of culture and the *idea* of commitment? What happens to a culture so rationalized that it seeks with full awareness for its own culture, its own commitments?

II

It was precisely the question of the relationship between experience and culture that fascinated a whole young generation of cultural critics from the years immediately preceding the First World War. Lewis Mumford's three path-breaking studies in American civilization and culture—*Sticks and Stones* (1924), *The Golden Day* (1926), *The Brown Decades* (1931)—might be viewed as a culmination of the concerns of a whole generation of intellectuals. By the end of the 1920s there was general agreement: America had indeed brought forth upon this continent a new civilization. In 1927 the distinguished French social scientist André Siegfried published a widely read and widely discussed analysis of that civilization, as hope and promise, as problem and menace. By 1929 his book *America Comes of Age* had gone through 14 printings and its message found acceptance and general reinforcement in other developments; it was no longer simply the concern of a small group of intellectuals. It had become part of the general national consciousness. "Today," Siegfried announced, "as a result of the revolutionary changes brought about by modern method of production, [America] has again become a new world. . . . The American people are now creating on a vast scale an entirely original social structure which bears only a superficial resemblance to the European. It may even be a new age. . . ."

Looking backward from their vantage point in 1936, Sheldon and Martha Cheney could declare that in 1927 "there was a spreading machine age consciousness." Other students since have pointed to some of the technological achievements of that year alone that heightened such consciousness: the establishment of radio-telephone service between New York and London, San Francisco, and Manila; the development of the first national radio networks; the opening of the Holland Tunnel, the first underwater vehicular tunnel in the world; the introduction of talking films; the production of Henry Ford's fifteen-millionth automobile. The list of such developments seems almost endless for that year, as Professor Robert A. M. Stern demonstrated in his important essay on 1927 as a turning point in the development of civilization.

As if the full consequence of living in a machine age—an age of an industrial civilization in which a new technology brought about changes in the material base of society that were altering patterns of social organization and structure—was not problem enough, there was also a growing awareness of subtle changes in the value structure as well, changes in part precipitated by the operations and needs of that very industrial civilization. Again writing from the perspective of the early 1930s, Malcolm Cowley shrewdly noted that the new ethical code, first promulgated by the Bohemians of Greenwich Village in revolt against the "business-Christian ethic then represented by *The Saturday Evening Post*," had become necessary to the new industrial order by the end of the 1920s. In his *Exile's Return* (1934)—a classic work of the 1930s although a study of the 1920s—he points out that the prevailing ethic was, in fact, substantially a production ethic: "The great virtues it taught were industry, foresight, thrift, and personal initiative." But after World War I, the mature capitalism of the new industrial civilization demanded a new ethic, an ethic that encouraged people to buy, a consumption ethic. Without attempting to exaggerate the role of the Bohemians and certainly not trying to point to Greenwich Village as the source of the revolution in morality, Cowley stated:

It happened that many of the Greenwich Village ideas proved useful in the altered situation. Thus, *self-expression* and *paganism* encouraged a demand for all sorts of products, modern furniture, beach pajamas, cosmetics, colored bathrooms with toilet paper to match. *Living for the moment* meant buying an automobile, radio or house, using it now and paying for it tomorrow. *Female equality* was capable of doubling the consumption of products formerly used by men alone. Even *changing place* would help stimulate business in the country from which the artist was being expatriated: involuntarily they increased the foreign demand for fountain pens, silk stockings, grapefruit and portable typewriters. They drew after them an invading army of tourists, thus swelling the profits of steamship lines and travel agencies. Everything fitted into the business picture.

Americans were conscious of living in the machine age, a new era vastly different from the vision of an agrarian world in which America had been founded and in which her fundamental institutions and social structure had been molded. Charles and Mary Beard in their greatest popular success, *The Rise of American Civilization* (1927)—a book widely distributed among middle-class readers by the new Book-of-the-Month Club, and which was to have significant impact on American thinking about its history for two decades—had called the first volume *The Agricultural Era* and the second volume *The Industrial Era*. But such awareness was further complicated by a sense of movement and conflict between an era of production and an era of consumption. Americans began to think and behave as consumers in a new way. No better symbol might be found for this shift than that offered by Henry Ford himself. In that same year, 1927, Ford ceased production of the old standard (and black) Model T and brought out the consumer-oriented (and available in many colors) high-styled Model A.

Thus a machine-age civilization could be seen in the physical world around Americans and could be sensed in a wide variety of social changes and patterns of living. Civilization, as Lewis Mumford had said, was "a material fact." But what of culture, which Mumford also defined in *The Golden Day* (1926) as "the spiritual form"? "Civilization and culture . . . are not," he assured his readers, "exclusive terms; for one is never found without at least a vestige of the other." The point was clear: what kind of culture would —and even more important what kind of culture could—emerge on the basis of such a new machine-age civilization? Initially a question that plagued intellectuals, more and more the whole idea of culture and most especially an American culture began to take hold in middle-class America. What did these obvious changes that had occurred in the material base *mean* for life? More and more concern grew over "ways of life," life-style, and as the debate moved on into the 1930s for what was to be called repeatedly "the American Way of Life." That concept was a product of the debate as well as a leading cliché in the debate during the post-Depression era: a search for forms in which to organize and express the experiences of a machine age in such a way that would lead (again in the 1926 words of Lewis Mumford) "to the nurture of the good life; [to permit] the fullest use, or sublimation, of man's natural functions and activities." The search for culture was the search for meaningful forms, for patterns of living. That search began in the 1920s and culminated in the 1930s.

By 1927 the words "modern" and "streamlined" were being used not only in reference to design of particular objects but also to a quality of living, a life-style. They are words of the new machine order looking for a culture. In 1934 The Museum of Modern Art (founded in 1929 and in a sense a product of the questions raised of culture in an industrial era) held an important show it called "Machine Art." Common household and industrial objects—stoves, toasters, kitchenware, chairs, vacuum cleaners, cash registers, laboratory equipment—were displayed as *works of art*. One of the themes of that exhibition had been provided by L. P. Jacks, the British social critic. "Industrial civilization must either find a means of ending the divorce between its industry and its 'culture' or perish." Alfred H. Barr, Jr., the director of the Museum, elaborated:

It is in part through the aesthetic appreciation of natural forms that man has carried on his spiritual conquest of nature's hostile chaos. Today man is lost in the far more treacherous wilderness of industrial and commercial civilization. On every hand machines literally multiply our difficulties and point our doom. If . . . we are to "end the divorce" between our industry and our culture we must assimilate the machine aesthetically as well as economically. Not only must we bind Frankenstein—but we must make him beautiful.

In April 1935, an Industrial Arts Exposition opened fittingly enough in the new Rockefeller Center, which was planned in the late 1920s and built in the early 1930s and designed as a new form to meet the new needs of the city in the machine age. The exposition proposed to exhibit "industry's present solution of the practical, artistic, and social needs of the average man." The exhibitors demonstrated through a series of model rooms new ideas for the ordinary house in which low cost and efficiency, labor-saving devices, and new ways of decoration were stressed. There were new ways of heating, air-conditioning for the home, new models of efficiency in bathrooms and kitchens—even a model of Frank Lloyd Wright's "Broadacre City," the planned city of the future. Moreover, Roy L. Gray, of Fort Madison, Iowa, who had several years before been chosen as the Average American, was selected to head a committee of one hundred Average Americans to judge the show and present an award to the winning exhibitor.

Yet all Americans did not respond in quite the same way to this search for a life-style in the machine age. In the same year, for example, in 1935, a volume of some two hundred pages was published that hardly sounds like a book of the 1930s at all. It was called *A Brief and True Report for the Traveller Concerning Williamsburg in Virginia* and was issued in connection with the opening to the public of a project that had also begun in the late 1920s: the restoration of Williamsburg, the old colonial capital, as it had existed in the eighteenth century. It, too, was a Rockefeller enterprise. The nonprofit corporation that made this unique effort not only to restore the old town physically but also to "re-create a living community" by showing living examples of craftsmen at their trade and hostesses wearing traditional garb of the era took as its motto "That the Future May Learn from the Past." It attempted to "tell the story of men of the 'middling sort' who conducted respectable, though small, businesses, and who provided support for the new nation in the making."

The restorers wanted not only to delight Americans with the charm of the place—considerably cleaned up socially (no real signs of slavery, for example) and physically (in order to get people to live and work there modern machine-age comforts such as electricity, indoor plumbing, camouflaged garages, screened porches, and the like had to be provided); they also wished to impress upon them a deeper significance by an "underlying appreciation of the moral and spiritual values of life" Williamsburg represented. Here, too, the stress was on the average man, defined as the small freeholder, although the restoration makes clear it was chiefly a planters' capital. The values that the restorers sought to stress with the enormous and expensive work they undertook they clearly stated: the concept of the integrity of the individual; the concept of responsible leadership; the belief in self-government; the concepts of individual liberty and of opportunity. Not only were these eighteenth-century virtues, they were of "lasting importance to all men everywhere."

And yet it seemed to many, in the late 1920s and early 1930s while the project was underway, that many of these very values had been threatened if not outmoded by the very advance of the United States into the machine age. André Siegfried had insisted, for example, that the "magnificent material achievement" that was American industrial civilization had been possible only by "sacrificing certain rights of the individual." And one might ponder what meaning as culture or way of life such a Williamsburg could possibly have for a machine age. That did not stop the steady and increasing flow of visitors, nor did it eliminate the spell that led to an increased demand by American consumers of Williamsburg-type houses and furnishings. Williamsburg houses, that is, with all the "modern conveniences." There were those critics who found the Williamsburg restoration of Perry, Shaw, and Hepburn as reactionary an influence on architecture and culture as Louis Sullivan and others had found the Renaissance boom fostered by the designs at the Chicago Fair of 1893.

By 1930 the debate over the nature of culture was being held in magazines, journals, books, and even newspapers. The poet Alan

Tate, whose 1927 "Ode to the Confederate Dead" called upon an older tradition as witness against the changes brought about by the newer order, joined eleven other distinguished Southern intellectuals at the end of the decade to issue a manifesto, *I'll Take My Stand*, questioning whether any culture could be created on the basis of industrialism and urging a reexamination of a culture based on a Christian-agrarian set of forms and patterns of living they presumably found buried in the South destroyed by the Civil War, that harbinger of industrialism. At about the same time, the so-called New Humanists—primarily Irving Babbitt and Paul Elmer More—offered the sanctity of the great classical civilizations as a cultural defense against the inroads of industrial barbarism. In 1931 Stuart Chase provided further ammunition in his *Mexico: A Study of Two Americas*. In this book, he compares two economic systems, handicraft and machine, and the resultant ways of life. He takes Tepoztlán, a village of 4,000 people that had been carefully studied by the anthropologist Robert Redfield, and shows how this community of machineless men carried on, and how it compares with the Middletown studied by the Lynds. While by no means rejecting all of the achievements of the machine age, he does most effectively rejoice in the basic qualities of life and values projected in that world without machines. Not all could be said to have found the answer to their culture search in the world of the "modern" and the "streamlined."

Thus the American people entered an era of depression and war somehow aware of a culture in crisis, already at the outset in search of a satisfactory American Way of Life, fascinated by the idea of culture itself, with a sense of some need for a kind of commitment in a world somehow between eras. In 1927 the German writer Hermann Hesse reported a supposed remembered conversation with his hero Harry Haller in the introduction to his novel *Steppenwolf*:

Every age, every culture, every custom and tradition has its own character, its own weakness and its own strength, its beauties and cruelties; it accepts certain sufferings as a matter of course, puts up patiently with certain evils. Human life is reduced to real suffering, to hell, only when two ages, two cultures and religions overlap.

As early as the 1920s there were those who were beginning to see that in a sense they were between two eras; they were in a machine age and yet somehow not completely of it; they were caught between an older order and older values and a new order with its new demands. As early as the middle of the decade, a citizen of the Lynds' Middletown could look at his fellow townsmen and sense: "These people are afraid of something; what is it?" That vague fear—in part at least of the consciousness of some suspension between two eras—was to be enormously elaborated under the threats imposed by the awesome experience of depression and war. But somehow, even before, there was already an ongoing sense that things were not quite right, in the natural order, in the moral order, in the technological order, and most especially in the relationships among them.

III

And the Depression did bring in its wake—in Harry Haller's words —"real suffering" to that group of Americans who most felt themselves suspended between two eras and who least expected their "progress" to yield such results: the enormous American middle class. For the story of American culture remains largely the story of this middle class. There is a tendency, when treating this period, for historians suddenly to switch their focus and concentrate on the newly discovered poor, the marginal men and women, migrant workers, hobos, various ethnic minorities deprived of a place in the American sun. There is equally a tendency to see the period in terms of the most radical responses to its problems, to see a Red Decade in which cultural as well as political life is somehow dominated by the Left. Yet the fact remains—and it is a vital one if we are to understand the period and the nature of American culture— that the period, while acknowledging in ways more significantly than ever before the existence of groups outside the dominant ones and even recognizing the radical response as important, is one in which American culture continues to be largely middle-class culture.

This is important because it is precisely the middle-class American for whom the experience of the Depression provided a special kind of shock and as a result a special kind of response. For those who were "marginal" in our society, the Depression was more of the same; suffering was not new to them since they had been denied a share in much of the progress and prosperity touted as characteristic of the achievement of American industrialism. If we keep our focus on the middle class, we may also be better able to understand why some shifts to the Left proved so temporary or even why the period proved in the end so fundamentally conservative as it concentrated on finding and glorifying an American Way of Life.

As early as 1944, the playwright Tennessee Williams could have his narrator in *The Glass Menagerie* define the period thus:

The time, that quaint period when the huge middle class of America was matriculating from a school for the blind. Their eyes had failed them, or they had failed their eyes, and so they were having their fingers pressed forcibly down on the fiery Braille alphabet of a dissolving economy. In Spain there was revolution. Here there was only shouting and confusion and labor disturbances, sometimes violent, in otherwise peaceful cities, as Cleveland—Chicago—Detroit. . . .

But what is of crucial importance here is the characteristic response to the experience rather than the experience itself, for this determined the forms—that is to say, the culture. The initial response, as Franklin Roosevelt brilliantly saw, was fear. It was a kind of fear brought about by insecurity. To the already great confusions produced by the growing consciousness of living in a new machine age, the Depression (and to a lesser extent World War II) added new insecurities. "One thing everybody in Middletown has in common: insecurity in the face of a complicated world. . . . So great is the individual human being's need for security that it may be that most people are incapable of tolerating change and uncertainty in all sectors of life at once." So the Lynds' report on their return to Middletown in the 1930s.

It would of course be a mistake to attribute such insecurity and such fear to the Depression alone. For example, the mobility provided to an increasing number of Americans by the machine age helped heighten the lack of security. Such mobility, long characteristic of civilization in the United States, became even more part of the way of life in the 1930s. Two Russian visitors to the United States in this period, the writers Ilya Ilf and Evgeny Petrov, were overwhelmed with the image, not of cities and skyscrapers, not of monuments or hills or factories, "but the crossing of two roads and a petrol station against the background of telegraph wires and advertising billboards." For them, "America is located on a large automobile highway," they wrote in *Little Golden America* (1937). Of all the new words and phrases of the period, none perhaps better symbolizes the problem that faced many Americans than the ironic idea contained in the concept of "mobile homes" and the growth of the trailer industry during the Depression years.

Such insecurity of course had its enormous consequences in the political and legislative history of the period. These have been profusely studied and documented. Less attention has been paid to the cultural consequences: middle-class Americans sought not merely political action and symbols; they readily attempted to translate these into more personally and easily identifiable cultural symbols as well. Witness, for example, the transformation of this sort in reference to President Roosevelt's political-economic objectives in the case of the famous Four Freedoms. When these were originally announced by the President in 1941, Freedom from Fear meant most specifically an effort to end by international agreement the frightening arms race, and Freedom from Want was related to a search for trade agreements that would mean easier access of all nations to the raw materials and products of others. By 1943, when the popular painter Norman Rockwell executed his famous four paintings of the Four Freedoms for that middle-class magazine *The Saturday Evening Post,* Freedom from Want had become a healthy and ample American family seated around a well-stocked table, being served an enormous, succulent stuffed turkey by an equally well-fed American mother; Freedom from Fear had become a sentimental visit to a children's bedroom with sleeping youngsters safely tucked in their comfortable bed, carefully watched over by kindly and loving parents. No other paintings ever so caught the American imagination or were so widely distributed in reproduction to eager American families.

Finding a sense of insecurity and a search for a pattern of culture and commitment to relieve such fears certainly provides no surprising discovery. But another overwhelming psychological reaction, even more important in analyzing the cultural developments of the period, may appear more unusual. A careful study of the evidence reveals an overwhelming sense of shame that seems to have engulfed so many of those middle-class Americans affected by the impact of the Depression—a shame felt by those who by no means starved but now found their accustomed way of life altered. So pervasive in fact was this sense that when Studs Terkel came some 40 years after the event to interview the survivors of that era, this feeling of shame, embarrassment, or even humiliation remained a vivid part of the remembering.

A well-to-do girl whose family could no longer pay her bills at a private boarding school: "I was mortified past belief." A girl who had lost her hair as a result of typhoid and could not afford a wig: "This was the shame of it." A middle-class surburbanite near Chicago: "Lotta people committed suicide, pushed themselves out of buildings and killed themselves, 'cause they couldn't face the disgrace. Finally, the same thing with me." Pauline Kael, the movie critic, remembering Berkeley in 1936: "There was embarrassment at college where a lot of kids were well-heeled." A distinguished theater producer and director: "I wonder if they remember the suffering and the agony and the shame they went through." A businessman: "Shame? You tellin' me? I would go stand on that relief line, I would look this way and that and see if there's nobody around that knows me: I would bend my head low so nobody would recognize me. The only scar that is left on me is my pride, my pride."

Such a brief sampling from Terkel's *Hard Times* can be duplicated many times over from this work alone as well as from our sources from the period. In an entirely different context, the Lynds may have provided us with an explanation of this particular kind of reaction, when they argue that when an individual "is caught in a chaos of conflicting patterns, none of them wholly condemned, but no one of them clearly approved and free from confusion; or where group sanctions are clear in demanding a certain role of man or woman, the individual encounters cultural requirements with no immediate means of meeting them." Perhaps in such a situation—and they see one existing in Middletown in the 1930s—the result is a sense of shame.

Terkel asks a distinguished psychiatrist in *Hard Times,* "Did any of the symptoms have to with status in society, say losing a job and thus losing face . . . ? The psychiatrist answers:

No, it was internal distress. Remember the practice was entirely middle class. I did a little field work among the unemployed. . . . They hung around street corners and in groups. They gave each other solace. They were loath to go home because they were indicted, as if it were their fault for being unemployed. A jobless man was a lazy good-for-nothing. The women punished the men . . . by withholding themselves sexually. By belittling and emasculating the men, undermining their paternal authority, turning to the eldest son. These men suffered from depression. They felt despised, they were ashamed of themselves . . . Thirty, forty years ago, people felt burdened by an excess of conscience. An excess of guilt and wrongdoing.

And still another psychiatrist—by the middle of the 1930s as we shall see, psychiatry was to become an important part of the established culture, an aspect of the American Way of middle-class life—reported:

In those days everybody accepted his role, responsibility for his own fate. Everybody, more or less, blamed himself for his delinquency or lack of talent or bad luck. There was an acceptance that it was your own fault, your own indolence, your own lack of ability. You took it and you kept quiet. A kind of shame about your own personal failure. I was wondering what the hell it was all about. I wasn't suffering.

Against such a psychological background—fear and shame—we can begin better to understand the cultural responses of the period. We can begin, for example, to sense the importance of a certain type of comedy that played such a vital role whether in the writing of a Thurber, the leading radio comedy shows (perhaps like "Fibber McGee and Molly"), or the classic film comedies of Frank Capra. All, in some degree, depend initially on a kind of ritual humiliation of the hero, a humiliation that is often painful and even cruel but from which the hero ultimately emerges with some kind of triumph, even though it be a minor one. The theme, of course, is not new to comedy in this era; but this was to be a golden age of comedy in all media, and rather than simple escape it provided a special kind of identification for those whose self-image had become less than favorable. This was especially to be the case for the enormously swollen radio and movie middle-class audiences.

Walt Disney, one of the true geniuses of the age who often created its most important symbols (and used the science and technology of the machine age to do it), seemed to know precisely how to take American fears and humiliations and transform them in acceptable ways so Americans could live with them. From *The Three Little Pigs* in 1933 to "Night on Bald Mountain" (the terrors of the natural order) and "The Sorcerer's Apprentice" (the terrors of the technological order), both episodes of *Fantasia* (1940), Disney provided a way to transform our most grotesque nightmares into fairy tales and pleasant dreams.

It is perhaps no wonder, then, that when Preston Sturges made his own remarkable film about film makers, *Sullivan's Travels* (1941), he told the story of a pretentious director of film comedy who decides, in response to the deplorable conditions in the world, to make a film of genuine social significance, *Brother, Where Art Thou?* To do so he proposes to prepare himself by setting out as a vagrant to see "how the other half lives"—carefully attended at a distance by a huge staff following him in a trailer. Through a series of accidents near the end of the film, however, he does find himself in a real-life situation, falsely imprisoned in one of the most evil of prisons. There he undergoes a singular experience. A black-people's church provides an occasion to share their poor happiness with the "less fortunate" prisoners: it invites them to attend a "picture show." The film is a typical Mickey Mouse cartoon. The director finds himself among the many laughing faces of the prisoners and the poor blacks, laughing with them. Thus he realizes at the end the enormous social importance of comedy. And perhaps we can also learn the cultural significance of the great comedies of the era if we realize the kind of social role they were to play for a middle-class America frightened and humiliated, sensing a lack of any order they understood in the world around them, and tending so often to internalize the blame for their fears, tending to feel shame at their inability to cope rather than overt hostility to a technological and economic order they did not always understand.

IV

Thus while political historians generally see the period as the age of Franklin D. Roosevelt, cultural historians are more likely to call it the age of Mickey Mouse, a culture-hero of international significance. The world of Walt Disney appears, initially, an absurd and even terrifying place; the inanimate become living things, men become artificial and nature human, accepted scientific laws thought to govern the world seem somehow no longer to apply, families are separated and children rarely have their real mothers. The Disney world is a world out of order: all traditional forms seem not to function. And yet the result is not a nightmare world of pity and terror, a tragic world, but a world of fun and fantasy with ultimate wish-fulfillment, ultimate reinforcement of traditional ways and traditional values. In *Fantasia*, for example, the terrors of the machine gone wild ("The Sorcerer's Apprentice") are followed by the sweet vision of nature in "Pastorale" and the terrors of nature gone mad in "Night on Bald Mountain" are exorcised in the almost cloying religious sentimentalism of the "Ave Maria." No matter how disordered the world appears, Disney and his Mickey Mouse any of his heroes or heroines—can find their way back to happy achievement by following the announced rules of the game.

Indeed, the leading games of the period stress this very fact: "Contract" Bridge, especially as developed into a fine art by Eli Culbertson, defied mere luck and chance in terms of the creation of an elaborate "system" of bidding and play; "Monopoly," Parker Brothers' widely played board game of the period based on speculation in real estate, stressed at one and the same time the extremes of luck and chance (a roll of the dice) and the importance of a complex set of stern rules and even drastic moral obligations (one might be forced, by a roll of the dice, to "Go Directly to Jail," for example); the pinball machine was the ideal toy of the machine age, with its spinning balls passing through a series of obstacle pins that meant points for the player if they met, although at the same time the solemn injunction "Do Not Tilt" severely limited the player's opportunity to interfere with the chance movements of the balls.

Here, then, was the middle-class American—already made uneasy by the new set of roles he was assuming in the machine age and the conflict he was increasingly aware of because of the different roles he was required to play, suddenly faced with a set of circumstances in the society that often made him unable to fulfill many if not all of the roles his culture demanded of him, he found himself fearful and ashamed. His world in all its aspects seemed out of order; luck, chance, irrationality greeted him everywhere at a time when he was himself generally a convert to, or a true believer in, the vision of greater order and increased rationality in the world and especially his own social and economic system. And yet in spite of this he knew there were stern moral injunctions he had long been taught he could violate only at his own peril.

Such an American, witnessing what we might call an "alienation of all familiar forms," strove first of all to find a commitment or a system of commitments that would enable him to continue, that would provide him with a mechanism to overcome his fears and his profound sense of shame. A product of the machine age, the American did not surrender his faith in science and technology. Rather, he often attributed his difficulties to the failure to apply himself more rigorously to the creation of a culture worthy of such achievements in science and technology. Science in the nation's service became increasingly the challenge and the scientist even more the hero. In the Academy Award–winning *The Story of Louis Pasteur* (1936), one of the many screen biographies of the period (not a few of which dealt with men and women of science), Paul Muni's portrayal of the eminent scientist first displays his genius with a cure for anthrax, a disease destroying the sheep and therefore vital economic resources of France. His achievement is hailed (not, it is true, without a struggle) because of the service it clearly renders the entire nation. But his later work has a rougher time in winning recognition because not only does it go counter to professional opinion and organization but also it is less easy to justify as a contribution to national power; it deals rather with the improved health and life of individuals.

The idea of scientific service to society is reflected in a series of activities often undertaken with government support. During World War II, for example, the distinguished social psychologist Kurt Lewin, supported by other social scientists such as the anthropologist Margaret Mead, set out on a government-sponsored campaign to change American dietary habits according to the latest scientific knowledge. Thus throughout the period science and social science joined together to find a way to improve the way of life. Such a commitment to science (which was to create deep and significant moral problems for the brilliant team of scientists whose work on atomic energy was to result in the building and detonating of an atomic bomb, the symbolic end of the period) was one characteristic response.

So, too, was the dedication not only to continued technological development and utilization, but also to an even more important voice for planning, organization, and designing of the future. From Technocrats such as Howard Scott at the beginning of the 1930s, through the neo-Veblenians like Rexford Tugwell in the New Deal administration itself, to the new industrial designers and the older but even more vigorous city, regional, and even national planners, the whole of the period stressed the need to design and reorder the world according to a more rational scheme of things. The great World's Fair of 1939 was a brilliant symbolic cultural act demonstrating this commitment. By the 1930s the trained, professional, expert human designer had in a sense replaced the eighteenth-century vision of God as a god of design. In a world increasingly out of order, increasingly on the verge or in the midst of apocalyptic disruptions, man as designer was called upon to find some new order in the world.

There were other kinds of commitments as well: to a tradition within the American experience like that of the Southern Agrarians or to a classical one propounded by the New Humanists; to the Left as an intense political, cultural, and even psychological experience wherein people might find themselves, and might establish some kind of identity by working closely with others for the creation of a better world, sentimentally, perhaps; to the myth of the "people" as expressed in Carl Sandburg's long poem—part of a larger search for mythic and symbolic sources of identity; to the New Deal itself because as a political movement (and through the keen sense Roosevelt and his administration had of the need of creating not only economic solutions to problems but of meeting psychological needs as well), it tried to establish a sense of personal identification by involvement of vast numbers of citizens, many of whom had never been involved before. Saul Alinsky, the professional social activist, recalls the lesson of the 1930s in Terkel's oral history:

In the Thirties, I learned . . . the big idea: providing people with a sense of power. Not just the poor. There is nothing especially noble about the poor. Everybody. That time may have been our most creative period. It was a decade of involvement. It's a cold world now. It was a hot world then.

Such a search for involvement and commitment had still further cultural consequences. It led on the one hand to a determined struggle for the attainment of the identity of an American Way of

Life, a definition of culture in America and for Americans with an increased emphasis on strengthening basic cultural institutions seriously threatened by newer cultural forms (especially those associated with the machine age), and the profound experiences of depression and war. At the same time, it sponsored a redefinition of the role of the individual, particularly in reference to such primary institutions, in ways that stressed the idea of *adjustment*. If the cultural historian can be permitted the use of metaphor, it might be helpful to think of the period as the age of Alfred Adler. This is not to suggest that the writings of that distinguished psychologist were a vital influence (although his *Understanding Human Nature* [1927] and *Social Interest* [an English translation of his *The Meaning of Life*, original 1933 and translation 1938] appear in this period). But the temper and direction of Adler's thought seem strikingly to fit the mood and response of the period in American culture generally. The problem is not the more traditional Freudian one of strengthening the ego. Rather, the effort appears to be—both in popular psychology and in the rising schools of professional analysis—to find some way for individual adjustment, for overcoming shame and fear—perhaps Adler's "inferiority complex"—by adopting a life-style that enables one to "fit in," to belong, to identify. Since man always finds himself in positions of inferiority, it is up to him to discover ways to overcome this. By finding and playing satisfactory roles in society, man can find his identity and lose his sense of inferiority.

The definition of success that that best seller of 1936, Dale Carnegie's *How to Win Friends and Influence People*—certainly a key work in any attempt to understand the culture of the period— proposes involves a view of individual personal achievement no longer simply measured by accumulation of wealth or even status or power. Success is measured by how well one fits in, how well one is liked by others, how well others respond to the roles one is playing. It is a strange kind of individualism for individualistic America. And what it often means is a stress on roles demanded by traditional and primary relationships. As the Adlerians would have it, "above all, it is the spontaneous acceptance to live in conformity to the natural and legitimate demands of the human community."

If we do think of this as an Adlerian age, we can find a context in which we can begin to understand much of the search for a way of life and the reassertion of the role of popular religion, the family, the school, and the community of the kind that occurs in the period. Even—by admittedly an extraordinary and literary stretching of the more precise scientific definition of Adler—the political leader of the era, Franklin Roosevelt, becomes an Adlerian hero: a man with an "organ inferiority" who "compensates" for that inferiority.

In 1927, André Siegfried found the American family already under the threat of destruction, "its field of action greatly restricted; for in the eyes of the apostles of efficiency, the family is regarded as a barrier impeding the current." Yet by the early 1930s all the devices of the media, the energies of psychology and social science, were enlisted in a major effort to revitalize and reassert the primary importance of the family. Scientific marriage counseling was born as a profession. The importance of child-rearing in a strong family setting was reemphasized; the role of women was again to be found in the home primarily and not outside it.

Counseling by scientific experts became a characteristic part of the American Way: to save the individual, the family, the worker as worker, even the community. Professional counseling was even now to be extended to the consumer to teach him how to be an effective consumer. In almost every area we can see the emergence of the professional counselor to help Americans *play those roles* they were having such great difficulty playing, *adjusting* to those situations and circumstances to enable them to overcome their own sense of fear and shame, their sense of their own ability to perform satisfactorily. By the time of World War II, the word "morale" had become commonly used and the problem of how to maintain such morale the concern of a growing number of experts. Thus social science and design joined hands with an Adlerian vision to reshape man and his culture in America as Americans themselves sought help in finding their culture and playing their required roles in it. Education joined the struggle. In the state of Montana, as one of many examples, a Rockefeller grant supported a study to provide "a workable play of education for enriching the life of small communities."

In 1942, Florence C. Bingham edited for the National Congress of Parents and Teachers a volume of essays prepared by leading social scientists and educators, *Community Life in a Democracy*. In it the Depression and the war were seen as rich opportunities to help create a true collective democracy in the United States. "Perhaps," wrote the Chicago sociologist Louis Worth, "the war, like other crises in the collective life, may bring to light further sources of community solidarity, mutual aid, and strength, which in the postwar period may be used for the building of a more genuine democratic order than we have known since the days of the American frontier." The entire volume stresses the role of community, family, school, church—the whole culture—in providing for a stable order for the future with clear, well-defined roles for all to play, in which children can be trained and in which such basic institutions can be reevaluated and reshaped by experts to produce the kind of children who will indeed know their roles and know how to play them. "When we think of the American way of life," an expert on child welfare reported, "we think of a pattern of community functions, each of which contributes in some fashion to the well-being of all who reside within the community. Thus, good schools, good clinical facilities, good social services tend to develop together."

From the agonized beginnings in dreadful fear and embarrassing shame there could emerge a new American. This was the ultimate myth of the combining of machine-age expertise and the characteristic vision of man in an Adlerian age. It is no better expressed than by the president of the National Congress of Parents and Teachers in *Community Life in a Democracy:*

America has awakened to a new conception of community life. From coast to coast and from border to border there has sprung up a sense of unity and solidarity that binds citizens together in their communities and our communities together in the larger life of the nation to an extent, that, with all our national reputation for neighborliness, we have never experienced before. Today we are keenly aware of each other as human beings and each other's children as potential leaders and saviors of humanity. There is a breakdown of the old rigid conception of "mine" and "thine," especially where children and youth are concerned. The extension of the parent's affection and the parent's concern beyond the limits of the family to children on the outside, wherever they and their needs are to be found and regardless of race, creed, or social status, is unmistakable, and it is an epic development.

Yet at the very time this work appeared Gunnar Myrdal and his colleagues were preparing *An American Dilemma* (published in 1944), one of many studies of basic social problems, in this case race relations, that by no means had been "solved" in the great era of adjustment. But Americans had begun to believe they had found the American Way of Life and had created a culture and that it was good. Believing so had become part of the culture itself, a response in finding roles to play, and learning—often through the help of "counselors"—how to play them, which reemphasized basic institutions and values and reinforced them in a wide variety of forms in the culture.

V

It was, then, an Adlerian age of adjustment, and consciously so, an age when men and women sought to find a place and play a role and turned increasingly to a set of newly institutionalized agencies designed explicitly to provide such adjustment, when new professions arose to meet these needs and older ones increasingly assumed these functions. Science—and most especially the social sciences and various schools of psychiatry—joined with popular religion and popular self-help movements. Strong efforts were made to strengthen basic institutions. Counselors like Dr. Paul Popenoe could point with great pride to their success in keeping families together; social scientists like Professor Elton Mayo could stress the role of proper "personnel management" in making industrial operations function more happily with less sense of worker alienation; and Dr. Karen Horney could show the way through meaningful adjustment to overcome the "neurotic personality of our time."

The popular arts, meanwhile, developed an extraordinary skill in providing a kind of comedy that stressed for its audiences a vicarious recovery from humiliation, shame, and fear, while the great political movement of the period, the New Deal, brilliantly used the new media (especially the radio, with the President's Fireside Addresses) and a set of significant symbols to give more Americans a sense of belonging and role. It was an era in which participation, or at least a sense of participation, became crucial, whether that participation was in sports, in block parties in urban communities, or in politics itself.

Even the Communist Party by 1935 was ready to play its role in an era of adjustment. The Popular Front was no doubt dictated by international as well as national political developments. But in the United States the enthusiastic effort to link Communism and "Americanism" created a firmer sense of belonging and involvement. The Party linked its movement to historic American tradition; it rewrote our history to find a place for itself so that the socialist movement would no longer be alienated from American life, meanwhile providing for its members a sense of participation in important work and roles that could be meaningfully played. It put ideological conditions to one side and stressed its relationship to the American Way of Life.

Yet the very culture produced in some measure by the Popular Front, and by other forces struggling to provide a sense of belonging and belief in an era of shame and fear, led finally beyond the Adlerian age of adjustment to a search for metaphysical certainty, a search for a sense of transcendent being, a collective identity deeply responding to deeply felt needs and aspirations. Especially for the period after the mid-1930s up to and through the war years, it is perhaps permissible to use another psychological metaphor and think of the age as Jungian as well. Once again, few perhaps were consciously reading or following the work of Carl Jung himself (although Philip Wylie specifically claims to base his critique of America, *Generation of Vipers* [1942], on his reading of Jung's analysis of human instincts revealed in myths and archetypes). It was an age that consciously sought new heroes, new symbols, even new myths; an age that rediscovered the "folk" and their work and deliberately sought to identify with this culture. It was an age that sought in established and regularized holidays and a host of new patriotic songs to return ritual to its "proper" place in American life.

A consumer culture in which advertising had become a crucial element of the economic life soon not only saw a series of clever advertising campaigns creating product identification, but also saw the advertising men behind these campaigns often turn their talents to the uses of the government to create symbolic means of citizen identification with their national administration and its objectives. Others, too, saw the importance of the manipulation of symbols— even words like "the people"—to create a sense of national morale, a national community "properly" directed toward "proper" ends. The importance of symbols is obvious for the builders of the World's Fair of 1939 and of the famous "Blue Eagle," the slogans, and the parades of the NRA.

An age of heroes: how important, especially perhaps for the young. Doc Savage in the pulps, the Shadow on the radio, Superman in the new comic books—these are but a few examples of the type that by the end of the 1930s began to dominate much of the media. Archetypes in a kind of boyhood fantasy world, these heroic figures joined others like the hard-boiled detective of Dashiell Hammett and Raymond Chandler, or the tough-guy heroes of the films. They tended to be men without attachments to any family (although often closely associated with a small group of trusted fellow workers or followers). They seldom obeyed any rules, whether those were laws of nature or requirements proscribed by any existing institutions. Their commitment was always to themselves (with a firm and strong belief in themselves, without fear, shame, or doubt about their role or identity). Such commitment, however, almost always involved a strong personal moral code that led them to "do good" and to devote themselves to overcoming the forces of evil. They triumphed precisely when and where traditional men and institutions could not. They worked for traditional American values and ends, but often—in a period that witnessed failures in the natural as well as the moral order to act "properly"—imposed their own order by themselves on a disordered world. And like the Lone Ranger, one of the earlier of such heroes in the world of radio, they rode off, after establishing such order, asking no thanks, going as mysteriously as they had come. Many such heroes, further, when not in their heroic disguises and regarded as ordinary citizens found themselves either humiliated or treated with some contempt by their fellows. Only in their hidden identities did they find praise and admiration.

Often such heroic figures merged into a special kind of myth becoming increasingly important, for example, in the films of the era: the new westerns of John Ford and a whole new range of urban westerns, the gangster films whose emergence as a significant genre can be traced to Von Sternberg's brilliant *Underworld* (1927). A new epic vision of the American past and present was being forged, its mythic sense of involvement and fulfillment created by the unfolding of the tale itself, in which the very form of the presentation—a kind of ritualized performance in which all expectations are satisfied in due and proper course—provided a sense of order and continuity.

A fascination with the folk and its culture, past and present, aided many to find a kind of collective identification with all of America and its people. There were, at the same time, efforts made to collect and preserve folk material from the past and an interest in the songs being created by singers in the present out of their own real experiences—not songs from Tin Pan Alley, but songs that came from the farms and mines, from the men on the road and the workers on strike. These songs, the expression of special experiences of special people, became widely adopted by many middle-class Americans as part of their own culture in spite of the fact that the experiences they spoke of were often alien to the middle-class citizens who now enjoyed singing and listening to them. Such vicarious experiencing often became a political as well as a cultural act. By 1939, in the heyday of Popular Front culture in America, two Left-leaning writers, John La Touche (lyricist) and Earl Robinson (composer), produced a special kind of pseudofolk ballad for a WPA revue. That work, later popularized in a recording by Paul Robeson and in a Hollywood film short starring Frank Sinatra, became enormously popular—a "hit" as song and record that was even performed at the Republican National Convention in 1940. "Ballad for Americans" represents the kind of new "folk" material being created in the Jungian age. It was about America and its history and those who made it. It was about the role of belief, about the "nobody who was anybody" and the "anybody who was everybody," about ultimate identification: "You know who I am: the people!" The ballad was a testament—as sentimental as Norman Rockwell's *Saturday Evening Post* covers—to the unity in a way of life that involved all ethnic groups, creeds, colors.

This search for some transcendent identification with a mythic

CULTURE AS HISTORY

America led Americans in a few short years from the deep concern for the Okies of the Dust Bowl as a profound social and human problem to the joyous "Oh! What a Beautiful Morning" with the "corn as high as an elephant's eye" of Rodgers and Hammerstein's *Oklahoma!* (1943), a hugely successful, if sentimental, effort to recapture the innocent vitality of the historic American folk. Sometimes, however, the efforts were of more interest and greater significance. In 1935 George Gershwin tried to make the daring fusion of pop and art, Broadway musical and grand opera, jazz, folk, and popular music, folk and mythic materials, and modern theater. Working from material supplied by the black author DuBose Hayward that itself relies on material from the folk, Gershwin's opera, *Porgy and Bess,* is set in a slum in what once had been a colonial palace. His theme, according to Wilfrid Mellers, is "the impact of the world of commerce on those who had once led, and would like to have led, may still lead, the 'good life,' " based on a close relationship between man and nature. Basic human relationships—mother and child, the rituals of a tight-knit community (like the picnic and prayer meetings), love—are contrasted with a world out of order, the violence and lure of gambling, and the vices of the big city, the alienation of "that lonesome road," the brutality of the fighting, the deformities of nature (Porgy's legs, the devastation of the hurricane).

The drama pits the longing for a return to an Eden before history or man, before consciousness ("I ain't got no shame"). And while there is a longing for the "reestablishment of the tribal innocence" and a return to Eden, the opera ends with Porgy's symbolic gesture: toward New York and his Bess, the recognition, again as Mellers suggests, that "the Promised Land *is* New York, where the new life can grow only when he and Bess can meet, accepting the city as a home." Thus in Gershwin's hands the folk material is used not to justify a refusal to accept the new order of things but to help us to understand what we must ultimately come to grips with, while his use of collective dreams and hopes, basic instincts, and illusions provides a sense of identity for those who find themselves aliens in an alien world.

The great American dancer Martha Graham was also drawn to a vision of theater as ritual in an almost classic sense. She early turned to a private world of myth as the basis of her best work, as in her highly personal *Primitive Mysteries* (1931), where she was the poetic Virgin, the woman inviolate of the Christian myth. By 1934 she was ready to explore America and her own Protestant background. As Leroy Leatherman suggests in *Martha Graham: Portrait of the Lady as an Artist:*

In *Letter to the World* (1940) . . . she confronted those dark inhuman forces. But the end was bleak. Then, in 1944, she was able to do *Appalachian Spring*. The doomful Ancestress of *Letter to the World*, a distillation of Cotton Mather and an archetypal figure of the past that drags one down to death, had undergone a marvellous transformation: In *Appalachian Spring* she is the Pioneer Woman, dominant, strong but loving and dedicated to the future. The Bride is joyous and will not be put down by a hell-fire-and-brimstone sermon.

Danced to a score by the American composer Aaron Copland, it was to prove one of her most popular and enduring works. In no sense is the work or even the music of the score "folk," nor does it pretend to be. But it does present itself as a special kind of American rite or series of rites—the sermon, the courtship, the marriage, the house-raising—which celebrates the American past and the American character (especially the American woman) with humor, joy, and tenderness. Copland's score, while it uses only one folk tune, makes an effort to relate to a body of characteristically American music, again uniquely in the composer's own gifted way. It was part of a body of music during the time demanded by the new media (radio and the movies) as well as by the development of the lyrical theatrical arts in America. Much of his music and much of Martha Graham's work of the period indicate a shift in mood, a desire to find a special collective relationship in which all Americans might share— not only in terms of a past but also in terms of a future. Composers, Copland himself tells us, felt "needed as never before"; this was combined with a "wave of sympathy for and identification with the plight of the common man." But at its very best the new lyric theater (and it was here that so many of the major cultural achievements of the period are, interestingly enough, to be found) strove to provide a new sense of common belief, common ritual observance, common emotional sharing that the psychological conditions of the era seemed to demand. Heroes, symbols, myths, and rituals: a Jungian age in America.

VI

All ages demand, in Ezra Pound's words, a symbol: none more self-consciously than the age we speak of here. We began with one symbol, the reconstruction of historic Williamsburg as a hedge against the new rising industrial order. We end with another, thought of at the time of its construction as the fitting monument to the new era itself: "The most interesting and efficiently designed mass office building. . . . The biggest in the world." It was rein- forced concrete, and its designers and builders (who immediately formed a Society of the Pentagon to perpetuate themselves and their achievement) prophesied it would be as "lasting as the Repub- lic." It was a "modern miracle of construction" built in a remarkably short time (in 14 months; in traditional and not war time it would have taken seven years) and provided a "stimulus to the wartime imagination." A complete world unto itself, it contained some 16 miles of corridors, 600,000 square feet of office space, room initially for 32,000 workers. It was to be the gigantic brain cell of the army and one critic called it a "World's Fair gone to war." Within those enormous corridors—painted in various shades of pastel to help one find his way—there were food services, medical facilities, even a private printing press. Its roads were patrolled by military police; and one author, visiting it while the approaches were being land- scaped, commented on the picture presented: "The work (of land- scaping) is being done almost entirely by squads of Negro women who all wear straw hats, cotton blouses, and blue trousers, giving the countryside something of a plantation aspect."

Yet a little different from the plantations of Colonial Virginia, one might suppose. The Pentagon, a final symbol of the great new world of industrial order and power, was made necessary by the venture into war. Perhaps, its defenders suggested, it would be un- necessary for the army after the war. In that case, it could easily be converted into an archive storage building. But such exigencies did not come to pass and the Pentagon is still with us. What its symbolic value is today, however, is far different from that it presented when erected in 1942. Or perhaps there were some even then who might have seen in its design another image, that of the Castle that the Czech author Franz Kafka had written about so chillingly back in 1927.

For the fact remains that by the early 1940s the culture often so self-consciously cultivated in response to the fear and shame that dominated so much of the early part of the period, and that gave way to a final celebration of the American Way of Life and strong sense of commitment to it, was under restudy and even attack. Many had begun to doubt that a rational or scientific order was enough; some had in fact allowed their commitments to wander to the idea of commitment itself—a whole new interest in the existential mode, in neo-orthodoxy in religion, in Neo-Thomism in philosophy, chal- lenging not only the dominant American pragmatism in schools of philosophy but also the philosophy of education itself (as at the University of Chicago under Robert M. Hutchins). Sidney Hook set off a lively debate in 1943 when he attacked this attack on pragmatism and science, on rationality and social engineering, as a new "failure of nerve." But already Philip Wylie had issued his bestselling blast at American myths, heroes, and values. The vision of a new order emerging out of a war was challenged by Carl Becker in 1942 in *How New Will the Better World Be?* and in 1943 Ayn Rand produced a blockbuster of a novel, *The Fountainhead*, that was to gain a wide readership especially on college campuses. It preached a new individualism—exalting, in fact, selfishness as a virtue—in the face of the collectivism, often happy, that provided "identity." The following year F. A. Hayek's *Road to Serfdom* reinforced Rand's individualism from the point of view of economic and social theory. The technological triumphs, even ultimate victory in war and the establishment of a total governmental structure after the war to put the finishing touches to the engineered welfare state, did not hold; the critics found neither meaningful culture nor a civilization perhaps worth keeping: "Civilization—Take It Away," a postwar song would have it.

An age of shame and fear had passed into history; it was somehow to be followed by an age that frankly thought of itself as an age of anxiety. An age of Adler and Jung, one might propose, gave way to an age of Wilhelm Reich:

Now there are times when a whole generation is caught . . . between two ages, between two modes of life and thus loses the feeling for itself, for the self-evident, for all morals, for being safe and innocent.

So Hesse's Harry Haller continues in a passage after the one quoted previously. And somehow this fits almost too perfectly the age that followed the technological achievements that built the Pentagon and the A-bomb. The age of culture and commitment, the age of adjustment, provided respite: fear and shame drove it back into a series of conservative postures, provided the use and strength of cultural forms that worked as temporary responses to the problems the experiences of the period demanded. But by 1945 these appeared exhausted and perhaps even detested forms that could and would no longer serve.

Thus it is that the Pentagon can be viewed as a two-faced symbol: for the age that it climaxed it was indeed the triumph of order, science, reason; the achievement of unity, purpose, morale;

the establishment of identity and role. And yet, for the age being born it was the home (spiritual, at least, in the most ironic sense) of the atom bomb and a frightening bureaucratic structure, the beginning of a brave new world of anxiety.

11 THE PEOPLE'S FAIR: CULTURAL CONTRA-DICTIONS OF A CONSUMER SOCIETY

In 1935 the American critic Kenneth Burke addressed the first of three American Writers' Congresses on the theme Revolutionary Symbolism in America. His intention was to convince the largely pro-Communist audience of the importance of myths as social tools for welding effective inter-relationships and for forging the organization to achieve common ends. The particular myth for which he pleaded, the positive symbol for which he called, was that of "the people."

> In suggesting that "the people," rather than "the worker," rate highest in our hierarchy of symbols . . . I am suggesting fundamentally that one cannot extend the doctrine of revolutionary thought among the lower middle class without using middle-class values. . . . The symbol of "the people" . . . also has the tactical advantage of pointing more definitely in the direction of unity. . . . It contains the ideal, the ultimate classless feature which the revolution would bring about—and for this reason seems richer as a symbol of allegiance. It can borrow the advantages of nationalistic conditioning and at the same time be used to combat the forces that hide their class preroga-tives behind a communal ideology.

"We convince a man by reason of the values we and he hold in common," said Burke, and in fact the idea of the people was basic to American folkways.

CULTURE AS HISTORY

We do not know whether the critic convinced his audience. We do know—any reading of the culture of the 1930s affirms it—that the idea of the people is in abundant evidence in the rhetoric of the period, a fundamental image that appeared to speak deeply of the American consciousness.

Because the rhetoric of an era often betrays the real—if often obscured—issues about the nature of a culture, it deserves serious examination. Certainly during the period from 1935 until the end of World War II, there was one phrase, one sentiment, one special call on the emotions that appeared everywhere in America's popular language: the people. It was not a new rhetorical flourish, to be sure, but the 1930s would see it acquire new functions. Never very precise as an ideological concept, it was now used to summon up notable outpourings of feelings to provide—somehow—an emotional base for an entire nation. With the birth of the so-called Popular Front in Western Europe, as well as in the United States, the people was a term meant to cut through divisions of class, ethnicity, and ideological distinctions of Left and Right to form a basic sentiment on which a national culture might be founded.

Thus Carl Sandburg gave us *The People, Yes;* the WPA projects offered Art for the People and The People's Theater; Frank Capra provided a series of enormously successful populist films in praise of "the little man"; and John Ford, most significantly in a number of films made near the end of the 1930s, rewrote American history in mythic and populist terms. And, while no statistical account is available, one might guess that more members of the audience responded tearfully than not to the image of Jane Darwell, playing Steinbeck's Ma Joad in Ford's film version of *The Grapes of Wrath,* when she delivered the final defiant speech with which the work closes: "We're the people that live. Can't nobody wipe us out. Can't nobody lick us. We'll go on forever. We're the people." Miss Darwell won a 1940 Academy Award for her performance. It was the heyday of the people.

The primary usefulness of this idea in the late 1930s was its ability to suggest that a basic unity underpinned the social and cultural structure of America. Divisions within society seemed superficial. Somehow, if they could only be allowed to talk or be instructed in what to say, the people could easily speak out in one voice. Perhaps because there seemed to be so many things that did divide, the idea of unity seemed crucial. A search was launched for some method of measuring and defining this unity and therefore of dealing with it properly. Statistics might very well prove the key. The concept of the average was born, a kind of statistical accounting of the people seen as a unit. For a culture that originally had enshrined individualism as its key virtue, interest in the average was now over-whelming. The Average American and the Average American Family became central to the new vision of a future culture. And by the 1930s additional statistical facts could be added to complete the picture of the average American: public opinion polls, from techniques developed in the mid-1930s, provided "scientific" evidence about thoughts and attitudes. Increasingly, this statistical creature —the average American—became central to cultural thinking and planning. He or she was soon invested as well with the sentimental aura that went with the more mystical notion of the people. If the people seemed pleasingly poetic and the average American suitably scientific, both versions of the idea nevertheless regarded society as a single entity. And both of these notions are essential to any serious assessment of American culture in the 1930s.

America's nineteenth-century seer Ralph Waldo Emerson once insisted about his countrymen, "We want our Dreams and our Mathematics." Frequently these are two sides of the same coin, that is, two sides of the same people, of the average American. The New York World's Fair of 1939–1940 pinched that coin and pinched it hard. It insisted it was the People's Fair and developed itself for the average American. The very appeal it sought, and gained, revealed basic contradictions that were crucial not only to the history of the Fair but to the culture from which it came.

Perhaps that was inevitable, for the Fair, almost as if it were consciously heeding Emerson's words, simultaneously demanded both Dreams and Mathematics. From the outset its ideological Dreams would be battering against the harsher realities of its Mathematics, its desire to please an America of consumers. This conflict was to pervade its history.

When the corporation that built the Fair ceased to be in 1945, it did an unusual thing: it left a small sum of money to commission the writing and publication of the Fair's history, "useful to those charged with organizing and operating future exhibitions." That little volume, *Making a World's Fair*, primarily was based on the 16 volumes of the minutes of the meetings of its board of directors. Written by a business reporter, Ed Tyng, it was not published until 1958, by a vanity press. It remains virtually unknown, and there is little evidence that it was, in fact, of value to anyone who was responsible for later fairs. But *Making a World's Fair* is remarkably fruitful for the historian who wishes to understand how the Fair-makers saw their own achievement, and especially how they understood the idea of the people and the average American, so central to their thought and rhetoric.

In his introduction to the book, Grover A. Whalen, the Fair's president, recalled that "the Fair was built for and dedicated to the people. It was built to delight and instruct them."

The statement reflects dozens of similar ones in speeches, news releases, and brochures issued from 1935, when Fair planning began, through the period of the life of the Fair. Whalen himself reiterated his populist appeal on the very first page of the Fair's *Official Guide Book:* "This is *your* Fair, built for *you,* and dedicated to you." In his autobiography, *Mr. New York,* he cited yet another brochure that announced that the Fair was for "everyone" and that its purpose was to "project the average man into the World of Tomorrow." *Making a World's Fair* also reprints an early statement, approved by the board of directors, that referred to their enterprise as "everyman's fair," dedicated to "bearing on the life of the great mass of the people," and offering special insights for "the plain American citizen."

No previous fair, either European or American, had developed such a rhetoric of popular concern, a rhetoric so closely in keeping with the idiom from which it had sprung. Previous fairs had shared what Whalen argued in his introduction was the demonstration of "the best industrial techniques, social ideas and services, the most advanced scientific discoveries of its day." But none had so openly articulated a message or lesson for the people. Again in Whalen's words, the Fair "conveyed the picture of the interdependence of man on man, class on class, nation on nation. It attempted to tell of the immediate necessity of enlightened and harmonious cooperation to preserve and save the best of modern civilization as it was then known."

Notice how significantly the rhetoric relates to the general concept of the people previously mentioned. The stress on unity, cooperation, interdependence, harmony—all relate in important ways to a general idea of the people. And while Fair literature contained much talk about the future—the World of Tomorrow—there was also considerable emphasis on *saving* "the best of modern civilization as it was then known."

All fairs may be said to educate, but this one insisted on a particular core curriculum, with particular lessons to be learned. As a key Fair document reprinted in the book reports, "The plain American citizen will be able to see here what he could attain for his community and himself by intelligent coordinated effort and will be made to realize the interdependence of every contributing form of life and work." Thus the Fair, in the eyes of its planners, proposed not only to invite the people, but to *create* the people in the most ideal sense of the concept.

Making a World's Fair is aware that all fairs have a more general and universal purpose: "They are designed directly to stimulate not only the larger interchange of goods domestically, but an increased international trade. In general, the success they attain in making business in every country aware of its own advantages and disadvantages as compared with others is very great."

In what sense does this perception of the nature of the Fair rest on an idea of the people? There are two significant issues at stake here. This Fair, more than had any previous effort, promoted as a major purpose the availability of consumer goods and services. It was a Fair that from the very start viewed the people not only as observers but also as potential consumers of the products it displayed. Indeed, as we shall see, the most popular exhibits tended to be those of producers of consumer goods. Thus, the advertising potential of the Fair and its promotion of the growing consumer culture of the time marked a subtle change in the role of the Fair— for the people. So important was this aspect to the World's Fair Corporation that it established an early Advisory Committee on Consumer Interests to develop some sort of effective consumer program. Yet in February 1939, several months before the Fair was to open, 21 members of that committee—government officials, consumer experts, academic and business—resigned, charging that the committee had been used to help sell exhibition space but that there had been "no opportunity to promote the interests of consumers in the planning of exhibits or to afford themselves any safeguard as to the values or reliability of information imparted to them by the Fair." This ambiguous relationship between the Fair and the people-as-consumers was to pervade the following two years.

While *Making a World's Fair* acknowledges that Fairs can be successful even if there is a financial loss, it is equally convinced that a Fair's contribution to world business and social progress would be more "limited" if this were the case. Thus from the start the Corporation assumed two additional and urgent functions: the Corporation itself would make money and its bondholding investors would reap a just profit. There was considerable confidence that New York City would also receive enormous financial gains. Whalen insisted that the Fair would bring to New York visitors who would spend a total of a billion dollars for merchandise, entertainment, hotels, and the like. Indeed, he calculated that an average Fair visitor would spend $56 in New York, of which $3.92 would be spent at the Fair itself.

It was in this way that the people, or the average Americans as the Fair executives called them, also meant what *Making a World's Fair* called "gates." The lesson is clear: "a cardinal principle of every fair is to have enough unusual, varied, and preferably 'revolutionary' spectacles and entertainments to attract masses of people, at an entrance fee that will not discourage volume attendance." In addition to their new role as consumers, the people were now customers.

Another aspect of the Fair's perspective on the people is more difficult to document, having received too little discussion in connection with almost all World's Fairs and perhaps especially with this one. In his introduction to *Making,* Whalen writes of the "color and rhythm and music and festivity" of the Fair; in his autobiography, he called the Fair "a rich and colorful festival." We know, of course, of the importance of color at the Fair and the special qualities attained through remarkable lighting. But let us consider the Fair as Festival, complete with parades, bands, pageants, and ceremonial occasions—the daily programs, the state salutes, and the vital participation of Fairgoers (the people) in these ritualistic activities. Whalen himself was a master of pomp and ceremony. He had arranged the extraordinary 1927 New York reception for Lindbergh and staged a brilliant National Recovery Act parade in New York City. Even the newspaper accounts of the many ceremonial events that made up the daily calendar at the Fair are alive with the spirit of popular involvement, with a sense of engagement ritualized.

If the Fair had been a small medieval festival in France or Italy, there undoubtedly would be a scholarly monograph on its meaning and significance. But in the United States we seldom take our festival life seriously. However, Whalen and the board of directors took the festival aspect of the Fair with all due seriousness. Whalen was a master showman who listed himself in *Who's Who* as a merchant, and his merchandising of the Fair often showed genius.

For the Fair was more than a plan, a well-ordered architectural and artistic display, brilliantly illuminated and effectively colored. It was as well a festival of sight and sound—always sound. The colorful tractor trains that toured the Fairgrounds played a few bars of "The Sidewalks of New York," and there were always bands, orchestras, and even, from some exhibits, the allure of interior sound floating out onto the general grounds. One *New York Times* item on May 5, 1939, speaks for a hundred or more similar reports:

Bands of strolling players—singers, dancers, musicians, acrobats, clowns, hired by the management Friday—roamed about the Fair. Seen in exhibit and amusement areas, they were strumming banjoes, singing popular songs, giving out swing music. They were always surrounded by crowds wherever they went.

Whalen knew the Fair could never be limited to the dream world of education and enlightenment its planners had envisioned; it had to meet the demands of its tenants, those commercial interests who regarded their participation as a simple money-making proposition. But in promising both enlightenment and consumer delights, Whalen was offering more than any fair could deliver.

The occasion for the Fair was the celebration of the 150th anniversary of the inauguration of George Washington as President, on the steps of Federal Hall in New York. When Fair ticket sales were not up to expectations in August 1939, Whalen organized a "jubilee Campaign" to sell 600,000 tickets in two weeks. Three hundred Fair employees—police, cashiers, guides, Haskell Indians, information clerks, and actors and actresses from Fair attractions—proceeded from the Fair grounds in a vast motorcade to Wall Street and the very spot at which Washington's inaugural ceremony had been held. There songs and stunts were performed at the base of the Washington statue; the music of the Trytons, the Fair Band, and the Dagenham Pipers (from the entertainment "Merrie England") helped delight the crowd of over 10,000. George McAneny, a banker and chairman of the Fair's board of directors, addressed the crowd, urging them to buy tickets to "your own Fair." It would be, he promised,

an experience and an opportunity to remember throughout your lives. We want you all to come, and we know that most of you will, but because there are still some slackers among so many thousands, some of the Fair employees have come to tell you a bit more about the Fair.

The famous black tap-dancer Bill Robinson, then appearing in *The Hot Mikado*, danced, and a group of chorus girls from another attraction did the Can-Can. Thus was historic celebration transformed for commercial gain; Fair attendance became equated with patriotic duty. The whole occasion had become a carnival.

One way in which the 1930s defined the people was in terms of public opinion. This concept had acquired an official aura after 1935, with the establishment by George Gallup of the American Institute of Public Opinion. Gallup's organization developed a method of polling that enabled all Americans to know what average or typical Americans thought about leading issues of the day. Thus in August 1939 Gallup was able to report that at least 85 percent of those who attended the Fair enjoyed it. Women were found to be significantly more enthusiastic about it than men. The "typical Fair visitor" visited the Fair an average of 2.3 times and only 3 percent of those attending did not like the Fair at all. Significantly, of those who did not attend the Fair, 63 percent felt they could not afford to attend.

In May Gallup reported that Fair visitors liked the following exhibits best: General Motors, the Theme Center (Democracity), American Telephone and Telegraph, Ford Motor Company, the Soviet Pavilion, the British Pavilion, and the Railroad exhibit.

During the same year Gallup reported other popular attitudes that might very well be important in a final assessment of the relationship between the people and the Fair. The majority of Americans thought the most serious issue facing the nation was not unemployment (the second most important issue) but keeping out of the war. The percentage for this as an overriding issue grew as the year came to an end. Few people seemed interested in buying television sets (13 percent), and there was still considerable doubt (47 percent) among the unemployed about whether one or the other spouse would be able to get a job within the next two years. And perhaps most interesting of all—given the Fair's enthusiasm for the World of Tomorrow and the wonders of machine technology—a June survey of those on relief disclosed that the reason most often given for the cause of their unemployment (23 percent) was the increased use of machines. Here was a paradox that Fair planners had hardly imagined in their optimistic vision of the technological future.

The real genius of the exhibitors at the Fair—and the Fair's board of design—was their understanding that the machine was not to be central, as it traditionally had been in all World's Fairs since 1851 and the Crystal Palace. Rather, they realized that in a consumer-centered society people ended up more fascinated with *process* than with machines. This Fair *showed* its visitors the processes. In this respect the intellectuals who planned the Fair and the people who attended it may have found some measure of interaction.

The people played yet another role. The designers and the theme committee did all they could to dramatize the sights of the Fair but the people of the People's Fair contributed a new element of singular innovation. It is perhaps best described in "Drama and Crowds—Direct Sources of and Materials for Design," an editorial that appeared in the August 1940 issue of *Architectural Record:* "Yet the greatest discovery in New York was the discovery of the crowd both as actor and as decoration of great power. The designers found out that the crowd's greatest pleasure is in the crowd." There followed a brilliant review of the most successful exhibits—American Telephone and Telegraph, Westinghouse, and General Motors— where the crowd took on a decorative pattern or where it was effectively used to fill space to excite the interest of other visitors. "Was not the finest element in the World's Fair 'theme center' the 'helicline,' with that long line of *people* held confidently against the sky?"

the reviewer asked. "The people themselves could well be the chief drama and decoration of a public architecture. . . ."

The official photographic version of the Fair experience—compiled in the commercial newsreels and the professionally commissioned photographs of the time—presents only one dimension of a much broader record. From opening day the people turned their Fair into something particularly special and vital to them: a setting for a series of important personal photographic souvenirs. No one can estimate the number of pictures—or the number of full photographic albums—that amateur photographers created out of their Fair. The newspapers were constantly reporting the rescue of amateur photographers who found themselves in dangerous situations while snapping pictures, and the Fair managers devoted more and more time to enabling camera-snapping visitors to accomplish their pictures without interfering with the life of the Fair. A study of the images they collected and how they visualized themselves and their families and friends within the Fair's environment would provide us with an invaluable understanding of the Fair from the people's perspective.

The Fair was not open for long before the people showed both the planners and the commercial interests how perverse they could be about following the arrangements so carefully made for them. One incident stands as a symbol for those who would dare to plan such an exposition in a world of modern capitalism. During the months of June and July 1939, the newspapers reported the dilemma frequently, and experts—planners, psychologists, and other professionals—provided their best official opinions and advice. What had happened was that 75 percent of the visitors who entered the Fairgrounds from subway and railroad terminals were turning to the right as they arrived, refusing absolutely to use both of the ramps provided for them. Fair officials and the newspapers insisted they did this in groups, "like sheep," and the situation not only created serious traffic problems but exasperated those exhibitors whose locations were on the left. In the end, in spite of the battery of official solutions, the people proceeded on its own way.

Nothing is more characteristic of the 1930s vision of the people than the concept of the typical or the average. While several suggestive examples already have been provided, a few more will confirm how central this vision was to the Fair during both its years.

Even before the Fair opened, in February 1939, the Consolidated Edison Company had announced that as a part of its theme it would display the high standard of living achieved by its 37,000 employees. This was to be accomplished by using the figure of Bill Jones, and a display of the living standard he had reached in 1938, as typical of all the Edison employees. A statue of Jones was to dominate the exhibit, which would highlight the facts that he was earning one-sixth more money for a shorter work week than in 1929, that he was a member of the Edison Savings and Loan Association, and that he was a happy participant in the Edison employee life insurance program. Bill was also portrayed as being safer from accidents than non-Edison workers, boasting a health rating more than 30 percent higher than the average industrial worker. Comprehensive medical insurance was his, as was the ability to get a low-interest loan that allowed him to be a homeowner.

In September 1940, the Fair selected New York City's typical boy on the basis of his appearance and his essay on the typical American boy. The winner, suitably enough, was to pose for a statue of the typical American boy. He was Alfred Roberts, Jr., an eighth-grader at P.S. 53, and his prize-winning essay was reprinted in *The New York Times*. It is a document clearly reflective of the values the Fair held dear:

> The typical American boy should possess the same qualities as those of the early American pioneers. He should be handy, dependable, courageous, and loyal to his beliefs. He should be clean, cheerful, and friendly, willing to help and be kind to others. He is an all-around boy—interested in sports, hobbies, and the world around him.
>
> The typical American boy takes good care of the public property he uses. He enjoys the comics, the movies, outdoor games, pets, and radio programs. He is usually busy at some handicraft or hobby and is always thinking up something new to do or make. That is why America still has a future.

One of the Fair's most popular films, *I'll Tell the World,* was shown every half hour at the Macfadden Publications exhibit; it followed the pattern of the family series so successful during the 1930s. Starring Jed Prouty, the Mauch Twins, and other leading performers of the day, it was the saga of how a typical American family, faced with the failure of its father's business, is "restored to happiness and security when father discovers the miraculous powers of advertising." (The quotation is from a *New York Times* report on March 5, 1939.) As expertly developed in the 1920s, the candid aim of advertising was to create a demand for its producers' goods and services. Then, as Silas Bent, the long-time investigator of American foibles in a machine-made nation, summed up in 1932, the four main emotions that advertising played on were humor, health, fear, and sentiment. A number of consumer advocates argued for resistance to such mass psychology. Stuart Chase, for example, maintained that if American society was to be truly functional, advertising would be used to teach people about the actual merits of new products, inventions, and opportunities; there would be no need to rely on psychological conditioning to foster artificial demand. In a *Survey* article on November 1, 1928, Chase referred to Russia as a country in which advertising was functional as well as beautiful.

The Fair took these arguments seriously, becoming in itself a gigantic advertisement both for a functional society and for the ideals and values that might produce such a society. Abandoning the old mass psychology appeals, the major exhibitors followed suit. In 1933 General Motors issued a pamphlet, "The Philosophy of Customer Research," detailing its newer version of its relationship with the public—the potential consumers of its products. A summary statement from the work, which was issued almost annually during the 1930s, reveals its perspective:

If a company can ascertain concretely and in detail just what the buyers would like to have, if it can build products in conformity with those desires and design its sales and advertising messages so that they will answer definitely the questions that are uppermost in the mind of the motorist, obviously there will be continued improvement in the merchandising process and a broadening of the service rendered.

Many of the most popular exhibits at the Fair attempted to follow this proposal by demonstrating *process* in order to involve the potential customer, by answering his or her questions, and by making the visitor feel part of the operation in a dramatic way. This is not to say that there were no hard-sell efforts to mold opinion and to stimulate interest in particular styles and approaches, but the fact of the visitor's involvement and participation shows that a new mode of advertising was pioneered in a major way at the Fair. This was indeed a new relationship between the people and the producers.

However, there were contradictions in the Fair's ideology concerning the people. Among them is the melancholy fact that the planners proposed, from the start, three important centers that were clearly off limits to the people. There were three private clubs at the Fair: Perylon Hall, the center of official entertaining, the Club of the National Advisory Committee, and the Terrace Club, of even more limited membership, restricted to certain major Fair bondholders.

Although the Fair planners saw to it that their experiences and ideology were preserved for posterity, we have fewer documents easily available to assess how the people in turn perceived the Fair. We can interpret only indirectly the impressions of those who attended, or who only read about it, saw pictures or movies of it, or received accounts from those who did attend.

The enterprise itself was an economic failure. The Chicago Fair in 1933 had made money; New York was convinced it could do even better. It did not. Attendance never matched expectations. Polls and press agents predicted that 50 million would attend during the first of the Fair's two seasons, but even two years of the Fair did not reach that mark. Why? A general explanation that seems to have satisfied most interpreters is the cost: the 75¢ admission charge was excessive.

Harvey Dow Gibson, a banker who served on the executive committee of the Fair board and who ran the Fair in 1940, insisted that a 50¢ admission, universal at all other fairs at the time, would have made the enterprise successful by drawing more people. Other critics agreed with Gardner Harding, in his generally approving *Harper's* analysis, that the "price ranges of the Fair are not . . . geared to the pocketbook of the fifty million people whom the Fair has staked its credit (and its return to its bondholders) on attracting through its turnstiles." He figured that an average tour of the Fair's high spots, with reasonable meals for two people, would cost an alarming $7.00.

Yet Gibson's privately printed autobiography, written in 1951, suggests another possibility (and incidentally offers an explanation for some of the changes that took place during the 1940 season, when he was in charge):

The Fair opened with overpowering ceremony, great pomp, and with regal splendor. So much so, that the common run of people, especially those from small places throughout the country, which were counted upon to comprise the backbone of the attendance, seemed to become sort of frightened in a way by it all and were ill at ease rubbing elbows or at the prospect of doing so, with what had unfortunately become known throughout the country as the high silk hat group which seemed to them as predominating. There seemed to be a growing feeling on the part of the masses expected to rush for the gates that they would be out of place in such an atmosphere.

But what of those who did come? The first conclusion that seems obvious from the published sources is that there was little interest in either the theme or the Fair's meticulous plan. The carefully articulated zones, the focal exhibits, the imaginative and symbolic use of color—they seemed to make no impression that in any way shaped consciousness in terms of what the Fair planners had seen as their message. Joseph Wood Krutch in *The Nation* carefully recommended that Fair visitors avoid "buildings given large inclu-

sive titles like 'Food,' 'Communications,' 'Consumers,' and the like.''
He stressed the Fair as a public playground and made fun of the
whole effort to define the World of Tomorrow. Debunking the
educational and cultural exhibits, he delighted in the "showmanship
. . . so good . . . that science and industry provide spectacles which
could easily compete with acrobats and trained seals of a conventional circus."

Life gave the Fair a major picture essay ("*Life* Goes to the
World's Fair," July 3, 1939) and detailed its favorite moments and
exhibitions but remained remarkably uninterested in the social message. Instead it saw "a magnificent monument by and to American
business." Walter Lippmann, in his influential column, did comment on the magnificent technological achievement of America, but
he found it ironic in view of men's lack of "moral unity with their
fellows and moral equilibrium within themselves."

Again and again, the critics admired and enjoyed the Fair's
entertainment but seemed unimpressed with its theme and higher
purpose. Krutch, in *The Nation*, was bored with the message of Democracity; he complained about its 25¢ admission charge and
fussed at some technical difficulties experienced during his visit.
But he was captivated by the spectacle of Bel Geddes' Crystal Las-
sies: "One stands on a platform just outside a huge crystal polygon
while nude dancers, deliriously multiplied by reflection, dance on
the mirror floors." So much for the Fair's message.

Gardner Harding, the Fair's friendliest critic, aired the most
fundamental objection to its practices by quoting an apologia from
a Fair administrator who had been with the project from the beginning: ". . . to be fully representative of community interests, the Fair
should have included the cooperative movement, the granges and
farmers' groups, the many useful and important social organizations that make up life in every American community. But you can't
sell space to those folks. They haven't any money." Harding's own
comment was that these folks without money were "anticipating the
World of Tomorrow with the rest of us" and that they were hardly
a minority of Americans. As an example of this failure he provided
a lengthy analysis of the Fair-sponsored Town of Tomorrow, which
he described as a "breach of faith." The exhibit intended to demonstrate that an actual modern residential community could be built
with the materials of the present for the pocketbook of everyman.
After reminding his readers that three-quarters of Americans
earned less than $3,000 a year, Harding pointed out that, of the 16
houses in the exhibit, only six "meet the absolute minimum require-
ment of social usefulness in costing less than $10,000 apiece."

The media that covered the Fair with perhaps the most intense interest and concern were the business magazines. For them the story of the Fair was a question of sheer marketing: advertising, merchandising, selling. *Business Week* did a long analysis on November 4, 1939, attempting to account for the success of the "shows that pulled at the Fair." General Motors' Futurama (*Business Week* felt people liked the comfortable moving chairs) was clearly the hit attraction. Others included: Eastman Kodak, with its brilliant show of photographs; American Telephone and Telegraph's audience participation, with free long-distance calls and the Voder, a device that talked like a human (*Business Week* felt the pretty operator who worked the keys and pedals was the secret of its success); and General Electric's House of Magic. ("Not many in the packed audiences understood the significance of the tricks they saw performed with thyratrons and stroboscopes. But they came away thrilled, mystified, and soundly sold on the company.") General Electric also featured a kitchen in which the appliances talked.

Reflecting the success of the general philosophy expressed in the General Motors pamphlet, *Business Week* observed: "Companies making consumer products did a better job of contacting the public than did the industrial goods producers." It admired the Ford exhibit for the comfort of its facilities and the quality of its attendants, who could explain technical matters in a layman's language. Macfadden Publications rated special praise for its clever use of films, "an ideal vehicle for the exhibitor who has something intangible to sell."

The magazine also approved of those solid exhibits that showed manufacturing operations, "sure-fire attractions" at Firestone, Ford, Chrysler, White Owl, and Swift. Exhibitors were critical of the architecture at the Fair, for merchandising reasons, it was reported. Exteriors, several felt, ought to be redesigned to "offer a stronger invitation to come on in."

Although the perspective is special, the list of the most popular exhibits is typical: account after account stresses showmanship above all other values. It is hard to believe that the people didn't respond overwhelmingly.

One major violation of the Fair's ideology turned out to be a remarkable success story in terms of significant profit on investment: Billy Rose's Aquacade, which rated the distinction of a *Time* cover story. The saga of Rose's triumph—approximately one out of every six visitors to the Fair paid 40¢ admission to see his show—is a show-business legend. In spite of the fact that many of the Fair managers thought his kind of production totally inappropriate for their lofty vision of the World of Tomororw, Rose had snagged the choicest ready-built concession for 10 percent under the highest bidders.

Walter Lippmann noticed the irony of General Motors' extraordinary success with Futurama. "General Motors has spent a small fortune to convince the American public that if it wishes to enjoy the full benefit of private enterprise in motor manufacturing," he wrote, "it will have to rebuild its cities and its highways by public enterprise." Did the people, from their comfortable seats at a fascinating show, notice the contradiction?

Many of the more than two hundred films shown at the Fair presented viewers with a complex new relationship between entertainment, education, and deceptively hard-sell commercial messages. *The New York Times* reported on June 18, 1939, that "only a handful" could be classified as pure entertainment. In Whalen's World of Tomorrow, the screen had been converted into a fast-talking salesman.

The *Times* analyzed at length the promotion and content of one of this new breed, *The Middleton Family at the New York World's Fair*. Produced by Westinghouse, it purported to be the story of a middle-class family from Indiana and their adventures at the Fair. In an elaborate advertising and distribution scheme, Westinghouse furnished prints to its local dealers throughout the country, ostensibly so that the people back home would not be deprived of experiencing the Fair's delights. But the Middletons were a fictitious family, portrayed by professional actors, and the Westinghouse Fair Building was the only one the film identified by name. The Fair had become a locus for pioneering what the *Times,* in its headline, dubbed "Tomorrow's Propaganda."

Other events raised questions of whether the American people were, in fact, ready for the World of Tomorrow. The Fair itself and its planners and administrators projected an optimism and an enthusiasm that often bewildered and even angered visitors from Europe, who were witnesses to the coming of a world war. But was this optimism characteristic? Were Americans truly committed to this vision of their future? One of the deans of American photography, Edward Steichen, thought not. Speaking at a meeting held to award prizes in a photography contest sponsored by the Citizens' Housing Council, Steichen took the occasion to attack the gloomy subject matter of American art. In the contest for photographs on How New York Lives, 702 photos were submitted, of which 678 portrayed slum scenes, and 24 pictured new model housing. Steichen felt called upon to comment on this in contrast to what he had seen in the photomurals at the Soviet Pavilion at the Fair. The photography itself, he remarked, was the kind any big American commercial house would regard as the lowest type of work: "But you leave that room after seeing those pictures with a sense of exhilaration. The pictures have joy, gaiety, and life. There's the message. They believe in what they are doing." Steichen seemed to forget the enthusiastic promise of the future that pervaded such art as *The City*, the classic 1930s film that premiered at the Fair. But which of these attitudes was closer to the truth of the people?

What is the historian to make of the fact that the lively and sustained discussion of the Fair's plan and theme, which occupied newspapers and popular magazines for three years before it opened, seemed to disappear once the Fair was a reality? Did the people refuse to accept its ideology, just as they insisted on going their own way, "like sheep"?

The contradictions of the Fair were the contradictions of the culture itself. How well anyone understood the people—except perhaps the newly developing geniuses of advertising and marketing—remains a serious question.

It is interesting to examine some of the major changes that were made when the Fair reopened in 1940 with Harvey Dow Gibson, the banker, in effect replacing Grover Whalen. Whalen stayed on as figurehead at a cut in pay from $100,000 to $75,000; Gibson worked for nothing in an effort to save the Corporation from bankruptcy. He didn't succeed, but he did manage a profit for the year.

The tone was changed. Gibson announced that the Fair would now be a "super country fair," and the description seems to have been an accurate one. He did away with any talk about the lessons of interdependence; even the World of Tomorrow tended to disappear under the new banner "For Peace and Freedom," Internationalism was played down, and the emphasis was distinctly American. The Fair's 1940 poster featured a rosy-cheeked, middle-aged middle-American signifying his great pleasure in same with a caption that read "Makes you proud of your country." A decade or so earlier, people might have called the posterman Babbitt, but the Fair chose to name him Elmer. Actors portraying him made personal appearances all over the country to urge fellow Americans to come to the Fair.

The Soviet Pavilion had been torn down. In its place, newly landscaped, a bandstand was built, and the area was rechristened the American Common. Here various Americanized foreign groups and other American folk performers presented weekly programs of song and dance. Robert Kohn, who from the beginning had been associated with the theme committee and with the board of design and had been the most outspoken proponent of the Fair's original ideology, was now reduced to presiding over the entertainment there. It is not without significance that an interest in *folk*—perhaps another way of defining the people—replaced the social ideas that had dominated the planning before 1939.

Except for the physical plan itself and its basic iconography, now almost quaint because it failed to function as part of a fundamental unity of thought and action, it was difficult to detect much that had survived from the first Fair season to the second. The Consumers Building was now the World of Fashion, complete with fashion shows. There were two new model houses, erected according to FHA standards, on the grounds before the Electrified Farm. These became homes for "more than forty representative American families, who will stay one week each. The families will be selected by newspapers in various parts of the country, and will consist of a father America, a mother America, and two little Americans, preferably a boy and a girl." One thing the Fair was not about to forget was its dedication to the average American and the average American family.

General Motors' 1940 additions included trains and still more cars on the roads of its exhibit. Bel Geddes, yielding to those who had found serious lapses in his vision of 1960, added 600 more churches, several hundred filling stations, and one university.

The 1940 emphasis on a folksy, comfortable Fair clearly suggested an event intended to entertain and amuse as opposed to one which challenged the mind. The Gibson administration renamed the Fair's entertainment area The Great White Way, and the Fair managers were more helpful to concessioners than they had been under Whalen's tenure.

The 1940 *Official Guide Book* was completely revised in a style designed to be snappier and more popular than the 1939 version. Stanley Appelbaum, in the excellent introductory essay to his *The New York World's Fair 1939/40*, a selection of professional photographs, compares a 1939 *Guide Book* entry with its 1940 successor: 1939's "In Steinmetz Hall, vivid lightning, thunderous noise, ten million volts flashing over a thirty-foot arc" became 1940's "In Steinmetz Hall, 10,000,000 volts of man-made lightning leap thirty feet through the air with a roar of thunder, scaring the daylights out of you."

The coming of war to Europe—and the well-documented fear of Americans that they somehow might be drawn into it—obviously cast a shadow on the Fair during both years of its existence. Wyndham Lewis, who came to visit the Fair from an England in the midst of struggle with Nazi Germany, provided a chilling comparison in his *America, I Presume* (1940). Unable to believe that the Fair could be as innocent as it seemed, he likened the Court of Power to the spectacle of the Nuremberg Rallies.

The managers decided early on not to broadcast news of the war at the Fairgrounds, but this could hardly obliterate the increasing consciousness of Americans about what the war meant. The theme committee had struggled to instill an understanding of interdependence that would assure peace; now the 1940 Fair was acknowledging the coming of war, sponsoring, for example, special occasions for peoples and governments in exile.

A final assessment of the People's Fair is difficult, for the people remain an anomaly. They were shown the possibilities of life as a festival, as a magic show, and they accepted consumer capitalism without critical reflection because of the wonders of process unfolded before them. So it was that the Fair became a rather generalized advertisement for something the 1930s had begun to call the American Way of Life.

The Fair's influence on the directions of science, technology, and the arts is a visible one. In an article about "Trends of Tomorrow," *House and Garden* predicted that the new ideas in home decoration displayed there "will surely bend the collective American mind to a much more widespread acceptance of the modern idiom —in architecture, decoration, and landscaping." The magazine's prediction was accurate, but the sectors it chose to feature—the Fair's three private clubs, the executive suites of the major exhibitors, the foreign pavilions of Poland, Finland, and Sweden—were either off limits to the people or sparsely attended in favor of the more spectacular attractions. It was the Fair *itself* that became a useful advertisement, in quite the same way that Thorstein Veblen had suggested in 1899: high culture becomes a kind of advertisement for the leisure class and those who would emulate it. For the people, the World of Tomorrow projected not a new world, but a new fantasy world based on the possibilities of modern technology, a world that could be enjoyed because it could be controlled—a veritable Disneyland.

Although physically vanished, the Trylon and the Perisphere remain as indelible as icons for all Americans. Although few can remember their specific symbolic import and what lesson they proposed to teach, all the people held on to the image; it is part of our legacy from the 1930s, a dazzling white reminder of a world that somehow science and technology might achieve, a neat and ordered geometric pattern that pleased aesthetically yet somehow, like a science fiction movie set, seemed alien to life as it is really lived.

If few remember what that image signified, fewer still are aware of what actually became of it. The four thousand tons of steel that went into the making of the Trylon and Perisphere became scrap destined to make bombs and other instruments of war. Designed to teach lessons of mutual interdependence that would make all future wars impossible, in its own final functioning the symbol became an instrument of war.

Given the contradictions between the planners' ideology and the demands of consumer capitalism, perhaps we can only guess what the New York World's Fair of 1939–1940 means as history. Perhaps, as John Bainbridge and St. Clair McKelvey observed in *The New Yorker* ("That Was the New York World's Fair") after it closed, the most eloquent summation of the whole incident "was made by a radio man named Dave Driscoll, an expert in double-talk" who worked for New York's station WOR:

On closing night, after everyone else said farewell to the Fair, Driscoll mounted the dais in the Court of Peace wearing top hat and tails and spoke impromptu in a tongue unknown to Barnum, as follows: "In this vast amphitheatre millions from all the Americas and from all corners of the world have heard addresses by statesmen, Whalen, graisnas, McAneny, cabishon, Gibson, forbine, and nobility. Here was the pledge of peace which might well have been the fiederness, bedistran, and goodle of this great expedition. Now that pledge is forgotten. Sleedment, twaint, and broint forbish the doldrum all over the world. Alas!"

We might all learn double-talk. Or perhaps we might better learn to face and resolve the contradictions.

IV | TRANSITIONS AND TRANSFOR-MATIONS

Library of Congress

The Alfred Stieglitz Collection 1949.
The National Gallery of Art, Washington

Our Town

*The urban experience
has been a source of
enthusiasm and energy,
dismay and despair.
There have been many
kinds of cities and city-
dwellers; not one urban
experience but many—
and equally many ways
of recording and thus
contributing to the cul-
ture of the city. These
intensely personal ren-
derings by two masters
of the art of photogra-
phy suggest how even
in an increasingly
mechanized urban
environment, indi-
vidual perspectives can
still illuminate our
own ways of seeing and
believing: Walker
Evans's "View of
Morgantown, West
Virginia, 1935," and
Alfred Stieglitz's "From
My Window, New
York, 1900–02."*

All good teachers should provide their students with at least one valuable practical tool useful after graduation. I give my students a model of an ideal history lecture good any time and place, whenever one might be called upon to perform in a learned manner. It provides a universal model of history yet requires only the most limited knowledge for its implementation. All you have to remember are four major propositions; all you have to have is some fast footwork and a quick tongue to get away with it.

The outline is as follows:

You start (some brief attention to place and time sets the proper tone) with the announcement that this (whatever time and place you are supposed to be discussing) was a time of crisis. After all, historians always are finding crises; some sort of crisis can always be found. So your audience will certainly believe you: it *was* a time of crisis, and who can possibly deny it?

Of course, the crisis (one should be sure to define it with sufficient vagueness or generality) leads naturally to your discussion of the cause of the crisis. That, too, is always easy: it was a period of transition. Once again, what kind of historian are you if you can't find some kind of transition? The world, it seems, is always betwixt and between: feudal to capitalist, rural to urban, the possible list is virtually limitless. Transitions seem the one really stable thing in this transitory world in which we live. There is always a transition occurring.

It now becomes slightly more difficult. That transition must somehow create a significant shift in the social structure: some class previously in control must, during the transition, slip and fall from power or grace. Frequently, it is an old middle class (somehow old classes, especially old middle classes, seem naturally destined to pass away); so let the old middle class go—not without some sorrowful words about its past glories and achievements, however.

Now we are ready for our triumphant conclusion: a new class—preferably here again a new middle class—is rising to take its rightful place in the order of things. Of course, some might prefer another class; that is optional as long as it rises and as long as you are aware that sooner or later there will be another lecture where you will have to arrange for it to fall, too.

My parody is crude and overdrawn. And yet I find myself (sometimes in this very volume) adopting a pattern that comes very close to this, convinced that after all it is not entirely foolishness and nonsense, that somewhere in the joke there is that famous kernel of truth. For history *is* the study of transitions and transformations. I suspect that the one proposition that all historians might agree to is that history is the study of change over time. That domain is in fact unique to the historian.

Because cultures are constantly in tension, because history is a fundamental part of culture, because being itself is essentially a contradiction, the dynamic of the historical process is composed of the working out of these tensions. In the most vigorous days of Enlightenment domination of much of the political and intellectual life of the eighteenth century, there was the constant challenge of religious enthusiasm and the growth of the Gothic and irrationalist tradition. There always has been, furthermore, the confrontation of a vision of reality not only with alternative visions, other ideologies, but also with hard-rock experience on which some ideologies can indeed shatter under certain circumstances.

Transformation was a key word in the late nineteenth and early twentieth centuries, becoming significant not only in the world of science and magic but in the world of history and social science as well. History increasingly had to confront the changing of forms in which experience was expressed—often rapid change because of technological innovation. Such transformations created the need for still others.

The three essays in this section are concerned with these general issues. The essay on the role of the city is an early one, reprinted in this place because it tries to deal with two important questions. First, the historian is often faced with words that continue to exist but whose essential nature or meaning has changed. *City* is one of those words. So is *family*. We can talk about Athens in the fifth century B.C. and New York in the nineteenth century and call them both cities, but it is obvious that what links the two cannot overlook the radically different experience each provided its residents. When we speak of families in the seventeenth century and families in the twentieth we can of course see a kinship, but in what sense are we talking about the same thing in terms of historical morphology? And second, the essay tries to put the discussion of pro- and anti-urbanism in a different cultural context. The urgency of its message is perhaps not so great as it was before the work of such distinguished cultural historians of the city as Thomas Bender and William Taylor, yet I believe it still makes a contribution.

"Culture and Communication" attempts to address the problem of transitions and transformation with a more careful examination of the cultural role of technology without yielding to the temptation of technological determinism.

The essay on the idea of "personality" makes a specific attack on the problem of transitions and transformation and is a key in my effort to define a new cultural configuration. Obviously, I believe in the importance for the cultural historian of a fundamental psychological base for the ordering of cultural materials. Cultures require some such psychological vision.

The concept of cultural change implies transformations in the social, technological, and moral order. They might not occur simultaneously or even in neat sequence. But such transformations indicate as well basic changes in the calculation of needs, wants, and desires. Each culture produces its own pattern of desire. Thus every culture, too, is predicated on a particular and unique psychological model essential to its own definition. All of this proposes a world of continuous transition and constant transformation.

12 THE CITY IN AMERICAN CULTURE

In 1950 the Director of the Census announced an important yet relatively unnoted change in reporting certain key data that revealed extraordinarily significant changes in American life and history. The urban population no longer could be reported in terms of so-called *cities* alone; one could only speak of *urbanized* areas. Nor did any meaningful definition of *rural* any longer exist (except for individual property holders' characterizations of their land as a ranch or a farm). In effect, the Director of the Census reported that the city no longer exists in America; rural and urban distinctions, statistically at least, are no longer meaningful. This "disappearance" of the city from American life calls upon us to reassess the overall meaning of the urban experience for the development of our culture. In a civilization that proposed to begin with a City on a Hill, we have learned a great deal about what happened to the hill but very little about what happened to the city.

The persistent myth of American anti-urbanism in a nation that from the start was more heavily urbanized than almost any nation on earth leads to a series of strange paradoxes. And a useful perspective on this emerges in taking that moment in history when a new consciousness of the city and its overwhelming importance to our development—cultural and intellectual as well as social and political—becomes obvious. Three "revolutions" occurred roughly between the 1820s and the 1870s. The first was a revolution in communications, a revolution that involved not only transportation but also all of the ways in which people might significantly communicate with one another, based upon the discovery and application of steam and ultimately electricity. A series of such dramatic inventions made it possible for a man in one lifetime to move from what appeared to be one kind of an era to another, from an era of difficulty in communication to a period of instant international communications. The second revolution was an "organizational revolution"—in a sense, a consequence of the first. Within the structure of industry as well as within all institutions of American society an increased premium was being put not simply on work and productivity, but also on bureaucracy and on organizers of work and production, consumption and distribution. This second revolution developed an entirely new class, a middle class not of property owners but of salaried workers, dedicated to engineering, to managerial tasks, to the science of administration. This class saw as its function a new kind of professional leadership for the engineer, manager, and technician within society. Coincident with these revolutions was a third occurence, the "organic revolution," which entailed a dramatic transformation in the basic images of intellectual discourse. The solitary, atomic image that dominated so much earlier thought was replaced by images of organic interaction, growth and evolution, process and outcome, groups and the identification of self in terms of its relationships to others.

The importance of these "revolutions" in themselves is not as significant in the present context as the growing awareness among Americans of the *existence* of these revolutions and their willingness to deal with their seeming consequences. For the city, the new city, seemed initially and inevitably the first consequence of these revolutions. Even more, this city was ultimately *the hope* of these revolutionary developments, the very ideal by which the problems resulting from these revolutions would be solved. This envisions a very special kind of city, a very special set of city images. And two of the most striking social developments of the nineteenth century —the greatest development of urbanization and the greatest increase in the number of Christians that the world had ever witnessed—are not unrelated.

Now, it would be relatively easy to provide a series of pro-urban images to counter the rather sterile and meaningless series of anti-urban sentiments by American intellectuals collected in Morton and Lucia White's *The Intellectual Versus the City*. But it would be more useful to look at Emerson, usually taken as a model of a person holding a certain kind of anti-urban sentiment. Emerson was no champion of the city—far from it—but his essay of 1844, "The Young American," is imbued with an optimistic involvement in an age of roadbuilding, of railroad construction, of science and engineering, and in their implications for the creation of American sentiments. Not only does Emerson seem to accept joyfully much of the communications revolution, but he also argues that certain organizational changes are of such great significance that they herald the approach of some kind of beneficent socialism. Certainly no positivist and no graduate of the École Polytechnique, Emerson is nonetheless prepared to state: "The community is after all only the continuation of the same movement which made the joint stock company for manufactures, mining, insurance, banking, and so forth."

Obviously, Emerson is concerned about the cities; cities "drain the country of the best" and as a result the country remains cultivated by "inferior men." In what is hardly a pastoral mood, Emerson bemoans the fact that the farmer often must sacrifice pleasure, freedom, thought, and love to his work and in the end is compensated only by bankruptcy! In his 1860 essay, on "The Conduct of Life," he makes clear his belief in the basic importance of wealth: "To be rich is to have a ticket of admission to the masterworks and chief men of each race." Speculative genius builds the mines, the telegraph, the mills, and as a result the public is the gainer. The country boy finds the town as his chance, an opportunity. While Emerson does not commit himself to an urban existence, he does argue that towns *ought* to exist for *intellectual* purposes, to harbor art and music, so that the public may reap the benefits. Perhaps the greatest problem of civilization is how to give all people "access to the masterpieces of art and nature." To this end, works of art, music, "intellectual production" should be owned by "states, towns and lyceums" in order that the bonds of neighborhood be drawn more closely. He is in fact proposing that the city be reconstituted so that it would exist "to an intellectual purpose." He praises "the aesthetic value of railroads [which] is to unite the advantages of town and country life, neither of which we can spare. A man should live in or near a large town, because, let his own genius be what it may, it will repel quite as much of agreeable and valuable talent as it draws, and, in a city, the total attraction of all the citizens is sure to conquer, first or last, every repulsion, and draft the most improbable hermit within its walls some day in the year." Emerson makes it absolutely clear that no one can be fully a person, in his sense, without the city. True, cities must be used "cautiously and haughtily," but "we can ill spare the commanding social benefits of cities; they must be used." And by 1867, in "The Progress of Culture," he is arguing even more strongly for cooperatives, societies of science and administration: "Who does not prefer the age of steel, of gold, of coal, petroleum, cotton, steam, electricity, and the spectroscope? All of this activity has added to the value to life, and to the scope of the intellect." Here, moreover, is a eulogy for the advancement of institutions and organization, the "new scope of social science," the "genius of science," of administration, of practical skill. The result is one of the first great testaments in praise of the new middle class of managers and technicians, organizers and engineers, what he calls the "rapid addition to our society of a class of true nobles." For Emerson, the chief value of all of this is metaphysical, never material, and the images he uses suggest that the "inviolate soul" that he seeks is "in perpetual telegraphic communication with the Source of events."

Such themes are not isolated in a few passages in Emerson; they are repeated over and over by him and by his contemporaries. The three revolutions—in communications, in organization, in perception of the world and its nature—implied a shift in basic values. Once they are accepted, so too, increasingly, is the belief not only in the inevitability of urbanization as a consequence of the revolutions themselves, but also in the possibilities of *the* city, or *a* city, in the wake of these new values. This does not mean an uncritical acceptance of urban life, but it does mean that acceptance of urbanization is not an unmitigated disaster; that, indeed, the city may have a special role to play in making a great civilization in America. Listen, for example, to George Tucker in his famous *The Progress of the United States* (1843):

The growth of cities commonly marks the progress of intelligence in the arts, measures the sum of social enjoyment, always implies excessive mental activity which is sometimes healthful and useful, sometimes distempered and pernicious. If these congregations of men diminish some of the comforts of life, they augment others; if they are less favorable to health than the country, they also provide better defense against disease and a better means of cure.

And in his revealing conclusion of this passage:

In the eyes of the moralist, cities afford a wider field both for virtue and vice; and they are more prone to innovation, whether for good or evil. The love of civil liberty is, perhaps, both stronger and more constant in the country than the town; and if it is guarded in the cities by a keener vigilance and a more far-sighted jealousy, yet law, order, and security are also, in them, more exposed to danger from the greater facility with which intrigue and ambition can there operate on ignorance and want. Whatever may be

good or evil tendencies of populous cities, they are the result to which all
countries that are at once fertile, free and intelligent, inevitably tend.

Tucker's passage provides many of the key ideas: the inevitability
of cities, the *necessary* relationship between cities and progress, the
very trials of the city that present such a profound challenge that
somehow improves men and institutions *if* met effectively.

Recall in this setting the image of the city as the great European capital of history that somehow each new city hoped to emulate (a new Carthage, an Athens of the Middle West). Let me
mention as examples a few bad lines from a poet named George
Lunt who wrote his poem "Culture" in 1843, dedicating it to the
members of the Boston Mercantile Library Association, whose purposes, Lunt insisted, proved "that the accumulation of wealth is
useful" and who "exemplify the character of a City, always distinguished for cultivation and liberality." (Just one very bad stanza will
make the point, I think.)

> And thou, fair city of the western wave,
> Built on the forest-hunter's vanished grave,
> Thou, whose whole story is a lesson taught
> How vanquished nature yields to conquering thought!
> As down their vista all thy years unveil,
> Fain would my heart prophetic read thy tale!
> A richer wealth than sea-born Venice bore,
> A nobler dower than golden Florence wore,
> No art has wrought it and no price can buy
> With Ophir's wedge or Tyre's imperial dye,—
> Daughters to grace and sons that built the state
> With deep foundations laid exempt from fate,
> Virtue in wealth and stable blessing given,
> Would man accept it, from indulgent Heaven!*

In 1839 Daniel B. Bernard called cities "the chief seats of
refinement and civilization in every land," as they always have and

---

* Admittedly great poets, too, found in the city and its scenes special joy as well as
special opportunities. Walt Whitman was ever the poet of that city. Declining almost
always to sentimentalize life in the country, he discovered that probably, "in *proportion*, there is as much wickedness in country as in towns." Further, life in the country
often meant misery, isolation, a hard struggle for existence, all of which nurtured
avarice, barbarous ignorance, alcoholism, and a strange sort of egotism. Bad diet and
hard work often destroyed young children, who lost the "elasticity of youth" and
became "round-shouldered and clumsy." The city possessed so many advantages,
libraries and art galleries not the least among them. Whitman concluded: "No matter
what the moralists and metaphysicians may teach, *out of our cities the human race does
not expand and improvise so well morally, intellectually, or physically.*"

always will of necessity be. The very concentration in cities means influence and power, Gardner Spring announced in 1850. And the Reverend E. H. Chapin saw that it was natural that rural youth should look hopefully to the city as the center of their dreams, the "magic world of their destiny." For the city was the "necessary agent of commercial enterprise, the builders of national greatness." To have a great nation meant, indeed, to have great cities: "The interest of the city is as superior to that of the country, as humanity to nature; as the soul to the forms and forces of matter; as the great drama of existence is to the theater in which it is enacted." But, more than this, all of these quoted—and literally hundreds more could be called as witnesses—agreed, as Chapin said, that "the city reveals the moral ends of being, sets the awful problems of life." Above all, the city is that testing ground, that fire necessary to temper steel, to strengthen by conflict man and morals.

The consequence of the three revolutions, in brief, was the acceptance of the city. And that city was now being thought of in terms of destined glory associated with a European past. Finally, the city as a moral challenge is repeated over and over in our literature —high-, low-, and middlebrow—at least from the 1830s to the present. This moral challenge is of greatest significance when it is put in the context of the growth of religious revivals leading to the special urban revivalism of the 1850s. Revivalism not only moves forcefully and centrally into the cities but also in the process becomes an effort to save the community and through this the salvation of the nation as a whole.

Obviously, the particular Christian moral challenge of cities is an older and more persistent theme in the literature of Christianity than we often realize. In his voyage, John Bunyan's Christian had to go through Vanity Fair in order to see and reach the Celestial City. Over and over, this notion of the need of Americans to pass through the necessary, the inevitable urban experience to reach the Holy City persists in our literature, especially in the last half of the nineteenth century. The theme is repeated almost without question not only by ministers, but also by laymen who often have a strong religious bent. The archetype remains important in spite of the fact that there is on most occasions no specific reference to Bunyan or to *The Pilgrim's Progress*. But Vanity Fairs *do* exist, and they do so meaningfully only in relationship to Celestial Cities. Nor is this an unusual idea to find in the literature of a Christian people for whom from the start "pagan" meant something connected with the rural countryside. After all, the religious vision of so great a Christian thinker as St. Thomas Aquinas insisted that to be a good Christian one must indeed live in the city.

If it is not unexpected to find an increasing interest in cities from a Christian people undergoing the most vigorous revivalist and missionary activity ever recorded, it is perhaps not too surprising to find a newer popular vision of the city also beginning to emerge in the post–Civil War years. Such images do not quite fit with a supposedly anti-urban America.

Currier and Ives, for example, those "printmakers to the American people" who operated from 1835 to 1907, not only printed rural, sporting, and historical scenes. but also devoted a good deal of their output to urban scenes bathed in as much nostalgia as any rural scene might be. This popular enthusiasm and even nostalgic or sentimental rendering of cities was common not only in popular prints but also in popular verse. Will Carleton, whose books sold in enormous quantities, felt, like all great poets, that true poetry was that which voiced the sentiments of its time and stirred the "blood of living generations." Carleton, who wrote "Over the Hill to the Poor House" and lived from 1845 to 1917, produced a huge series of successful volumes of poetry that Harpers published. The first volume, *Farm Ballads,* appeared in 1873. It was followed by *Farm Legends* and, finally, in 1881, *Farm Festivals.* But, like Currier and Ives, Carleton did not simply dwell on American rural nostalgia. In the next few years, he produced *City Ballads* (1885), *City Legends* (1889), and, of course, *City Festivals* (1892). If one looks at Carleton's verses (it is perhaps not fair to call them poems) one discovers a strange phenomenon: as with Currier and Ives, rural and urban experiences can be regarded with the same sentimentalism, the same full-blooded enthusiasm, the same sense of values. It is in fact difficult to distinguish between the two kinds of experiences. Carleton delights in both, and he was, on his own admission and by evidence of the sales figures, trying to express the basic sentiments of a wide American audience. "The Burning of Chicago" is a marvelous long poem that ends:

O Crushed but invincible city. . . .
And happily again they will prosper, and bask in the blessings of God
Once more thou shalt stand mid the cities, by prosperous breezes caressed
O grand and unconquered Chicago, still Queen of the North and the West!

Thus the structure of his verses, the similiarity between essentially rural and urban treatments, is a popular parallel to the work of Currier and Ives and indicates a more complex popular pattern than most critics have allowed.

Another popular vision emerged in this period of the city, a familiar one, though perhaps not in quite the way I propose to treat it. Horatio Alger published, between 1867 and 1910, an enormous series of books. So popular were the books, however, that the publisher continued the series after his death (he died in 1889). The Alger books are of course normally treated as hymns to American middle-class concepts of success, and although this is important such a concentration of attention has blinded most cultural historians to the whole of their cultural significance. For whatever the Alger books may have to say about success, they were directed toward a rural, and not an urban, population. The urban, at least big-city, response to his books was not in any sense as overwhelming as the response of rural or at least small-town America. In fact, many city dwellers found the works foolish and without interest. They realized how little of what Alger had to say corresponded with the reality of life in the city.

Of even greater significance is that many of the books are about New York City—and go into enormous detail. This is a crucial point, for in large part these books existed and thrived because they provided an easy and terror-free way of making possible rural adaptation to urban life. You could find out *what* to do, *where* to go, *how* to begin, and *how* to proceed in the city. They are effortless guidebooks, not simply to success but to life in the city. They were how-to-do-it books, not simply how to discover wealth but how to adapt easily to the pattern of living expected in the city. A young man from the country could brief himself on transportation around the city, the ways to obtain lodging and employment. This aspect of the Alger books has been too often overlooked and deserves greater stress; they are *not* anti-urban. Indeed, they may even have been enthusiastically purchased by many who did not believe in their basic value structure or who were not interested in the story as much as in the wealth of realistic detail. In fact, there is a great need for a study of the many devices available for such adjustment to urban living, a subject every bit as important as the Americanization of the immigrant.

Thus some key developments in late-nineteenth-century American intellectual history help prepare the way for an easier acceptance of certain features of the newly developing culture, especially elements of the urban experience. Robert H. Walker's often obtuse study, *The Poet and the Gilded Age,* almost inadvertently points to apparent paradoxes. One chapter is devoted to showing how the bad but popular poets he studied reacted negatively to the city; yet his own statistics reveal that 19 percent of his poets pay tribute to urban achievements while 23 percent react to city "evils." Further, while his poets are enthusiastic about the American West, a sizable number are really talking by the 1890s about the glories of new and major cities arising in the West. Their West is the West of Chicago and San Francisco, not of prairie and mountains alone.

To all this should be added a reminder of that older and constant minor theme in our intellectual life that reaches a peak in the last decades of the nineteenth century and early decades of the twentieth—the discovery of the degeneracy and the fundamental isolation of rural life. In literature, at least since Howe's *Story of a Country Town* (1883), there appears a persistent discussion of the vicious, narrow, and even pernicious life of rural America, its degeneration from older, more ideal forms. When one joins these well-known fictional accounts with the newer development in "rural sociology"—the work of such people as Gilpin and Liberty Hyde Bailey—the increasing concern for the disappearance of meaningful country life becomes evident. No longer do we find a kind of gay primitivism ascribed to backwoods communities. There are, for example, a series of penetrating and bitter articles about the country mountain folk in Kentucky. Their original discovery in the 1870s and 1880s by local colorists had suggested a kind of romance, but by the 1880s and 1890s there emerged instead serious discussions of degeneracy, of crime, of poor elements among them. Social action to "uplift" them is called for. In a long article in the *American Journal of Sociology* "The Smoky Pilgrims," an extraordinary treatment complete with photographs, the march to the city is shown leading the "superior" people away; seemingly only the vicious and the vagabonds, the tramps and the ineffectual remain behind. The dangers of farm life are depicted: the lack of variety, the basic moral weaknesses, the lying, the use of vile language. The author of the article insists that "a man without a place in the world is as much crowded out when he faces the broad fields as in the large city amidst the rush of hurrying industry." The issue is not simply, therefore, rural versus urban. Article after article suggests that somehow progress and civilization have passed these people by. Now, it is true that one can find in the same period an enormous body of literature testifying to the persistence of rural nostalgia. Americans often *did* try to maintain the rural community; they tried to rehabilitate it through the new rural church, the new and expanding functions of the Department of Agriculture, Theodore Roosevelt's Country Life Commission, and hundreds of meetings and volumes by rural sociologists. But the story is not so simple; there persist enormous and basic doubts about supposedly rural ideas that led to a whole rethinking of values of rural *and* of urban experience.

Max Weber brilliantly illuminated the basic dilemma. Invited to participate at one of the many great conferences held in conjunction with the too-little-studied World's Fair at St. Louis in 1904, Weber was assigned as his subject "The Rural Community." He began by expressing some mystification: surely all the committee that has invited him could mean was "rural society" and surely this could not be taken literally: "For the rural society, separate from the urban social community, does not exist at the present time in a great part of the modern civilized world." The American farmer is, after all, simply an enterpriser like the others. Certainly, there are technical agricultural problems (most frequently relating to the "politics of communication"), but, according to Weber, "there exists not yet any specific rural social problem." Weber insisted on seeing American rural life as it was affected (very much like that of Europe) by the spread of capitalism, and almost the only special or characteristic feature of rural conditions (primarily in the wheat-producing West) was "the absolute individualism of the farmers' economics, the quality of the farmer as mere businessman." Many studies by sociologists and many treatments by writers of fiction were in fact establishing the same conclusions. Indeed, Veblen was to state these even more bitingly in later essays. The point was that there was no ideal rural community, no nostalgic escape from the reality of an urbanized America; the utopias of the 1880s tended often to be particular kinds of cities, frequently military in organization, technological in development. Seldom were they rural heavens.

As a matter of fact, taking our literature, our art, our political development as a whole, American culture around 1890 reached a kind of synthesis of some significance. For the first time, we achieved what might be called a national literature, with writers like Crane, Norris, Dreiser. We began to develop a vigorous, self-conscious American school in painting, again largely urban-centered (Sloan, Henri, and the Ash Can School), sometimes painfully self-conscious but frequently also sentimental, even nostalgic, in its urban vision. The triumph of a new architecture centered in the building of great cities like Chicago, and the evolution of a brilliant concept of urban design with the skyscraper. And perhaps most characteristic of all, the literature of social and political commentators began to regard the nation as a kind of federation of different kinds of cities and towns. The definition of America is largely now seen in terms of the New Yorks, the Chicagos, the Clevelands, the San Franciscos: a striking image of a nation as a series of large and small towns, of cities and their immediate rural backgrounds. Our "realistic" national literature defines itself in vividly precise local color that is yet national in its implications. In spite of profound local and regional distinctions, notions of national character paint a Yankee as the distinctive representative American.

Further, this emerging national synthesis stresses the values of communication, of organization, of newer technological developments and engineering skills. By the 1890s, our tripartite revolution had fulfilled itself in the new synthesis. By this time, Americans had gone through a period of severe questioning. There had been over a decade of utopian novels (not to mention the great utopian movement associated with them). These utopian novels frequently were neither pro- nor anti-urban. One of the most characteristic works is a novel of 1893, *A City-less and a Country-less World*, a title suggestive of the emergence of a new social form resulting from the tensions between the rural ideal and the industrial urban ideal. And this ideal form is aesthetically significant its end is an aesthetic experience of some sort, thought of in almost religious terms (though perhaps the aesthetic and the religious experience desired are actually the same experience). Consider, too, another utopian novel like *The Making of the Millennium* (1903). The new social form developed in the book is called a city, but it is a special vision of the city. Down to the 1930s this image is central to American experience.

A symbolic event occurred at the same time as the first great national synthesis did—the Chicago World's Columbian Exposition of 1893. The fair, called the "White City," reveals two facts of great importance. What is most significant is the idea that there could be a city that is ordered, organized, planned, yet beautiful, meeting the needs and the interests of the people. Enthusiasm for the White City on the banks of Lake Michigan can be traced in source after source. Supposedly one of our anti-urban intellectuals, William Dean Howells was often quoted for his remarks on the unpleasantness of New York City. In a letter to *Cosmopolitan*, however, he expresses a quite different view. Here is a vision—aesthetic, religious, social, political—of what is possible, of what a city might be: the beauty of it, the social efficiency of it, the brilliant organization of its services, the triumph of its use of technological innovation, the ease of communication within it, all effectively contrasted with the dark slums brooding along Chicago's fringes. The image of the White City, in fact, is one of the crucial moments in the history of so-called American Progressivism. Its significance may well be international: Sun-Yat-sen asked the planner Daniel Burnham to come to China to build a progressive capital exactly like the White City. Thus the city, a special vision of the city, suddenly becomes realized in model form at the White City at just that moment when the national synthesis also comes to being. Its millennial hope emerges in a distinctive way in American thought.

Yet at the very time that this ideal of a new America emerges, it is threatened by materialism, by the business corporation, by the new ethnic groups and their problems. Many therefore turn to saving the city. No one can fail to be impressed with the enormous amount of the literature on urbanism and urban reform and on the nature of the city itself from the 1890s through the 1930s. If rural sociology dominates the scholarly world of the early period, by the First World War urban sociology certainly comes into its own. Many historians have argued that Progressivism was an urban phenomenon, but too few have seen that Progressivism in its very nature begins with an urban image. Its vision of a new America is a vision of a land transformed into a series of ideal cities. And in this vision we find merged the religious drives toward the great community, the hungering for the richer aesthetic experience, the artisan ideals of a newer administrative- and engineering-minded middle class. All are the outcomes of the three revolutions—in communication, organization, organic thinking. Listen to Josiah Strong at the end of *The Twentieth Century City* (1898):

The city is to control the nation. Christianity must control the city, and it will. The first city was built by the first murderer and the crime and wretchedness and vice have festered in it ever since. But into the last city shall enter nothing that defileth. Neither shall there be any more sorrow, or crime, for former things shall have passed away. Shelley said "Hell is a city much like London." But the city redeemed is a vision of the revelation, the symbol itself of Heaven, Heaven on Earth, the Kingdom fully come.

Notice the combination of images, wrapped in a marvelous pseudoscience, a physical geographical "study" that the optimistic Oliver Babcock—surely an extraordinary crackpot—called *Cosmonics of the United States*. Originally written in anticipation of the World's Fair of 1876 (mistakenly, in Babcock's opinion, held in Philadelphia) and then republished in 1893, Babcock talks of the search for a capital, the need for some force to achieve the integrity of the whole union. All this he saw happening in the Mississippi Valley, the center of both commerce and agriculture, the combination of all the elements that guarantee success. Naturally, Chicago must be queen of all of this; here the World's Fair must be held (and of course this time it was). In this grand area, Babcock sees a future in which will be enacted, successively, the dramas that will unfold the mysteries of Providential design concerning the whole continent, the nation, and human freedom itself. Here, in Chicago, will "finally stand revealed His purposes and plans, born amidst trial and trust, fear and faith, anxiety and expectation."

Writing in 1909, Simon N. Patten worries about a social order increasingly interested in production at the price of what he calls "climax," and "demand . . . for satisfaction that renews men." For him the traditional agencies of civilization—the school, the church, the library—are repressive rather than expressive. While he believes that legitimate climax is contained in "passionate citizenship," such could not be achieved without a series of steps leading to this desired end. The place to begin is in the city streets:

The street is the city man's substitute for Nature's highways of forest and stream and the city boy becomes as adept in its lore as the savage does upon the hunting trail. . . . We must make of our streets an Institution that shall express, direct, and gratify men's thwarted necessities for vital excitement as definitely as the church has been used to express his longing for spiritual excitements.

And William Allen White, in 1910, identifies steam as the creator of the new democracy. He sees the major problem of his age as the "socialization of steam" (presenting in brief a philosophy of history naming as key to the history of the world the problem of the socialization of invention). For White, the city is the answer to the questions posed by the changing of the old order.

We are in the youth of our race life. Yet we hold to the racial institutions that made us conquerors of the Mongol and the Semite: the home and the folkmoot. . . . We still see visions. And the genius of a people that can conceive and accomplish self-government under a king or a monarch or a republic, will keep self-government pure and undefiled. . . . What we have gained in three thousand years of pilgrimage westward across the earth we have kept, and we are stronger than ever before in our struggle for the retention of home and home rule. And the city, which seems to be in a fair way of becoming the prevailing type of local government on this continent, will be a free city. A curious miracle—but how old—is this city life of ours. . . . And so these cities of ours—spindles in the hands of fate—dirty though they are, and befouled, must keep moving incessantly as they weave the garment.

The need to maintain the city, to see it as the center of what will be the new life is the recurrent refrain; our literature exudes this theme. Here, in 1930, is William B. Munro, not in a personal polemic but in *The Encyclopedia of the Social Sciences:*

The city, in any event, is bound to be a controlling factor in the national life. As the city is, so will the nation be. Its population supplies most of the national leadership. Through its daily press the city dominates public opinion far outside its own bounds. It is stronger in its influence upon political thought than its ratio of population warrants. It sets the fashions—in morals and in manners as in attire. The demeanor of the city is not, therefore, a matter of concern to itself alone. It is the vital concern of all who desire high national aspirations to be established and maintained, for the ideals of the nation are determined by the most influential among the various elements of its population. Being so determined, they are constantly in process of change, Hence the saying that although men make cities, it is equally true that cities make men. He who makes the city makes the nation, and it is indeed the cities of the future that will determine the character of the world.

The United States did not come close to creating in the 1920s an equivalent of Europe's Oswald Spengler, no real equivalent—in spite of some genuine enthusiasm for Spengler's work—of the kind of agrarian mysticism that saw the death and destruction of the city as a desirable aim of civilization. While there was indeed an agrarian vogue that persisted from the 1880s (and flourished extraordinarily in the 1930s), we also find article after article talking of the emergence of a new American civilization that will be unique because it is a "real" civilization—"a city-civilization," as one writer in *Harper's* in 1924 called it. Here we find the extraordinary image of America as a grouping of cities, a civilization made up of and characterized by a variety of different cities, each operating in its own way, somehow federated, to form this overall city-civilization. This image of the city and of America dominates much of the literature: there is a need to save the city, to create the ideal city.

Obviously, this city is *not* the traditional industrial city. In its ideal form it is in one sense Christian and in another pre-industrial; the ideal city is always beautiful and always affords people the experience of community and communion, the final experience of the beauty of the spirit (somehow). It is this ideal that had led—or misled—writers to assume that American intellectuals were anti-urban. For Americans still sought that City on the Hill. These ideas persist; Americans still can and do regard the city in these political, social, and religious terms. In a recent (1962) study of the history of the New York Mission Society, *The People Are the City*, Kenneth and Ethel Miller end this way:

Who shall praise the city? Surely only a lover of the place. The city has been a long time growing and shows the dark patina of her age as well as the scars of abrasive experience with defeat and calamity. Her willful pride, the wild arrogance of sheer size and power, these have been reduced by the inevitable pains and humiliations of life. The true lover of the city is struck by her continuing glory, by every shining facet in the upthrust of her vigor and vitality. . . . The city is an ancient monument. Aristotle, thinking on Athens, admitted it was built first for the safety of the citizens, but, more importantly, that men might find within it the advantages of leading the good life. The same idea was implicit in the parable of the city set on a hill, where nothing was hid, where lofty ideals could lift people in the pursuit of beauty and truth. For the people *are* the city—the shape of the physical assemblage of brick and mortar is the outward expression of the city's material success, the symbols of civilized living. Within, invisible, but all-vital, is the spirit and the soul of the real city, its treasury of people. The city is a sacrament, instituted of God. God so loved the world that He sent a Man, a man of the people to mingle with the throngs of humans, to transform and transmute the crowded ways into highways for the City of God. The Son of Man wept over the city, with God-filled compassion; and there is need for weeping today. But there is cause for rejoicing too, when men of independence, linked by one great aim—the common-weal—are each so "in love with the city" that they will spend themselves utterly in her service. All great cities have their origins in religion: the primary factor for good or evil from Athens to Byzantium, from Rome to London, to Paris and New York was religion. Can religion transform and change the city? Will men of good will ensure the refining away of the dross in the golden material of mankind to build the New Jerusalem?

Such a characteristic statement could have been written at almost any time in American development from 1620 to the present. If we honestly examine American thought, we will find no persistence of an anti-urban image. There is something more important than a hunger for an idyllic rural past. For in between the myth of the primitive and the myth of the city-centered nation-state—poles of the European experience that Henri Baudet makes such brilliant use of in his marvelous little book *Paradise on Earth*—there is another myth of a special kind of city toward which Americans have directed their attention. And if they found that the city as it exists was full of problems, these very problems have been accepted as challenges, necessary challenges to them as men, as Christians, and as Americans. If they have found the city materialistic and industrial in ways they believed unsatisfactory, they have refused to give up the whole thing as a lost cause and instead invented for themselves another image of the city, an ideal to which they wished to transform it. For American thought, at least from 1830 to 1930, was built in large part on a structure that assumed the growth of the ideal of a great city.

13 CULTURE AND COMMUNI-CATIONS

Any essay that discusses, however informally, the history of mass communications must of necessity take note of the significance of form. And thus the form of one's discourse itself comes to be a significant matter.

The ideal essay would be formulated to include a few carefully chosen texts, preferably anthropological. The texts would be followed by several significant caveats, as prelude to a series of assertions—bold ones, of course—that in a speculative essay may stand free of ordinary proof or demonstration. And one should finish with a peroration sufficiently eloquent that one's readers would fail to recall the author's many errors. Texts, caveats, assertions, peroration: certainly enough formal apparatus to satisfy the most devout historian of culture and communications.

My texts (anthropological):

Communication constitutes the core of culture and indeed of life itself.
Edward T. Hall (1966)

Culture communicates; the complex interconnectedness of cultural events itself conveys information to those who participate in those events. . . . We must know a lot about the cultural context, the setting of the stage, before we can even begin to decode the message.
Edmund Leach (1976)

My caveats:

First, too many of us who study mass communications have tried to decode the messages we have discovered without sufficient awareness of a larger cultural context. That "complex interconnectedness" of which the distinguished British social anthropologist speaks should alert us to the difficulties we face and the risks we run when we isolate aspects of the larger, more general communicative process that in fundamental ways is culture itself. Our work, for practical and reasonable concerns, often forces us to examine a part, a particular medium, a special theme; but we must never forget that that part, medium, or theme is perforce related to others, sharing in some greater whole. Unless we have sensitivity to this fact —for indeed we are all aware that media somehow affect the general culture and that at the same time the general culture shapes the media—we will miss the crucial issue of *relationships,* perhaps the most essential of all cultural questions. Too often, we have become insistent on thinking in rigid and awkward causal terms; instead we ought to be thinking "ecologically," in terms of a total, interacting environment. The environment of communications should be our central concern. And if we can remember Leach's fundamental statement, "culture communicates," we will begin to know better what we mean when we write about communications.

All my other caveats follow from this approach.

My second caveat warns against any kind of technological determinism. The acceptance of any technological innovation obviously depends on the nature of the culture into which any proposed innovation is introduced. Even more significantly, the *form* such innovation takes is culturally shaped. When we speak of the impact of the automobile on American society, for example, we do not mean simply a technological achievement but also a particular form of that engineering accomplishment. Henry Ford's genius lay not only in his mastery of the technique of mass production. Rather we can attribute to him a real cultural revolution as well: the "invention" in some real sense of the "form" this automobile would take. For it was Ford who created the idea of the "family" car, owned, operated, and repaired by the family head, and used by the family primarily for leisure purposes. Ford did not invent the automobile or even the important new engineering details. But he transformed the invention from a plaything of the well-to-do to the necessity of every family. He took a technological innovation and from it created a special cultural form.

Culture also shaped the motion picture, even though its inventors had a limited vision of the nature and function of film. At the outset of the creation of film as form in France, two entirely different propositions for cultural form seemed to compete: the brothers Lumière concentrated on brief films of everyday life, using the motion picture camera to record and document; Georges Méliès (present when the Lumière brothers showed their first films in 1895) concentrated his efforts on the world of illusion made possible by the use of trick photography. Further, the significant form of film best known today can be said to have been created in 1915, by D. W. Griffith for American middle-class audiences with *The Birth of a Nation*. This development occurred more than ten years after the "birth" of a film industry, and it was to be the cultural form in which American films have made their great impact ever since. My point is not simply to spotlight creators of cultural forms, but that it is only in a fuller comprehension of the cultural context in which each creator worked and in which each work was accepted that we can begin to understand: I stress the ecological approach.

Third, we must pay careful attention to the problems raised by form *and* content and the precise relationship between them. We should see technologies concretely within the culture and avoid abstract discussions of formal matters and issues of content. Here we run into several problems. We begin with the almost inevitable separation of cultural products: for example, high, popular, and folk. Or at least, since the days of Van Wyck Brooks, highbrow and lowbrow. This separation leads us to assume that popular culture is radically different from high culture. And so in fact it may be. Yet my ecological vision forces me to think again; there must be some relationship, if not in form, in content (issues, problems, themes), or if not in content perhaps in form ("advanced" literature's fascination for the "forms" of modern art, the film, etc., as literary devices). Do popular cultural matters operate by "formulas" and high cultural ones by "conventions"? How different are they? Or, better, how do these cultural products relate to each other, how do they or can they coexist? These questions suggest a series of other problems, one of the most difficult of which is the precise relationship between form and content, especially in the popular culture provided by the media. New technological developments too often seem to signal radical cultural transformation. A Whig theory of change results, generally: not only are the cultural and social orders transformed, but those transformations also "modernize" and improve life. In fact, given a culture that preexists and has consequences ("culture communicates"), there is no reason to assume either that overwhelming change is necessary or that what is basic to that culture actually has changed. Certain formal elements may change without any deeper social or even psychological changes.

Even more startling, many examples specifically reveal that the most radical change in form may still retain the most traditional content.

D. W. Griffith, for example, is in reality an avant-garde artist. His methods of editing, his brilliant and complex use of a variety of shots to special effect, all suggest a master modernist, an innovator creating new possibilities for motion pictures readily recognizable by critics and students alike. So advanced were some of his techniques that audiences were sometimes puzzled and confused (witness *Intolerance*, 1916). Yet for all of his formal radicalism, there is nothing very radical or even new about the basic content of his films, the story line, his ideas about women, masculinity, family, virtue. Here Griffith remains a mid-nineteenth-century Victorian.

A better example would be the conservative content of the radio soap operas of the 1930s. Soaps were the source of countless jokes. And yet, the formal method of the lowly soaps has exceptional aspects. Time is stretched out almost endlessly. Several weeks of programs can be only a few minutes in the "lives" of those in the story itself. Such a radical readjustment of formal temporal order has significant consequences for the listener. A form is created that in some ways appears radically different from the supposed real-life content. Thus changes in medium may effect changes in both form and content or in one or the other or in the relationship between them. The matter is far from simple in this world of relationships.

There remains at least one final problem in relation to this caveat: when analysts attempt to read the message of the soaps in the responses of the audience, to what, in fact, is the audience reacting? Are they reacting to both form *and* content? To one or to the other? The form of the soap may be considered at least as important as or even more important than the content: the daily ritual of repeated programs, the ritual closing, even the ritual placement of the commercials, might have communications consequences. The entire ritual itself might indeed be the message. I know this kind of analysis offends those who believe the pill is more important than the ritual of taking it, but I am one of those who will continue to wonder what the role of instructions ("take every three hours") plays in the efficacy of the pill-taking. Even the act of listening or seeing has cultural consequences, if only because the cultural setting proposes a meaning to these acts.

Fourth, the ecological model should alert us to the dangers of complete surrender to the media or to a new technological innovation as a characteristic cultural response. Too many critics of contemporary culture assume that audiences give way before every new technology and are easily manipulated by powerful media. Complex cultures, however, operate this way; moreover, there is often resistance both to new technologies and to what the media propose. This resistance is a cultural fact of profound significance too seldom explored. Not sufficiently interested in the holdouts and their achievements, cultural historians, like military historians, are too often interested in the victors and what they have won. Further, when this audience resistance is analyzed along with the modifications required because of existing cultural patterns, a very different story often surfaces from the one that historians of communications like to tell.

My fifth caveat is perhaps implicit in those that have gone before. Since culture shapes experience, it obviously shapes the way we respond to new technologies and new media; it shapes the anticipations we have of them and of the world in which we live. Thus, in the between-the-wars period, there were expectations built into the complex culture we are discussing. Culture offers us ways to anticipate; and it gives us methods of coping with the unanticipated. We must pay careful attention to the expected and unexpected, and to the ways the culture provides for dealing with both.

A few examples from my own work will suggest what I mean. In the New York World's Fair of 1939–1940, communications played a crucial role in visualizing the future. Yet the Fair refused to recognize the beginnings of a Second World War, surely something of consequences for a World of Tomorrow. Furthermore, with all the enthusiasm for human use of new technology, the Fair's experts were often mistaken; they were trapped in their own world. Norman Bel Geddes, whose Futurama for General Motors was the hit exhibit of the Fair, projected the new cities demanded by the automobile, General Motors' main product, yet he failed to consider anywhere near the number of filling stations such a volume of cars would require.

Like the Fair experts, Franklin Roosevelt also failed to perceive the future. As a war President, he tried to get appropriations for an enormous new headquarters for the military (the Pentagon); Congress, however, resisted. They could not imagine the military needing such a vast structure—then the world's largest office building—after the war. So FDR, in order to obtain the necessary funds, sent a letter pledging to use the space to house national archives when the war ended. The point is that anticipation is cultural, as are the ways we cope with the unexpected. Imagination in real ways, and therefore the imaginary, are shaped by culture.

My last caveat: always remember that investigators are a product of the culture they are investigating. When we think about communications or culture, we are participants in a debate that has been characteristic of American culture for a long time. One of the reasons we talk so persistently about the impact of media is because thinking and talking about its role, and about the role of technology generally, have become cultural characteristics. In a sense, we are hardly able *not* to think and talk about the media. And we engage in this enterprise with a particular set of questions and a special language provided for us from the start. Not only do the media help shape the way we think about the media, but thinking about the media also helps shape the way the media operate within the culture. There is a complex relationship between the way the media are used and the way we think about those uses.

The time has come for some assertions. I have already suggested the first: from at least the middle of the nineteenth century on, there occurred what historians have called a "communications revolution." By this is generally meant a fundamental way in which goods, services, people, and ideas are put in motion over space by the application of new forms of energy (steam and electricity) and newly developed machines. Those who have studied this revolution have been concerned primarily with its economic and social consequences, the creation of a world market, vast physical mobility, development of an international audience. Fundamental to these changes as well was a new way of thinking about the world. Of course, the very conception of time and space was transformed. But along with this change came different ways of thinking about man and society. While generally known, these changes have been too seldom examined as a group, too seldom analyzed as a foundation of much of our thinking about culture and communications today.

My assertion: by the 1920s, there had developed a way of thinking about society, culture, and communications that was to have significant consequences for the world of communications. A few examples of late-nineteenth- and early-twentieth-century thinkers will make the point. American thinkers worried increasingly about community. They were haunted by the fears that the new urban, industrial world of mass communications would destroy real community. Thus, thinkers often began with a definition of community. For Josiah Royce, America's leading idealist thinker, all knowledge had to be mediated through signs. As Royce put it, the human self knows himself through a process of interpretation, what others tell him about himself, what he sees in others about himself. Community, therefore, is essential if there is to be any self-knowledge, and any real community is in fact a community of interpretation. What is important about this assertion is that it defines the community in terms of a process of communication.

George Herbert Mead, the American pragmatist at the University of Chicago, defined society as a series of social acts. A social act, he said, is a communicative process. And the sociologist Charles H. Cooley at the University of Michigan defined society, in *Social Organization* in 1909, as a mental complex held together by communications. The nature of the words, he believed, clearly link community and communications. In the wake of a revolution in communications, social and economic thinkers such as David Wells and Francis A. Walker concerned themselves with the immediate impact of such changes in communications. Social thought generally began redefining its terms, reassessing its process in communications metaphors and realities. The nature and function of communications became basic to American social thought.

Perhaps the best evidence for this shift can be found in the new University of Chicago established in the 1890s, where philosophers, sociologists, and educationalists showed exceptional concern for the problem of communications. Any examination of the work of Park, Small, Burgess, Thomas, or their students, as well as of the work of Dewey and Mead and their students, establishes this concern. Not only did these people study the role of the media and of groups such as the ghetto and the neighborhood in which communication was important, but they also expressed deep concern over the disappearance of face-to-face communication previously thought to constitute the family, the group, the community possible. This concern often represented a real fear of modern civilization. In 1881 another observer, George Beard, a distinguished American physician, attempted to explain what he called "American nervousness":

The modern differ from the ancient civilizations mainly in these five elements—steam power, the periodical press, the telegraph, the sciences, and the mental activity of women. When civilization, plus these five factors, invades any nation, it must carry nervousness and nervous diseases along with it.

For Beard, the problem is psychological dimension. Others viewed communications as a problem of public policy. Thus Woodrow Wilson in a 1919 message to Congress:

I can only suggest in the case of the telegraph and telephone as in the case of the railroads, it is clearly desirable in the public interest that some legislation should be considered which may tend to make these indispensible instruments of our modern life a uniform and coordinated system which will afford those who use them as complete and certain means of communication with all parts of the country as has been long afforded by the postal system of the government. An exhaustive study of the whole question of all electrical communications and the means by which the central authority of the nation can be used to unify and improve it would certainly result in great public benefit.

By 1919, the new communications, the source of dis-ease and even disease, could be addressed by the President of the United States as "indispensable instruments of modern life."

Along with expressions of fear, however, came new optimism. Having redefined the community as communications, many of the social theorists pragmatically began to see mass communications as an answer to the problem of the disappearance of face-to-face communication. These theorists argued that instruments of communication might help create communities based on electronic communications and no longer on geography or on any kind of contiguity. Could the new community be forged from the instruments of the new communicators? The most sanguine glimpsed enormous possibilities here.

At the start of the period between the wars, thinkers were examining both the great potential and the terrible price these possibilities might entail. Edward Sapir captured these tendencies in his article on Communications for *The Encyclopedia of Social Sciences* (1930). He wrote that the increase in the sheer radius of communication, the lessening of the importance of geography, can be had only at some cost. Communication cannot be kept "within desirable bounds." It tends to cheapen literary and artistic values.

All effects which demand a certain intimacy of understanding tend to become difficult and are therefore avoided. It is a question of whether the obvious increase of overt communication is not being constantly corrected . . . by the creation of new obstacles to communication. The fear of being too easily understood may, in many cases, be more aptly defined as the fear of being understood by too many—so many, indeed, as to endanger the psychological reality of the image of the enlarged self confronting the not-self.

At the same time, Sapir spoke with enthusiasm of the new communications making the whole world the "psychological equivalent of a primitive tribe."

These analyses are premature echoes of Marshall McLuhan. The philosophers and sociologists at Chicago, in fact, helped train Harold Innis, Canada's great historian of communications, who, in turn, helped train Marshall McLuhan. When the University of Chicago was founded, in the logic of ecological cultural history, the coming of Marshall McLuhan's ideas seemed almost inevitable. Most fittingly, the debate over the role of communications in the media in the 1880s and 1890s and found a specific center in Chicago, that hub of communications. The discussion was an important aspect of the story of communications.

The period from 1920 to 1940, an era when the study of communication becomes virtually a field in its own right, holds a special place in this history. By 1928, I. A. Richards, a literary critic, is able to offer one of the first definitions of communication as a discrete aspect of the human experience:

Communication takes place when one mind so acts upon its environment that another mind is influenced, and in that other mind an experience occurs which is like the experience of the first mind, and is caused in part by the experience.

By the time we reach the 1920s, there is a sharpening and a focusing on the issue of culture and communications. Significant doubts flourish amid significant hopes. But all agree that there was a new world and that communications in large part had helped make it.

Perhaps a literary reference will make my assertion more dramatically clear. In 1919, Sherwood Anderson published a volume of short stories about a small midwestern town, Winesburg, Ohio, that he called "a book of grotesques." Each of these stories deals with a psychological transformation in the life of one or another residents of Winesburg, which Anderson explains from a nearly sociological perspective:

In the last fifty years a vast change has taken place in the lives of our people. A revolution has in fact taken place. The coming industrialism, attended by all the roar and rattle of affairs, the shrill cries of millions of new voices that have come among us from overseas, the going and coming of trains, the growth of cities, the building of the interurban car lines that weave in and out of towns and past farmhouses, and now in these later days the coming of the automobiles has worked a tremendous change in the lives and in the habits of thought of our people of Mid-America. Books, badly imagined and written though they may be in the hurry of our times, are in every household, magazines circulate by the millions of copies, newspapers are everywhere. In our day a farmer standing by the stove in the store in his village has his mind filled to overflowing with the words of other men. The newspapers and the magazines have pumped him full. Much of the old brutal ignorance that had in it also a kind of beautiful childlike innocence is gone forever. The farmer by the stove is brother to the men of the cities, and if you listen you will find him talking as glibly and as senselessly as the best city man of us all.

CULTURE AND COMMUNICATIONS

In the world before such changes, Anderson tells us, men didn't need words in books and magazines and newspapers. By implication, one might assume, they didn't need motion pictures and radios. For they had God, not in a book, but in their hearts. Now, "Godliness," the title of the story from which this passage comes, is problematic.

The genius of *Winesburg, Ohio* is its formulation of what became a brilliant and central paradox. Here in the age of easy and mass communications—press, movies, radio, automobile, telegraph, telephone, photograph—here in an age when it appears that everyone can know what everyone else knows and everyone can know what everyone else thinks, here no real, private, human communication is possible. Significantly, the hero in Anderson's book, George Willard, is a newspaperman and the hotel he lives in, run by his mother, is next to the railroad that will take him out of town forever in the final story. The telegraph, as well as the newspaper, is featured in several stories. One of Anderson's characters, in fact, is a telegraph operator who becomes a poet. Yet, it is ironic that the citizens of Winesburg are totally unable to communicate with one another in a world of vast communications networks. "The communion between George Willard," Anderson tells us, "and his Mother was outwardly a formal thing without meaning." Anderson even uses the word "communion," attaching a religious significance to genuine communication. This newspaperman, however, is a creature of forms without significance (is that the world of mass communications?).

This theme—the fundamental problem of public versus private communication and the suggestion that one makes the other impossible—dominates aspects of the culture and is crucial to any understanding of it in the twentieth century. It lies at the heart of many questions that have been defined basically as sociological and psychological. The problem itself was definitively presented in these years, and no more brilliant examples of this presentation can be found than in one of the greatest literary achievements of the period. Very early in Robert Musil's *The Man Without Qualities* (1930), the Austrian novelist offers a discussion of a possible place where one might spend one's life, or at least, a place where it would be smart to stay. Musil's analysis represents an ideal toward which Americans strive while at the same time indicating the price that might have to be paid:

For some time now such a social *idée fixe* has been a kind of super-American city where everyone rushes about, or stands still, with a stopwatch in his hand. Air and earth form an ant-hill, veined by channels of traffic, rising storey upon storey. Overhead-trains, overground-trains, underground-trains, pneumatic express-mails carrying consignments of human beings, chains of motor-vehicles all racing along horizontally, express lifts vertically pumping crowds from one traffic-level to another. . . . At the junctions one leaps from one means of transport to another, is instantly sucked in and snatched away by the rhythm of it, which makes a syncope, a pause, a little gap of twenty seconds between two roaring outbursts of speed, and in these intervals in the general rhythm one hastily exchanges a few words with others. Questions and answers click into each other like cogs of a machine. Each person has nothing but quite definite tasks. The various professions are concentrated at definite places. One eats while in motion. Amusements are concentrated in other parts of the city. And elsewhere again are the towers to which one returns and finds wife, family, gramophone, and soul. Tension and relaxation, activity and love are meticulously kept separate in time and are weighted out according to formulae arrived at in extensive laboratory work. If during any of these activities one runs up against a difficulty, one simply drops the whole thing; for one will find another thing or perhaps, later on, a better way, or someone else will find the way that one has missed. It does not matter in the least, but nothing wastes so much communal energy as the presumption that one is called upon not to let go of a definite personal aim. In a community with energies constantly flowing through it, every road leads to a good goal, if one does not spend too much time hesitating and thinking it over. The targets are set up at a short distance, but life is short too, and in this way one gets a maximum of achievement out of it. And man needs no more for his happiness; for what one achieves is what moulds the spirit, whereas what one wants, without fulfillment, only warps it. So far as happiness is concerned it matters very little what one wants; the main thing is that one should get it. Besides, zoology makes it clear that a sum of reduced individuals may very well form a totality of genius.

What I intend to suggest here in my use of this passage from Musil, as well as in my caveats, is a simple and obvious, but often overlooked, fact: various technologies come into the culture adjusted in terms of a form and function shaped by that culture itself. This is evident in what the forms and functions of radio, telephone, television—every media technology—became in an American cultural circumstance. In many instances, these forms and functions were different from those in other nations, other cultures.

The movies suggest this quite well. The early masters of cinema in the United States developed an ability to deal with huge crowds ("crowd splendor," Vachel Lindsay called it in his superb *The Art of the Moving Picture*). To this development, the genius of D. W. Griffith added the closeup shot, that unique concentration on the human face quite unavailable in a real world and possible only because of the camera. These two images became crucial to film: the mass on the one hand and the individual on the other. Montage allowed a juxtaposition of such images.

Is it farfetched to argue that this was a formal aesthetic response to an intellectual issue? Any examination of the rest of the culture reveals a fundamental and deep-seated anxiety about the problem of the individual in a mass society. Film enabled a demonstration and probing of that problem iconographically. In addition, "motion" pictures dealt with and were exemplars of mobility in space. (Is any particular kind of motion implied? Early films confined motion to the frame.)

To many Americans, movement in space was the equivalent of social mobility. But for a long time Americans had a special fondness for vast panoramas of space, movement in space. In my view, many of the nineteenth-century Luminist paintings now attracting so much critical attention used their vaunted light to heighten a sense of vast and endless space. And if we discover, too, that such space, such an opportunity to move in space, was somehow joined ideologically with ideas of freedom or social movement as well, then all the more reason to examine film as an inheritor of that tradition. It is difficult to think of film as using the technological capabilities unique to it without such movement over space and even over time: the chase is fundamental—automobile, train, Indians, men in armies, men on foot pursuing other men, men pursuing women. Further, the film adopted, and made iconographically its own, the traditional story of a journey (as old at least as Homer). In Westerns, film often made the journey myth as well. These films yield technically to iconographic demonstration of our fundamental cultural problems and concerns.

One more assertion about iconography: one of the characteristics of modern American culture has been the conversion of means of communication into icons; objects of everyday life attain iconographic significance in the modern world, and none are more useful, it would seem, than icons from the realm of communications. This is especially the case with visual media, but it even operates in the world of sound and print as well. For example, fast-moving trains suggest something beyond the image, as do the roar of engines and the toot of whistles on radio. Leo Marx and others have shown how often the locomotive was the "machine in the garden," and at least since 1876 and the writing of Tolstoy's *Anna Karenina,* that same locomotive has had powerful significance as it chugged through the landscape of modern literature. In more recent times, Watty Piper has used that train to provide a moral example for children in the famous *The Little Engine That Could.* By the late 1930s and early 1940s, so pervasive were the instruments of modern communication in our literature that they served as something more than symbol or metaphor in a series of what have become classic American short stories: Delmore Schwartz's "In Dreams Begin Responsibilities," (motion pictures); John Cheever's "The Enormous Radio"; Lionel Trilling's "Of This Time, of That Place" (photography).

Even the commonplace telephone quickly found itself adapted for popular cultural use. A catalog of such iconographic usage often reveals the telephone as an image, emphasizing the problem of communication, the theme of the inability to communicate in spite of the existence of the technological means for such communication. In Irving Berlin's song the singer is "All Alone by the Telephone." In film, both Luise Rainer's great telephone scene in *The Great Ziegfeld* (for which she won an Academy Award) and Shirley Booth's memorable call to her mother in *Come Back, Little Sheba* link the telephonic act with disappointment and even tragedy. And in *Sorry, Wrong Number* and *Dial M for Murder,* the telephone becomes an object of terror and even murder. In the bright Broadway musical comedy *Bye Bye Birdie,* the kids we see as the second act begins are all busily talking on the phone without seeming to communicate. The phone company keeps advertising, "Reach out and touch someone," but the iconography of popular culture often suggests the inability to do that very thing, or perhaps even a danger in trying. (I should add parenthetically that when I call my mother she invariably asks immediately, "What's the matter?" She cannot quite believe that anyone would use the phone except to deliver bad news.) Thus the culture takes an attitude, if I may be permitted a strange turn of phrase, toward the devices of communication that becomes clear as a message when we see these devices used iconographically in cultural works.

Frank Capra's *It Happened One Night* captures this tension brilliantly. Of course, we all know it is about a journey; another one of those. We know it is about a spoiled rich girl and an arrogant newspaper reporter who are somehow transformed on a cross-country bus trip. Yes, certainly. And it is a story about love and marriage characteristic of 1930s cultural concerns. But let me show you what I mean, drawing on Robert Riskin's script. I know of no other film so compellingly dependent upon communications icons to establish virtually every scene.

A brief review of the initial location of each part of the screenplay may be of assistance. Part I opens in a yacht carefully anchored among many other yachts. It ends with the sending of telegrams. The setting of Part II and the series of shots that establishes the action in the first instances of the meeting of our hero and heroine are particularly important. To quote from Riskin's screenplay:

CULTURE AND COMMUNICATIONS

The RAILROAD STATION of an active terminal in Miami fades in. The view moves down to the entrance gate to the trains, passengers hurrying through it; then picks out two men, obviously detectives, who have their eyes peeled on everyone passing through. Then the view affords a glimpse of ELLIE, who is standing watching the detectives. This scene wiping off, we see an AIR TRANSPORT, with several detectives standing around in a watchful pose. This scene wiping off, the front of a WESTERN UNION OFFICE comes into view. Several people walk in and out. At the side of the door, two detectives are on the lookout.

This scene also wipes off, revealing the WAITING ROOM of a BUS STATION. Over the ticket window there is a sign reading "BUY BUS TICKETS HERE," and a line forms in front of it. Here too there are two detectives.

Part III begins in a telegraph office before moving to a bus station where we hear (barely) an announcer calling bus departures over a public address system.

Part IV opens at night on a road where the bus has been forced to stop by a washout on the road ahead. This leads to the first night at Duke's Auto Camp, an institution created by the communications revolution, and suggests a new life style to which the wealthy heroine, Ellie Andrews, is completely unaccustomed. This is an important aspect of the film, rich in comedy but also indicative of how much life has been transformed by new methods of communication, in this case the automobile. Part V finds us in the sky and, more specifically, in the cockpit of an airplane. While Part VI begins in a newspaper office with a flood of telegrams, it culminates with "That Night" when "It Happened": a pastoral in a cow pasture, removed from the world of mechanical communications. The road (and this leads to the famous hitchhiking scene) is the setting for the beginning of Part VII. Part VIII is the only portion of the script that fails to begin with some aspect of the devices of communication. We are in the office of our heroine's father. The last part, IX, also might appear to be an exception because it opens on the lawn of the Andrews estate. We soon discover, however, that this lawn is a launching pad for airplanes, an autogyro, and, finally, the wedding car.

Our leading characters are identified iconographically. We meet Ellie Andrews on her father's yacht, which offers us an immediate vision of spoiled wealth. We meet Peter Warne, the hero, in a phone booth in a station. He is drunken, arrogant, unpleasant, and his phone-booth setting somehow enhances these qualities as his drunken fellow reporters hover around him, urging him to resign from his paper. There is virtually no known means of communication left unexploited icongraphically in the film: telegrams, radios, police calls, newspapers and newspaper headlines, newsreel cameras and cameramen, photographs, telephones (often in a crucial role and generally leading to misunderstanding), police cars and motorcycles, typewriters. There is every kind of car from Model T to limousine. Indeed, the famous hitchhiking scene is almost an excuse to review every car and truck on the American road in the early 1930s. Further, the iconography is extended to the newer institutions housing the devices of communication: bus stations, auto court, diners—the whole range. This modern litany includes demands for a new life-style, not only in the auto court but also in the diner, and especially on the road itself (the hitchhiking lesson is an example).

Further, the hero is a newspaperman, a typical figure in many American films. The whole film centers on the question of "getting a story." The hero starts out to get one; the heroine thinks she has been used because she *is* a story. In the end, the hero is less interested in the story than in the woman herself: a characteristic American tale, but one that tells us something about attitudes toward the press and toward public communications as well. (At the same time, it should be noted, the press delighted in detailing every aspect of the Hollywood story. Movies and stars were news.)

It Happened One Night is a story about communications. It exemplifies in a nearly archetypical twentieth-century American way the inability of individuals to communicate privately in the world of such awesome, constant, universal public communications. Adrift in a world of communications, where every private act (especially of the rich and famous) is public property, our hero and heroine can communicate only when they leave that world totally. In one wonderful moment, when these two leave the road at night, they climb over barbed wire (a product of industrial America that cuts off communication) into a haystack. There is little light, and therefore, without the daylight vastness of the road, the endless spaces of the journey, space is confined. Here in a limited, unpretentious world, a natural world of cantaloupe and carrot, they can find out who they are and at last be themselves in face-to-face communion.

The next scene, the hitchhiking scene—it is morning and light and the vast road beckons—dramatically counterposes the image of the human body with the image of the run of speeding machines, the automobiles. Our hero and heroine's first contact with a third party who picks them up turns out disastrously: he steals their belongings and leaves them behind. Finally, dependence on mechanical means of communication leads to misunderstanding and almost to an act of destruction: Ellie is preparing to marry her playboy lover of the airplane and autogyro. There is, of course, a happy ending, indeed a Capra ending. Peter and Ellie elope in a jalopy, and in the famous last scene they are back in the auto court. This time we *see* nothing; we learn what we can learn from our ears. As on their initial stay at the auto court, the unmarried couple erect a blanket on a line between them. They call it the "walls of Jericho." Now, at the film's end, with a marriage assured, we hear the bugle sound, announcing the pulling down, we suppose, of those walls— surely an act of communication but an act not of the twentieth century but rather of some Biblical or mythical time before modern means of communications. *It Happened One Night* expresses one of the fundamental myths of modern American culture.

Robert Musil's *The Man Without Qualities* deals in a special way with this situation in the United States. Recall when you read Musil's reference to "cow-eyed gaze . . . that so enraptured the Greeks" that the crucial moment in *It Happened One Night* occurs in a cow pasture.

It is by no means certain that things must turn out this way, but such imaginings are among the travel-fantasies that mirror our awareness of the unresting motion in which we are borne along. These fantasies are superficial, uneasy and short. God only knows how things are really going to turn out. One might think that we have the beginning in our hands at every instant and therefore ought to be making a plan for us all. If we don't like the high-speed thing, all right, then let's have something else! Something, for instance, in slow-motion, in a gauzily billowing, sea-sluggishly mysterious happiness and with that deep cow-eyed gaze that long ago so enraptured the Greeks. But that is far from being the way of it: we are in the hands of the thing. We travel in it day and night, and do everything else in it too: shaving, eating, making love, reading books, carrying out our professional duties, as though the four walls were standing still; and the uncanny thing about it is merely that the walls are traveling without our noticing it, throwing their rails out ahead like long, gropingly curving antennae, without our knowing where it is all going. And for all that, we like if possible to think of ourselves as being part of the forces controlling the train of events. That is a very vague role to play, and it sometimes happens, when one looks out of the window after a longish interval, that one sees the scene has changed. What is flying past flies past because it can't be otherwise, but for all our resignation we become more and more aware of an unpleasant feeling that we may have overshot our destination or have got on to the wrong line. And one day one suddenly has a wild craving: Get out! Jump clear! It is a nostalgic yearning to be brought to a standstill, to cease evolving, to get stuck, to turn back to a point that lies before the wrong fork. And in the good old days when there was still such a place as Imperial Austria, one could leave the train of events, get into an ordinary train on an ordinary railway-line, and travel back home.

Americans, in short, think of their culture as one of communications; their social theory and their cultural works often reflect these basic concerns. So much of our culture is self-reflexive in its cultural products: we delight in works about the media, works about newspapers, television, radio, the theater, the railroad, the automobile, the airplane. In public, we engage almost constantly and excessively in discussion of and worry about both our rapidly developing system of universal and even interterrestrial communications and in private worry equally about our inability to communicate.

A final example from the World's Fair of 1939: here was an effort to highlight achievements in technology, especially in communications and transportation technology. Here many witnessed the very first television broadcasting. It was an exciting Fair and the exhibits of General Motors, General Electric, and Bell Telephone were among the most popular. Yet at the same moment that Americans flocked to these exhibits and stood in fascinated awe at the wonders of new means of communications and new possibilities of technology, the Gallup Organization discovered by its polling that most Americans thought that the Depression from which they suffered was the consequence of the development of modern technology. The same people who believed they were jobless because of modern technology flocked to the Fair to see in awe the "achievements" of this technology.

The period from 1920 to 1940 is characteristically read in terms of dramatic tensions that shaped the culture. Complex cultures are often the products of "things"—ideas, structures, classes, life-styles—held in tension rather than the exemplum of one dominant vision. Surely, then, one of the most significant tensions is evident in how the same Americans who have dreamed about the possibility created by new methods of communication and who continue to delight in even further possibilities have at the same time created a culture in which significant creative works use these new methods of communication as icons against themselves. Americans are quite caught up in wanting the world, that Land of Oz, and yet are anxious to get home again; they want that magic and exciting world of constant motion and yet want to yell, "Get off, jump!" to all who will listen.

The world of modern communications has other dangers. We know that it creates stereotypes; we know that it repeats "facts" until lies often become "true" in their constant retelling. One hears so often that which is *not* the case that one can no longer resist believing it.

Years ago, I did a study of the American expatriates in France.

Long before it was in vogue, I decided to do what is today known as oral history. As I began to interview Americans who lived in France between the wars, I soon discovered that frequently they knew less about their lives than I did from reading other sources. I came to realize that often they were not telling me what had happened to them. What they now called their own memory was actually a recollection of what had appeared in the media about American expatriates. They had read all the autobiographies of others, all the many articles, had seen some of the shows and movies, had taken in the various journalistic accounts. They remembered being in places and with people when I knew from indisputable sources that they had arrived in France only later and had never been there when the others they claimed as comrades were. Finally, I had to surrender my oral historical effort; it was causing me more work rather than less. But I was both too young and too ignorant to see what I really had uncovered: the nature and function of a myth that had been created by the media, a myth so powerful that even bright people (or perhaps especially bright and imaginative people, who after all had shared, at least in a spiritual sense, the mythic expatriate experience or perhaps the expatriate travel-fantasy) believed it true for themselves.

Rather than casting a critical glance at those I interviewed, I must offer my own confession about the myth-making power of the media. In my researches on the expatriate project, I read three English-language daily newspapers published in Paris from 1919 until 1939. I was unbelievably immersed in the period and in Parisian life. I spent eight to ten hours a day with these newspapers for almost a six-month period. This had its consequences. Months after, I would remind my wife of things we had done or seen: "Remember . . . ?" "No," she would gently chide, "You just read about that. We really weren't there." This happened more than once. I have always regretted that I somehow did not persuade my wife to read all the papers with me. Would she, too, have "remembered" and would we have remained in a travel-fantasy of our own?

The media issue their own stereotypes, folktales, and myths, and students of communications should therefore beware. (You see, yet another caveat.) Perhaps I have been felled once again by the media endlessly repeating the very tension I have tried to describe. Even so, this only reinforces one major point: we live in a world of modern communications with whatever consequences that may exact for culture. We also live, however, in a world and in a culture where constant discussion of the media and their role, of communications and their consequences for good and evil, is a fundamental aspect of culture as environment. Those of us who study this world must remain aware of both and of the profound interrelationship between the two.

Given the approach in this paper, I must provide the reader with some sense of where I am coming from intellectually and the cultural base of my own interest. When I was an undergraduate, I had little special interest in land policy and the frontier, but nevertheless I found myself a student of Paul Wallace Gates' at Cornell. In the several courses I took from him, I learned things that to this day I am not sure he knows I learned, and it is to him that I owe the opening of a whole world. For him I read Harold A. Innis, Canada's most distinguished historian, on the fur trade and was led to Innis' other writings on communications: *Empire and Communication, The Bias of Communications,* and other works.

Through Gates I also came upon the remarkable learning of James C. Malin of the University of Kansas. Gates was fascinated by Malin's work on John Brown although more than a little skeptical of most of his work and his intensely, it seemed, reactionary bias. Yet Malin was a brilliant critic of F. J. Turner and was the very first scholar I read on the communications revolution and its consequences. In a series of personally published books of exotic essays, Malin always excited a young man's interest in questions of the consequence of views of time and space, in the role of perception in history, in the consequences of communications shifts and new forms of energy. His book *The United States since the War* was published in 1930. Malin makes central, as does no other historian, the fundamental role of communications in shaping that postwar world. Written almost exclusively from the public record and immediately after the events discussed, it remains a remarkable work for all its limitation. Malin's interests—and Innis' and Gates'—were also the interests of a young graduate student of Gates' when I was an undergraduate at Cornell. He bullied me intellectually and taught me a great deal. But it was one early publication of his that fundamentally changed my thinking in this area. Lee Benson wrote an exhaustive essay (most easily available in his collection *Turner and Beard*) on the essential historiographic setting of the famous Turner thesis. What, among other things, Benson did in this exceptional piece was to study with care the nature of the communications revolution and the implications that a series of economists, political scientists, social theorists, and historians drew from the experience. The piece shaped my own thinking about the problems I have discussed above more than even I am probably aware. I am delighted to have this occasion to thank him.

14 "PERSONALITY" AND THE MAKING OF TWENTIETH-CENTURY CULTURE

P*erhaps the greatest problem which any historian has to tackle is neither the cataclysm of revolution nor the decay of empire but the process by which ideas become social attitudes.*
J. H. Plumb

I have always observed a singular accord between supercelestial ideas and subterranean behavior.
Montaigne

The whole history of ideas should be reviewed in the light of the power of social structures to generate symbols of their own.
Mary Douglas

No ideas but in things.
William Carlos Williams

One of the things that make the modern world "modern" is the development of consciousness of self. The European world that produced the Reformation, the new capitalist order, and the growing system of nation-states also gave us a new vocabulary that re-

vealed a new vision of the self. "Consciousness" became a key word
in the seventeenth century; the new language of self announced
what Owen Barfield has called "the shifting of the centre of gravity
of consciousness from the cosmos around him into the personal
human being himself."[1] The results of such a shift were significant.
Impulses that control human behavior and destiny were felt to arise
more and more *within* the individual at the very time that the laws
governing the world were seen as more and more impersonal. Not
only was it more difficult to feel spiritual life and activity immanent
in the world outside the self; as the rituals of the external church
grew feebler, the needs of inner self grew also stronger.

This story is familiar to the historian of modern thought. He
has charted the way of this newly developed self in a stormy and
changing world from its beginnings in Luther and Calvin, Descartes
and Locke. To insist that the history of thought in the modern era
is the history of thinking about that self may be an exaggeration.
But the consequences of this vision of a self set apart have surely
been felt in every field of inquiry, whether it be psychology or political theory, epistemology or economics. Freud, in one of his rare
moments of historical analysis, pointed in 1917 to a series of blows
that had been administered by modern science to the fragile self. In
the sixteenth century, Copernicus gave it a cosmological buffeting
by removing man from the center of the universe and insisting that
he dwelled on a small fragment of matter, only one of a countless
number of them. In the nineteenth century, Darwin made a biolog-
ical assault on the self when he argued man's essential affinity with
all animals and brought into doubt the special role of reason and
civilization. The final blow, Freud thought, was that delivered upon
our own century, the psychological blow. This vision (his own) denied that the center of personality was the ego or the soul, and it
further suggested, from its new view of the unconscious, that man
in the traditional sense did not have full control over himself.[2] In
Freud's vision, the history of science is especially important because
of its effect on man's view of himself.

All of this has been the stuff of the intellectual historian. He
has studied each "crisis" in thought—as he calls it—brought about
by a newer vision of new knowledge. He has attempted to assess the
"influence" of major and even minor "thinkers" and has examined
new "patterns" of thought emerging from the reconsideration of
old problems in new contexts or from new problems arising in
changed circumstances. On occasion, he has made an effort to relate
"ideas" to the particular social structure in which they appear to
have been generated. We have "seen" ideas become social attitudes.
We have been made aware of the "impact" of Locke, Darwin, and

Freud. Seldom do we even ask the question whether social attitudes do indeed become "ideas." When the historian talks of "popular" ideas, he rarely sees them as part of the world in which "ideas" (real ideas?) are born.

Yet that world—that combination of new social, economic, political, and religious structures—in which the new idea of self-consciousness developed belonged to others than just Hobbes and Locke—and I do not mean Descartes and Pascal! The same problems of self so important in the systematic thinking of the modern era were already widely felt. The changes in language and usage, the new words and word forms we find in the seventeenth and eighteenth centuries, are at least suggestive. It is striking, for example, to see the interest as early as the seventeenth century in what was called "character"; and how significant a cultural form character study became. Surely by the nineteenth century *character* was a key word in the vocabulary of Englishmen and Americans.

Philip Rieff has pointed out that as cultures change so do the modal types of persons who are their bearers.[3] By 1800 the concept of character had come to define that particular modal type felt to be essential for the maintenance of the social order. The term itself came to mean a group of traits believed to have social significance and moral quality, "the *sine qua non* of all collective adjustment and social intercourse."[4] In the age of self-consciousness, a popular vision of the self defined by the word "character" became fundamental in sustaining and even in shaping the significant forms of the culture. Such a concept filled two important functions. It proposed a method for both mastery and development of the self. In fact, it argued that its kind of self-control was the way to fullest development of the moral significance of self. But it also provided a method of presenting the self to society, offering a standard of conduct that assured interrelationship between the "social" and the "moral." The importance of character can be most easily established by examination of the hundreds of books, pamphlets, and articles produced during the century, the character studies providing examples for emulation, and the manuals promising a way to character development and worldly success. These were clearly a popular and important cultural form, but further examination of other aspects of the culture—literature, the arts, popular music, and the like—helps reinforce the importance of the concept of character to the culture of the nineteenth century. It was a culture of character.

It is significant in this context to call attention to the other key words most often associated with the concept of character. A review of over two hundred such items reveals the words most frequently related to the notion of character: *citizenship, duty, democracy, work, building, golden deeds, outdoor life, conquest, honor, reputation, morals, manners, integrity,* and above all, *manhood.* The stress was clearly moral and the interest was almost always in some sort of higher moral law. The most popular quotation—it appeared in dozens of works—was Emerson's definition of character: "Moral order through the medium of individual nature."

The problem of self, even as vaguely as it is defined here, thus becomes a fundamental one for almost all modern cultural development. The effort to achieve both a moral and a social order and a freely developing self shapes the cultural products of the times— high, middle, and low culture. The very existence of manuals (obviously necessary among the middle class in terms of their numbers and sales) indicates the reality of the problem. Further investigation would establish, I think, that the patterns of behavior, the institutions developed, the persistence in nineteenth-century America of a predominantly Arminian vision, the insistence on the so-called Protestant ethic, with emphasis on work as essential in a society that was constantly stressing producer values—all these are part of what I have suggested is a culture of character.

These are assertions, not proofs; these are not established propositions. Yet they illustrate my conviction that we can best understand modern cultural developments in all forms if we see and define the particular vision of the self basic to each cultural order. But my fundamental interest in the culture of character lies in the signs of its disappearance and the resulting call for a new modal type best suited to carry out the mission of a newer cultural order. It was not that the culture of character died suddenly or that books and manuals stressing the "character" vision of the self disappeared. In fact they are still being published. But, starting somewhere in the middle of the first decade of the twentieth century, there rapidly developed another vision of self, another vision of self-development and mastery, another method of the presentation of self in society. First, there is clear and growing evidence of an awareness of significant change in the social order, especially after 1880. Symptoms are easily suggested: what was called "American nervousness" and the various efforts at its diagnosis; the rash of utopian writings; the development of systematic sociological and economic analysis in the academic world; the development in government and public journals of a view of the need for "objective" and "scientific" gathering of data and treatment of social ills; and, even more important, the development of psychological and psychiatric studies. This awareness of change also suggested the need for a new kind of man, a new modal type to meet the new conditions. Perhaps few were as specific as Simon Patten and *The New Basis of Civilization* (1909), in which he argued that a society moving from scarcity to abundance required a new self. But it is hard to read the social theorists of the period—Sumner, Ward, Veblen—without some sense of the keen interest in the relation between social orders and psychological types, the belief that a change in the social order almost demanded a change in the people in it.

Writing in the middle of the century about the Renaissance in Italy, Jacob Burckhardt, the greatest of cultural historians, suggested:

In the Middle Ages both sides of human consciousness—that which was turned within as well as that which was turned without—lay dreaming or half awake beneath a common veil. The veil was woven of faith, illusion, and childish prepossession. . . . Man was conscious of himself only as a member of a race, people, party, family, or corporation—only through some general category. In Italy this veil was first melted into air; an *objective* treatment and consideration of the State and all of the things of this world became possible. The *subjective* side at the same time asserted itself with corresponding emphasis. Man became a spiritual *individual* and recognized himself as such. . . . It will not be difficult to show that this result was due above all to the political circumstances of Italy.[5]

This analysis is valuable to us as a model. There is general agreement among historians that some significant material change occurred in the period we are considering. Whether it is a change from a producer to a consumer society, an order of economic accumulation to one of disaccumulation, industrial capitalism to finance capitalism, scarcity to abundance, disorganization to high organization—however that change is defined, it is clear that a new social order was emerging. But even more important than this was the growing awareness on the part of those living through the change that it was in fact occurring and that it was fundamental. The ability to treat this change with increasing "objectivity" made it possible to face the subjective or psychological changes that seemed to be mandated.

All of this is preface to the discovery of the beginnings of a radical shift in the kinds of advice manuals that appeared after the turn of the century, and to new preoccupations, which strike at the heart of the basis of the culture of character. In an important sense, however, the transition began in the very bosom of the old culture. For it was what might be called the other side of Emerson—his vision of a transcendent self—that formed the heart of that New Thought or Mind Cure movement so important in the process from a culture of character to a culture of personality. The key figures— Ralph Waldo Trine, Ella Wheeler Wilcox, Annie Payson Call, Horatio Dresser, Orison Swett Marden—attempted to combine the qualities of the works on character with a religious and even mystical stress on a spiritual vision of the self; they insisted not only on a higher moral order but also on the fulfillment of self by a striving to become one with a higher self. As New Thought work proceeded, it was possible to note an increasing interest in self-development along these lines, with somewhat less interest in moral imperatives.

Meanwhile, in the American heartland, a careful reader of Ralph Waldo Trine was developing a method of production along with a new philosophy of industry. The results in all areas were revolutionary. When he made his famous 1907 announcement promising a motor car for the great multitude, he was favoring production, mass consumption, mass society. But he also stressed both the family (it would be a family car) and the individual (the owner could run and care for it). Everyone could have one. It would be made of the best materials by the best men. It would be simple in design. And what was its purpose? To "enjoy . . . the blessings of hours of pleasure in God's open spaces." A machine for pleasure. How much Ford's world sounds like that of Simon Patten. No more austerity and sacrifice but rather leisure and rational enjoyment for all.[6] The world of the man of Dearborn—with its new ideas of production, consumption, and use—is not part of the culture of character.

It is further a striking part of the turn-of-the-century decade that interest grew in personality, individual idiosyncrasies, personal needs and interests. The vision of self-sacrifice began to yield to that of self-realization. There was fascination with the peculiarities of the self, especially the sick self. Miss Beauchamp, in Dr. Morton Prince's 1905 study *The Dissociation of Personality*, became a figure of popular discussion. At least five major studies of Jesus appeared in the same decade. But in these works the Nazarene is not the healer, the social problem-solver, the achieving man of character and moral exemplar. Rather he is a sick personality, a miserably maladjusted fanatic. So serious was the debate on this analysis that Albert Schweitzer felt called upon to reply to these studies in 1913 with *The Psychiatric Study of Jesus*. And our literature produced the strange heroine of William Vaughan Moody's *The Great Divide* (1909), with her peculiar problems of personality (in its way a precursor of the drama of Eugene O'Neill), and Gertrude Stein's remarkable portraits in *Three Lives* (1906), perhaps in its way a model for Sherwood Anderson's *Winesburg, Ohio* (1919). Literature was interested increasingly in probing personality and less in studying moral or social achievement in the more traditional way of a culture of character.

But even without these hints the evidence is readily available in hundreds of manuals and guides for self-improvement published between 1900 and 1920. One of Raymond Williams' "keywords," *personality*, is a modern term.[7] It appears in the late eighteenth century, and there is some evidence of its modern usage in the nineteenth century. While there are examples of its use by Emerson and Henry Adams, Walt Whitman alone, to my knowledge, made frequent and consistent use of the word in its current sense in the last century. By the first decade of this century, it was an important part of the American vocabulary. It is in that decade as well that a series of volumes and articles began to appear addressed to the problem of helping people develop their personalities. From the start *personality* was distinguished from *character*. In 1915 Funk and Wagnalls published a series of self-help books, their *Mental Efficiency Series*. (*Efficiency* and *energy* are also important words with significantly increased usage in the new culture of personality.) The series contains volumes on both character ("How to Strengthen It") and personality ("How to Build It"). From the beginning the adjectives most frequently associated with personality suggest a very different concept from that of character: *fascinating, stunning, attractive, magnetic, glowing, masterful, creative, dominant, forceful*. These words would seldom if ever be used to modify the word *character*. One writer makes the point: character, he insists, is either good or bad; personality, famous or infamous.[8]

"Personality is the quality of being Somebody."[9] This definition—repeated in various ways in almost all of the manuals I have analyzed—is also a major theme of this literature. The problem is clear. We live now constantly in a crowd; how can we distinguish ourselves from others in that crowd? While the term is never used, the question is clearly one of life in a mass society (*crowd* is the most commonly used word). Since we live in such a world it is important to develop one's self—that is, those traits, "moral, intellectual, physical, and practical," that will enable us to think of ourselves and have others think of us as "somebodies." "To create a personality is power," one manual writer insists.[10] One does this by being "conscious of yourself and of others," by being discerning and sincere, by showing energy, by paying attention to others so that they will pay attention to you.

To be somebody one must be oneself (whatever that means). It is an almost too perfect irony that most of the works published and sold in large numbers as self-help in developing an effective personality insist that individuals should be "themselves" and *not* follow the advice or direction of others. The importance of being different, special, unusual, of standing out in a crowd—all of this is emphasized at the same time that specific directions are provided for achieving just those ends. In virtually the same breath, the reader is also urged repeatedly to "express your individuality" and to "eliminate the little personal whims, habit, traits that make people dislike you. Try in every way to have a ready command of the niceties, the manners, the ways of speech, etc. which make people think 'he's a mighty likable fellow.' That is the beginning of a reputation for personality." [11] Thus "personality," like "character," is an effort to solve the problem of self in a changed social structure that imposes its own special demands on the self. Once again, such a popular view of self proposes a method of both self-mastery and self-development as well as a method of the presentation of that self in society. Both methods differed from those proposed in the culture of character and they underpin the development of a new culture, the culture of personality.

This was also, of course, the age of Freud and psychoanalysis. Philip Rieff has argued that "psychoanalysis defends the private man against the demands of both culture and instinct." He asserts that this era was one dominated by a new character type, "psychological man.":

We will recognize in the case history of psychological man the nervous habits of his father, economic man, he is anti-heroic, shrewd, carefully counting his satisfactions and dissatisfactions, studying unprofitable commitments as the sins most to be avoided. From this immediate ancestor, psychological man has constructed his own careful economy of the inner life . . . and lives by the mastery of his own personality. [12]

In a general sense, the popular personality manuals I have investigated establish essentially the same new character type Rieff sees as the consequence of Freud's influence. I do not mean to suggest that Freudian theory is implicit in these works (although in the 1920s Freud was often explicitly cited on occasion to support the general position advanced). I mean rather that a vision of the self and its problems generated in large part by an awareness of a significant change in the social structure contains certain basic attitudes comparable to those of Rieff's "psychological man." Freud, without doubt an intellectual genius, lived after all in the social world. What I am suggesting is that general social attitudes exist in popular thought before formal "ideas" expressing them rise to the level of general understanding. This is perhaps why so many ideas of major thinkers do finally win popular acceptance.

In the particular case under study, there is a striking example. Even in the early personality manuals in the first decade of the century there is singular emphasis not only on the need for self-confidence but also on the importance of not feeling "inferior." Not only are there constant warnings against the dangers of feeling inferior (if one harbors such feelings, one can never impress others and will always exhibit, as a result, a weak personality), but there is a positive injunction to appear superior (but not overly or aggressively so). This attitude was important long before Alfred Adler explained to the world the significance of the "inferiority complex" late in the 1920s.

A brief examination of two works by one of the most popular writers of the period will serve to press home the importance of the change in emphasis from character to personality. In 1899 Orison Swett Marden published *Character: The Greatest Thing in the World.* Crowded with character studies of special historical heroes as exemplars, this book dwells most particularly on the "mental and moral traits," the "high ideals," the "balance" that make character and therefore bring success in the world. Being a true Christian gentleman, pure, upright, intelligent, strong, and brave, possessing a sense of duty, having benevolence, moral courage, personal integrity, and the "highest kinship of soul," devoting service to mankind, being attentive to the "highest and most harmonious development of one's powers" to achieve "a complete and consistent whole"— these are the key words and phrases used in support of the argument. In the course of the volume, Marden stresses the basic values necessary in a producer-oriented society, including hard work (the "sacredness of one's work.") and thrift. He ends the book with a powerful appeal. Quoting President Garfield ("I must succeed in making myself a man"), Marden insists that character above all means, for those interested in developing it, "Let him first be a Man."

In 1921 Marden published *Masterful Personality.* It suggests a remarkably different set of interests. In this book Marden addresses himself to "man's mysterious atmosphere," the aura and power of personality that can "sway great masses." Against the profound dangers of feeling inferior, he proposes a search for supremacy. Much attention is focused on "personal charm." He urges women not only to rely on physical beauty but also to develop "fascination." The ability to attract and hold friends is important. "You can," Marden insists, "compel people to like you." "So much of our success in life depends upon what others think of us." Manners, proper clothes, good conversation ("to know *what* to say and *how* to say it"), energy, "life efficiency," poise—these are the concerns of this volume. In the course of 20 years Marden had come to see the need for a different character type.[13]

The older vision of self expressed in the concept of character was founded in an inner contradiction. That vision argued that the highest development of self ended in a version of self-control or self-mastery, which often meant fulfillment through sacrifice in the name of a higher law, ideals of duty, honor, integrity. One came to selfhood through obedience to law and ideals. Brilliantly sustaining the human needs of a producer-oriented society, it urged in effect a sublimation of self-needs or their redefinition in Arminian terms. But the newer vision of personality also had its paradox. It stressed self-fulfillment, self-expression, self-gratification so persistently that almost all writers as an afterthought gave a warning against intolerable selfishness, extreme self-confidence, excessive assertions of personal superiority. But the essentially antinomian vision of this, with its view not of a higher law but of a higher self, was tempered by the suggestion that the self ought to be presented to society in such a way as to make oneself "well liked." There is an obvious difficulty here. One is to be unique, be distinctive, follow one's own feelings, make oneself stand out from the crowd, and at the same time appeal—by fascination, magnetism, attractiveness—to it.

Both visions of self—visions I argue shaped the very nature of the culture—are assumed from the start not to be natural but to be things that can be learned and practiced, through exercise and by study of guidebooks to success. Both visions relate to the needs of a particular social structure and do not develop in an atmosphere of pure philosophical speculation. The older vision no longer suited personal or social needs; the newer vision seemed particularly suited for the problems of the self in a changed social order, the developing consumer mass society.

The new personality literature stressed items that could be best developed in leisure time and that represented in themselves an emphasis on consumption. The social role demanded of all in the new culture of personality was that of a performer. Every American was to become a performing self. Every work studied stressed the importance of the human voice in describing methods of voice control and proper methods of conversation or public speaking. Everyone was expected to impress and influence with trained and effective speech. Special books and courses were developed to meet demands in this area alone. In these books and articles exercise, proper breathing, sound eating habits, a good complexion, and grooming and beauty aids were all stressed. At the same time, clothing, personal appearance, and "good manners" were important, but there was little interest in morals. Poise and charm top the list of necessary traits, and there was insistence that they could be learned and developed through careful practice. The new stress on the enjoyment of life implied that true pleasure could be attained by making oneself pleasing to others.

Often the books stressed the role of personality in business success. *Personality in Business*, a series of 50 articles on every aspect of business activity by some of the most distinguished businessmen and publicists of the period, was first issued in 1906 and then reprinted in 1910 and 1916. The new stress on personality in business, in fact, led to a reaction by some of the older character-based authors. George Horace Lorimer, in his 1902 best seller, *Letters from a Self-Made Merchant to His Son*, specifically warned against the attempt to be popular, suggesting that the effort took too much time and was not always successful in a business way. But in general the personality manuals move away from an interest in business or even financial success and provide a newer definition of what constitutes genuine success in life.[14]

The new interest in personality—both the unique qualities of an individual and the performing self that attracts others—was not limited to self-help authors in this period. It extended to participants in the high culture as well. In 1917 Ezra Pound pleaded for the struggle that would assure what he called "the rights of personality," and even earlier he had insisted to a friend that mass society created a world in which man was continually being used by others. For him, *the* issue of the modern world was "the survival of personality." Earlier, Herbert Croly explained in *The Promise of American Life* (1909) that "success in any   pursuit demands that an individual make some sort of personal impression." Painters, architects, politicians, all depend "upon a numerous and faithful body of admirers." Emancipation, self-expression, excellent work are all meaningless unless such gifted individuals have the support of a following. This is only one of many works in the period that stress the role of personal magnetism in leadership. And in 1913 Randolph Bourne pleaded with young radicals to understand the new order of things, which included the importance of personality, sincerity, and the like, and which is interpreted in terms of these attainments. In stressing the importance of influence Bourne proposed that nothing was so important as a "most glowing personality." Self-cultivation, he maintained, "becomes almost a duty, if one wants to be effective towards the great end (the regeneration of the social order). And not only personality, but prestige."[15]

At the outset of the century, Nathaniel Southgate Shaler wrote in *The Individual* (1900), which he insisted was a purely scientific analysis, a central chapter on "Expression of the Individuality." Here he demonstrated the importance of what he called "modes of externalization," the ways people gain the attention of others. He believed these things are done not simply for gain or esteem but because there is an instinctive need "to externalize the self." He saw this in dress and fashion, in song and speech, in the richness of language. Each culture, he suggested, has different "motives of self-presentation." The key to all expression of self, however, is the face. We are, in Shaler's view, all actors, and the face has the power of an instrument able to express intellect as well as emotion.

The test of the general approach proposed in this paper would be a more specific analysis of the cultural forms of our century to see whether in fact they share the characteristics of a culture of personality, whether they can be examined as manifestations of the working out of the basic ideas central to this vision of self. Investigations have convinced me that most cultural forms studied to date reveal a kinship to the culture of personality. Comic strips, radio programs, even beauty pageants have yielded evidence of significant dependence on these ideas. For purposes of this paper, however, I want to offer only one example. I am convinced that the nature and form of the modern motion picture as it developed as a middle-class popular art between 1910 and 1915 clearly show its participation in the culture of personality. Technically, the film, especially in the hands of its major developer as a middle-class art, D. W. Griffith, and those who followed him, depended on two major modes and used them dramatically in startling juxtaposition. The first was the handling of vast groups of people. Vachel Lindsay in his brilliant 1915 book on film speaks of the role of what he calls "crowd splendor" in motion pictures.[16] Films are not only a mass medium, they also represent one of the major ways in which a mass society can examine itself as mass. There was from the start of serious motion pictures an intimate relationship between it and the portraying of the role of crowds. To the depiction of the crowd, and often in striking contrast to it, Griffith added the extraordinary form of the closeup. Almost as if he were following the teachings of Shaler, the face, bigger than life and abstracted from it, provides a brilliant expression of self, of an individual. The importance of this contrast—the mass and the isolated individual apart from that mass —to the development of film, and thus of film's role in the culture of personality, cannot be exaggerated.

Up to 1910, motion picture studios generally concealed the identity of most screen players. In 1910, however, the idea of the movie star was born. The creation of the star changed the nature of the role of motion pictures in our society. It brought into even more prominent use the press agent and modern advertising. "Henceforth, a screen player was to be marketed for her admirers as a personality, an image and, to an increasingly sinister extent, an object," the historian of the star system suggests.[17] This immediately leads to fan magazines and to a new consciousness of the importance of personality. It leads, in fact, to a new profession—that of being a movie star or a celebrity. In the culture of character, the public had insisted on some obvious correlation between achievement and fame. Now that insistence is gone. The very definition of reality was altered, as Richard Schickel explains in his suggestive study of Douglas Fairbanks, Sr.: "Indeed, it is now essential that the politician, the man of ideas, and the non-performing artist become performers so that they may become celebrities so that in turn they may exert genuine influence on the general public."[18] Fairbanks himself was dedicated not to his art but to himself. As early as 1907 a famous actress said of him that he would be famous in films: "He's not good looking. But he has worlds of personality."

Fairbanks is important to us in this analysis. He becomes one of those symbols social structures generate—and in this case an active agent as well. Not only was he a star and a topnotch public relations man, but he also wrote his own kind of self-help books (*Make Life Worth-While, Laugh and Live*) and a column in one of the leading movie magazines. He provided a link between the pioneers of the new self-help literature and the new social world that Henry Ford was building. In 1928 Ralph Waldo Trine published *The Power That Wins*, the report of an intimate talk on life with Henry Ford. Trine begins his conversation with Ford by recalling a trip to Hollywood and a visit to Douglas Fairbanks. He assumes, of course, that Fairbanks doesn't know who he is

> "Don't I?" he replied. "Just wait until I show you a specially inscribed copy of *In Tune with the Infinite* that Henry Ford sent me."
> MR. FORD. Yes, I remember sending that book to Mr. Fairbanks. Back in 1914, when my associates and I were working out some very difficult problems here, some of your books were of great help to me. I used to keep a stock of your books in my office, to give to friends or associates who, I thought would be benefited by them the same as I.[19]

Trine, Ford, Fairbanks, three major figures in the transition from a culture of character to a culture of personality, are here neatly linked together.

If Fairbanks was at the beginning of this world of stars and press agents, we know that it was only the beginning. There *are* ideas in things (maybe *only* in things, as William Carlos Williams insists), but we are only beginning to understand our cultural developments in terms of the system of ideas on which they are in fact based, the system of ideas inherent in the cultural forms we study.

Movies suggest many explorations not yet undertaken. For films have been an agency fundamental for the generation of the key symbols of our social structure. Complete with stars and even gods and goddesses, housed in places that (even down to the massive organ) resemble huge cathedrals, motion pictures became for thousands a new religion (perhaps a special religion for the antinomians of the twentieth century). No wonder some more fundamentalist Protestant religionists forbid movie-going to their congregants. They know a surrogate or competing religious order when they see one.

A CONCLUDING, MOST UNSCIENTIFIC, POSTSCRIPT

Some unproven assertions about the emergence of a culture of personality in twentieth-century America lead me to attempt to confirm these speculations. Convinced that the nature of cultural development specifically depends for its forms on the existing vision of self —in terms of its definition of its problem in development and presentation in society—I am also anxious to press the analysis further and account for the significant changes clearly visible in our cultural history during the century. Thus within the culture of personality there are divisions based on special readings of the problem of personality at different times within the whole range and in response to shifts in social structure. In the period from 1910 through the late 1920s, the problem was most often defined in terms of guilt and the need to eliminate guilt. One might think of this period, at least metaphorically, as the age of Freud—not so much in terms of direct influence but rather in terms of the point of view from which the culture viewed its problem of self. I have already argued elsewhere that the period from 1929 to 1938 might be seen as one dominated by the problem of shame, and I have, again metaphorically, called this the age of Alfred Adler. From 1939 through the late 1940s we do not need to invent a name. The period self-consciously thought of itself as the age of anxiety. The major concern for moral, national identity and character led increasingly to an interest in myth, to a search for some collective unconscious brought to awareness. Let me call this the age of Jung. From the end of the 1940s to almost the end of the 1950s the problem was fundamentally redefined as that of personal identity. Who could object to seeing this as the age of Erik Erikson? The 1960s and the profound interest in liberation, especially sexual liberation, provided still another modification in the culture of personality. Perhaps this will be known as the age of Wilhelm Reich. I refuse to speculate on the immediate present for fear I will be regarded as irresponsible. Yet, wild as these speculations may seem, I remain convinced that the changes in culture do mean changes in modal types of character and that social structures do generate their own symbols. Intellectual historians would do well to begin to see ideas in things and to see that there is in fact some connection between the most ethereal of ideas and common, and even basic, human behavior.

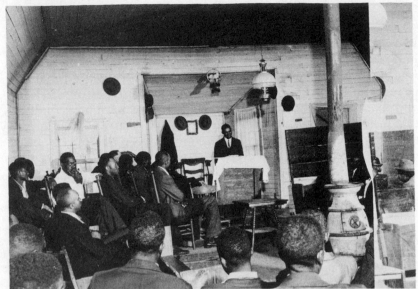

Library of Congress

Our Church

Religious experience in America today is often defined in terms of traditional institutions and traditional structures. In fact, there have been a wide range of religious visions and associated practices. Americans have shown a remarkable facility for creating formal and informal "churches," architectural icons suited to their particular needs. Here are but two of the many such sites of religious "events": a rural black church captured by Jack Delano in 1942 and, twelve years later, a New York street scene from William Klein.

William Klein

AFTERWORDS
PAST AND PRESENT IN THE TWENTIETH CENTURY

One of the most important things about the present—any "present"—is its past. The historian is engaged in the present in a study of that past. But what are the consequences of the knowledge that his work reveals? This question has sparked an important debate characteristic of our culture. Early in the nineteenth century John Keats could have Apollo in "Hyperion" boast: "Knowledge enormous makes a God of me." It is precisely historical knowledge that deifies him: "Names, deeds, gray legends, dire events, rebellions . . . Creations and destroyings." Yet almost exactly one hundred years later T. S. Eliot's "Gerontion" warns us: "After such knowledge, what forgiveness?" For history has "cunning passages." It "deceives with whispering ambitions"; it guides us "by vanities." As the poets disagree, so too do the historians. Thomas Buckle in the middle of the last century assumed that the knowledge of origins—how things came to be—would enable men to solve basic human problems. Yet approximately one hundred years later Arthur Schlesinger, Jr. warned us that history was no "redeemer" and that there were fundamental human problems impossible of easy solution no matter how much we knew and that, in fact, knowledge of the past established human history as "tragic."

It is not hard to reject both positivist optimism and neo-orthodox tragic vision. It is harder to specify precisely the uses of historical knowledge. Jacob Burckhardt once defined history as "the

breach with nature caused by the awakening of consciousness."
Thus it is an aspect of the growing awareness and understanding
that enable us to experience the world, function in it, and even
change it. The task is never to gather facts or develop intellectual
structures alone. For history, like the culture of which it is a part, is
something lived, something used.

The cultural historian, as Johan Huizinga insisted, is primarily
a morphologist and cultural history the study of the forms men,
women, and children develop and use in experiencing the world.
This concern for forms leads us to the problem of the particular
form historical writing itself must take.

Many of the "facts" about a culture are not expressed directly
in the culture but are rather assumed. In what Franco Moretti has
called "the unconscious culture" lie the deep, buried, invisible pre-
suppositions of every world view. A careful study of the conventions, the unassuming everyday acts, the rhetorical devices in speech
and song, the unconscious patterns of behavior, all help to uncover
that "implicit knowledge" and those fundamental assumptions that
members of such cultures share.

Anthony Wallace has rightly argued that no real culture that
any historian can understand is "one giant harmonious pattern felt,
understood, and practiced by all members of a society." There is,
rather, a "structure of conflict." Separate parts are "maintained,
developed, and changed by different groups, and in many aspects
experienced in a slightly different way by every individual." The
world may be more Hegelian than many would like to believe: contradiction may indeed be the essence of being. A culture is in fact
defined by its tensions, which provide both the necessary tensile
strength to keep the culture stable and operative and the dynamic
force that may ultimately bring about change or complete structural
collapse. Great events, the wars and the depressions, may intrude in
significant ways, but may themselves be explained by the view that
cultures are special patterns of tensions and structures of conflict.

Cultures can actually be arguments or debates themselves.
Each group, class, faction, or party attempts to persuade the others
to its vision of the world or to mock or destroy some contrary vision.
They seize and manipulate all the possible instruments of persuasion the culture provides: symbols, central icons, devices to achieve
laughter and those to create tears, rhetorical flourishes of all kinds
including the enormously effective use of key words or phrases.
The word "culture" itself can become a weapon in the struggle. The
illustrations in this volume indicate some of the debates and some
of the instruments in the argument. But this way of seeing culture
as a debate still assumes some measure of common understanding

and even common language, as well as separate and special under-standings and languages that belong almost singularly to those groups, classes, factions, and parties.

Such a view of culture also throws doubt on many traditional ways of dealing with its history. The notion of popular culture, for example, takes on different force. Can it be treated independently of the whole range of structures of conflict, especially in the twentieth-century world of mass communications, which often obliterate sharp distinctions? When figures from the world of popular culture (the world of the comic book) begin to appear in the paintings of artists considered high cultural figures and the life and work of difficult avant-garde painters appears, as Jackson Pollock's for example has, to have entered the popular consciousness, serious questions must be asked. And even in recent studies of early modern European popular culture we have begun to see the fruitful gains that come from the examination of the "circularity" (as Mikhail Bakhtin has called it) between the culture of dominant classes and that of subordinate classes, reciprocal influences which have traveled from low to high and from high to low.

Such a view threatens as well our neat and simple visions of historical determinacy. American historians too easily give way before the force of the machine: changing technology is claimed as the source of all cultural change. As I see it, technological change is the consequence of the existing pattern of tensions, the result of the operation of the structures of conflict. Aspects of that culture provide the very aspirations and other conditions that make innovation possible while at the same time themselves determining how the resulting technology is shaped and used—or not used, in some cases.

This definition will allow us as well to examine aspects of our recent past that we have not, in the realm of cultural history, probed sufficiently. Burckhardt proposed that there were three great forces that shaped the nature of civilizations: Culture, Religion, The State (the capital letters are essential to his meaning here). In different civilizations different individual forces have dominated. American cultural historians are surely now more willing to see the role of religion in shaping our culture, although perhaps not sufficiently so for our own century. And there has been almost always an interest in the role of Culture with a capital C. The State, however, when it is thought about at all, is considered the province of the political, economic, and perhaps social historians. Of course, until very recently few historians were willing to admit we had a State in the European sense. I've argued in this book that that State—administrative, bureaucratic, and far from the Republic of which our

Founding Fathers dreamed—came into existence in the nineteenth century largely under the auspices of the new middle class that appeared around the same time. This hypothesis surely needs fuller examination, but so, too, does the role this new State took in shaping the nature of the culture, the lives and experiences, of Americans of many kinds. It helped us in raising our children and in shaping our diet; it used the most effective means of persuasion to make us into the kind of citizens and even the kind of consumers it wanted us to be. Thus we need to broaden the scope of our cultural analysis to include the newer institutions and agencies the culture itself creates which become a piece of the structure of conflict, an element of the pattern of tension itself.

Of all the tensions, however, it may be that the great confrontation, that significant relationship between past and present, defines the most serious. If this is the case (and this book has argued its importance), the historian finds himself in a special role: in acting out his search for answers to his own personal problems and needs amidst the specific cultural situation in which he finds himself, the historian performs crucial cultural work in his effort to deal with that confrontation. There are obvious political and ideological implications of the work he does, whether intended or not. History as an expression of consciousness is also the shaper of perceptions of the world (another name, after all, for ideology). This, too, has been a key theme of this book. When Vico—our first cultural historian and therefore the father of us all—discovered early in the eighteenth century that men make their own history, he was not simply illuminating the past for his present; he was also unveiling a vision that was to have (as Edmund Wilson among many others has clearly demonstrated) significant ideological consequences for the nineteenth and even more especially our own twentieth century. But recall Carl Becker once again. Historians do not monopolize the study of the past. Surely he was right and everyman—and every woman and child—is in some fundamental sense his own historian. This, too, is a cultural fact of enormous importance. For the truth —whatever Mr. Jefferson thought that might be—may not set you free. But from it can come an understanding, an awareness, that may in fact enable us to continue to make our own history.

NOTES

CHAPTER 1
HISTORY AND THE AMERICAN
INTELLECTUAL:
THE USES OF A USABLE PAST

1. This is the first sentence of their introduction to *The Rise of American Civilization* (New York, 1927), p. vii.

2. An earlier version of this paper was read to a joint American Studies Association/American Historical Association luncheon held in New York, December 28, 1960.

3. This distinction, so important in modern historiographical discussion, is made effectively in Benedetto Croce, *History: Its Theory and Practice* (London, 1920).

4. History arose in an effort to analyze new problems in a changing social order, problems now believed possible of such analysis by rational inquiry. Scientific inquiry had its origins in similar circumstances, with the realization that the nature of the physical world was also amenable to such analysis. In both instances, of course, a special kind of professionalism developed. But again, in both instances, the existence of a special class of trained inquirers failed to give these men a real monopoly over their fields: others could use the results of such inquiries for their own purposes. This continues to be especially true in the study of history, where special technical difficulties such as exist in today's scientific inquiry have really never developed. I am, of course, aware that there is in fact a kind of sociology of historians; not everyone was interested in history in every period. In the classical world, history was generally written by and for members of the

NOTES

governing classes, for example. My point is simply that history *could* in fact be available to all who could read. It presented no special mysteries. Also, in the discussion that follows I am interested only in professional historians when they have an impact on the more general intellectual community. Obviously, after 1885 the professional historian is an important cultural fact, but I am more interested in the cultural consequences of the uses of history by intellectuals who may indeed not be professional historians.

5. I realize that my social categories are "ideal types" that are perhaps not acceptable for more sophisticated social analysis, but I believe that they can still be useful in a more general way, a rough background for my analysis. I am sorry, too, to insist on my own usage for the words *myth, ideology, history,* and *utopia.* I am well aware that others use these terms differently and, since precise definition would take more space than I may have, I hope that my meanings are clear from the context. I have been influenced in part by Kenneth Burke, "Ideology and Myth," *Accent,* VII (Summer 1947), 195–205. Mr. Burke sees myth as a way of stating a culture's "essence" in narrative terms. Two very important recent discussions of myth and ideology have been published by Ben Halpern: "The Dynamic Elements of Culture," *Ethics,* LXV (July 1955), 235–249, and " 'Myth' and 'Ideology' in Modern Usage," *History and Theory,* I (1961), 129–149.

6. While this point is obvious, it unfortunately escapes too many writers. Stow Persons is consistently excellent in indicating these differences and their significance in his *American Minds* (New York, 1958).

7. W. Lloyd Warner, *The Living and the Dead* (New Haven, 1959), pp. 101–225.

8. For examples of this transformation, see Upton Sinclair's extraordinary anthology of the literature of social protest, *The Cry for Justice* (Philadelphia, 1915). Book VII, 345–382, is called "Jesus" and in it appear many examples of the use of the historical Jesus as a figure of social protest.

9. Stow Persons, "The Cyclical Theory of History in Eighteenth Century America," *The American Quarterly,* VI (Summer 1954), 147–163. This seems to me one of the most important articles on the Enlightenment in America and yet it is not sufficiently well known or used by those who continue to talk about the period in traditional ways, be they the ways of a Becker or a Boorstin.

10. I have often wondered whether there is any significance in the fact that most of those who were originally headed for a career in law generally selected European history as their field of inquiry, while those who had prepared for the ministry, like Sparks and Bancroft, devoted themselves to the American story.

11. *History as a Romantic Art* (Stanford, Calif., 1959).

12. *The American Adam* (Chicago, 1955), p. 161.

13. V. L. Parrington, Jr., *American Dreams* (Providence, R.I., 1947), is an account of utopian works with a good checklist of titles.

14. It is important at this juncture to recall Turner's extraordinary essay "The Significance of History," which antedates his more famous paper of 1893 and which is really one of the earliest statements in the "New History" position that Beard and Robinson were to espouse. This essay is reprinted in *The Varieties of History,* ed. Fritz Stern (New York, 1956), pp. 197–208. For the setting out of which the Turner thesis itself came see Lee Benson, "The Historical Background of Turner's Frontier Essay," *Agricultural History,* XXV (April 1951), 59–82.

15. I have discussed this point in my article "The Useless Past: American Intellectuals and the Frontier Thesis, 1910–1930," *The Bucknell Review*, XI (March 1963), 1–20. For ideological consequences of the kind I mean see, for example, William Appleman Williams, "The Frontier Thesis and American Foreign Policy," *The Pacific Coast Historical Review*, XXIV (November 1955), 379–395.

16. See Morton White, *Social Thought in America* (New York, 1949), and Cushing Strout, *The Pragmatic Revolt in American History* (New Haven, 1958).

17. This present paper barely suggests one of the major attacks on the Puritan past. Also see especially Frederick J. Hoffman, "Philistine and Puritan in the 1920's," *The American Quarterly*, I (Fall 1949), 247–268.

18. William Carlos Williams, *In the American Grain* (New York, 1925), pp. 188, 109, 189. Italics in the original.

19. It might be well to recall at this point that the two novels I discussed in the first section of this paper in effect mark the beginning and end of the period under discussion, Melville's novella at the start of the era and Faulkner's novel marking in some real sense the end of an era.

20. This is, of course, from Arthur Schlesinger, Jr.'s, famous *Partisan Review* essay "The Causes of the American Civil War: A Note on Historical Sentimentalism," written in 1949. The essay is most conveniently found in *The Causes of the American Civil War*, ed. E. C. Rozwenc (Boston, 1961). The passage I have quoted appears on pp. 189–190 in that text.

CHAPTER 2
THE FRONTIER THESIS AND
THE AMERICAN INTELLECTUAL

1. An earlier version of this paper was read at the April 1960 meeting of the Mississippi Valley Historical Association in Louisville, Kentucky. Van Wyck Brooks' article "On Creating a Usable Past" can be found in *The Dial*, LXIV (April 11, 1918), 337–341.

2. Waldo Frank, *Our America* (New York, 1919), pp. 132–133.

3. John Gould Fletcher, *Europe's Two Frontiers* (London, 1930), p. 3.

4. Brooks, op. cit., pp. 337, 338, 339.

5. By "Turnerism" I mean the whole body of doctrine in reference to the West and the frontier as what Henry Nash Smith calls "myth and symbol." His important book *Virgin Land* (Cambridge, Mass., 1950) is crucial as an introduction to the problem of the frontier myth as ideology, but he stops his analysis in 1893 with a discussion of Turner's famous essay. Anyone who wishes to understand the historical and ideological setting for Turner's own work (with several important insights for our own century as well) would do well to see Lee Benson's classic article "The Historical Background of Turner's Frontier Essay," *Agricultural History*, XXV (April 1951), 59–82. One of the few efforts to examine the consequences of Turnerism for thought and action in our own century is William Appleman Williams' brilliant "The Frontier Thesis and American Foreign Policy," *The Pacific Historical Review*, XXIV (November 1955), 379–395.

6. It was in this period that the Turnerian approach was applied more specifically to various cultural aspects of American life, especially in the fields of religion and literature. See, for example, Peter George Mode, *The Frontier Spirit in American Christianity* (New York, 1923); Henry K. Rowe, *The History of Religion in the United States* (New York, 1924); W. W. Sweet,

NOTES

The Story of Religions in America (New York, 1930); Harold E. Luccock, *Jesus and the American Mind* (New York, 1930); Dorothy Dondore, *The Prairie and the Making of Middle America* (Cedar Rapids, Iowa, 1926); Lucy Lockwood Hazard, *The Frontier in American Literature* (New York, 1927). This last volume has an extremely interesting final chapter on the period under discussion, which Mrs. Hazard considers an age of "spiritual pioneering." This is an important document. Henry Nash Smith has summed up rather vaguely: "The fact that Turner's influence seems to have increased very rapidly after about 1920 is likewise suggestive in relation to the general development of American thought. This was the period when the revolt against the Genteel Tradition reached its climax, when the Young Intellectuals were proclaiming the liberation of American literature and thought from the dominance of conservative critics in the tradition of the New England Brahmins. Turner's reinterpretation of American history was highly destructive of the earlier tendency to view our history, especially our intellectual development, as having its focus along the Atlantic seaboard or even more narrowly within a thirty-mile radius of the Harvard Yard. Many critics and writers who ordinarily paid little attention to academic historical scholarship found Turner a useful weapon in the all-out campaign against 'Puritanism' and the out-worn 'ideality' of nineteenth-century official artistic theory." "The West as an Image of the American Past," *The University of Kansas City Review*, XVIII (Autumn 1951), 36. Obviously, I am interested in a different kind of problem, but I wish to make it clear that I am here concerned with only one aspect of Turnerism in the twentieth century. This piece is part of a much longer study aimed at a fuller discussion of the various implications of the frontier thesis as American ideology from 1900 to 1960.

7.   In his Introduction to Perry Miller and Thomas H. Johnson, eds., *The Puritans* (Boston, 1938), p. 17

8.   *The United States in 1800* (Ithaca, N.Y., 1955), p. 128. This volume reprints the first six chapters of Vol. I of Adams' *History of the United States of America During the First Administration of Thomas Jefferson* (New York, 1889).

9.   "Contributions of the West to American Democracy," reprinted in George Rogers Taylor, ed., *The Turner Thesis* (Boston, 1949), p. 23. But see also Rush Welter, "The Frontier West as Image of American Society: Conservative Attitudes Before the Civil War," *Mississippi Valley Historical Review*, XLVI (March 1960), 593–614. Professor Welter ably indicates how American conservatives in this early period overcame their initial repugnance for frontier life sufficiently to use the image of the frontier to further their own ideological ends. Thus Welter makes an important contribution in the discussion of the relationship between the frontier and American ideology.

10.   *The Rediscovery of the Frontier* (Chicago, 1931). This brief volume provides an interesting, if superficial, examination of the new interest in the American frontier, especially among novelists and literary critics.

11.   Harold Waldo, "New Wests for Old," *Bookman*, LI (June 1920), 396–400.

12.   Duncan Aikman, ed., *The Taming of the Frontier* (New York, 1925). Ten authors, including Bernard DeVoto, write on some Western city where somehow sturdy individualism has long withstood the onrush of standardization. The whole volume becomes a kind of "salute to a passing spirit."

13.   Katherine Fullerton Gerould, *The Aristocratic West* (New York, 1925).

14.   There are two excellent articles, both written during the period under discussion, that indicate a keen awareness of many of the major trends and

issues involving the use of the frontier and the pioneer: Mark Van Doren, "The Repudiation of the Pioneer," *The English Journal* (College Edition), XVII (October 1928), 616–623, and especially Carey McWilliams, "Myths of the West," *North American Review*, CCXXXII (November 1931), 424–432. It is important to note that the ambiguities in Turnerism sometimes lead to similarly ambiguous treatments of the pioneer in the hands of an individual author. While in general the pioneer and the frontier were the enemy, occasionally this attitude was combined with an almost eulogistic treatment of the pioneer spirit that "constitutes the real American national genius." Harold Stearns, therefore, can praise this spirit—unafraid in the face of any hazard—at the same time, and on the same page in which, he attacks "belligerent individualism" and "pioneer social docility," which went with it. *America and the Young Intellectual* (New York, 1921), p. 18. See also page 36 and his chapter in his symposium *Civilization in the United States* (New York, 1922), pp. 138–139.

15. Ibid., p. 57. This view becomes a commonplace in serious treatments of the history of American law in this period. See, for example, Roscoe Pound, *The Spirit of the Common Law* (Boston, 1921).

16. "Our Deep-Rooted Lawlessness," *The New York Times Magazine* (March 9, 1930), pp. 1–2. James Truslow Adams was in many ways a thoroughgoing Turnerian, but was more likely to see the dangers of frontier attitudes when carried over into his own time. He was a very popular, widely read historian. See also his *The Epic of America* (Boston, 1931) and " 'Rugged Individualism' Analyzed," *The New York Times Magazine* (March 8, 1934), pp. 1–2, 11.

17. Meredith Nicholson, *The Valley of Democracy* (New York, 1918), a discussion of Midwestern "folks," their types and diversions, the farmer, Chicago, the politics of the area, and, of course, "The Spirit of the West." William W. Cook was a conservative New York corporation lawyer and writer on legal subjects. I am quoting from his more general study of America, *American Institutions and Their Preservation* (New York, 1927), pp. 300–327.

18. Randolph Bourne is directly answering Meredith Nicholson in his review of *The Valley of Democracy*, reprinted in *The History of a Literary Radical and Other Papers* (New York, 1956), pp. 286, 287. This volume was originally published in 1920.

19. "Our Legacy from a Century of Pioneers," *South Atlantic Quarterly*, V (October 1906), 311–333. The exact quotation appears on page 320.

20. *The New Frontier* (New York, 1920), p. 290. This is an almost incredible volume (published in the same year and by the same publishers as Turner's *The Significance of the Frontier in American History*) that makes almost ludicrous all the clichés about frontier individualism and initiative, but it is not atypical in the writing on business by businessmen during this period. The whole question of the search for "new frontiers" as a replacement for the old frontier that made America has been dealt with in a shrewd and witty manner by Walter P. Webb in *The Great Frontier* (Boston, 1952).

21. Archer Hulbert, *Frontiers: The Genius of American Nationality* (Boston, 1929), pp. 220–231. The entire volume is an important document in the ideological uses of frontier history.

22. There is at present no analysis of the vast literature or any bibliography (Everett E. Edwards, *References on the Significance of the Frontier in American History*, United States Department of Agriculture Library, Bibliographic Contributions, No. 25, 2nd ed., April 1939, mimeographed, does contain some pertinent titles). But see, for example, the slim volume published by the Middle West Utilities Company, *America's New Frontier* (Chicago, 1929), and in a later decade the chapter "New Pioneers on a New Frontier" in Ralph E. Flanders, *Platform for America* (New York, 1936). Mr. Flanders was at that time president of the Jones and Lamson Machine Company.

23. "The Frontier and Literature," *The New Republic*, LXVIII (September 2, 1931), 78. Josephson takes the occasion, while reviewing Percy Boyton's *The Rediscovery of the Frontier*, to discuss the problem of the frontier and American culture.

24. In "Letters and Leadership," reprinted in *Three Essays on America* (New York, 1934), p. 129. The original volume first appeared in 1918.

25. *America and the Young Intellectual*, p. 36. But see note 14 above.

26. Reprinted in *The Works of Theodore Roosevelt* (New York, 1926), p. xvi.

27. *The Price of Freedom* (New York, 1924), p. 37. Mr. Coolidge believed that President McKinley "belonged to the race of pioneers," p. 301.

28. This statement, written while Hoover was Secretary of Commerce, appears in his Foreword to F. W. Wile, *A Century of Industrial Progress* (New York, 1928). Perhaps his best statement on this theme appears in his *American Individualism* (Garden City, N.Y., 1922), pp. 63–72.

29. *The Challenge to Liberty* (New York, 1934), p. 149. I do not mean to suggest that the Republicans held a monopoly over the use of the frontier myth for political purposes; they merely happened to be in control during much of the period discussed in this paper. When the New Deal arrived— even during the campaign of 1932—it tried to make the theme of New Frontiers its own, although it disowned "rugged individualism." There is as yet no study of the New Deal's use of Turnerism, but there is a provocative beginning for one in Curtis P. Nettels, "Frederick Jackson Turner and the New Deal," *Wisconsin Magazine of History*, XVII (March 1934), 257–265, especially brilliant when one considers its date. See also Henry A. Wallace, *New Frontiers* (New York, 1934); Harold L. Ickes, *The New Democracy* (New York, 1935); Rexford Tugwell, "No More Frontiers," *Today*, IV (June 22, 1935), 3–4. In spite of the attempt of the New Dealers to appear as frontiersmen on a new frontier, their opponents could level attacks against them in the name of what they considered true frontier ideals. See, for example, Ogden L. Mills, *Liberalism Fights On* (New York, 1936), p. 157: "We must scotch the pernicious notion that the frontier is closed." Mills, who served in the Hoover administration and was a leading businessman, of course believed that New Deal governmental interference and bureaucracy were denying frontier opportunities to the people. The historian of American ideas was not at all surprised to discover Senator John F. Kennedy, as the Democratic candidate for the Presidency, calling for still newer frontiers and promising to lead the American people to them.

30. "Exit Frontier Morality," *The New Republic*, XXXVII (January 2, 1924), 137–138. This editorial is clearly, in part, an answer to Hoover's book of 1922.

31. Perhaps it was for this reason that these intellectuals had a high regard (almost unanimously in the 1920s anyway) for Emerson and the transcendentalists, for those who seemed out of the mainstream of American life or the "real America," as Harold Stearns called the pioneer mind and attitude. *Civilization in the United States*, p. 138. Pioneer and industrial America was the real America, but Emerson and those like him constitute the real

culture heroes to intellectuals like Stearns, Brooks, Mumford, and Josephson, to name a few who regarded the transcendentalist era as "The Golden
Day."

32. This particular passage is from John Gould Fletcher, op. cit., p. 205.

33. While almost all the intellectuals of the period seemed to use social
conditions to account for personality development, there were some who,
in what I would consider a more accurate Freudian approach, suggested
that the neurotic personality sought out the particular kind of environment
best suited for him because of his essential personality difficulties. The end
result, of course, made the frontiersman no more appealing as a character.
The best example is perhaps in the work of Alfred Booth Kuttner, who had
studied Freud with some care and had been responsible for several translations of the work of the master. In his chapter on "Nerves" in the Stearns
symposium, *Civilization in the United States,* Kuttner insisted that the frontier
provided an excellent "loophole," a mechanism by which the neurotic personality might escape from the demands of civilization. Thus the neurotics
were initially attracted to America and the frontier. Kuttner's comments are
worth quoting at length: "Certainly our pioneers have been too much romanticized. The neurotic legacy which they bequeathed to us can plainly be
seen in many characteristics of our uncouth Westerners with their alternate
coldness toward visitors and their undignified warmth toward the casual
stranger who really cannot mean anything to them. There is something
wrong about a man as a social animal when he cannot live happily in a valley
where he sees more than the distant smoke of his neighbour's chimney.
When at least the pressure of population forces him to live socially his
suspicion and distrust are likely to turn him into a zealot and reformer and
make possible the domination of American life of such a sub-cultural type
as Bryan or the beatitudes of a State like Kansas. The favorite Western
exhortation to be able to look a man in the eye and tell him to go to Hell is
worthy of an anti-social community of ex-convicts, and the maxim about
minding your own business can only be understood as a defence against the
prevalent tendency of everybody to mind his neighbour's business. Thus
the self-isolating neurotic ends by revenging himself upon society by making it intolerable." Stearns, op. cit., p. 429.

34. I am convinced that a thorough study of both Freudianism and Marxism in the United States will reveal the remarkable impact Turnerism, in
the hands of American practitioners, had on both of these analyses. Certainly, the Neo-Freudians in this country show this influence with their
special stress on the role of environment as conditioning factors for personality, and especially the frontier environment. See, for example, Franz Alexander, *Our Age of Unreason* (Philadelphia, 1942), especially Chapter VII,
"The American Scene" (a Turnerian analysis), and Chapter VIII, "New
Frontiers."

35. Waldo Frank, op. cit., p. 28.

36. "The South—Old or New?" *The Sewanee Review,* XXXVI (April 1928),
140. Ransom is trying to establish that fact that the South did not go
through the same pioneering process insofar as it refused to yield to the
pioneering spirit (which leads to materialism, belligerence, an anti-nature
attitude, a belief in progress and service). Rather, the South built its culture
on European principles. Along with every other intellectual discussed in
this paper, Ransom insists, "Industrialism, of course, is the contemporary
form of pioneering." Thus he is opposed to the New South, which pins its
hopes on an introduction of the pioneering spirit he most opposes.

37.   Lewis Mumford, *The Golden Day* (New York, 1926), p. 80
38.   *The Ordeal of Mark Twain* (New York, 1920). The other great obstacle to Twain's fulfillment as an artist was American Puritanism. But see note 47 below.
39.   Op. cit., p. 358
40.   An unusual view of the frontier and the problem of intolerance can be found in Alfred Booth Kuttner, "A Study of American Intolerance," *The Dial*, LXIV (March 14, 1918), 223–225. Kuttner maintains that there could be no question of tolerance while the frontier remained as a means of escape from organized social life. Only in well-ordered communities can one discover anything like true tolerance. Thus the frontier was largely responsible for delaying the development of any true tolerance.
41.   See, for example, Charles P. Howland, "America's Coming of Age," *Survey*, LVIII (August 1, 1927), 437–440. Howland welcomes the end of the pioneering process in the hope that it will hasten the development of sophistication and the end of simple frontier morality.
42.   "Exit Frontier Morality," op. cit.
43.   New York, 1912, pp. 23, 24, 36.
44.   "Exit Frontier Morality," *The New Republic*, op. cit., and Matthew Josephson, "The Frontier and Literature," (September 2, 1931).
45.   Matthew Josephson, ibid.
46.   "The American Intellectual Frontier," reprinted in his *Character and Events* (New York, 1929), I, 448. This article first appeared in *The New Republic* on May 10, 1922, a fact that seems to reinforce the magazine's interest in this theme.
47.   The best brief discussion of the Puritan as scapegoat for the intellectuals of the 1920s can be found in Frederick J. Hoffman, *The Twenties* (New York, 1955), pp. 314–327. Since at least the days of Tocqueville, commentators have insisted that American character and culture were molded by three forces, the Puritan theology and philosophy, the pioneering experience, and the push of business enterprise or materialism. This last force was further considered in large part to be the result of the first two. Almost every volume that purported to be a "balanced" treatment of the American mind gave attention to both the Puritan legacy and the frontier inheritance. See, for example, Harold E. Luccock, *Jesus and the American Mind* (New York, 1930), Chapters III and IV. What happened generally among the Young Intellectuals of the period and their teachers was the development of a new view that made all three forces the product of one and the same historical experience. On the relation of the frontier to Puritanism, see also William Allen White, "Kansas: A Puritan Survival," in Ernest Gruening, ed., *These United States* (New York, 1923), Chapter I, p. 1–12.
48.   Van Wyck Brooks, *Three Essays on America*, p. 131. "Puritanism was a complete philosophy for the pioneer, and, by making human nature contemptible and putting to shame the charms of life, it unleashed the acquisitive instincts of men, disembarrassing those instincts by creating the belief that the life of the spirit is altogether a secret life and that the imagination ought never to conflict with the law of the tribe." Thus Puritan, Pioneer, Businessman, and Philistine become one and the same person.
49.   *Character and Events*, pp. 451–452. It is perhaps especially interesting to see John Dewey take this view with reference to the influence of the frontier. Dewey had been one of the teachers and heroes of the Young Intellectuals before the First World War, but Dewey's position on the war and other intellectual considerations had brought Dewey and especially

NOTES

American pragmatism as a philosophy into discredit with this group. In fact, pragmatism was specifically attacked on the grounds that it was simply the philosophy of the pioneer and the result of the frontier process. Waldo Frank bitterly maintained. "Pragmatism, in its servility to Reason, is supine before the pioneer reality whose decadent child it is. . . . The legs of the pioneer had simply become the brains of the philosopher." *Our America*, p. 29. Lewis Mumford's analysis was perhaps more sophisticated but issued in the same general condemnation. *The Golden Day*, pp. 254–264.

50. The younger intellectual leaders of the 1950s have perhaps added a new cultural villain, a fourth "P," to the list and regard him as most deadly of all—the populist. Treatments of the populist as cultural scapegoat are very reminiscent of the writings of the period 1910 to 1930; again, it is an attack on the Middle West and on frontier influences. The leaders again are largely Easterners: Richard Hofstadter, Daniel Bell, Peter Viereck, Talcott Parsons, Seymour Martin Lipset. See especially Daniel Bell, ed., *The New American Right* (New York, 1955), and the brilliant critique by C. Vann Woodward, "The Populist Heritage and the Intellectual," *The American Scholar*, XXIX (Winter 1959–60), 55–72.

51. I am well aware of the extensive critical attack upon the Middle West by intellectuals and especially artists from that area. Edgar Lee Masters, Sherwood Anderson, Sinclair Lewis, Glenway Wescott—the list could go on for pages. See Frederick J. Hoffman's brilliant account "The Midwest as Metaphor" in his *The Twenties*, pp. 327–335. Both Percy Boynton and Lucy Lockwood Hazard spend considerable space on this phenomenon in their books (previously cited). But I believe that research will indicate that these attitudes, while superficially the same in attacking the sterility of contemporary Midwestern life, have a different basis. Frequently, these writers looked back to history, to the days of pioneering, with greater nostalgia than any of the Eastern intellectuals discussed in this paper did. They were intrigued, it is true, with the problems of the frontier past, but on many occasions seemed to have regretted the passing of those days.

52. "On Creating a Usable Past," *The Dial*, LXIV (April 11, 1918), 337.

53. Generally, John C. Almack, "The Shibboleth of the Frontier," *Historical Outlook*, XVI (May 1925), 197–202, is regarded as the first published assault. Almack's piece is especially interesting because he finds Turner's theory "dangerous" with special reference to the social and ideological consequences that seem to follow from it. Thus he is in line with many of the intellectuals discussed in this paper. Charles A. Beard also attacked "the agrarian thesis" in "Culture and Agriculture," *The Saturday Review of Literature*, V (October 20, 1928), 272–273. During this period, Beard had spent some time considering the role of the city in American life. His critique, too, seems to fall in line with many of the views of the other intellectuals discussed above. The detailed criticisms of the Turner thesis were not published until after the onslaught of the Great Depression, indeed in the early 1930s.

54. In many ways, of course, Beard is a key member of the group of intellectuals discussed here. He published in their magazines, *The Dial*, *The Freeman*, *The New Republic* (among others). In Harold Stearns' symposium *Civilization in the United States*, although Turner's frontier is a menace second only to Puritanism, Turner's writings themselves are never specifically referred to, in the text or in the recommended bibliographies. Beard is cited several times with approval.

NOTES

CHAPTER 5
SOCIALISM AND AMERICANISM

1.   Frank Tannenbaum, *The Labor Movement* (New York, 1921), pp. 64–65. My italics.

2.   On this whole subject see R. Laurence Moore, *European Socialists and the American Promised Land* (New York, 1970). The last chapter deals with American socialists.

3.   Elwin H. Powell, *The Design of Discord* (New York, 1970), p. 104. A provocative study by a sociologist with some ideas worthy of considerable development. Chapter VII, "Class Warfare in Buffalo," is of special interest to those concerned about the questions raised in this volume.

4.   I have developed this notion as a significant aspect of the 1930s that contributed to the essential conservativism of the period in two essays: "The Thirties," in S. Coben and L. Ratner, eds., *The Development of American Culture* (Englewood Cliffs, N.J., 1970), and "Introduction," to my own *Culture and Commitment* (New York, 1972).

5.   This is a most important essay. It appears in Lasch's volume *The Agony of the American Left* (New York, 1969). The sentence quoted is on page 40, but the whole essay must be read by anyone interested in social movements in America.

6.   All of the quotes in this paragraph are taken from the first chapter of James B. Gilbert, *Writers and Partisans* (New York, 1968), pp. 12, 33, 14. Gilbert's book is the most valuable book we have on literary radicalism. But see also Daniel Aaron, *Writers on the Left* (New York, 1961).

7.   Tannenbaum, op. cit., p. 208.

8.   Powell, op. cit., p. 93.

9.   Malcolm Cowley, *Exile's Return* (New York, 1934), pp. 72–73.

10.   Irving Howe and Lewis Coser, *The American Communist Party* (New York, 1962). The quotation appears on page 338. While many writers on the Left have been critical of this volume I find that Chapter VIII on the Popular Front is especially brilliant, and its conclusions are bolstered by my own research in the period.

11.   Gilbert, op. cit., p. 147.

12.   Harold Stearns, ed., *Civilization in the United States* (New York, 1922), p. 541.

13.   Twelve Southerners, *I'll Take My Stand* (New York, 1962), pp. xxi–xxii. The original edition was 1930.

14.   I am thinking in particular of R. L. Bruckberger, *Image of America* (New York, 1959), pp. 195–97 especially. There is a section comparing Ford to Marx and Lenin in this book and it is very suggestive.

15.   Twelve Southerners, op. cit., p. xxiii.

16.   Howe and Coster, op. cit., p. 358.

CHAPTER 6
THE PERSISTENCE OF REFORM

1.   Frederick C. Howe, *The Confessions of a Reformer* (New York, 1925), pp. 17, 55.

2.   Ibid., p. 189.

3.   Paul Goodman, *Growing Up Absurd* (New York, 1960), pp. 80–81.

4.   Op. cit., p. 340.

CHAPTER 9
THE CULTURE OF THE THIRTIES

1. Josephine Herbst, "A Year of Disgrace," in S. Bellow and K. Botsford, eds., *The Noble Savage 3* (Cleveland, 1961), p. 160. Herbst's memoirs (of which two sections have thus far appeared) are one of the classic accounts of the intellectual life of the 1920s and the 1930s.

2. Ibid.

3. Ibid., p. 145.

4. Erich Auerbach, *Mimesis: The Representation of Reality in Western Literature*, trans. W. R. Trask (Princeton, 1953), p. 20.

5. Alistair Cooke, in *Generation on Trial* (New York, 1952), his study of the Hiss trial, makes this point vividly, especially in his first chapter, "The Remembrance of Things Past," one of the best essays on the 1930s.

6. Daniel Aaron presents an excellent account of this problem based on his own research difficulties in writing his study of Communism and American writers in the 1930s in an important article, "The Treachery of Recollection: The Inner and the Outer History," in Robert H. Bremmer, ed., *Essays on History and Literature* (Columbus, Ohio, 1966), pp. 3–27.

7. See especially the collection of articles by Daniel Bell, *The End of Ideology* (New York: 1960). Most relevant are "The Mood of Three Generations," pp. 286–299, and "The End of Ideology in the West," pp. 369–376. See also Leslie Fiedler, *The End to Innocence* (Boston, 1955).

8. See Daniel Aaron, *Writers on the Left* (New York, 1961); also his previously cited article (fn. 6), as well as "The Thirties—Now and Then," *The American Scholar*, XXXV (Summer 1961), 490–494. Frank A. Warren III, *Liberals and Communism: The "Red Decade" Revisited* (Bloomington, Ind., 1966), throws further light on this question.

9. Josephine Herbst, "Moralist's Progress," *The Kenyon Review*, XXVIII (Autumn 1965), 773. George K. Anderson and Eda Lou Walton, eds., have an interesting discussion of the importance of this work in their anthology *This Generation* (Chicago, 1949), pp. 545–546. Obviously, I do not mean to suggest that there were no "ideologies" or ideologists in the 1930s. I mean rather that there were several; that ideological thinking was not as striking an aspect of intellectual life as has been supposed or indeed that can be discovered in earlier periods (such as the Progressive era, for example).

10. See notes 42, 43, and 44 below.

11. George Orwell, "Inside the Whale," reprinted in *A Collection of Essays* (New York, 1954), p. 236, in the Anchor paperback edition. This brilliant essay written in 1940 provides a stimulating view of the whole period.

12. See, for example, "Making the 1930's Pay Off—At Last," *Business Week* (August 20, 1966), pp. 128–132.

13. The original sales of Fuchs' novels are as follows: *Summer in Williamsburg* (1934), 400 copies; *Homage to Blenholt* (1936), 400 copies; *Low Company* (1937), 1,200 copies. So Fuchs reports in a new preface to the paperback edition (New York, 1965), p. 7. These novels were also reprinted in hardcover in 1961. West's *Miss Lonelyhearts* (1933) sold only 800 copies in its original edition, according to Robert M. Coates in his Afterword to the Avon paperback reprint of the McCoy novel (New York, 1966), p. 134. McCoy's novel of 1935 may be regarded as almost a best seller in this company: it sold 3,000 copies. It was reprinted in paperback in 1948, in 1955, and for the third time in 1966 (which text I am using).

14. Harvey Swados, ed., *The American Writer and the Great Depression*, The American Heritage Series (Indianapolis, Ind., 1966), has a fine introductory essay and a good bibliography; Jack Salzman, ed., *Years of Protest* (New York, 1967), covers many issues and has especially useful headnotes. Louis Filler, ed., *The Anxious Years* (New York, 1963), is wide-ranging and the introduction provides useful information but also some strange opinions.

15. See Henry Dan Piper's valuable collection of Malcolm Cowley's important pieces of reportage, controversy, and criticism from the 1930s, *Think Back on Us* (Carbondale, Ill., 1967). On this point, see especially pp. 51–55. Caroline Bird, *The Invisible Scar* (New York, 1966), is in many ways a good social history. On this question see pp. 89–90. In addition to Paul Conkin's solid work *Toward a New World* (Ithaca, N. Y., 1959), see the valuable essay (the third chapter) in Warren French, *The Social Novel at the End of an Era* (Carbondale, Ill., 1966), for important data on this point.

16. A. L. Kroeber and Clyde Kluckhohn, *Culture: A Critical Review of Concepts and Definitions*, originally published as Vol. XLVII, No. 1, of the Papers of the Peabody Museum of American Archeology and Ethnology, Harvard University, in 1952 and reprinted in paperback (New York, 1963), is the crucial work in the whole area of definition and use and a starting point for any study. It deals largely with professional social scientists, however, and does not deal with what I would call the acculturation of the concept. Charles and Mary Beard wrote an important book as part of their series of volumes *The Rise of American Civilization*, a final volume called *The American Spirit* (New York, 1942). This volume, too often overlooked and much more significant than scholars have hitherto acknowledged, was the study of the idea of civilization in the United States that the authors felt was the key American idea and a molding force in the development of American civilization itself. In my own work I have argued that the idea of culture always existed somehow opposed to and in tension with the idea of civilization, but the Beards' book is significant. Kroeber and Kluckhohn also discuss the distinction between culture and civilization. In a different context, using very different material, the anthropologist Clifford Geertz has provided a very stimulating essay, "The Impact of the Concept of Culture on the Concept of Man," in John R. Platt, ed., *New Views of the Nature of Man* (Chicago, 1965), pp. 93–118.

17. Robert S. Lynd, *Knowledge for What? The Place of the Social Sciences in American Culture* (Princeton, N.J., 1967), pp. 16, 19.

18. F. R. Cowell, *Culture in Private and Public Life* (New York, 1959), p. 5.

19. Mitford M. Matthews in his *Dictionary of Americanisms* (Chicago, 1951) does list a use of "the American Way" as early as 1885, but his other references reinforce the opinion that it came especially into vogue in the 1930s and 1940s. There were at least four books in the period that used the phrase in a title (including a collection of essays edited by Newton D. Baker in 1936 and Earle Looker's 1933 study of FDR in action). Kaufman and Hart used it as the title of a play in 1939. The play traces the history of an immigrant family in America and ends with patriotic flourishes. There is, I suspect, little significance in the fact that it was the first Broadway play I ever saw. Certainly, there were more books and articles using the phrase in the 1930s than ever before. Merle Curti has some extremely interesting things to say about the idea of an American Dream in his article "The American Exploration of Dreams and Dreamers," *Journal of the History of Ideas*, XXVII (July–September, 1966), 391. He believes that James Truslow Adams invented, or at least publicized, the phrase in 1931. George O'Neil's play of that name was produced in 1933 and showed the progressive deterioration of the ideals and character of a New England family through American history. The word "culture" itself begins to appear commonly. Many titles are cited in this essay. Others include Jerome Davis, *Capitalism and Its Culture* (New York, 1935).

20. On this issue see Matthews, op. cit., as well as Raven I. McDavid, Jr.'s revised one-volume abridgement of H. L. Mencken's *The American Language* (New York, 1963), p. 183. An important book of the 1930s published as the result of a symposium organized by the Department of Agriculture, with a Preface by Charles Beard that stressed the key role of agriculture as a base for any democracy in America, was M. L. Wilson, *Democracy Has Roots* (New York, 1939). We need further studies of the rhetoric of American history.

21. From "America Was Promises," *Collected Poems 1917–1952*. Copyright 1952 by Archibald MacLeish. Reprinted by permission of the publisher, Houghton Mifflin Company. Reprinted in Louis Filler, ed., *The Anxious Years*, pp. 225–226.

22. Leo Gurko, *The Angry Decade* (New York, 1947), has some useful information, especially on the context of American reading in the period, although its analysis is not very penetrating. James D. Hart, *The Popular Book* (New York, 1950), is invaluable.

23. See the perceptive essay by Reuel Denney, "The Discovery of Popular Culture," in *American Perspectives,* Robert E. Spiller and Eric Larrabee, eds., (Cambridge, Mass., 1961), p. 170.

24. Stuart Chase, *Mexico: A Study of Two Americas* (New York, 1931). This book, written in collaboration with Marian Tyler, begs for more extensive treatment, especially since Hart, *The Popular Book*, indicates it was a best seller in the period. I have quoted almost at random: pp. 170, 130, 154, 171, 128.

25. William Fielding Ogburn, *Social Change with Respect to Culture and Original Nature* (New York, 1922)

26. Robert Lynd, *Knowledge for What?*, pp. 3–4. Lynd also speaks, in the passage immediately preceding, about what has spoiled "the American Dream."

27. Carl Becker, *Progress and Power* (Palo Alto, Cal., 1936), p. 91.

28. See note 16. I have developed this argument at length in my paper "The Nature of American Conservatism," which I delivered at the First Socialist Scholars Conference, September 1965, and which is included in Part Two of the present work.

29. I have not dwelled in this essay on what happened to Progressive ideas in the period. Obviously, there was considerable continuity at least in some aspects of the culture of the period. Otis L. Graham, Jr., *An Encore for Reform* (New York, 1967), is enlightening on differences as well as similarities, but Rexford G. Tugwell has written a most brilliant essay, "The New Deal—The Progressive Tradition," *Western Political Quarterly,* III (September 1950), 390–427, which can be missed by the cultural and intellectual historian only at great peril.

30. Herbst, "A Year of Disgrace," *The Noble Savage 3*, p. 159.

31. Nelson Algren, *Somebody in Boots* (New York: 1965), pp. 82–83. Originally published in 1935.

32. In addition to works already cited, Alfred Kazin, *On Native Grounds* (New York, 1942), has an extraordinary analysis, considering the date of its appearance, in his section on the 1930s, especially the chapter "America, America." We need an extended study of the newly awakened popular interest in anthropological and archeological studies in the 1920s and 1930s, which produced not only an outpouring of scholarly discoveries and works but also a considerable popular literature as well.

33. Brooks edited a collection of Rourke's essays and provided a most significant preface, *The Roots of American Culture and Other Essays* (New York, 1942). Vico and Herder play an important role in the new concern for culture. Brooks quotes Herder to the effect that "folk-forms were essential to any communal group, they were the texture of the communal experience and expression." All of the key words were, as we shall see, especially important in the 1930s.

34. See the essay of Harvey Swados with which he introduces his 1966 anthology, *The American Writer and the Great Depression.*

35. In 1928 Niebuhr published his *Does Civilization Need Religion?*, the first of many important works really on this theme; in 1934 Mumford began his series of four volumes pleading for a harnessing of science and technology in the interest of a better life for man with his *Technics and Civilization.* The series as a whole is called The Renewal of Life. The decade saw the publication of *The Dictionary of American Biography* as well as *The Encyclopedia of the Social Sciences, Recent Social Trends,* and *Recent Economic Trends.* Many of these works had been begun, of course, during the 1920s. But the 1920s and the 1930s produced an enormous body of literature on the nature of history, culture, and the social sciences as well as the gathering of significant data about our history and society. See Merle Curti, ed., *American Scholarship in the Twentieth Century* (Cambridge, Mass., 1953).

36. For a brief introduction to this subject treated historically, see Stow Persons, *American Minds* (New York, 1958), Chapter 21.

37. Hadley Cantril has provided us with a social-psychological study of this affair in *The Invasion from Mars* (Princeton, N.J., 1940).

38. Beaumont Newhall provides a good starting point for further analysis in *The History of Photography* (New York, 1964), Chapter 10.

39. Quoted in T. V. Smith, "The New Deal as a Cultural Phenomenon," *Ideological Differences and World Order,* F. S. C. Northrop, ed. (New Haven, 1949), p. 212.

40. The best analysis of the "soaps" is still the delightful series James Thurber did for *The New Yorker,* reprinted in his *The Beast in Me* (New York, 1948) as "Soapland."

41. Kenneth Burke, "Revolutionary Symbolism in America," in *Perspectives on Modern Literature,* Frederick J. Hoffman, ed. (New York, 1962), p. 181.

42. Kenneth Burke, "The Rhetoric of Hitler's 'Battle,' " reprinted in his *The Philosophy of Literary Form* (Baton Route, La., 1941). This is an important collection of pieces for purposes of this essay.

43. Thurmond Arnold, *The Folklore of Capitalism* (New Haven, 1937). I have a reprint edition that indicates that at least ten printings of this work occurred between 1937 and 1941. There is an extended analysis of the work in Richard Hofstadter, *The Age of Reform* (New York, 1959), pp. 317–322. Previously, Arnold had published *The Symbols of Government* (New Haven, 1935).

44. Lasswell's career began with a study of *Propaganda Technique in the World War* (New York, 1927). In 1930 he published *Psychopathology and Politics* and in 1936 *Politics: Who Gets What, When, How.*

45. "The New Deal as a Cultural Phenomenon," in F. S. C. Northrop, ed., op. cit., p. 209.

46. It was in 1938 that the distinguished Dutch cultural historian Johan Huizinga published his landmark study of play and civilization, *Homo Ludens.*

47 In addition to the Bird volume already cited (note 15), see the excellent social history of Frederick L. Allen, *Since Yesterday: The Nineteen-Thirties in America* (New York, 1940), Chapter 6. There are some illuminating suggestions in Robert M. Coates' Afterword to the Horace McCoy novel previously cited (note 13). See also Foster Rhea Dulles, *A History of Recreation* (New York, 1965), a revised edition of his *America Learns to Play.*

48. Roger Caillois, *Man, Play and Games* (New York, 1961), especially Chapters 3 and 4.

49. Ibid., p. 55.

50. Robert Sherwood's *Idiot's Delight* (1936) is reprinted in Harold Clurman, ed., *Famous American Plays of the 1930s* (New York, 1959). This passage appears on p. 253. Quoted by permission of Charles Scribner's Sons.

51. William Saroyan's *The Time of Your Life* (1939) is also reprinted in *Famous American Plays of the 1930s.* The passages quoted appear on pp. 388 and 463. Quoted by permission of William Saroyan.

52. Robert S. Lynd and Helen Lynd, *Middletown in Transition* (New York, 1937), pp. 233–234, and Robert Lynd, *Knowledge for What?*, pp. 236–237

53. Neil Leonard, *Jazz and the White Americans* (Chicago, 1962), Chapter 6.

54. A good deal that follows is based on Meyer's superb analysis in *The Positive Thinkers* (New York, 1965), certainly one of the most important recent studies in the field of American civilization. See especially Chapters 14, 18, and 19.

55. James D. Hart, *The Popular Book,* (New York, 1950), pp. 255–256, is excellent here. Carnegie's book sold 750,000 copies by the end of its first year in print. By 1948 it had sold over 3,250,000 copies in all editions. Also popular were Walter B. Pitkin's *Life Begins at Forty* and Dorothea Brande's *Wake Up and Live,* among the hundreds of best-selling do-it-yourself books devoted to self-help.

56. All the social historians comment on this point. Caroline Bird, *The Invisible Scar* (New York, 1966), p. 277, has some especially interesting material.

57. Mayo deserves more serious treatment than I have given him. He influenced Harold Lasswell's studies, for example, and his books *The Human Problems of an Industrial Civilization* (Cambridge, Mass., 1933) and *The Social Problems of an Industrial Civilization* (Cambridge, Mass., 1945) are important works. Meyer discusses Mayo briefly in his book, cited above (fn. 54), and Loren Baritz has an important analysis in *The Servants of Power* (Middletown, Conn., 1960).

58. Clara Thompson has a brief analysis of the Neo-Freudians in the last chapter of her *Psychoanalysis: Evolution and Development* (New York, 1950), and there is a stimulating critique of the movement in the Epilogue to Herbert Marcuse's *Eros and Civilization* (Boston, 1955).

59. The word was perhaps not widely used in the decade, certainly not as widely used as it was to become in the 1940s and 1950s. It did not quite gain the currency that the word *culture* did. But the idea was a concept important to the period. On the whole question of the word, its origins and meanings in contemporary discussion, see Edmund Wilson, "Words of Ill-Omen," in his *The Bit Between My Teeth* (New York, 1965), pp. 415–416.

60. Hart, op. cit., p. 259, points out that nearly a quarter of all new novels published in the decade were detective-mystery stories. Only 12 books of this type appeared in 1914; only 97 in 1925. By 1939 the production of new titles (to say nothing of reprints) had reached 217.
61. *The Yale Review*, XXXIX (September 1949), 76–95.
62. I am using the Dell paperback reprint (New York 1966), pp. 188–189.
63. John Dewey, *Freedom and Culture* (New York, 1939), p. 21.
64. Karen Horney, *The Neurotic Personality of Our Time* (New York, 1937) p. 47ff. It is interesting, in passing, to note how much Professor Lynd makes use of Horney's analysis in his own book *Knowledge for What?* previously cited.
65. In "Symposium: The First American Writers' Congress," *The American Scholar*, XXXV (Summer 1966), 505.
66. Ibid., p. 500.
67. In her reply to the *Partisan Review* questionnaire "The Situation in American Writing," first published in 1939 and reprinted in William Phillips and Philip Rahv, eds., *The Partisan Reader* (New York, 1946), p. 617.
68. "The Starched Blue Sky of Spain," *The Noble Savage 1* (Cleveland, Ohio, 1960), p. 78
69. From *For Whom the Bell Tolls* (1940), quoted in Norman Holmes Pearson, "The Nazi-Soviet Pact and the End of a Dream," in Daniel Aaron, ed., *America in Crisis* (New York, 1952), p. 337. *For Whom the Bell Tolls* was originally published by Charles Scribner's Sons.
70. Josephine Herbst, "The Starched Blue Sky of Spain," op. cit., pp. 79–80.
71. Introduction, *Marginal Manners* (Evanston, Ill., 1962), p. 7. This excellent anthology of Professor Hoffman's has an important section on the 1930s: "The Expense of Poverty: Bottom Dogs," pp. 92–126, with material reprinted from Dos Passos, Steinbeck, Dahlberg, and Maltz and very intelligent headnotes by Hoffman.
72. Josephine Herbst, "Moralist's Progress," *The Kenyon Review*, XXVIII (Autumn 1965), 776.
73. An article by Norman Holmes Pearson, "The Nazi-Soviet Pact," is excellent on this whole question. It is an important piece on the intellectuals and the Left in the 1930s. The works of Daniel Aaron previously cited (notes 6 and 8) are basic.
74. Malcolm Cowley, "Symposium: The First American Writers' Congress," op. cit., p. 500
75. On this subject, Donald B. Meyer has produced a key book in our understanding of the 1930s with his *The Protestant Search for Political Realism* (Los Angeles, 1960)).
76. Josephine Herbst, op. cit., p. 777.
77. Granville Hicks, *Small Town* (New York, 1946). This is the autobiographical account Hicks has given us of his involvement in a New York community after his break with the Communists.
78. Allen Tate, in his answer to the 1939 *Partisan Review* questionnaire, reprinted in *The Partisan Reader*, p. 622.
79. Morgan is quoted from a pamphlet published by the organization, "About Community Service Incorporated," n.d.
80. *The Culture of Cities* (New York, 1938), the second volume in the already-cited Renewal of Life series (note 35). Mumford had begun his career

in the 1920s with a study of various utopias men had devised through the ages.

81. See Edward Dahlberg's interesting piece on the communitarian tradition, reprinted in *Alms for Oblivion* (Minneapolis, Minn., 1964), "Our Vanishing Cooperative Colonies," pp. 91–103. Dahlberg as well as Hart Crane and Archibald MacLeish became interested in pre-Columbian Indian life and its extinction by the Conquest. William Carlos Williams may have led the way in his *In the American Grain* as early as 1925. At the end of the Dahlberg essay cited, he asks, "Is the solitary American superior to the communal Indian?"

82. Quoted in Louis Rubin, Jr., *I'll Take My Stand* (New York, 1958), p. xiii.

83. See Malcolm Cowley's critique, "Angry Professors," written in 1930 and reprinted in *Think Back on Us*, pp. 3–13.

84. Robert M. Hutchins, *The Higher Learning in America* (Chicago, 1936), pp. 73, 77, and 95.

85. *Pragmatism and American Culture*, Gail Kennedy, ed., (Boston, 1952), is an excellent anthology with a good bibliography to help the reader trace this development. One of Dewey's own best answers appeared in 1943 in *The Partisan Review:* "Anti-Naturalism in Extremis." It is reprinted in *The Partisan Reader*, pp. 514–529.

86. *Proletarian Literature in the United States,* ed. Granville Hicks et al., with a critical Introduction by Joseph Freeman (New York, 1935), p. 10.

87. Ibid., p. 19.

88. Jack Conroy, in his contribution to "The 1930's: A Symposium," *The Carleton Miscellany*, VI (Winter 1965), 39.

89. In his answer to the 1939 *Partisan Review* questionnaire, reprinted in *The Partisan Reader*, p. 622.

90. Alfred Kazin, *Starting Out in the Thirties* (Boston, 1965), p. 15.

91. The story is told by Burke in his comments in "Symposium: The First American Writers' Congress, *The American Scholar*, XXXV (Summer 1966), 505–508.

92. Herbert Agar, *Who Owns America?* (Boston, 1936), p. vii

93. Edward Dahlberg, "The Proletarian Eucharist," in *Can These Bones Live?* (New York, 1941), pp. 73–74.

94. William Phillips, "What Happened in the '30s?" *Commentary*, XXXIV (September 1962), 204–212; Robert Warshow, "The Legacy of the '30s," reprinted in his *The Immediate Experience* (New York, 1962).

95. Warshow, op. cit., p. 7.

96. William Phillips. "The Intellectuals' Tradition," reprinted in *The Partisan Reader*, p. 489. This essay originally appeared in 1941.

97. George Orwell, *An Age Like This: 1940–1943*, ed. Sonia Orwell and Ian Angus (New York, 1954; Harcourt Brace Jovanovich, 1968).

98. Ibid., pp. 248 and 249.

99. Ibid., p. 256.

100. Sydney E. Ahlstrom, "Theology in America," in *The Shaping of American Religion*, Vol. I, ed. James Ward Smith and A. Leland Jamison (Princeton, N.J., 1961), p. 312.

101. Ibid., pp. 315–316. See also Donald Meyer, *The Protestant Search for Political Realism* (Berkeley, 1960).

102. James Agee and Walker Evans, *Let Us Now Praise Famous Men* (Boston, 1941), p. xv.

103. Ibid., p. 12.

104. The Trilling criticism comes in his excellent review of the work that appears in *The Mid-Century*, XVI (September 1960), 3–11, on the occasion of the appearance of the newly revised edition. On the subject of the various attacks on American "innocence" in recent American scholarship and criticism see the interesting article by Robert A. Skotheim, " 'Innocence' and 'Beyond Innocence' in Recent American Scholarship," *The American Quarterly*, XIII (Spring 1961), 93–99.

CHAPTER 14
"PERSONALITY" AND
THE MAKING OF
TWENTIETH-CENTURY CULTURE

1. Owen Barfield, *History in English Words* (London, 1954), p. 166.

2. The essay "A Difficulty in the Path of Psycho-Analysis" is reprinted in *Standard Edition of the Collected Psychological Works of Sigmund Freud*, 23 vols. (London, 1955), XVII, 135–144.

3. Philip Rieff, *The Triumph of the Therapeutic Uses of Faith after Freud* (New York, 1966), p. 2.

4. A. A. Roback in the article "Character" in the *Encyclopaedia of the Social Sciences*, 14 vols. (New York, 1930), III, 335.

5. Jacob Burckhardt, *The Civilization of the Renaissance in Italy* (New York, 1954), pp. 100–101.

6. I have developed this analysis at greater length in a piece on Henry Ford, "Piety, Profits, and Play: The 1920s," in *Men, Women, and Issues in American History*, ed. A. Quint and M. Cantor, 2 vols. (Homewood, Ill., 1975), II, Chapter 10.

7. Raymond Williams, *Keywords: A Vocabulary of Culture and Society* (New York, 1976), pp. 194–197. The word "character" does not appear in Mr. Williams's study.

8. Henry Laurent, *Personality: How to Build It* (New York, 1915), p. iv. This volume was translated from the French by Richard Duff.

9. Ibid., p. 25.

10. Ibid., pp. iv, 29. I have used this manual as typical. Part 1 deals with the "building" of personality, and Part 2 with "how to impress." It stresses self-control as a way to control others. I find all of the themes of other manuals studied stated here more boldly and precisely.

11. B. C. Bean, *Power of Personality* (Meriden, Conn., 1920), p. 3. This is one of a series of pamphlets called The Science of Organizing Personal Powers for Success.

12. Philip Rieff, *Freud: The Mind of a Moralist* (New York, 1961), pp. 391–392. The whole of Chapter 10, "The Emergence of Psychological Man," makes an important statement.

13. Orison Swett Marden, *Character, The Greatest Thing in the World* (New York, 1899), pp. 7, 11, 16, 21, 25, 30, 37, 50; idem, *Masterful Personality* (New York, 1921), pp. 1, 3, 17, 23, 33, 68, 291.

14. George Horace Lorimer, *Letters from a Self-Made Merchant to His Son* (New York, 1902). See especially pp. 40, 88–89. This is striking in almost all the self-help manuals studied. There is clearly a relationship between this new definition of success and the contemporary religious interest in personality. I address this issue in another paper, "The Religion of Personality and Personality as a Religion." This issue is of considerable importance to the theme I am attempting to develop. In this context let me cite only one of many theologians and philosophers on the importance of personality, J. Herman Randall, in *The Culture of Personality* (New York, 1912), p. xiii. "[Personality] is by far the greatest work in the history of the human mind. [It is the key] that unlocks the deeper mysteries of Science and Philosophy, of History and Literature, of Art and Religion, of all of man's ethical and social relationships."

15. Ezra Pound, "Provincialism the Enemy," *The New Age*, XXI (July 19, 1917), 268–269. See also letter to Margaret Anderson, reprinted in her *My Thirty Years War* (New York, 1930), p. 171. Herbert Croly, *The Promise of American Life* (New York, 1909), p. 432. His whole analysis of individualism and leadership can be best understood in terms of the premises of this paper. In another paper, "Leadership and Public Opinion in a Culture of Personality," I deal with the implications in political theory and especially in political rhetoric in the period from 1890 to 1920. Randolph Bourne, *Youth and Life* (New York, 1913), p. 294.

16. Nathaniel Southgate Shaler, *The Individual: A Study of Life and Death* (New York, 1900), Chapter 7. Vachel Lindsay, *The Art of the Moving Picture* (New York, 1915). There was a revised edition in 1922. It remains a classic work for all cultural historians.

17. Alexander Walker, *Stardom: The Hollywood Phenomenon* (New York, 1970), p. 36.

18. Richard Schickel, *His Picture in the Papers: A Speculation on Celebrity in America Based on the Life of Douglas Fairbanks, Sr.* (New York, 1974), p. 9.

19. Ralph Waldo Trine, *The Power That Wins* (Indianapolis, Ind., 1928), pp. 2–3.

INDEX

INDEX